GRAND OLE OPRY®
FAMILY ALBUM
97TH ANNIVERSARY

GRANDIN HOOD
Publishers

Grand Ole Opry Family Album

Copyright © 2022 by Grandin Hood Publishers and Grand Ole Opry®, LLC: opry.com

All rights reserved. No part of this book may be reproduced in any form or by any electronic or mechanical means, including retrieval systems, without permission in writing from the copyright holders, except in brief quotations or approved images used in a review.

All photography contained in this book is copyright by the individual photographers. For information concerning photography please contact the Grand Ole Opry.

Designed by:
Jeff Carroll
Franklin, Tennessee
www.jeffcarrolldesign.com

Published by:
Grandin Hood Publishers
1101 West Main Street
Franklin, Tennessee 37064
www.grandinhood.com

Printed in South Korea by PACOM Korea
ISBN: 978-1-7339304-8-2

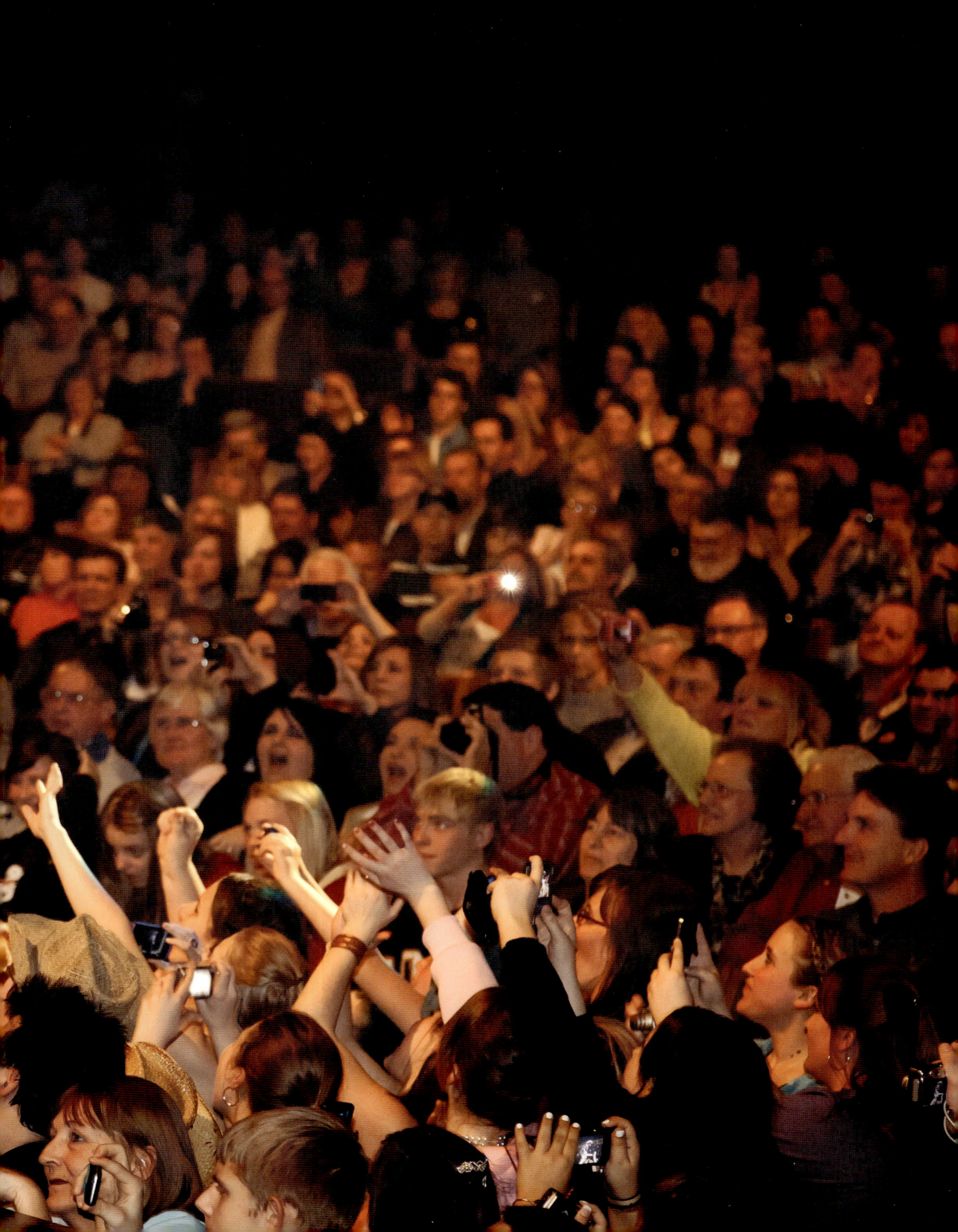

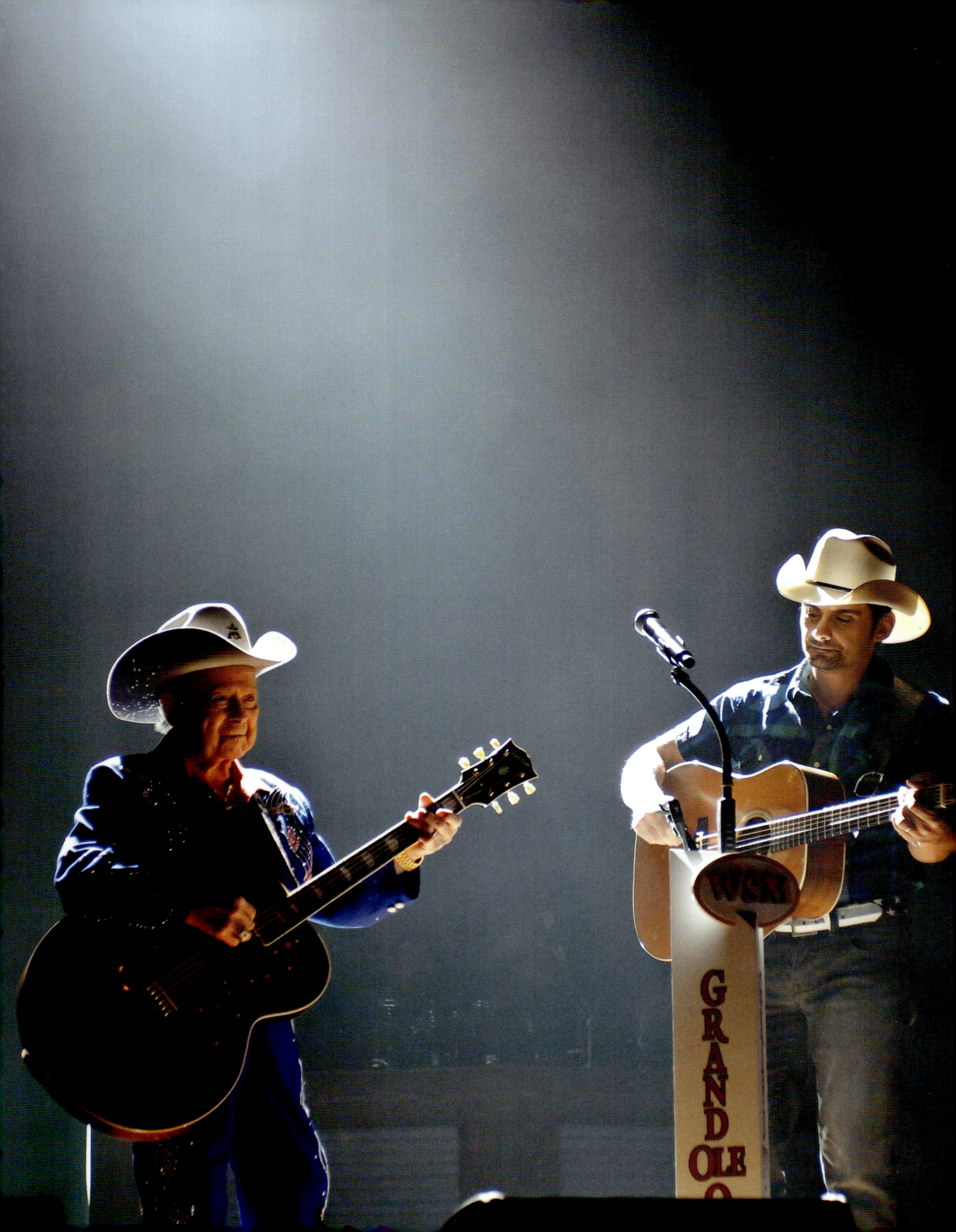
WSM
GRAND
OLE

DEDICATION

THE OPRY'S LITTLEST BIGGEST STAR

The Opry lost a member regarded as its greatest treasure, Little Jimmy Dickens, at the dawn of its 90th Anniversary year. Brad Paisley thought of Dickens as a fishing buddy, hero, and best friend.

The Grand Ole Opry has always been a stage that showcases the past, present and future of country music. It has presided and watched over decades of this art form's growing, expanding, and changing with the times. And throughout eight or so of those decades, a little legend also presided from the stage and watched in the wings as everything unfolded. Debuts, returns, milestones, all these highlights seemed to revolve around Little Jimmy Dickens. He was an instant favorite when he first appeared on the show on February 21st, 1948, and was still everyone's favorite when he last performed on Dec. 20th, 2014. In that time, from Tater's perspective (a nickname Hank Williams gave him), what must it have been like to see country music become what it is today? To make friends with every single performer who ever made a difference in this town? To feel the love from so many generations of fans, and witness this institution become the greatest country music show on earth? Well, we invite you to sit in the pews, enjoy the legend, and watch history unfold for yourself. And know that our littlest-biggest star is probably watching from on high as the rest of our history unfolds. May the circle be unbroken.

—BRAD PAISLEY

GRAND OLE OPRY FAMILY ALBUM 10

RY
2022
DECADES
A 97 YEAR TRADITION

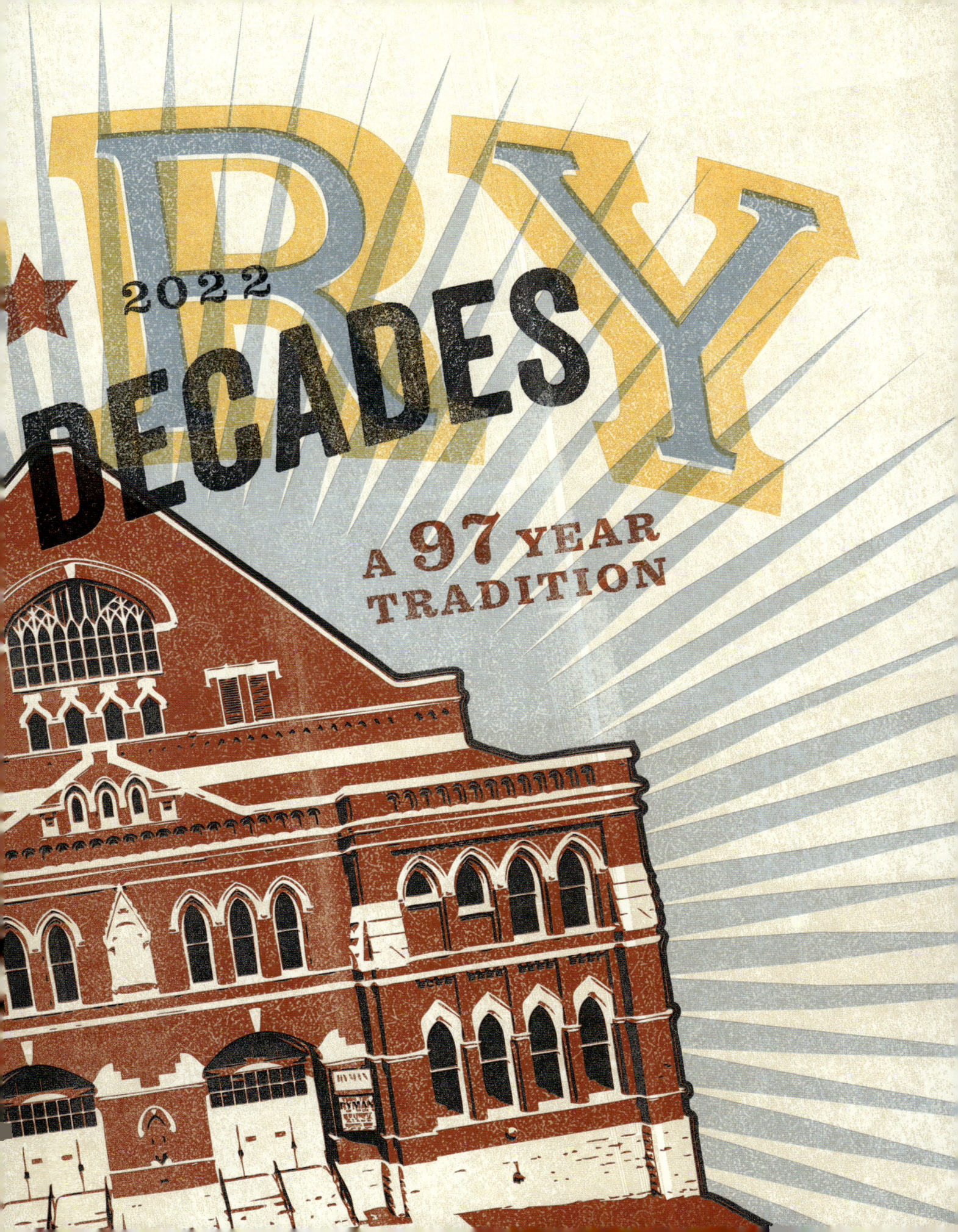

OPRY BY THE DECADES
1925–1934

Even in its early days, the Grand Ole Opry presented a broad range of what would become known as country music. Born as a barn dance program in a downtown office building, the show emphasized old-time fiddlers and harmonica players. It also featured what Opry founder George D. Hay called "hoedown bands" like the Possum Hunters and the Gully Jumpers, along with Uncle Dave Macon — the artist many regard as the Opry's first super star act— which gave the show a rural feel. While most of its first decade was spent in residence at the National Life and Accident Insurance Company headquarters, the show moved to the Hillsboro Theater, now known as the Belcourt Theatre, in 1934.

**OPRY INDUCTEES
1925-1934:**
DeFord Bailey
Henry Bandy
Dr. Humphrey Bate and his Possum Hunters
The Binkley Brothers and their Dixie Clodhoppers
The Crook Brothers
Kitty Cora Cline
The Fruit Jar Drinkers
The Gully Jumpers
Theron Hale and his Daughters
Sid Harkreader
Uncle Dave Macon
Uncle Joe Mangrum and Fred Schriver
The Pickard Family
W. Ed Poplin and his Barn Dance Orchestra
Arthur Smith
Melvin Garfield Smith
Uncle Jimmy Thompson
Mazy Todd

NOVEMBER 28, 1925

WSM's Barn Dance – forerunner of the Grand Ole Opry – broadcasts for the first time from a 15'-by-20' fifth-floor studio in the National Life and Accident Insurance Company headquarters (below). A white-bearded, 77-year-old fiddler named Uncle Jimmy Thompson (left), who claimed he knew a thousand songs and could "fiddle the taters off the vine," plays a set that began with "Tennessee Waggoner."

NATIONAL LIFE AND ACCIDENT INSURANCE CO. BLDG.-7TH AVE. AT UNION-NASHVILLE-TENN

MAY 1, 1926

Uncle Dave Macon (with the banjo) becomes a Barn Dance regular. The 55-year-old former vaudevillian is the show's first performer with a national reputation, and he will entertain Opry audiences with his old-time banjo picking and comedy until three weeks before his death on March 1, 1952, at age 81. At left is Opry founder George D. Hay's famous steamboat whistle which he is playing in the image above.

JUNE 19, 1926

DeFord Bailey, the Opry's first African American member, makes his first documented Opry appearance. Bailey, billed as "The Harmonica Wizard," will be a regular on the show until 1941, and his signature tune, "Pan American Blues," will often open the broadcasts.

OPRY BY THE DECADE

★ **DECEMBER 1927** ★

Following an NBC network broadcast of conductor Walter Damrosch's Music Appreciation Hour, WSM program director George D. Hay, nicknamed "The Solemn Old Judge," proclaims, "For the past hour we have been listening to music taken largely from Grand Opera, but from now on we will present the Grand Ole Opry." The new name sticks. The photo above is the 1927 cast of the Grand Ole Opry.

OPRY BY THE DECADES 1925–1934

OCTOBER 5, 1932

WSM begins transmitting with what is then the world's tallest radio tower (878 feet) in Brentwood, Tennessee, increasing the station's broadcast power to 50,000 watts. On Saturday nights, the Opry can now be heard from New York to California and into Canada and Mexico.

FEBRUARY 1934

To accommodate growing Saturday night crowds at the National Life building, the Opry moves into WSM's recently constructed Studio C, which seats 500.

★ **JULY 4, 1934** ★

Nearly 8,000 people show up for an all-day Opry-sponsored show in West Tennessee that features Uncle Dave Macon (front row, right), Fiddlin' Arthur Smith, the Gully Jumpers, and the Crook Brothers (above). As a result of the show's success, George D. Hay starts the Artists Service Bureau to book Opry stars on concerts throughout the South.

OPRY BY THE DECADES 1925–1934

Dr. Humphrey Bate's string band, the Possum Hunters, included his daughter, Alcyone (front row, center), who is recognized as the first female vocalist to appear on the Grand Ole Opry. Asher Sizemore and his son Little Jimmie (right) joined the Opry cast in 1933.

★ OCTOBER 1934 ★

The Opry rents the 800-seat Hillsboro Theater, a former silent film house in the Vanderbilt University area. The show's segmented format begins here, as the performers play two 15-minute sets in front of separate audiences. Known today as the Belcourt Theatre, the venue continues to house film and music events.

OPRY BY THE DECADES
1935–1944

The Opry's popularity grew rapidly in its second decade, forcing the show to move first from the Hillsboro Theater to the Dixie Tabernacle, then to War Memorial Auditorium, and finally to the Ryman Auditorium. Eventually during its second decade the show also began charging admission. But nothing seemed to dampen the public's enthusiasm for stars like the Delmore Brothers, the husband-and-wife duo Curly Fox & Texas Ruby, and long-bow fiddler Arthur Smith and his band with Sam and Kirk McGee, the Dixieliners. Comedy acts took their place on the Opry, including the most enduring comedy act in country music history, Cousin Minnie Pearl. Stylistically, the show's emphasis moved from old-time instrumentals to modern country singers, and three of the Opry's most prominent figures for decades to come—Roy Acuff, Bill Monroe, and Ernest Tubb—were among the artists who joined the cast during this time.

OPRY INDUCTEES 1935–1944:
Sarie and Sallie
Jack Shook and his Missouri Montaineers
Pee Wee King and his Golden West Cowboys
Curly Fox and Texas Ruby
Roy Acuff and his Smoky Mountain Boys
The Tennessee Valley Boys
Hilltop Harmonizers
Jamup and Honey
The Andrews Brothers
Bill Monroe and his Blue Grass Boys
Ford Rush
John Daniel Quartet
Paul Howard and his Arkansas Cotton Pickers
Minnie Pearl
Mack McGarr
David "Stringbean" Akeman
The Duke of Paducah (Whitey Ford)
Bradley Kincaid
Curley Williams and his Georgia Peach Pickers
Ernest Tubb
The Smith Sisters
Eddy Arnold
Pete Pyle and his Mississippi Valley Boys
The Bailes Brothers
The Cackle Sisters (Carolyn and Mary Jane Dezurik)
Clyde Moody
The Poe Sisters
Rod Brasfield
The Happy Valley Boys
The Old Hickory Singers

JUNE 13, 1936

The Opry relocates to the Dixie Tabernacle – a 3,500-seat religious revival house with wooden benches, sawdust floors, and no dressing rooms – at 410 Fatherland Street in East Nashville.

OPRY BY THE DECADES 1935–1944   18

★ JUNE 1939 ★

The Opry moves to the War Memorial Auditorium in downtown Nashville. Because the auditorium's seating capacity – 2,200 – is a third less than the Dixie Tabernacle, the show begins charging admission – 25 cents.

★ FEBRUARY 5, 1938 ★

Roy Acuff (left) makes his second Opry appearance with his band, the Crazy Tennesseans, after a lackluster debut four months earlier. Acuff's rendition of "The Great Speckled Bird" generates an avalanche of mail, prompting WSM to add him to the official cast two weeks later. With the addition of Acuff, the Opry begins shifting emphasis from instrumental music to vocal performers.

Grand Ole Opry cast of 1939 at the War Memorial Auditorium

OPRY BY THE DECADES 1935-1944

OCTOBER 14, 1939

The NBC radio network begins carrying a half-hour Opry segment, hosted by Roy Acuff and sponsored by Prince Albert Tobacco. The show attracts mostly regional affiliates.

OCTOBER 28, 1939

Bluegrass patriarch Bill Monroe (second from left) joins the Opry cast and performs "Muleskinner Blues." George D. Hay is so taken with Monroe's performance, he declares that if Monroe ever wants to leave the Opry, he'll have to fire himself.

JUNE 25, 1940

Republic Pictures releases Grand Ole Opry, in which George D. Hay, Roy Acuff, and Uncle Dave Macon help Ozarks residents wrest control of the state government from crooked political interests. Nashville's Paramount Theatre hosts the film's local premiere on June 28.

NOVEMBER 1940

Comedienne Minnie Pearl joins the Opry cast. Though many of the signature elements of Minnie Pearl are present already, the gossip of Grinder's Switch has not yet added the famous price tag to her flowered straw hat. That will come a few years later as an accident, when a tag inadvertently left on a new bunch of silk flowers flops out during a performance and draws laughter from the cast backstage. Minnie will decide to leave the tag as a part of the costume and a testament to "human frailty."

★ JANUARY 16, 1943 ★

Ernest Tubb makes his Grand Ole Opry debut. He brings with him the guitar of his idol, Jimmie Rodgers, given to Tubb by Rodgers' widow, Carrie.

★ JUNE 5, 1943 ★

The Opry moves to the Ryman Auditorium on Fifth Avenue in downtown Nashville. The building, a former tabernacle, features oak pew seating and exceptional acoustics, but no air-conditioning.

23   OPRY BY THE DECADES 1935-1944

OPRY BY THE DECADES
1945–1954

In its third decade, Opry stars like Red Foley and Eddy Arnold became ambassadors for country music, traveling throughout the nation during the week and returning home on the weekend to the Opry stage. In this era, the Opry welcomed debut performances by Jimmy Dickens, Hank Williams, Lefty Frizzell, and Elvis Presley, to name just a few. During this decade, Ernest Tubb took an Opry troupe to New York's Carnegie Hall, and the show made its first European tour.

OPRY INDUCTEES 1945–1954:

Lew Childre
The Tennessee Sweethearts (Clyde and Marie Dilleha)
Cousin Wilbur and his Tennessee Mountaineers
Wally Fowler and his Georgia Clodhoppers
Grandpa Jones
Red Foley
The Willis Brothers
Annie Lou and Danny Dill
Milton Estes and his Musical Millers
Johnnie and Jack
Lonzo and Oscar
Cowboy Copas
Jimmy Dickens
George Morgan
The Jordanaires
Hank Williams
Hank Snow
Cedar Hill Square Dancers
Cousin Jody (James Clell Summey)
Chet Atkins
Mother Maybelle Carter and the Carter Sisters
Moon Mullican
Lefty Frizzell
Ray Price
Carl Smith
Ralph Sloan and his Tennessee Travelers
Martha Carson
Faron Young
Kitty Wells
Webb Pierce
Marty Robbins
Goldie Hill
The Wilburn Brothers
The Ladells
Benny Martin
The Carlisles (Bill Carlisle)
Del Wood
Ferlin Husky
Red Sovine
Slim Whitman

DECEMBER 8, 1945

Earl Scruggs makes his debut with Bill Monroe's Blue Grass Boys (above), completing the historic line-up that would serve as the prototype for the bluegrass sound — Monroe on mandolin, Scruggs on banjo, Lester Flatt on guitar, Chubby Wise on fiddle, and Howard Watts on bass. Pictured at right is Bill Monroe's famous hat.

SEPTEMBER 18 AND 19, 1947

Ernest Tubb and Minnie Pearl headline an Opry troupe that plays two shows at New York's Carnegie Hall. "The radio and newspaper people ignored us the first night we were there," Tubb says, "but we turned away six thousand people and the next night every reporter was there." *Billboard* magazine reports, "Such screaming and wild applause after each number hasn't been heard in town since Frank Sinatra brought out the bobbysoxers at the Paramount."

25 OPRY BY THE DECADES 1945–1954

FRIDAY NIGHT FROLIC

★ SEPTEMBER 1948 ★

To keep Eddy Arnold (pictured at right) on WSM via his syndicated radio show, the station agrees to create a new live show for broadcast in the adjacent timeslot, to lure more listeners. The show, called the Friday Night Frolic, would move to the Ryman in 1964 and become the Friday Night Opry. Below, Opry announcer T. Tommy Cutrer joins Jim Reeves on stage.

OPRY BY THE DECADES 1945–1954   26

JUNE 11, 1949

Hank Williams makes his Opry debut. The audience calls him back six times to reprise his song, "Lovesick Blues." Opry legend Little Jimmy Dickens says more than 50 years later it was the Opry performance by another artist he most vividly recalled. At left are Hank Williams' boots.

OPRY BY THE DECADES

NOVEMBER 13, 1949

The Opry partners with the USO to send Opry stars Roy Acuff, Rod Brasfield, Jimmy Dickens, Red Foley, Minnie Pearl, and Hank Williams on a tour of U.S. Air Force bases in England, Germany and the Azores. It's the first overseas trip for the Opry.

Roy Acuff entertains the Opry crowd with his classic fiddle balancing act.

OPRY BY THE DECADES 1945–1954

MAY 29, 1950

"Mother" Maybelle Carter and the Carter Sisters — June, Anita and Helen — join the Opry.

The cast of the Grand Ole Opry, circa 1953

29 OPRY BY THE DECADES 1945–1954

OPRY BY THE DECADES
1955–1964

The Opry's fourth decade had it all—honky tonk, bluegrass, crooners, comedy, even a little rock 'n' roll. At home at the Ryman, the show not only brought in established acts like Lester Flatt and Earl Scruggs, it could also turn an unknown like Stonewall Jackson into a star. The Opry began the '60s by inducting a bevy of young talent. Patsy Cline, Hank Locklin, George Hamilton IV, and Billy Walker all joined in the first year alone. The era also had its share of tragedy, including the untimely deaths of Cline, Cowboy Copas, Hawkshaw Hawkins, Johnnie & Jack's Jack Anglin, Jim Reeves, Texas Ruby, and Ira Louvin. As the recording industry in Nashville took hold, Opry membership and hit records often went hand in hand.

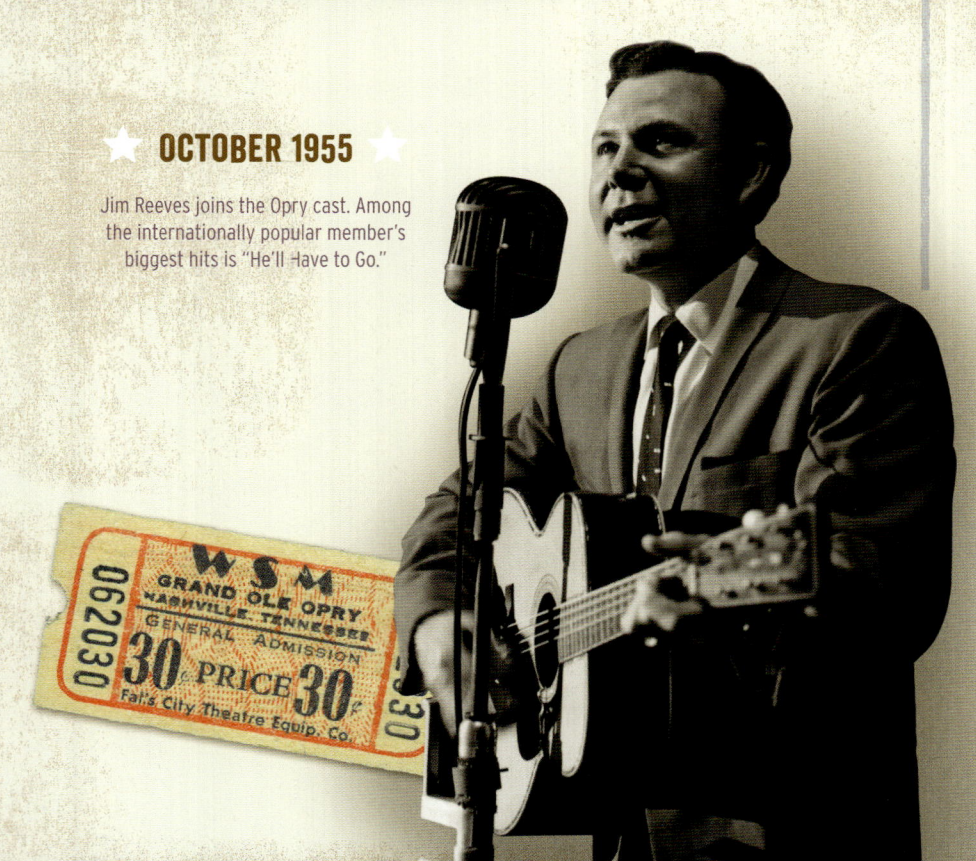

★ OCTOBER 1955 ★

Jim Reeves joins the Opry cast. Among the internationally popular member's biggest hits is "He'll Have to Go."

OPRY INDUCTEES 1955–1964:

The Louvin Brothers
Hawkshaw Hawkins
Hank Thompson
Justin Tubb
Jim Reeves
Jean Shepard
Johnny Cash
Jimmy C. Newman
George Jones
Rose Maddox
Stonewall Jackson
Lester Flatt and Earl Scruggs
Wilma Lee and Stoney Cooper
Porter Wagoner
The Everly Brothers
Rusty and Doug Kershaw
Archie Campbell
Don Gibson
Carl and Pearl Butler
Roy Drusky
Ben Smathers and the Stoney Mountain Cloggers
Billy Grammer
Margie Bowes
Skeeter Davis
Billy Walker
Patsy Cline
The Glaser Brothers
Bobby Lord
Hank Locklin
George Hamilton IV
Bobby Bare
Bill Anderson
Charlie Walker
Merle Travis
Jimmy Driftwood
Loretta Lynn
Leroy Van Dyke
Sonny James
Marion Worth
Norma Jean
The Browns
Jim and Jesse
Ernie Ashworth
Dottie West
The Osborne Brothers
Willie Nelson

★ **JULY 7, 1956** ★

Johnny Cash joins the Opry. Johnny meets his future wife, June Carter, backstage at the Opry the same year. Pictured with Johnny is Carl Smith. At left is Johnny's tie from 1956.

The 1956 cast of the Grand Ole Opry

MAY 11, 1957

The Everly Brothers make their Opry debut the same week their first single, "Bye Bye Love," enters the country charts.

Opry program from the era

Backstage at the Opry in 1957: Ferlin Husky, Elvis Presley, Faron Young, Hawkshaw Hawkins and Tom Perryman

33 OPRY BY THE DECADES 1955–1964

NOVEMBER 29, 1961

An Opry troupe featuring Patsy Cline, Jim Reeves and Grandpa Jones (pictured below), as well as Marty Robbins (bottom photo) and Bill Monroe, travels to New York's Carnegie Hall to perform for a sold-out crowd. The performance benefits the Musicians Aid Society.

Opry lineup from December 15, 1962

MARCH 9, 1963

A silent prayer is held during the Opry in tribute to members Patsy Cline, Cowboy Copas, and Hawkshaw Hawkins, who died March 5 in a plane crash near Camden, Tennessee. Also remembered is Jack Anglin of the duo Johnnie and Jack, killed en route to a prayer service for Cline. Opry manager Ott Devine encourages the audience "to keep smiling, and to recall the happier occasions. I feel I can speak for all of them when I say… let's continue in the tradition of the Grand Ole Opry."

Loretta Lynn backstage with the Willis Brothers in June 1962

35 OPRY BY THE DECADES 1955–1964

OPRY BY THE DECADES
1965–1974

The Opry found a new home during its fifth decade, leaving the urban surroundings of the Ryman for the suburban splendor of the new Grand Ole Opry House and an adjoining theme park. The cast celebrated guest visits from astronauts, a Beatle, and –for the first time in its history— a U.S. President.

OPRY INDUCTEES 1965–1974:
Tex Ritter
Bob Luman
Connie Smith
Ray Pillow
Del Reeves
The Four Guys
Stu Phillips
Jeannie Seely
Jack Greene
Dolly Parton
Tammy Wynette
Tom T. Hall
Jan Howard
David Houston
Barbara Mandrell
Jeanne Pruett
Jerry Clower

1965 cast of the Grand Ole Opry

★ 1965 ★

Johnny Cash drags his microphone stand across the front of the Ryman Auditorium stage, breaking all the footlights. He is banished from the Opry but, four years later, returns to the Ryman stage as host of his own ABC television series. Pictured at right are Cash and Jeannie C. Riley on the set of his new show in 1969.

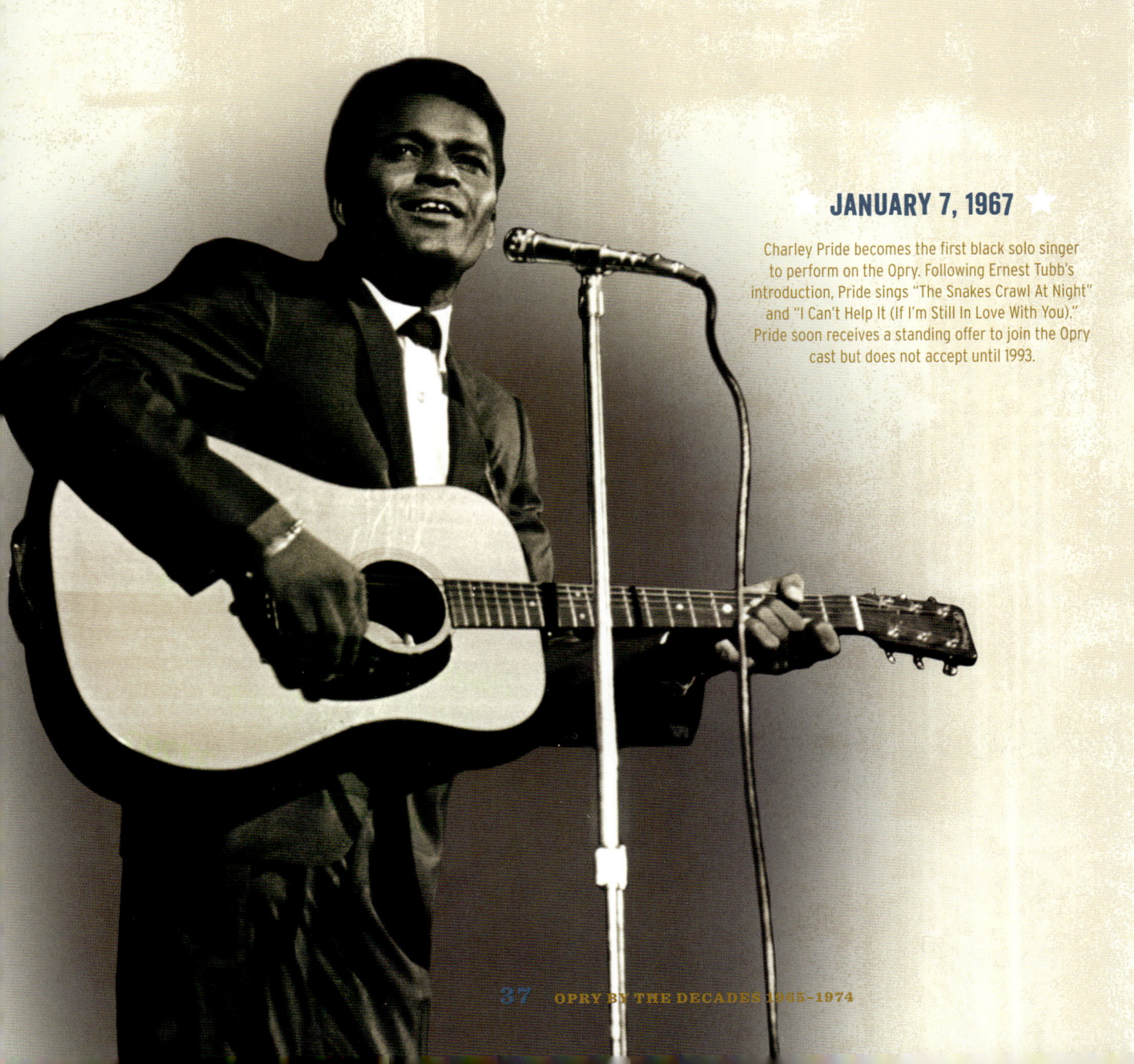

★ JANUARY 7, 1967 ★

Charley Pride becomes the first black solo singer to perform on the Opry. Following Ernest Tubb's introduction, Pride sings "The Snakes Crawl At Night" and "I Can't Help It (If I'm Still In Love With You)." Pride soon receives a standing offer to join the Opry cast but does not accept until 1993.

37   OPRY BY THE DECADES 1965–1974

★ **MAY 13, 1967** ★

Merle Haggard debuts at the Opry.

★ **MARCH 15, 1968** ★

Rock group The Byrds, featuring Gram Parsons and future Desert Rose Band member Chris Hillman, perform on the Opry. The group sings Bob Dylan's "You Ain't Goin' Nowhere," then substitutes their own "Hickory Wind" for a previously announced cover of Merle Haggard's "Sing Me Back Home."

OPRY BY THE DECADES 1965–1974

★ NOVEMBER 10, 1973 ★

Popular Opry member David "Stringbean" Akeman appears on the Opry for the final time. When Stringbean returns home from the Opry that night, he and his wife, Estelle, are ambushed and murdered by two men who plan to rob the couple of money Stringbean reputedly had hidden in his home. Twenty-three years later, some $20,000 will be found, rotted and worthless, in the chimney of the house.

★ MAY 11, 1968 ★

The Opry pays tribute to founder George D. Hay, who died in Virginia on May 8. Opry announcer and Hay protégé Grant Turner says: "He called himself The Solemn Old Judge. If he was solemn, it was only in the face of those who sought to change or corrupt the purity of the barn-dance ballads he sought to preserve. We, the performers and friends of the Grand Ole Opry, salute the memory of one whose influence is felt on the stage of the Opry tonight – The Solemn Old Judge, George D. Hay."

39 OPRY BY THE DECADES 1965–1974

Grand Ole Opry from the Ryman Auditorium, circa 1973

★ MARCH 15, 1974 ★

The Opry broadcasts its last Friday show from the Ryman. George Morgan's "Candy Kisses" ends the show. After the Opry, Johnny and June Carter Cash sing "Will the Circle Be Unbroken" on the *Grand Ole Opry Gospel Time* show to end the final broadcast from the Ryman. A young writer named Garrison Keillor covers the Opry's final Ryman show and is inspired to create his own unique radio show, *A Prairie Home Companion*, which goes on the air four months later in Minnesota. In the photo at right, Minnie Pearl sheds a tear as she says farewell to the Ryman.

★ MARCH 16, 1974 ★

Roy Acuff opens the new 4,400-seat Grand Ole Opry House with a performance of "The Wabash Cannonball." President Richard Nixon attends and leads the Opry audience in singing "Happy Birthday" to First Lady Pat Nixon, who is 62. Acuff attempts to teach the President how to yo-yo before the Opry audience. Pictured below is Roy's actual yo-yo.

41 OPRY BY THE DECADES 1965–1974

OPRY BY THE DECADES
1975–1984

The Opry settled in to the Grand Ole Opry House in its sixth decade, also broadcasting live on television in its entirety for the first time and later moving on to a half-hour weekly cable broadcast. The Opry's roster additions ranged from the country pop modern sounds of Ronnie Milsap, to the Western harmonies of Riders In The Sky, to the traditional country and bluegrass-influenced music of Ricky Skaggs and The Whites.

OPRY INDUCTEES 1975–1984:
Ronnie Milsap
Don Williams
Larry Gatlin and the Gatlin Brothers
Melvin Sloan Dancers
John Conlee
Boxcar Willie
B.J. Thomas
Ricky Skaggs
Riders In The Sky
The Whites
Lorrie Morgan

The cast of the Grand Ole Opry celebrates its 50th anniversary in October 1975.

WSM Presents...
THE GRAND OLE OPRY AT 50
A NASHVILLE CELEBRATION

A VIDEOTAPING
October 22 & 23, 1975
AT THE GRAND OLE OPRY HOUSE

GRAND OLE OPRY
50 YEARS
SINCE 1925

ABC-TV
November 11, 1975
sponsored by
THE BORDEN COMPANY

Souvenir Program
GRAND OLE OPRY

★ OCTOBER 25, 1975 ★

Four members of the Apollo-Soyuz crew (three Americans and one Russian astronaut) visit the Opry following the spacecraft's historic flight.

43 OPRY BY THE DECADES 1975–1984

★ JANUARY 29, 1977 ★

Andy Warhol and Jamie Wyeth visit the Opry at the invitation of Tex Ritter's widow, Dorothy, the official Opry hostess and patroness of the Nashville arts scene. The two artists are in Nashville to attend a reception at Cheekwood Botanical Garden and Museum of Art for an exhibit of portraits they painted of each other.

Poster promoting an Opry 1977 visit to Boston Garden

MARCH 4, 1978

The Grand Ole Opry is televised live in its entirety for the first time, as part of a PBS pledge-drive special. Pictured above is Barbara Mandrell.

JUNE 17, 1978

Marty Robbins drives his new, custom-made Panther DeVille onto the Opry stage. Roy Acuff gets a security guard, who writes Robbins a parking ticket. Pictured at the far right is Marty's guitar.

Waylon Jennings and Johnny Cash on the Opry stage in 1978

★ JANUARY 27, 1979 ★

Actress Sissy Spacek joins Loretta Lynn and Ernest Tubb on the Opry stage as Spacek prepares for her starring role in the motion picture *Coal Miner's Daughter*. Spacek will later win an Academy Award for her portrayal of the Opry legend.

Riders In The Sky is inducted into the Grand Ole Opry by Ernest Tubb in June 1982.

MARCH 10, 1979

At the invitation of Porter Wagoner, R&B superstar James Brown performs on the Opry. Brown's set includes "Your Cheatin' Heart" and "Tennessee Waltz," as well as his own "Papa's Got a Brand New Bag."

Roy Acuff warms up before his Opry performance, circa 1980.

47   OPRY BY THE DECADES 1975–1984

OPRY BY THE DECADES
1985–1994

Country's popularity exploded during the Opry's seventh decade, creating a new generation of music superstars, many of whom became official members of the Opry family in addition to delivering chart-topping hit after hit.

**OPRY INDUCTEES
1985–1994:**
Johnny Russell
Mel McDaniel
Reba McEntire
Randy Travis
Roy Clark
Ricky Van Shelton
Patty Loveless
Holly Dunn
Mike Snider
Garth Brooks
Clint Black
Alan Jackson
Vince Gill
Emmylou Harris
Travis Tritt
Marty Stuart
Charley Pride
Alison Krauss
Joe Diffie
Hal Ketchum

One of Porter Wagoner's many rhinestone jackets and boots

OPRY BY THE DECADES 1985–1994   48

MAY 18, 1985

Then-Vice President and Mrs. George H.W. Bush visit the Opry. Ten years later, the couple will celebrate their 50th anniversary at the Opry House.

FEBRUARY 20, 1988

During a show honoring Roy Acuff's 50th Opry anniversary, superstar Dolly Parton and her musical mentor Porter Wagoner perform together for the first time in 14 years.

★ OCTOBER 6, 1990 ★

Garth Brooks joins the Opry cast during a show that also features one of Alan Jackson's first Opry appearances. Introduced by Johnny Russell, Brooks performs "Friends in Low Places," "If Tomorrow Never Comes," and "The Dance."

★ NOVEMBER 3, 1990 ★

On the occasion of her 50th anniversary with the Opry, Minnie Pearl receives 50 dozen – that's 600 – roses from Dwight Yoakam. President and Mrs. George H.W. Bush send a congratulatory telegram, and Dolly Parton shares her good wishes via videotape. After seeing Dolly's message, Pearl quips, "I wear a hat so folks can tell us apart."

★ FEBRUARY 29, 1992 ★

Porter Wagoner welcomes Travis Tritt as he joins the Opry, while future member Trisha Yearwood debuts on the show, singing "She's in Love With The Boy."

★ OCTOBER 23, 1992 ★

Opry patriarch Roy Acuff makes his final performance. "The King of Country Music" dies exactly one month later, at age 89.

Roy ACUFF
Sept. 15, 1903 – Nov. 23, 1992

★ **MAY 1, 1993** ★

Charley Pride joins the Opry, 26 years after first appearing on the show as a guest. Jimmy C. Newman celebrates with him.

★ **JUNE 3, 1994** ★

Ryman Auditorium – the "Mother Church of Country Music" – reopens as a premier performance hall and museum after a major renovation.

OPRY BY THE DECADES 1985–1994

★ **JULY 3, 1993** ★

Alison Krauss becomes the first bluegrass artist in 19 years to join the Opry cast when she is inducted by Garth Brooks.

In one of his last known portraits, blugrass legend Bill Monroe is joined by Hatch Show Print's Jim Sherraden as they inspect one of the print shop's timeless works of art.

OPRY BY THE DECADES
1995–2004

The dawn of a new century brought more ways than ever for fans to experience the Opry, including the internet. While the Opry bid farewell to some of its most storied members including Minnie Pearl and Bill Monroe, its member additions reflected a commitment both to country music's glorious past and its bright future.

OPRY INDUCTEES 1995–2004:
Bashful Brother Oswald (Beecher Ray Kirby)
Martina McBride
Steve Wariner
Johnny Paycheck
Diamond Rio
Trisha Yearwood
Ralph Stanley
Pam Tillis
Brad Paisley
Trace Adkins
Del McCoury
Terri Clark

NOVEMBER 30, 1995
Martina McBride joins the Opry during a taping of a CBS special celebrating the Opry's 70th anniversary, inducted by one of her greatest influences, Loretta Lynn.

JANUARY 3, 1998

Grandpa Jones makes his final Opry appearance. The 84-year-old entertainer suffers the first of a series of strokes shortly after his performance and goes straight from the Opry to a Nashville hospital. He will pass away on February 19.

NOVEMBER 7, 1998

Jimmy Dickens celebrates his 50th Opry anniversary with friends and cohorts Carl Smith, Waylon Jennings, Bobby Bare, and Bill Anderson on hand. He joins Herman Crook, Roy Acuff, Minnie Pearl, Bill Monroe, and Grandpa Jones as the only Opry members to have celebrated 50 years as cast members to that point. Since then, Bill Anderson, Jim Ed Brown, Wilma Lee Cooper, Billy Grammer, George Hamilton IV, Stonewall Jackson, George Jones, Charlie Louvin, Loretta Lynn, Jesse McReynolds, Jimmy C. Newman, Osborne Brothers, Jean Shepard, Porter Wagoner, and Teddy Wilburn have also reached that milestone.

1997-1998

Over a nine-month period, Vince Gill makes more than 40 Opry appearances as he prepares for the release of his album *The Key*, often testing new material on Opry audiences.

JANUARY 15-16, 1999

The Grand Ole Opry broadcasts all three of its weekend shows from the Ryman Auditorium for the first time in 25 years. During the run, Trisha Yearwood is surprised with an invitation to join the cast. She will become an Opry member on March 13, 1999.

OPRY BY THE DECADES 1995-2004

★ JUNE 10, 2000 ★

The Opry unveils its first major set redesign in 25 years. Designed by Emmy-winning production designer Rene Lagler, the new set features a barn-shaped backdrop made of aluminum, wood, and projection materials, as well as large projection screens flanking the stage.

★ FEBRUARY 17, 2001 ★

Steve Wariner congratulates Brad Paisley as he is inducted into the Opry while wearing the bright yellow jacket that Buck Owens wore on the cover of his 1966 *Live at Carnegie Hall* album.

★ FEBRUARY 16, 2002 ★

Marty Stuart, Travis Tritt, and Hank Williams Jr. pay tribute to Waylon Jennings, who died the previous Wednesday. Williams sings his song "Eyes of Waylon," and the three entertainers spend an hour singing such Jennings hits as "Only Daddy That'll Walk the Line," "This Time," "I've Always Been Crazy," and "Are You Sure Hank Done It This Way." Porter Wagoner calls the night "the most exciting night I can ever remember on the Opry."

★ SEPTEMBER 7, 2002 ★

Alan Jackson, Kenny Chesney, Lee Ann Womack, and Jim Lauderdale serenade Opry member George Jones with versions of his classic hits during a birthday celebration. Jones takes the stage himself for a performance of "I Don't Need Your Rocking Chair." Little Jimmy Dickens is shown giving his well wishes.

★ NOVEMBER 30, 2002 ★

Tim McGraw makes his Grand Ole Opry debut on a bill that also includes Brad Paisley.

★ DECEMBER 14, 2002 ★

Toby Keith makes his Opry debut. Keith Urban and Trace Adkins also appear that night.

★ JANUARY 4, 2003 ★

Hank Williams Jr. and Hank Williams III both perform during an Opry show commemorating the 50th anniversary of Hank Williams Sr.'s death. Hank Jr. introduces the son of Rufus "Tee Tot" Payne, the street musician who mentored Hank Williams. Vince Gill, The Whites, and Jimmy Dickens also perform during the tribute.

★ FEBRUARY 17-21, 2003 ★

Syndicated television game show *Wheel of Fortune* airs a week of shows taped on the Grand Ole Opry stage the previous month. Among the country stars who appear on the show during the week are Terri Clark, Montgomery Gentry, Lorrie Morgan, and Trisha Yearwood.

★ JULY 10 AND 13, 2004 ★

Camera crews shoot the video for Alan Jackson's "Too Much of a Good Thing." The crew shoots B-roll footage backstage during the Saturday Opry on the 10th and Alan's performance at the Tuesday Night Opry on the 13th.

59 OPRY BY THE DECADES 1995-

OPRY BY THE DECADES
2005–2015

Throughout the Opry's ninth decade, the invitation and induction of each addition to the Opry family has been presented with great fanfare. Opry management takes the decision to add a cast member very seriously. After all, each new member has the potential to shape the show for decades to come. In this most recent decade, each new member has not only added to the musical breadth of the show, but also possesses a great love for the Opry's rich 90-year tradition. Also during this decade, advancements in digital technology have allowed the Opry's voice to be spread worldwide and for Opry fans to connect like never before thanks to social media and mobile devices. A 2010 flood tested the Opry's mettle and sent the show on a tour of various venues around Music City after more than four feet of water inundated the Grand Ole Opry House. The flood's end result, however, was that a completely refurbished Opry House re-opened less than six months after the flood as a true country music showplace. Brad Paisley sang his No. 1 smash, "Welcome to the Future," to celebrate the opening of the remodeled Opry House.

OPRY INDUCTEES 2005–2014:
Dierks Bentley
Mel Tillis
Josh Turner
Charlie Daniels
Carrie Underwood
Craig Morgan
Montgomery Gentry
Blake Shelton
Oak Ridge Boys
Rascal Flatts
Keith Urban
Darius Rucker
Old Crow Medicine Show
Little Big Town

SEPTEMBER 1, 2006

Taylor Swift makes her Opry debut. A video of her performance of "Tim McGraw" from that night is later included on the deluxe version of her debut CD.

OCTOBER 15, 2005

Garth Brooks, in retirement, returns to the Opry for the first time in five years, performing on the Opry's 80th anniversary show with Porter Wagoner, Bill Anderson, and Jimmy Dickens. Garth also sings "Longneck Bottle" with Steve Wariner.

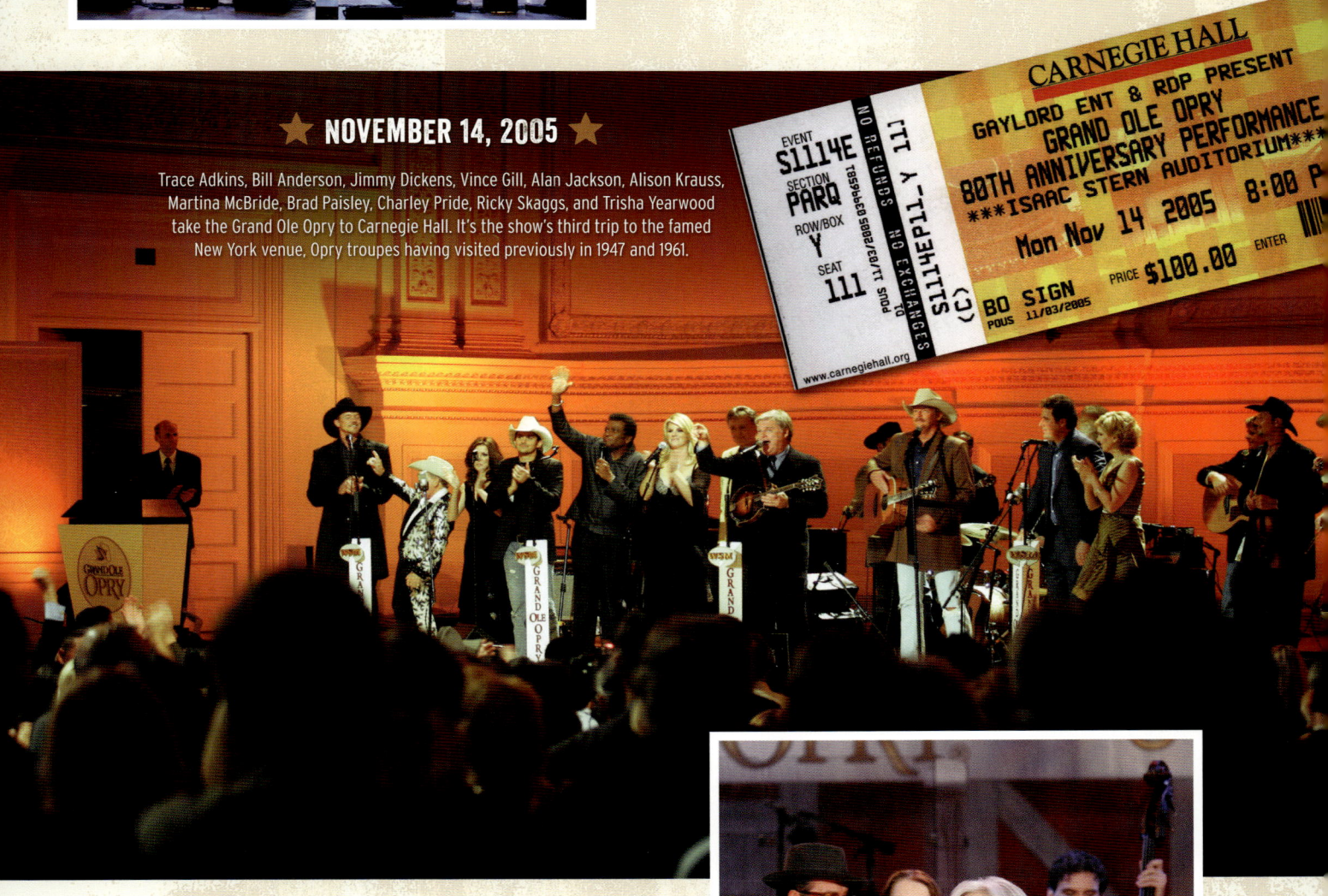

NOVEMBER 14, 2005

Trace Adkins, Bill Anderson, Jimmy Dickens, Vince Gill, Alan Jackson, Alison Krauss, Martina McBride, Brad Paisley, Charley Pride, Ricky Skaggs, and Trisha Yearwood take the Grand Ole Opry to Carnegie Hall. It's the show's third trip to the famed New York venue, Opry troupes having visited previously in 1947 and 1961.

FEBRUARY 18, 2006

Emmylou Harris brings Rock and Roll Hall of Famer Elvis Costello to the Opry for the weekend, and the two sing several songs together including "I Still Miss Someone," "Must You Throw Dirt in My Face," "Love Hurts," and "Mystery Train." During the Saturday show, Costello's wife, jazz singer Diana Krall, and Vince Gill perform an impromptu duet of a song called "Faint of Heart," which they recorded earlier that day.

61 OPRY BY THE DECADES 2005–2015

★ MAY 19, 2007 ★

Porter Wagoner celebrates his 50th anniversary with the Opry. As part of the festivities, Wagoner's former duet partner Dolly Parton joins him to sing "Just Someone I Used to Know," "The Last Thing on My Mind," and "I Will Always Love You." It's the last time the two appear together on the Opry stage.

★ MAY 10, 2008 ★

Garth Brooks officially welcomes fellow Oklahoma native Carrie Underwood into the Opry family, presenting her with the Opry Member Award.

OPRY BY THE DECADES 2005–2015

OCTOBER 5, 2008

As part of the activities leading up to the presidential debate between Senator Barack Obama and Senator John McCain at Nashville's Belmont University on October 7, the Ryman Auditorium hosts a special Grand Ole Opry featuring Opry members (and Belmont alumnus) Brad Paisley, Trisha Yearwood, and Josh Turner, along with guests Julie Roberts, Darius Rucker, and CBS News journalist Bob Schieffer & Honky Tonk Confidential. Schieffer, who will moderate the presidential debate at New York's Hofstra University later in the month, performs two songs, then joins Paisley for a show-closing rendition of Paisley's hit "Alcohol."

MAY 30, 2009

Steve Martin plays the banjo as he makes his Opry debut to promote his album, *The Crow: New Songs for the Five-String Banjo*. Also appearing with the award-winning actor, comedian and musician that night: Opry member Vince Gill and Gill's wife, Amy Grant, as well as musicians Stuart Duncan, Tim O'Brien, John McEuen, and others. "I can't tell you what a thrill it is for me to be standing on this stage with you and all these great people," Martin tells Vince shortly before they and the band launch into the Flatt & Scruggs' classic "Foggy Mountain Breakdown."

MAY 1-2, 2010

During a two-day flood that devastates much of Nashville, the Grand Ole Opry House sustains major damage that leaves the venue's stage underwater. As a result, the Grand Ole Opry is forced to broadcast from various locations around the city, including the undamaged Ryman Auditorium and the War Memorial Auditorium, the show's home from 1939-1943. Marty Stuart opens the first show since the flood, saying "Our family, our songs, and our spirit live on." The Opry makes a triumphant return to the Opry House, restored as a true country music showplace, on September 28. Among those appearing that night are Keith Urban, Jason Aldean, Martina McBride, Charlie Daniels, and Blake Shelton, who is invited to become an official Opry member.

★ SEPTEMBER 25, 2012 ★

Loretta Lynn marks her 50th anniversary as a member of the Opry family with a star-studded show featuring, among others, Trace Adkins, four CMA Female Vocalist of the Year winners: Loretta, her sister Crystal Gayle, Lee Ann Womack, and Miranda Lambert.

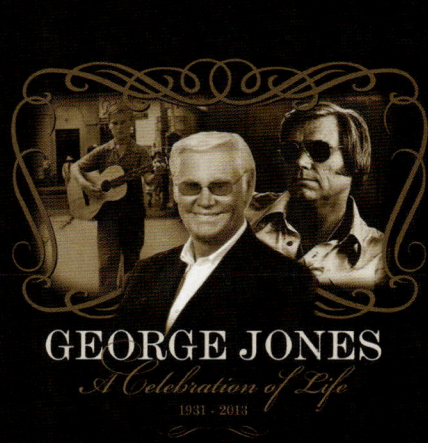

HAPPY 50TH

GEORGE JONES
A Celebration of Life
1931 - 2013

★ MAY 2, 2013 ★

The Opry family comes together at the Opry House to mourn the loss of Opry great George Jones during a service carried live via television, radio, and the internet. Among the many sharing words and songs were Vince Gill, Patty Loveless, Alan Jackson, Brad Paisley, and First Lady Laura Bush.

OPRY BY THE DECADES 2005–2015 64

★ SEPTEMBER 17, 2013 ★

Old time string band Old Crow Medicine Show stages an impromptu performance on the Opry Plaza before becoming an official Opry member later in the evening. Among the group's first Nashville gigs was entertaining Opry guests on the Plaza in the shadow of the Opry House more than 10 years earlier.

★ MARCH 16, 2014 ★

The Opry celebrates 40 years at the Opry House with performances by Blake Shelton, Miranda Lambert, Bill Anderson, and more as well as an all-cast show opener led by Old Crow Medicine Show and reminiscent of Roy Acuff's show opener 40 years earlier.

GRA

FA
ME

Grand Ole Opry Family Members

The Heart & Soul of the Opry

TRACE ADKINS
MEMBER SINCE 2003

The Grand Ole Opry stage holds many fond memories for Trace Adkins, beginning with his 1996 debut performance. In 2003, the 6'6" singer was invited to join the Opry by 4'11" veteran Little Jimmy Dickens, who stood on a stepladder to ask him face to face. Later that same year, one of Adkins' heroes, fellow Opry member Ronnie Milsap, welcomed him into the family.

Country music fans first embraced Trace's rich, resonant baritone nearly two decades ago. His lengthy list of hits includes "(This Ain't) No Thinkin' Thing," "Every Light in the House Is On," "Then They Do," "Honky Tonk Badonkadonk," "You're Gonna Miss This" and "Just Fishin'."

BIRTHPLACE: Sarepta, Louisiana
BIRTH DATE: January 13
OPRY INDUCTION: August 23, 2003

> "I ONLY RECORD SONGS THAT I REALLY LIKE AND BELIEVE IN AND CAN SING WITH CONVICTION."

Trace grew up in Sarepta, La. and developed an interest in music when his father taught him to play guitar. During high school, he joined a gospel group called the New Commitments. He spent time working on an oil rig before moving to Nashville to pursue a career in country music. After a record executive saw Adkins playing at a small club just outside of Nashville, he was soon signed to his first record deal.

Trace, who has worked as a spokesman for the Wounded Warrior Program, is well known for his staunch support of the U.S. military. He has performed for troops in Kuwait, Iraq, and Afghanistan. In 2007, he was honored with the USO Merit Award in recognition of his dedication to assisting others through charitable works. In 2007, Random House published his autobiography, *A Personal Stand: Observations and Opinions from a Freethinking Roughneck*.

In 2008, Trace expanded his fan base beyond the country audience when he finished second on Donald Trump's *Celebrity Apprentice*. Because his daughter Brianna has severe food allergies, he used the time on that show to raise money and awareness for the Food Allergy and Anaphylaxis Network. Trace won *All-Star Celebrity Apprentice* in 2013, raising money for the American Red Cross. He's also acted in several films including *An American Carol*, *The Lincoln Lawyer* and *The Virginian*.

CLOCKWISE FROM TOP LEFT:
1. With Blake Shelton, October 23, 2010
2. May 3, 2011
3. July 17, 2007
4. June 28, 2005
5. Opry induction with The Opry's Pete Fisher, Ronnie Milsap, and Lorrie Morgan. August 23, 2003.

WSM
GRAND OLE OPRY
GRAND OLE OPRY

GRAND OLE OPRY

GRAND OLE OPRY

LAUREN ALAINA
MEMBER SINCE 2022

Lauren Alaina's affinity for the Grand Ole Opry has deep roots. "Since I was a little girl, I dreamed of this moment," she said during her induction. "Most little girls dreamed of their weddings. I dreamed of this."

A proud Georgia girl, Lauren grew up singing in children's choirs, pageants, and at family gatherings. At age 15, she auditioned for *American Idol*. After her audition, judge Steven Tyler said, "I think we found the one today." Lauren went on to become the season ten runner-up and *American Idol* catapulted her country music career.

BIRTHPLACE: Rossville, Georgia
BIRTH DATE: November 8
OPRY INDUCTION: February 12, 2022

DID YOU KNOW? Lauren invited her dad, a U.S. Army Veteran, and her brother onto the Opry stage to perform the Keith Whitley classic "When You Say Nothing At All" with her during the Opry's annual "Salute The Troops" show in 2021. She has said that it was her dad's dream to perform on the Grand Ole Opry stage.

> "EVERY TIME I GET TO PERFORM IN THIS AMAZING BUILDING, I JUST HAVE CHILLS AND I FEEL THE PRESENCE OF ALL THE PEOPLE WHO CAME BEFORE ME AND PAVED THE WAY FOR ARTISTS LIKE ME."

Lauren's musical hero-turned-friend Trisha Yearwood had the honor of inviting her to join the world-famous Grand Ole Opry family on December 18, 2021.

"You are exactly the kind of artist the Opry loves and wants and looks for," Trisha said during her induction.

Through tears, Lauren said, "I promise to do everything I can to represent country music … I promise to represent this family well."

And she has, with countless Opry performances and multiple nominations for ACM Awards, CMA Awards, CMT Music Awards, *Billboard* Music Awards, and more. Lauren won the 2017 ACM New Female Vocalist of the Year, CMT Breakthrough Video of the Year for her "Road Less Traveled," and CMT Collaborative Video of the Year for "What Ifs," with her childhood friend Kane Brown.

"Everyone that makes up this family, I respect, I've listened to, I've believed in, I've fangirled over," she said in 2022, as the youngest member of the family. "This place is just different, and magical, and so special for country music to have for newcomers like me."

CLOCKWISE FROM TOP LEFT:
1. Lauren performs on the Opry on June 8, 2021.
2. Lauren hosts a Grand Ole Opry livestream in 2020.
3. The Opry House audience sings back to Lauren during her performance on November 11, 2021.
4. Lauren on stage after being invited to join the family by Opry member and friend Trisha Yearwood.
5. Lauren sings to a little girl in the audience during a performance in 2021.

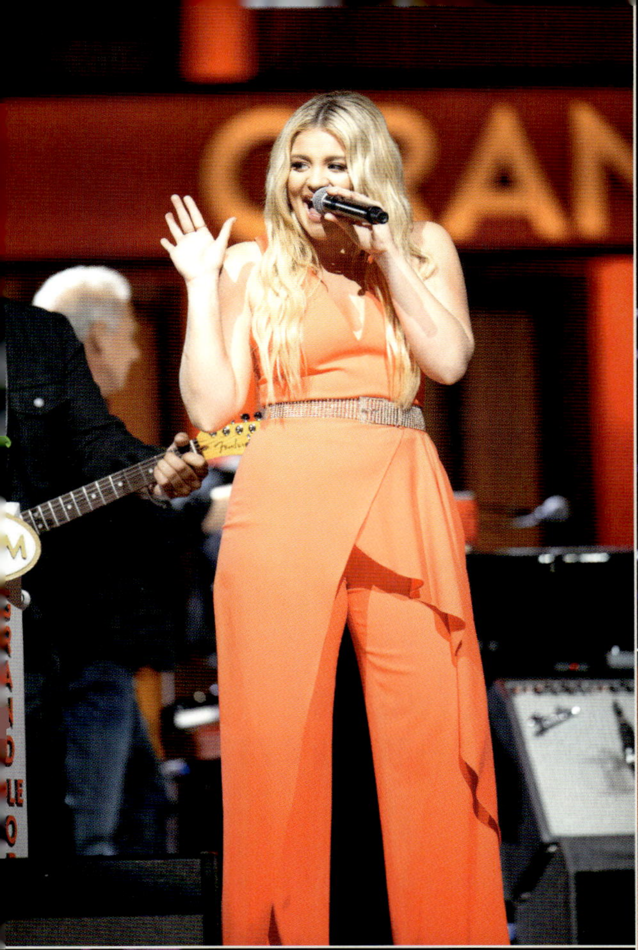

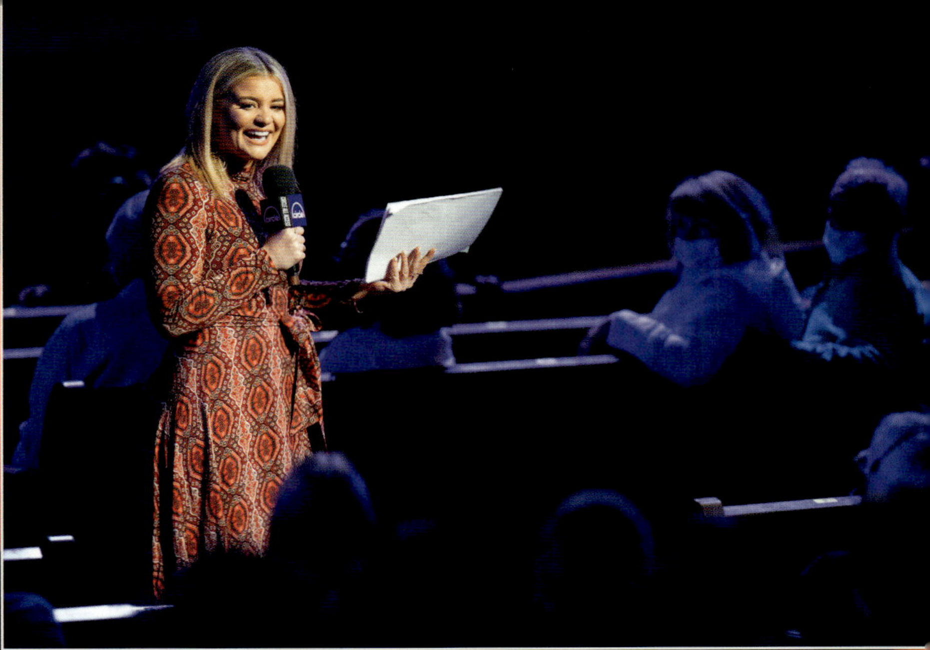

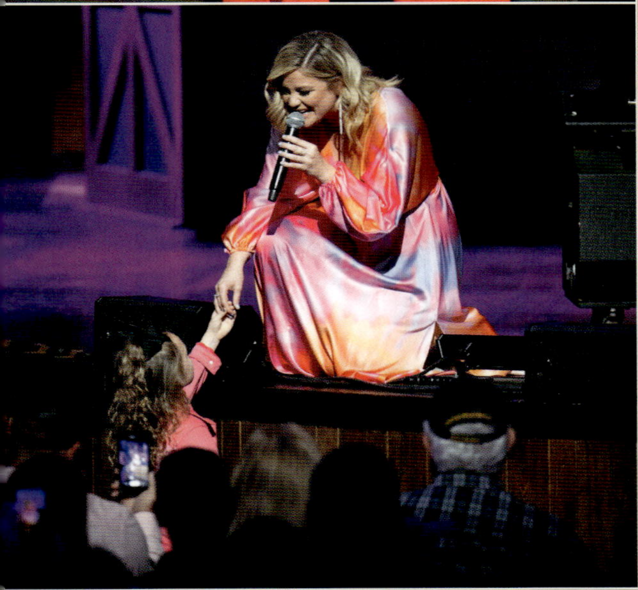

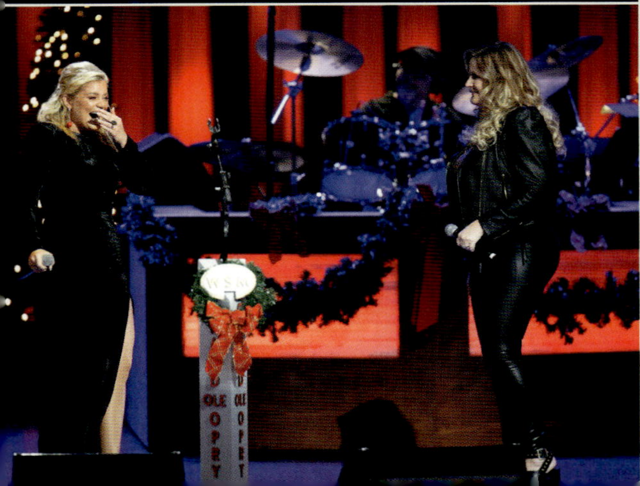

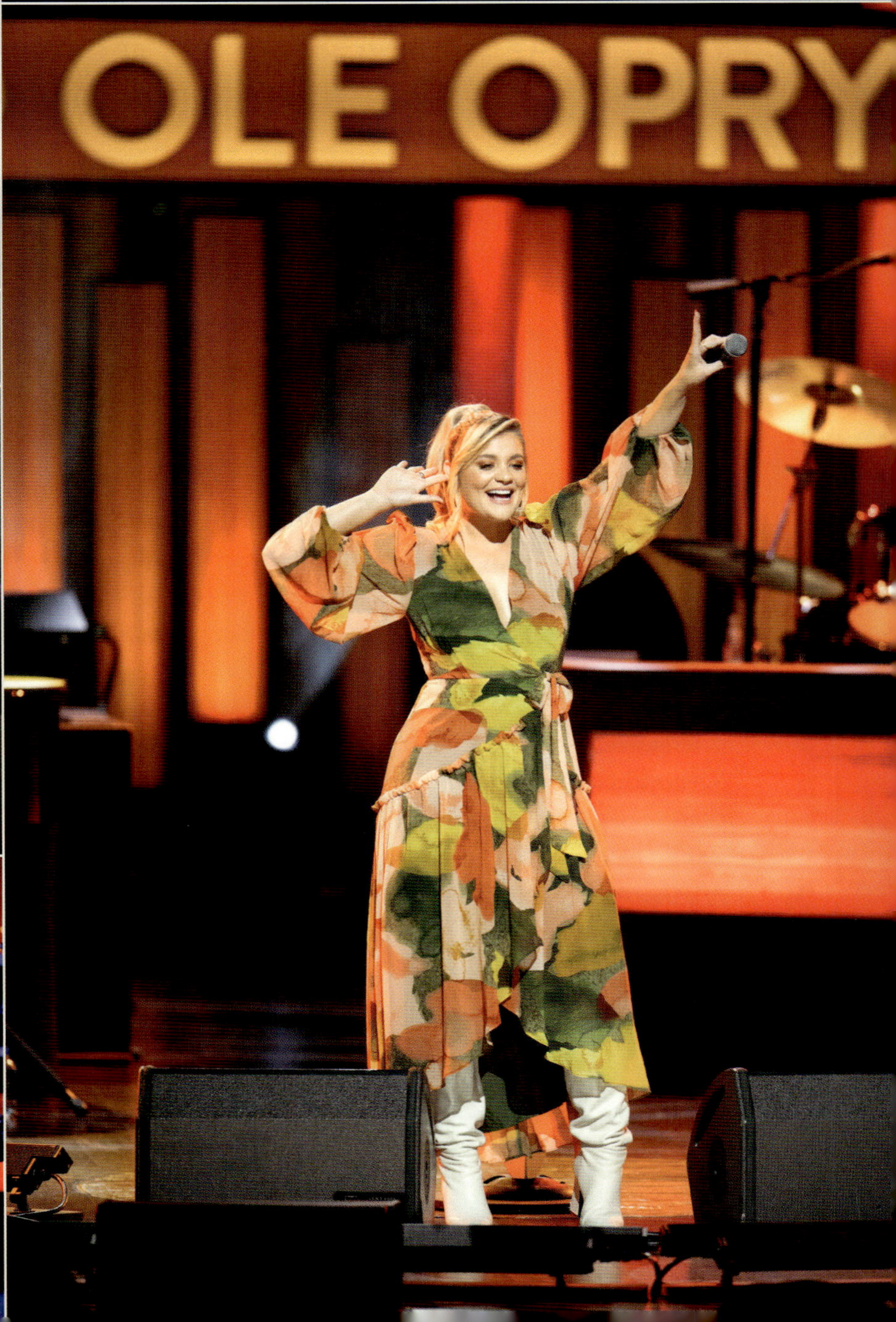
OLE OPRY

BILL ANDERSON
MEMBER SINCE 1961

Bill Anderson started his career as a sportswriter and disc jockey in Georgia, but he moved to Nashville in 1958 when Ray Price recorded his song "City Lights" and put it at the top of *Billboard* magazine's country charts for 13 weeks. Bill soon signed with Decca Records and made his Grand Ole Opry debut just weeks before his 21st birthday, singing his Decca debut, "That's What It's Like to Be Lonesome."

BIRTHPLACE: Columbia, South Carolina
BIRTH DATE: November 1
OPRY INDUCTION: July 15, 1961

DID YOU KNOW? Bill Anderson penned No. 1 country singles in six consecutive decades.

> "BILL ANDERSON HAS BEEN ONE OF MY FAVORITES SINCE I WAS BORN. MY DAD WAS ABSOLUTELY OBSESSED WITH WHISPERIN' BILL." —TAYLOR SWIFT

Even as Bill had huge hits of his own with songs including "Still," "Po' Folks," "I Love You Drops" and "Bright Lights and Country Music," he continued to write for other artists, too. He discovered Connie Smith at an Ohio talent contest and wrote her debut smash, "Once a Day," along with many of her subsequent hits. Many other Opry stars also cut Bill's songs.

"Connie Smith, Charlie Louvin, Jean Shepard, Porter Wagoner — these people were so good to me back in those days," says Bill. "Each one of them recorded multiple songs of mine, and we had hits together. It was always great. They would come up and say, 'What have you got new?'" But it wasn't just Opry members recording Bill's tunes. He has written a number of songs now considered country classics, including Lefty Frizzell's "Saginaw, Michigan" and Conway Twitty's "I May Never Get to Heaven."

The man the late Opry star Don Gibson called the "sweet singin', songwritin' boy from Georgia" joined the Country Music Hall of Fame in 2001, but he hasn't been content to rest on his laurels. Since then he has written hits for the likes of Kenny Chesney ("A Lot of Things Different"), and George Strait ("Give It Away"), as well as fellow Opry stars Brad Paisley and Alison Krauss ("Whiskey Lullaby"), with the last two on that list earning the Country Music Association's Song of the Year award.

Bill also continues to record his own popular albums.

Q: What is your most memorable "Opry Moment"?
A: As you might expect, in over 50 years as an Opry performer, I have had quite a few memorable moments. The most recent took place in the fall of 2014 when I was standing on stage and learned that a group of World War II soldiers were in our audience. When I heard the news, I quickly told the band I was changing my song from the one we had rehearsed to "Old Army Hat," a song based on the true story of a Tennessee soldier from that war. At the end of the song, the group of soldiers from hometowns all across America and ranging in age from their early 90s to 101 years old stood and applauded me. In turn, my band and I along with 4,400 people in the audience stood and applauded them. I thought the ovation was never going to stop. You don't forget moments like that!

CLOCKWISE FROM TOP LEFT:
1. Circa 1960s
2. With Dolly Parton October 9, 2010
3. Opening night at the Grand Ole Opry House, March 16, 1974
4. April 26, 1975
5. With Hawkshaw Hawkins, Jean Shepard, Stonewall Jackson, Marty Robbins. 1958. Anderson was a special guest at WSM, as "Mr. Deejay, USA" from Commerce, Georgia.
6. --
7. Welcoming the Tennessee National Guard to the Opry May 2013

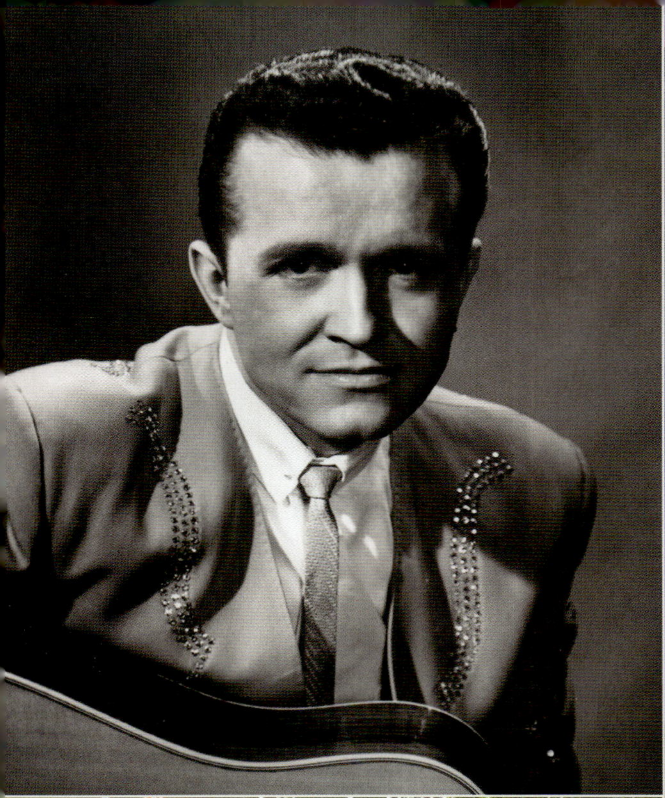

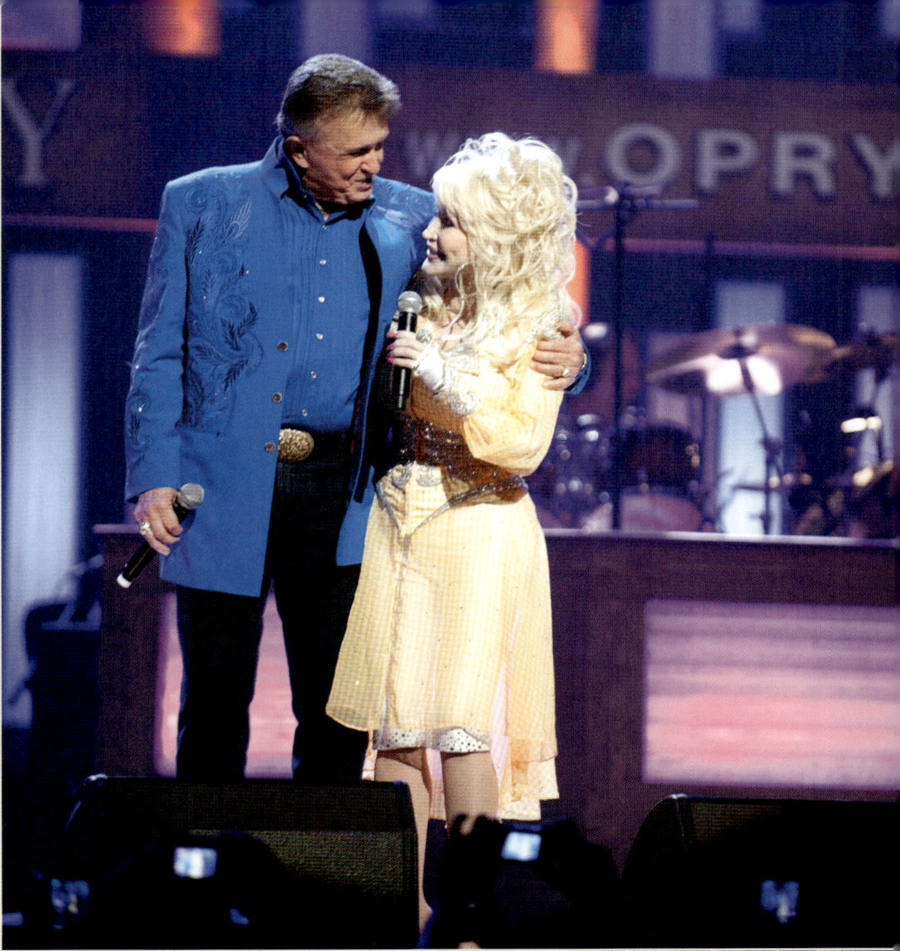
OPRY

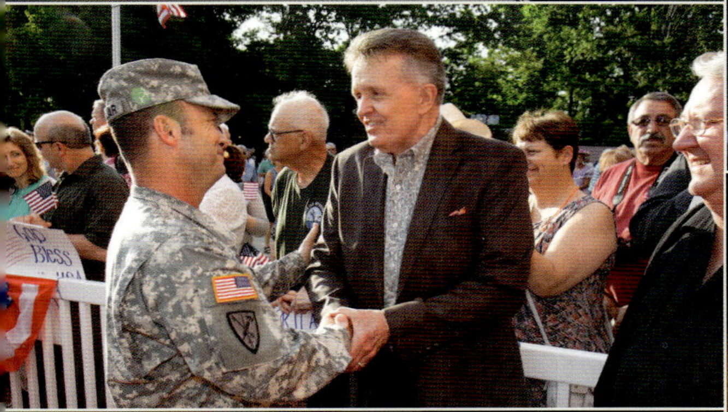

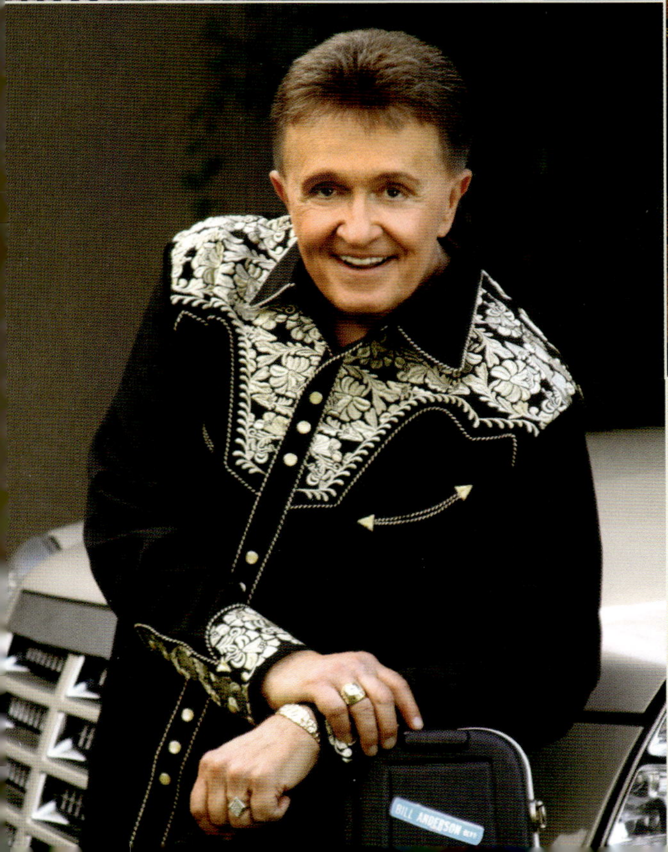
BILL ANDERSON

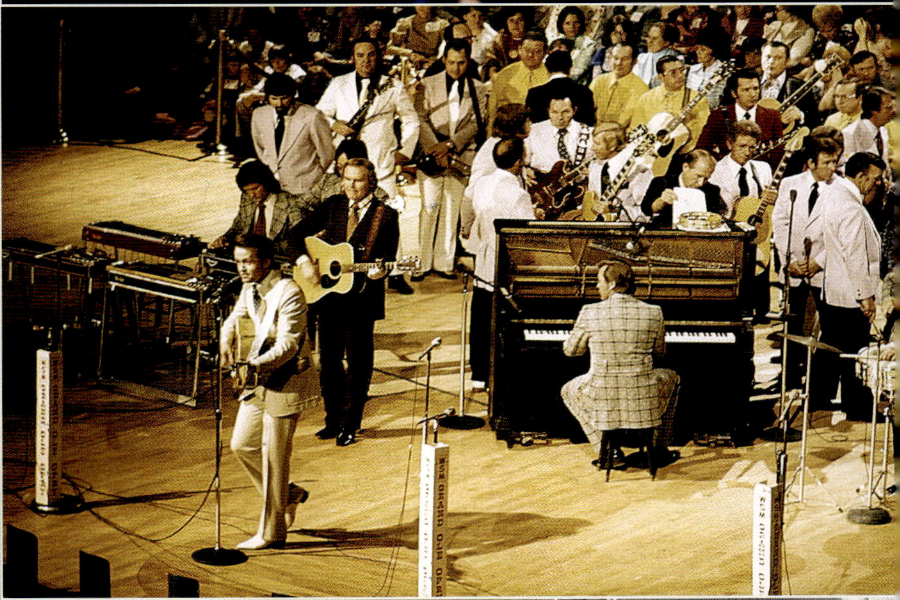

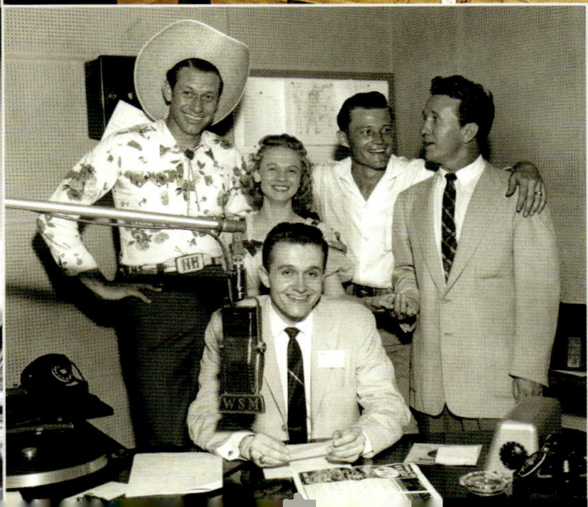
WSM

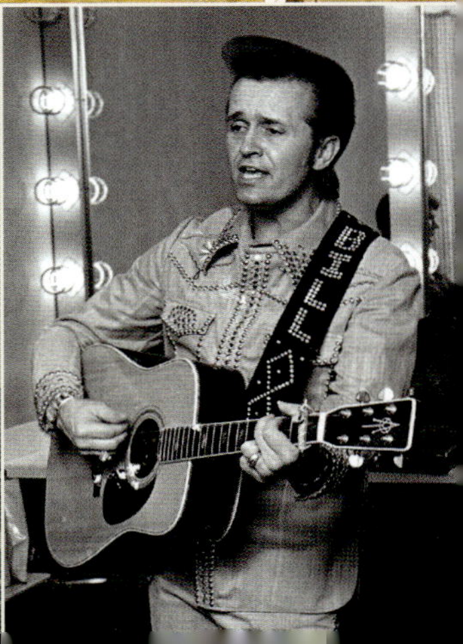

KELSEA BALLERINI
MEMBER SINCE 2019

As the first female country artist since Wynonna Judd to see her first three singles reach No. 1 on the charts, Kelsea Ballerini hasn't had many opportunities to step back and take it all in. But one moment stands out to her with such clarity: February 14, 2015, the night she made her Grand Ole Opry debut.

On that Valentine's Day night, she performed her breakout single "Love Me Like You Mean It." Opry audiences quickly grew smitten as she'd perform in the coming years.

Playing on the Opry had been at the top of her list of goals since she fell in love with music. Growing up in nearby Knoxville, Tennessee, she'd visit the Opry with her mom to watch their favorites like Josh Turner perform.

BIRTHPLACE: Mascot, Tennessee
BIRTH DATE: September 12
OPRY INDUCTION: April 16, 2019

DID YOU KNOW? Kelsea was the youngest member of the Opry cast at the time of her induction.

> "GRAND OLE OPRY, THANKS FOR SEEING SOMETHING IN ME AND FOR BELIEVING THAT I'LL ALWAYS LOVE YOU LIKE I DO BECAUSE I DO, AND I WILL."

As time went on after her debut, Kelsea began to dream bigger dreams, hoping one day she'd have the honor of actually becoming a member of the Opry — she just didn't see it coming four years after making her debut.

But on March 5, 2019, when Little Big Town invited her on stage to sing along to the group's hit "Girl Crush," Kelsea didn't realize that it was a ruse. In the final line of the song, bandmates Kimberly Schlapman and Karen Fairchild switched up the lyrics with their harmony, "Kelsea Ballerini, want to join the Opry?"

A month later, Kelsea would be inducted by one of her personal heroes, Carrie Underwood. "The Opry has been and will always be the heart and soul of country music, the family. You are in it," Carrie said. It became another moment that Kelsea knows she'll remember forever, regardless of what lies next for her.

"It's so nice and comforting to know that no matter where life takes me and no matter if the radio stops playing me tomorrow — whatever happens — I can always come here and I can always play country music."

CLOCKWISE FROM TOP LEFT:
1. Kelsea makes her Opry Debut in 2015.
2. Kelsea appears on Opry Goes Pink in 2017, dancing alongside guest of honor Chrissy, a young breast cancer survivor.
3. Kelsea and Carrie Underwood perform Trisha Yearwood's "Walkaway Joe" on the night of Kelsea's induction.
4. Little Big Town surprises Kelsea with an invitation to join the Opry after they perform "Girl Crush" together.
5. During this 2016 performance, Kelsea performs "Ghost In This House," a song originally recorded by Shenandoah and then Alison Krauss. Kelsea's portrait now hangs next to Alison's in the Women of Country dressing room.

OPRY FAMILY MEMBERS

WSM
GRAND OLE
GRAND OLE

RAND OLE
WSM
GRAND OLE OPRY
GRAND OLE OPRY

WSM
GRAND OLE OPRY
GRAND OLE OPRY

WSM GRAND
WSM
GRAND OLE OPRY
GRAND OLE OPRY

LE OPRY
OPRY.CO
WSM
GRAND OLE OPRY
WSM
GRAND OLE OPRY

BOBBY BARE
MEMBER SINCE 1964

Bobby Bare knew there'd be cake — it was the night of his 83rd birthday — but he had no idea that he'd be celebrating something much bigger on April 7, 2018: his return as an official Opry member.

Garth Brooks was there on stage to welcome him back home. "The Grand Ole Opry is family. Family is forever. So, Mr. Bare, young man — as my dad would say — it is my honor, it is the Grand Ole Opry's honor, to officially welcome you back, the great Bobby Bare, to the Grand Ole Opry," Garth said.

BIRTHPLACE: Ironton, Ohio
BIRTH DATE: April 7
OPRY INDUCTION: 1964

DID YOU KNOW? Bobby had nearly five dozen Top 40 hits from 1962 to 1983.

> "BEING A MEMBER OF THE OPRY IS PROBABLY EVERYBODY IN COUNTRY MUSIC'S DREAM. I'VE REALIZED ALL THOSE DREAMS I'VE EVER HAD."

"I've got to tell you that this is quite a surprise," Bobby said, taking in a standing ovation from the crowd. "I was a member of the Opry for 10 years, but then I just drifted away. Thank you to everybody on the Grand Ole Opry."

Bobby first joined the Opry in 1964 and remained a member of the cast in the 1960s and '70s, after which his official membership lapsed.

But Garth said it best: "Standing shoulder-to-shoulder with Bobby Bare, it makes the Opry better. It makes me better as an Opry member to be standing next to him."

Bobby could stand next to anything and make it better. Dubbed "The Springsteen of Country," he is one of the best storytellers in the business, blending country and folk at a time when few people were doing it.

Never afraid to venture out, he has recorded material by the likes of Shel Silverstein and Bob McDill and written songs cut by Loretta Lynn, Kris Kristofferson, Bob Dylan, and Johnny Paycheck. Bobby's straight-talking style on tracks like "Miller's Cave" and "(Margie's at) The Lincoln Park Inn" raised eyebrows, but that's his music: unapologetically real and true to form for an "original outlaw."

Bobby Bare: Country Music Hall of Fame member, Grammy winner, and Grand Ole Opry member, once again and forever. You really can go home again.

CLOCKWISE FROM TOP LEFT:
1. Bobby sings alongside his young son, Bobby Bare Jr.
2. Bobby Bare Jr. joins Bobby on stage for a performance of his father's 1970 hit "Come Sundown." It was the pair's first Opry collaboration in more than 40 years.
3. Bobby appears on the Opry stage in 2012, his worn guitar a testament to his virtuoso.
4. Bobby performs on stage.
5. Bobby addresses the crowd after being welcomed back as a member on April 7, 2018.

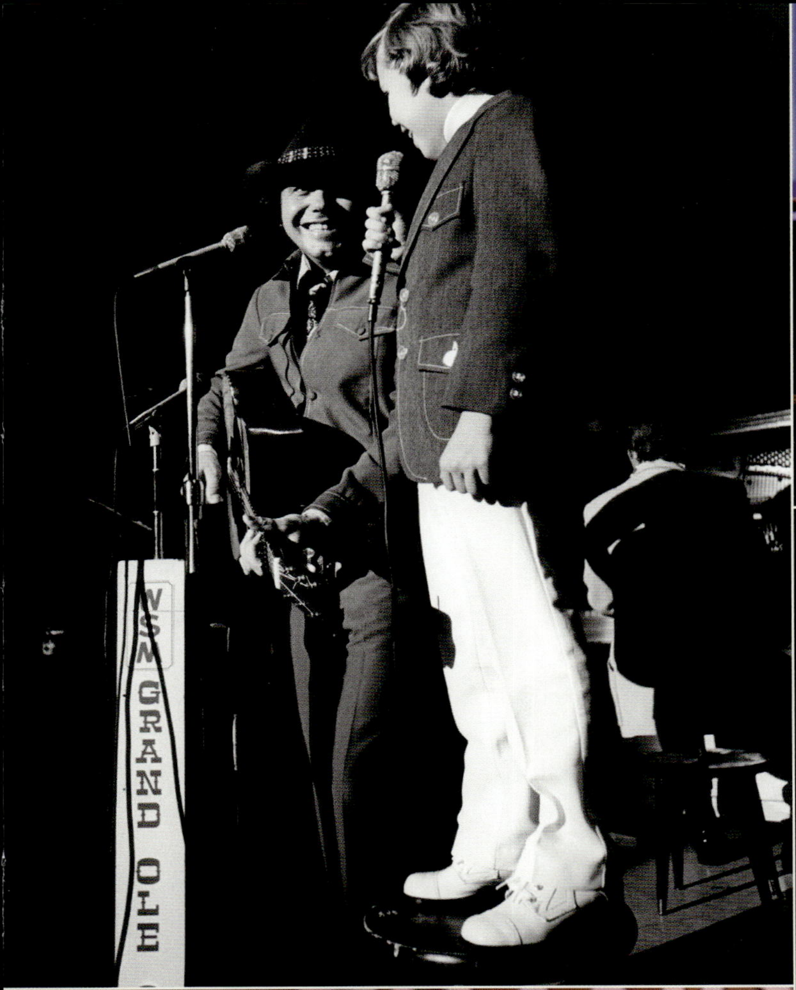
WSM
GRAND OLE
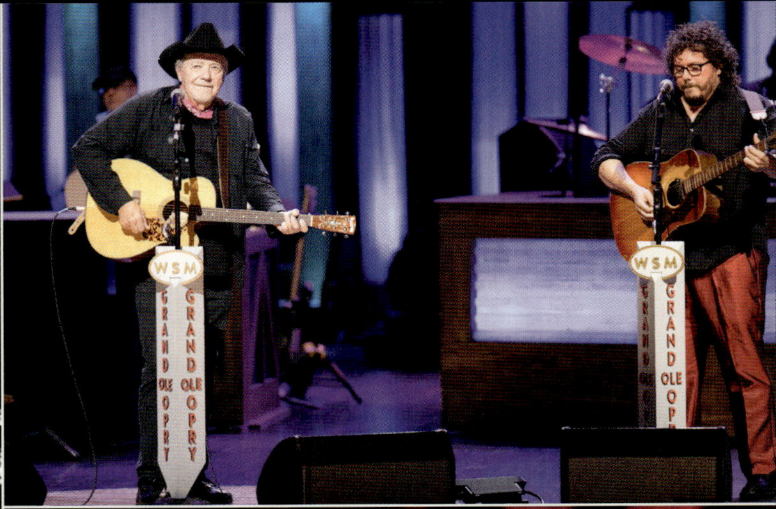
WSM
GRAND OLE OPRY
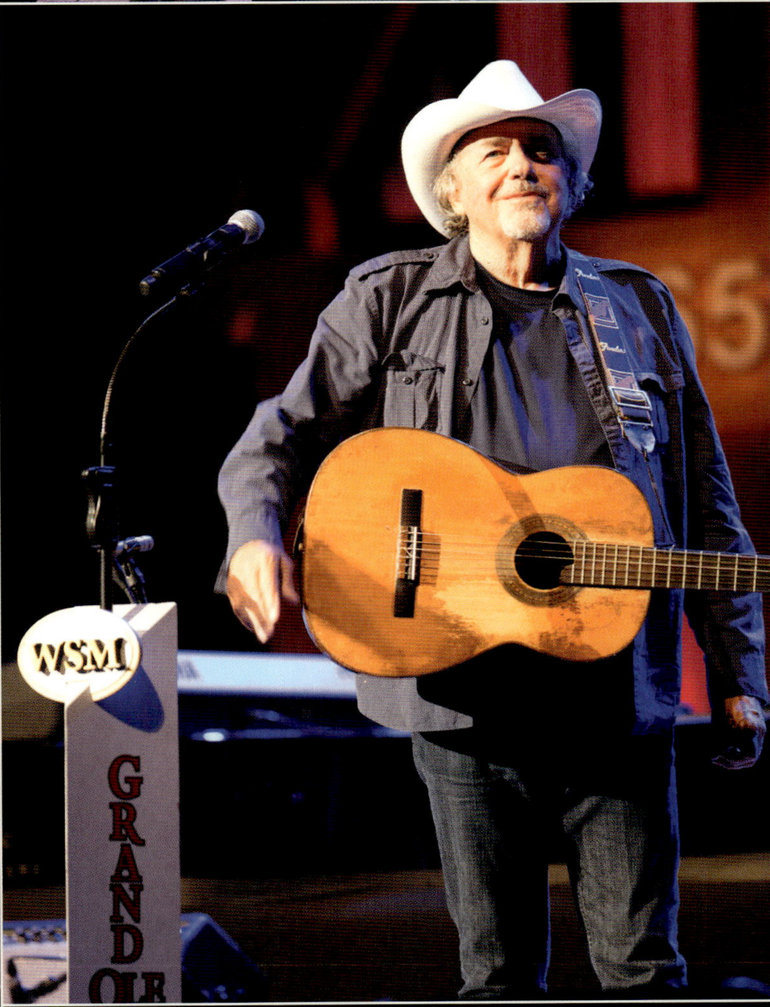
WSM
GRAND
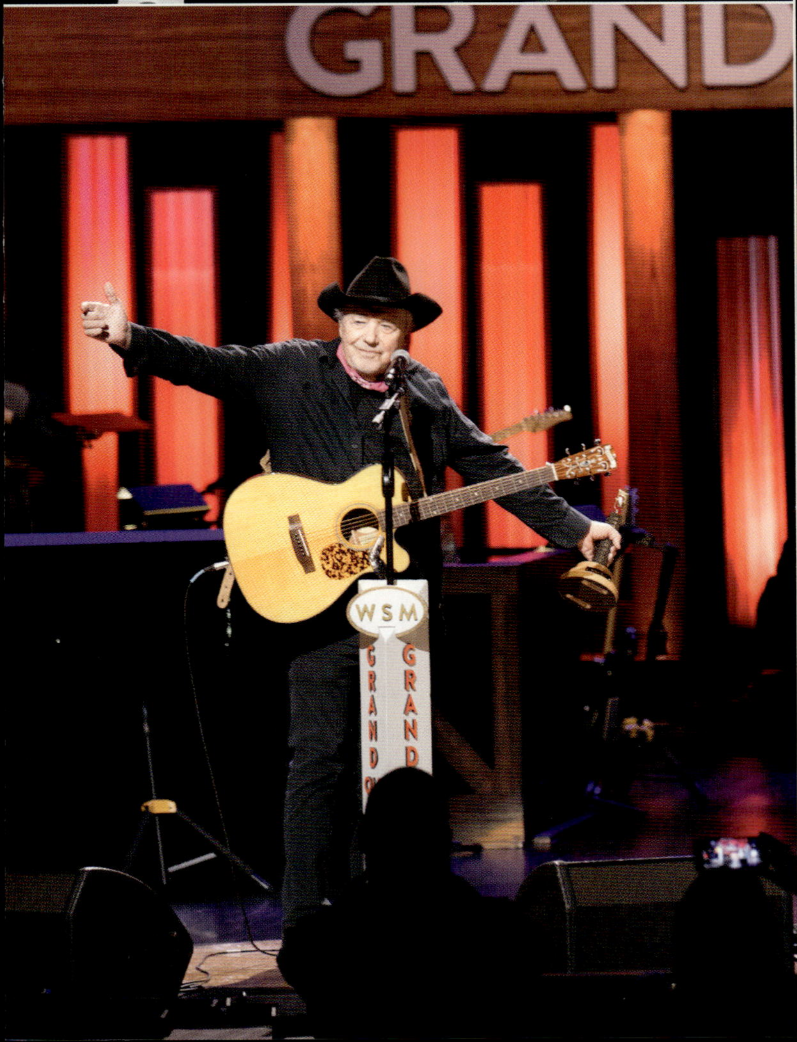
GRAND
WSM
GRAND
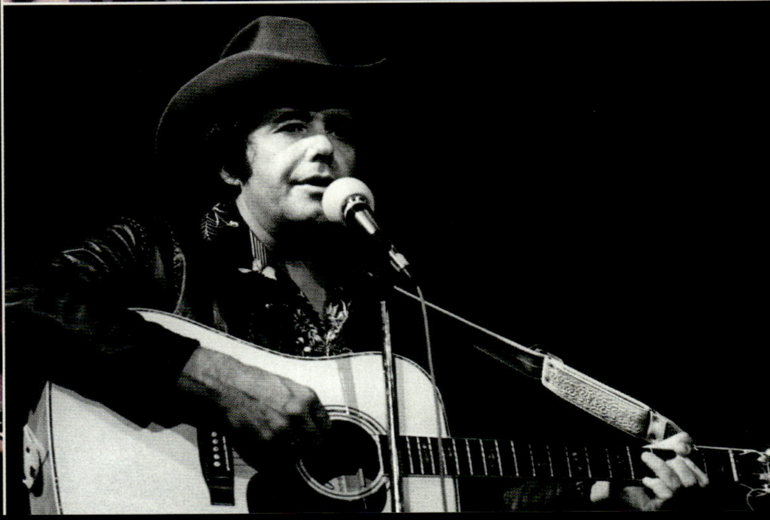

MANDY BARNETT
MEMBER SINCE 2021

Called "the Judy Garland of our time" by *American Songwriter*, Mandy Barnett has built a reputation for her commanding voice and unwavering devotion to classic country.

The celebrated vocalist began working with famed producer Jimmy Bowen – who worked with Frank Sinatra, Reba McEntire, Kenny Rogers, and more – at the age of 12. She moved to Nashville as a teenager and began visiting the Grand Ole Opry and singing backstage. When she turned 18, she began performing center stage, in the world-famous wooden circle.

On her birthday in 2021, after over 500 appearances spanning 27 years, Mandy was honored by Opry member and country legend Connie Smith with a surprise invitation to become an official member of the Grand Ole Opry.

BIRTHPLACE: Crossville, Tennessee
BIRTH DATE: September 28
OPRY INDUCTION: November 2, 2021

> "I'VE KNOWN SINCE THE FIRST TIME THAT I STEPPED ONTO THE OPRY STAGE THAT IT WAS SPECIAL AND ALWAYS WANTED TO BE A PART OF THE OPRY FAMILY. BECOMING A GRAND OLE OPRY MEMBER WAS A LIFELONG DREAM FULFILLED!"

Mandy has recorded eight critically applauded albums and her music has been featured in many major film and television soundtracks. She often contributes tracks to multi-artist compilation albums of all genres — from country to Great American Songbook collections. *Variety* named her album *Every Star Above* one of the best albums of 2021. *USA Today* called Mandy one of Nashville's "finest classic country and torch singers," while the *Chicago Tribune* said she's "a torch singer in the grandest sense of the word."

CLOCKWISE FROM TOP LEFT:
1. Opry members Marty Stuart and Connie Smith help induct Mandy into the family.
2. Mandy looks to the audience from the Opry stage during her induction.
3. Mandy performs during her induction on November 2, 2021.
4. Opry member Connie Smith joins Mandy on stage to invite her into the Opry family.
5. Brenda Lee welcomes applause for Mandy during a performance on December 11, 2021.

DID YOU KNOW? Mandy first gained national notice as the original star of the "jukebox" musical *Always...Patsy Cline* at Nashville's famed Ryman Auditorium, where she performed as Cline hundreds of times. She is the only actress to have played the role on the stage where Cline's legend began.

A Tennessee Music Pathways historical marker in Mandy's hometown, presented by the Tennessee Department of Tourist Development, honors her contributions in making Tennessee the "Soundtrack of America."

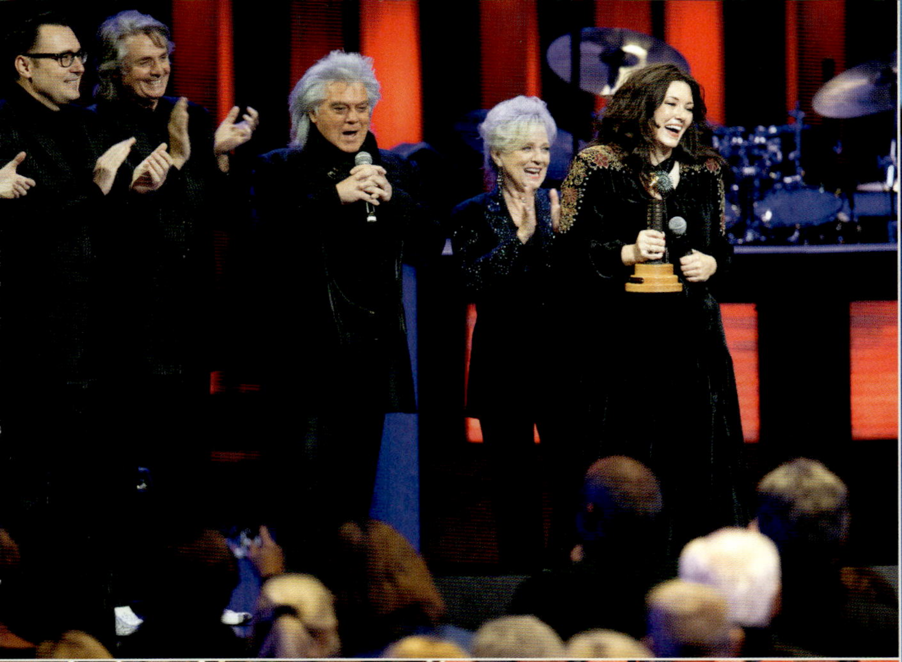

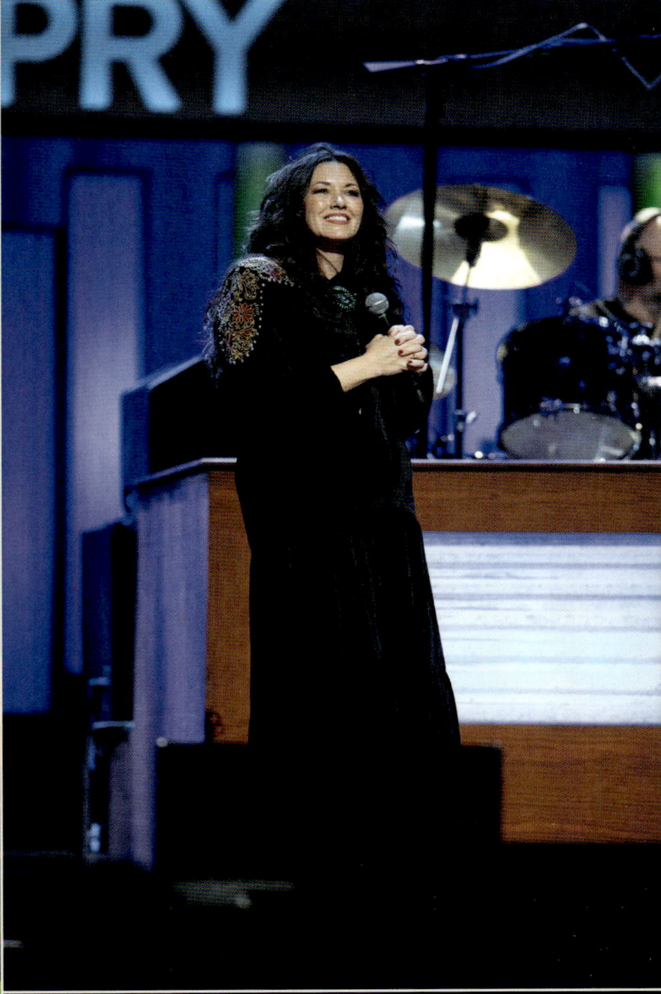
PRY

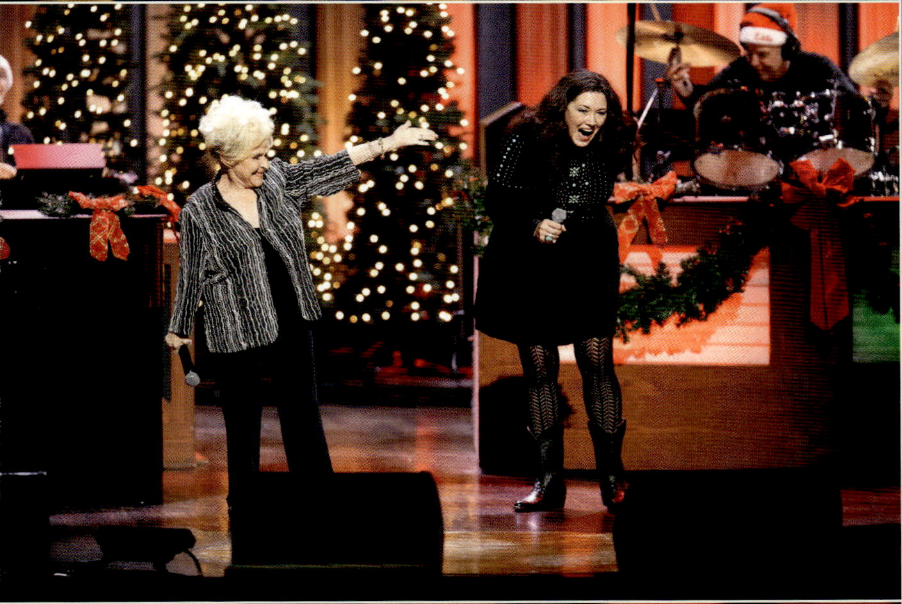

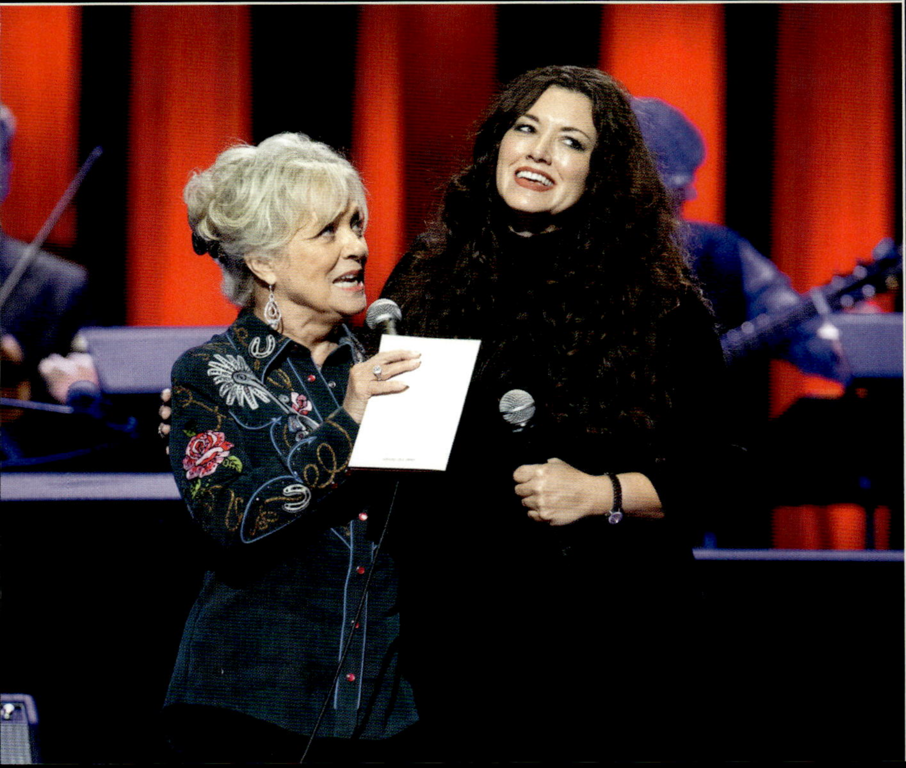

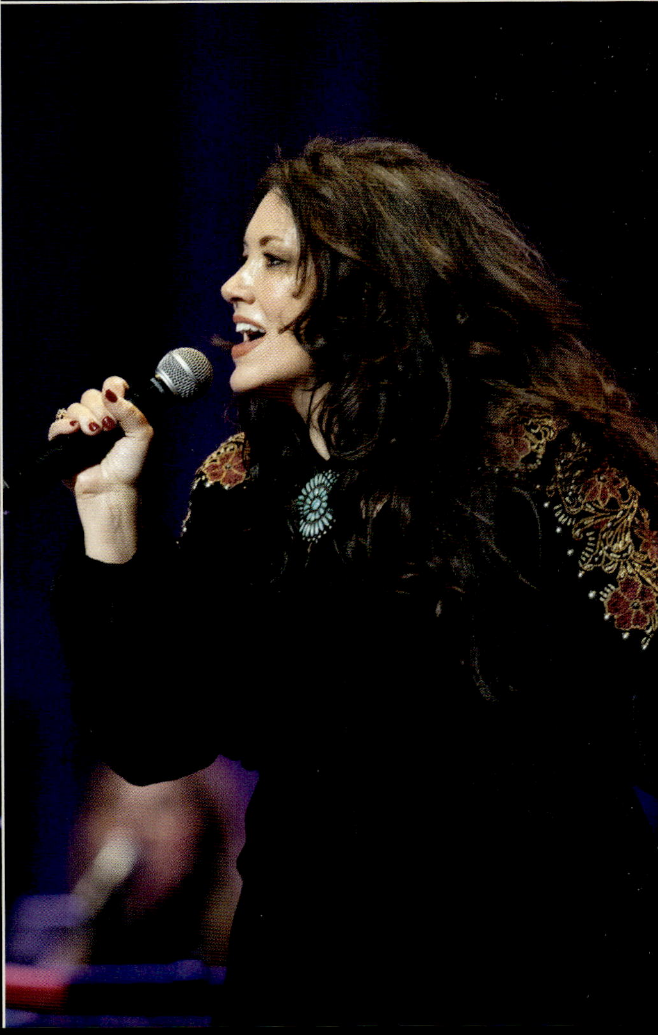

DIERKS BENTLEY
MEMBER SINCE 2005

Dierks Bentley may be the only singer banned from the Grand Ole Opry before he even got to sing there. During his early days in Nashville, Dierks got a job as a researcher for The Nashville Network, which was headquartered in the same complex as the Opry House. Dierks made sure to stay late on weekends so he could slip backstage at the Grand Ole Opry House to watch the show and visit the musicians. Dierks did this so often that Opry management finally asked to limit his access. These days, of course, Dierks is always welcome at the Opry.

"I actually come to the Opry even when I'm not playing," says the singer of hits including "Come A Little Closer," "Every Mile A Memory," "I Hold On," and "Drunk on A Plane."

BIRTHPLACE: Phoenix, Arizona
BIRTH DATE: November 20
OPRY INDUCTION: October 1, 2005

DID YOU KNOW? Dierks' beloved dog Jake appeared with him on stage on the night of his Opry induction.

> "I LOVE KNOWING THAT DOWN THE ROAD, NO MATTER HOW MUCH WE'RE TOURING OR WHAT'S GOING ON IN MY LIFE, THERE'S ALWAYS ONE CONSISTENCY, AND THAT'S THE GRAND OLE OPRY AND GETTING A CHANCE TO PLAY THERE ON SATURDAY NIGHT."

Dierks made his Opry debut in April 2003 and sang his breakthrough hit, "What Was I Thinkin'" — a song inspired by a girl he'd met backstage at the Opry during those early visits. "I just want to add my name to the list of people that said this was the biggest night of their life," he said that night after Ricky Skaggs introduced him, "because this really is a dream come true." Two years later, Dierks had been officially welcomed into the Opry fold.

Dierks has broad-ranging musical tastes. He's a student of history, but he also knows how to appeal to the young girls who come to his shows wearing the little white tank tops mentioned in "What Was I Thinkin'." He loves bluegrass (at the same time he was hanging around the Opry, he was also a regular at Nashville bluegrass club, the Station Inn), but he also has ties to the Texas and alternative country scenes. And while he's a regular at the top of the country charts, his 2010 bluegrass-infused *Up on the Ridge* album featured guest spots by fellow Opry stars Vince Gill, Alison Krauss, and Del McCoury.

CLOCKWISE FROM TOP LEFT:
1. May 15, 2007
2. With Marty Stuart on Opry induction night, October 1, 2005
3. With Sam Bush and Del McCoury
4. Backstage with the Del McCoury Band, September 28, 2010
5. With The Grascals
6. February 7, 2014

OPRY FAMILY MEMBERS

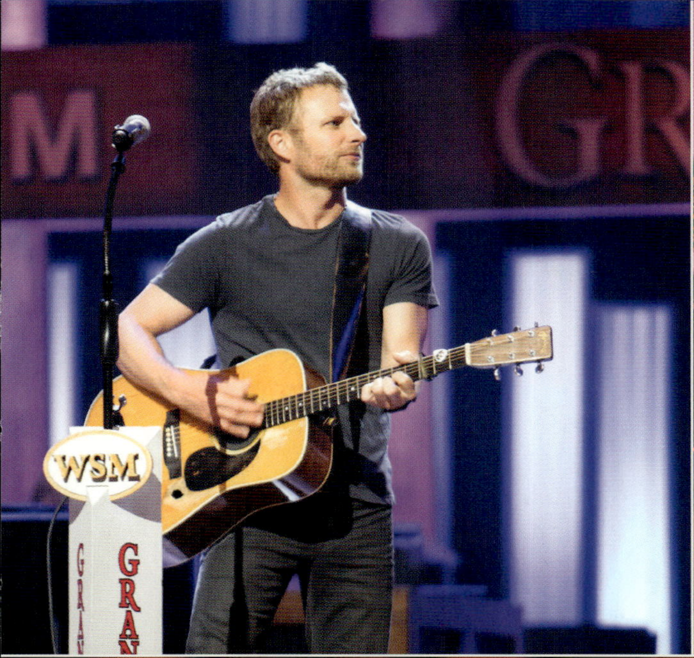
WSM
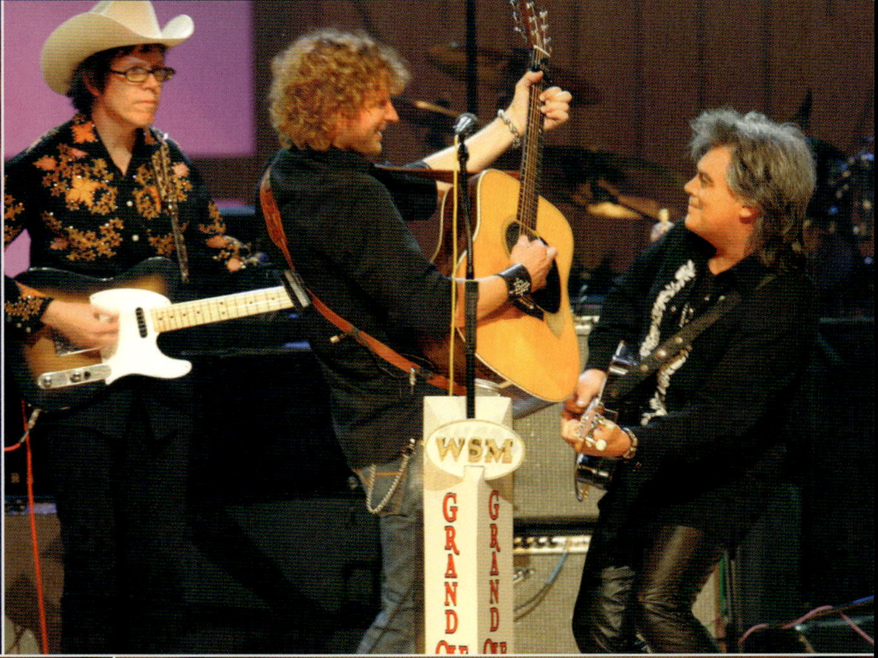
WSM
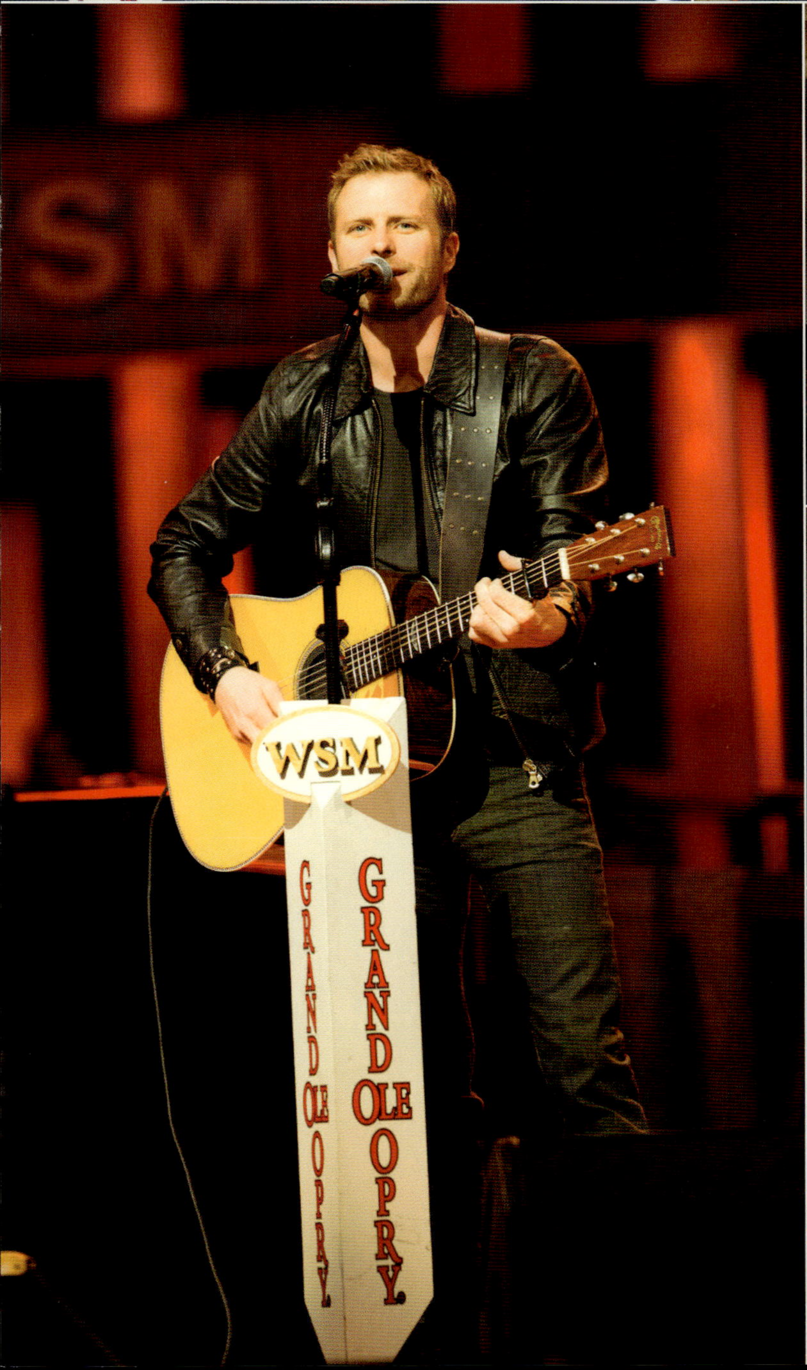
WSM
GRAND OLE OPRY
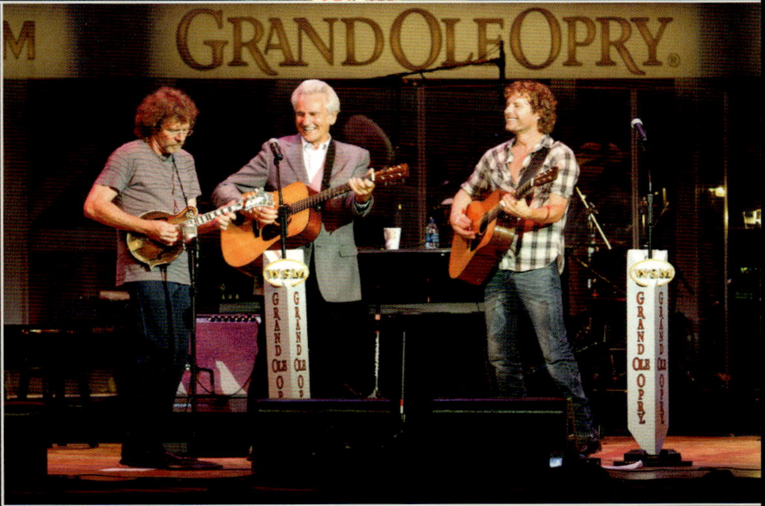
GRAND OLE OPRY
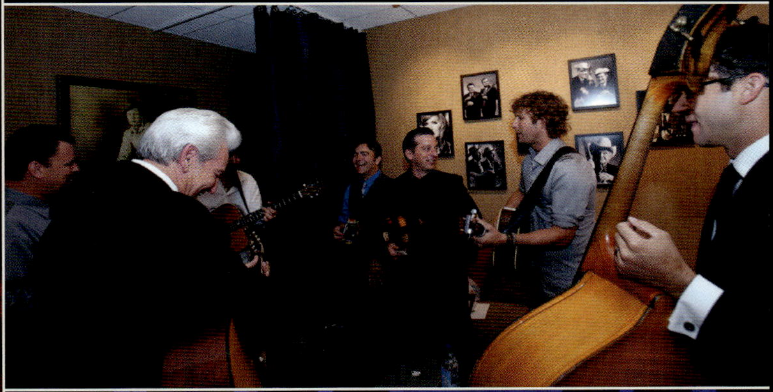
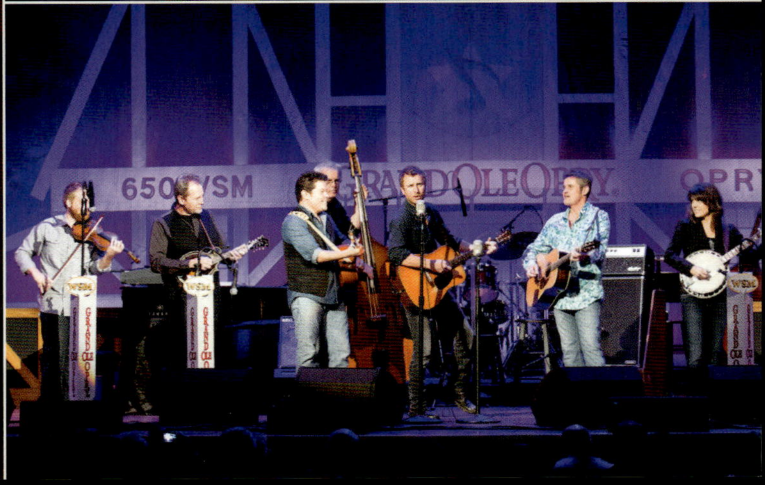

CLINT BLACK
MEMBER SINCE 1991

As part of country music's "Class of '89," Clint Black was one of a handful of country stars who achieved their initial success that year, then went on to dominate country music for a decade. Clint's career got off to an unusually fast start when his first four singles all zoomed straight to No. 1 on the *Billboard* country chart. He won the Country Music Association's Horizon Award in 1989 and in 1990 was voted Male Vocalist of the Year.

Those first four hits — "A Better Man," "Nobody's Home," "Nothing's News" and "Killin' Time" — all came from his triple-platinum debut album, *Killin' Time*. The Grammy-nominated singer went on to land nine more No. 1 singles and sell more than 20 million albums worldwide. Seven of his albums have achieved platinum or multi-platinum sales status.

He's been equally successful as a songwriter. He wrote or co-wrote all 13 of his No. 1 hits, as well as all but one of his 17 other Top 10 hits. Known primarily as a vocalist and guitarist, Clint is also proficient on drums and harmonica.

Clint was raised in the Houston suburb of Katy, Texas, and began singing professionally as a teen at the Benton Springs Club in Houston. After marrying actress Lisa Hartman in 1991, Clint caught the acting bug himself, beginning with a cameo appearance in the 1994 film *Maverick*. He also has appeared in the films *Going Home* and *Anger Management*. He had a starring role in 1998's *Still Holding On: The Legend of Cadillac Jack*. In 2010, he co-starred in the film *Flicka 2*.

In 2010, Clint claimed a spot on *Billboard* magazine's list of the top 25 country artists of the past 25 years. He continues to tour regularly.

BIRTHPLACE: Long Branch, New Jersey
BIRTH DATE: February 4
OPRY INDUCTION: January 10, 1991

Q: What makes the Opry unique?
A: The backstage "hang" is unparalleled. You can sit and talk with Charlie Daniels, or jam with Steve Wariner; hear the Riders in the Sky warming up..., hear a joke from Little Jimmy Dickens, or Bill Anderson..., that's not happening backstage at my shows! Only at the Opry.

> "WALKING OUT INTO THE HALLS AND GETTING YOUR PICTURE TAKEN AND PEOPLE WANTING AUTOGRAPHS—THAT'S WHAT NORMALLY IS HAPPENING BACKSTAGE AT THE OPRY. YOU SEE ALL THE PEOPLE THAT YOU KNOW AND YOU ALSO SEE FANS. IT'S THAT CRAZY FEELING THAT YOU GET—THERE'S EXCITEMENT BACKSTAGE AT THE OPRY."

CLOCKWISE FROM TOP LEFT:
1. With Garth Brooks after having been introduced as the Opry's newest member during the show's 65th Anniversary network television special
2. Circa 2000
3. October 13, 2003
4. --
5. With wife Lisa Hartman Black March 15, 2014

OPRY FAMILY MEMBERS 82

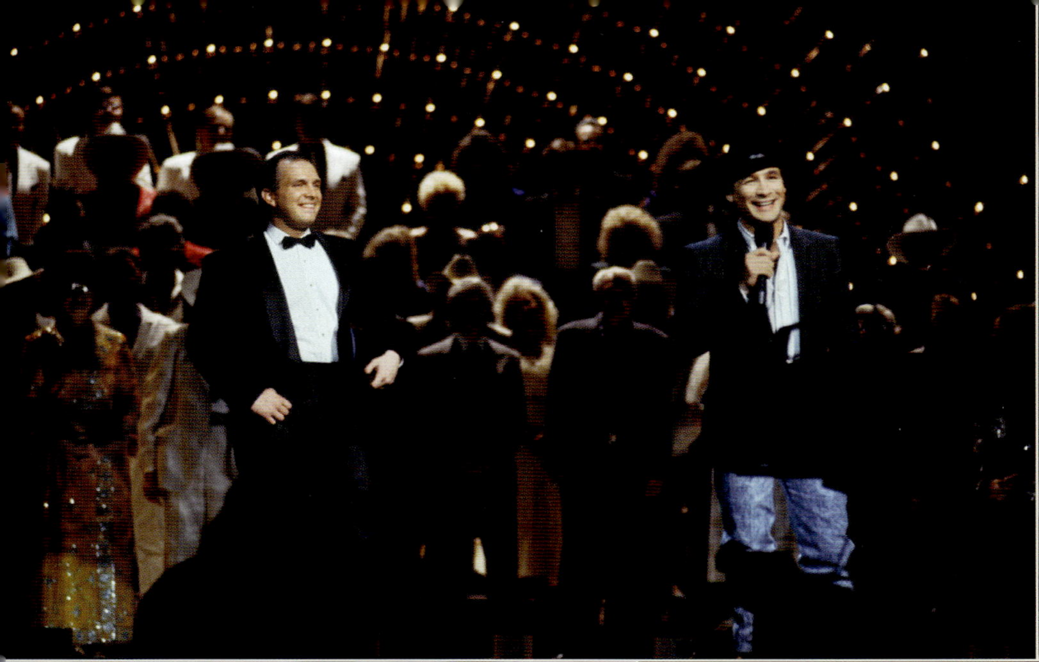

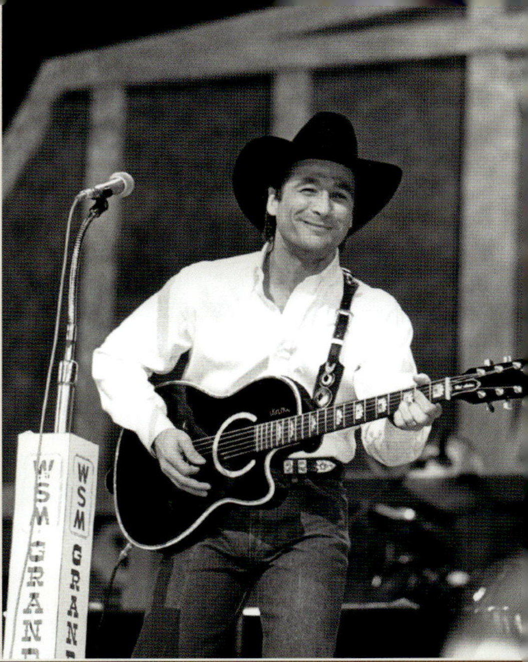
WSM

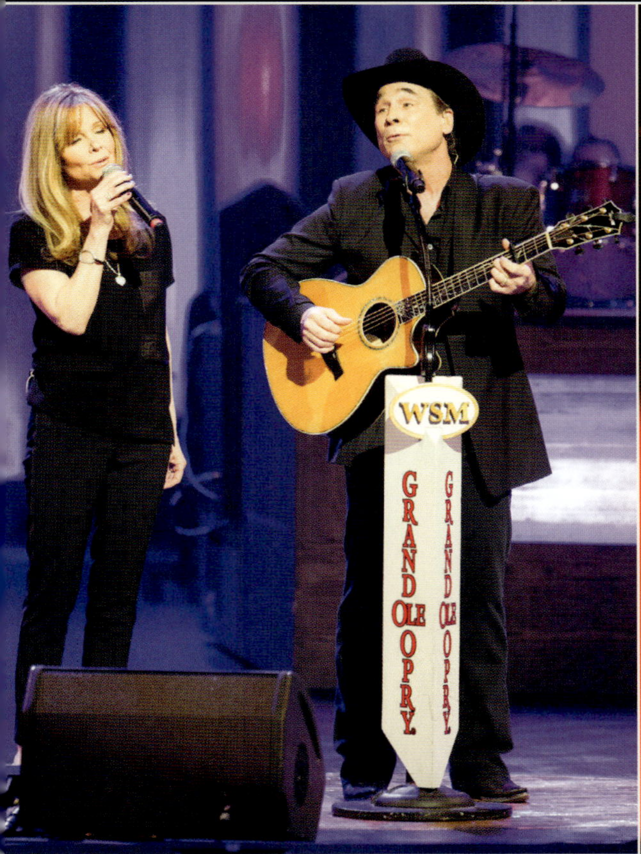
WSM
GRAND OLE OPRY

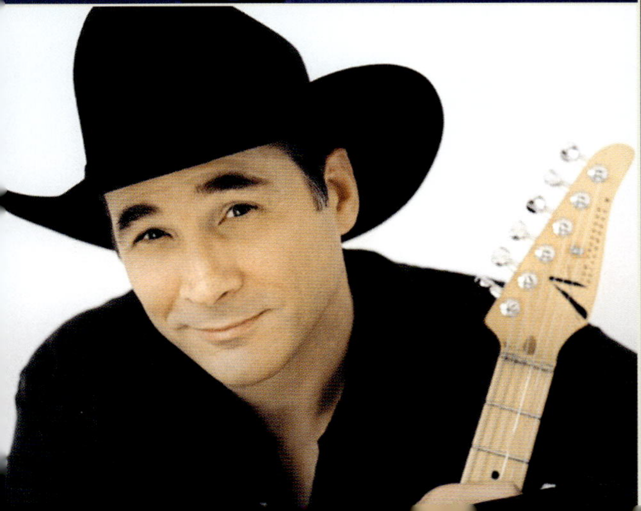

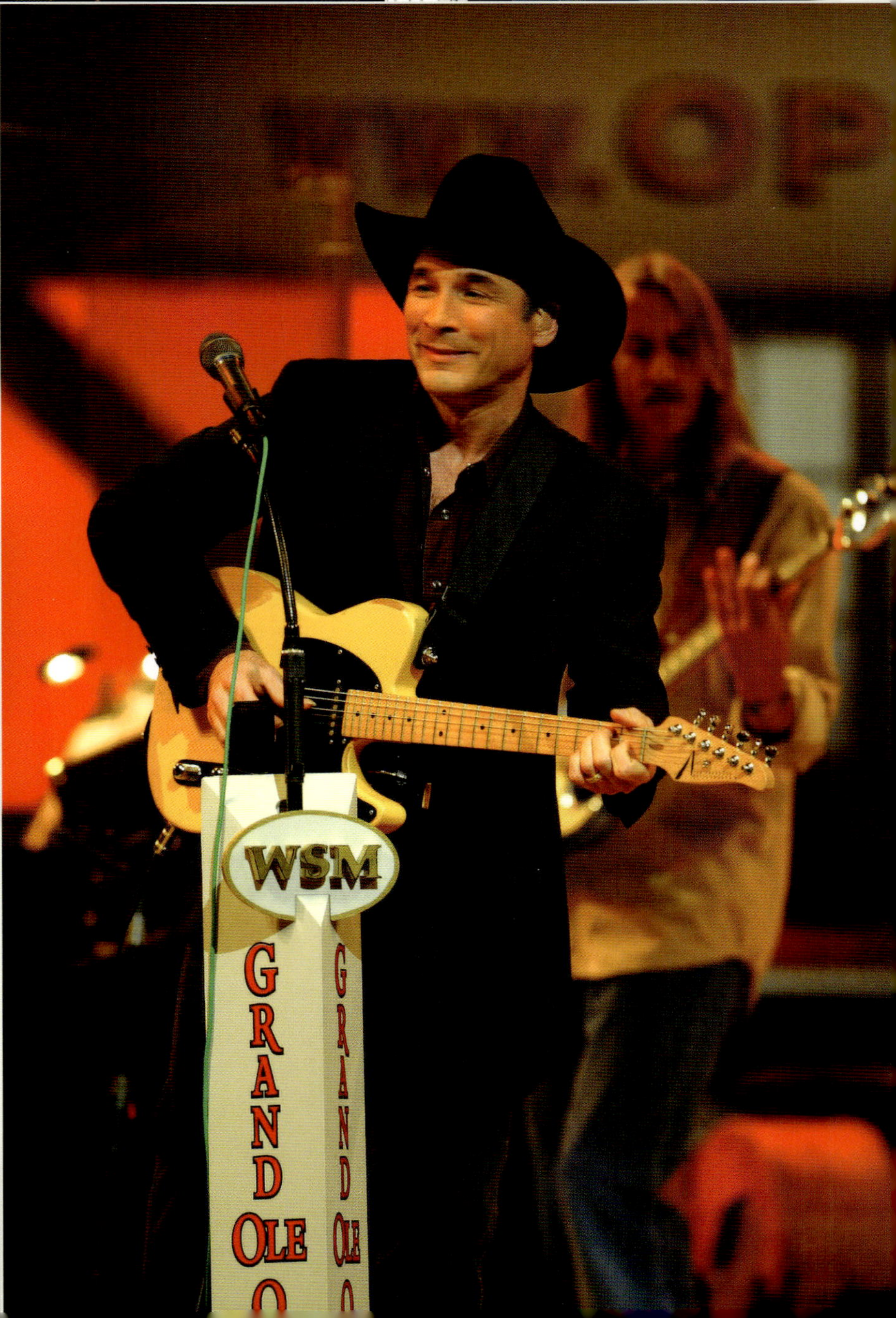
WSM
GRAND OLE

GARTH BROOKS
MEMBER SINCE 1990

The Grand Ole Opry stage has long been hallowed ground to the man who has sold more albums than any other country act. Garth made his debut on June 24, 1989, and wept tears of joy on the occasion. He joined the show's cast a year later, and he has always called that night one of the proudest moments of his unparalleled career.

The youngest of six children, Garth grew up in Yukon, Oklahoma, an oil town near Oklahoma City. He first moved to Nashville in 1985, only to return home 23 hours later. After completing a degree in advertising at Oklahoma State University, he ventured back to Music City in 1987 and within six months signed a recording contract with Capitol Records.

BIRTHPLACE: Tulsa, Oklahoma
BIRTH DATE: February 7
OPRY INDUCTION: October 6, 1990

> "TO BE RECOGNIZED AS A MEMBER [OF THE GRAND OLE OPRY] IS AMONG THE CLASS OF HONORS THAT WILL NEVER BE TOPPED, NO MATTER HOW LONG OR HOW FAR MY CAREER GOES."

Garth's first single, "Much Too Young (To Feel This Damn Old)," from his self-titled debut album, hit No. 8 on the charts. More big hits followed: "Not Counting You," "The Dance," and "If Tomorrow Never Comes."

The only male artist to have four albums — *No Fences*, *Ropin' the Wind*, *The Hits*, and *Double Live* — each exceed sales of 10 million, Garth places second only to The Beatles as the best-selling act of all time, according to the Recording Industry Association of America.

Garth has received nearly every accolade the recording industry can bestow upon an artist, including two Grammys, 11 Country Music Association awards and 24 *Billboard* Music awards. He's also earned a star on the Hollywood Walk of Fame. In 1997, Garth's Central Park concert in New York drew the largest crowd the park had ever seen. The HBO special *Garth Live from Central Park* was that year's most-watched cable television special.

CLOCKWISE FROM TOP LEFT:
1. February 17, 2014
2. Circa 1990
3. Porter Wagoner presents triple platinum sales award to Garth Brooks for No Fences album. Circa 1990
4. With Porter Wagoner, Bill Anderson, and Little Jimmy Dickens during the Opry's 80th Birthday Bash

OPRY FAMILY MEMBERS

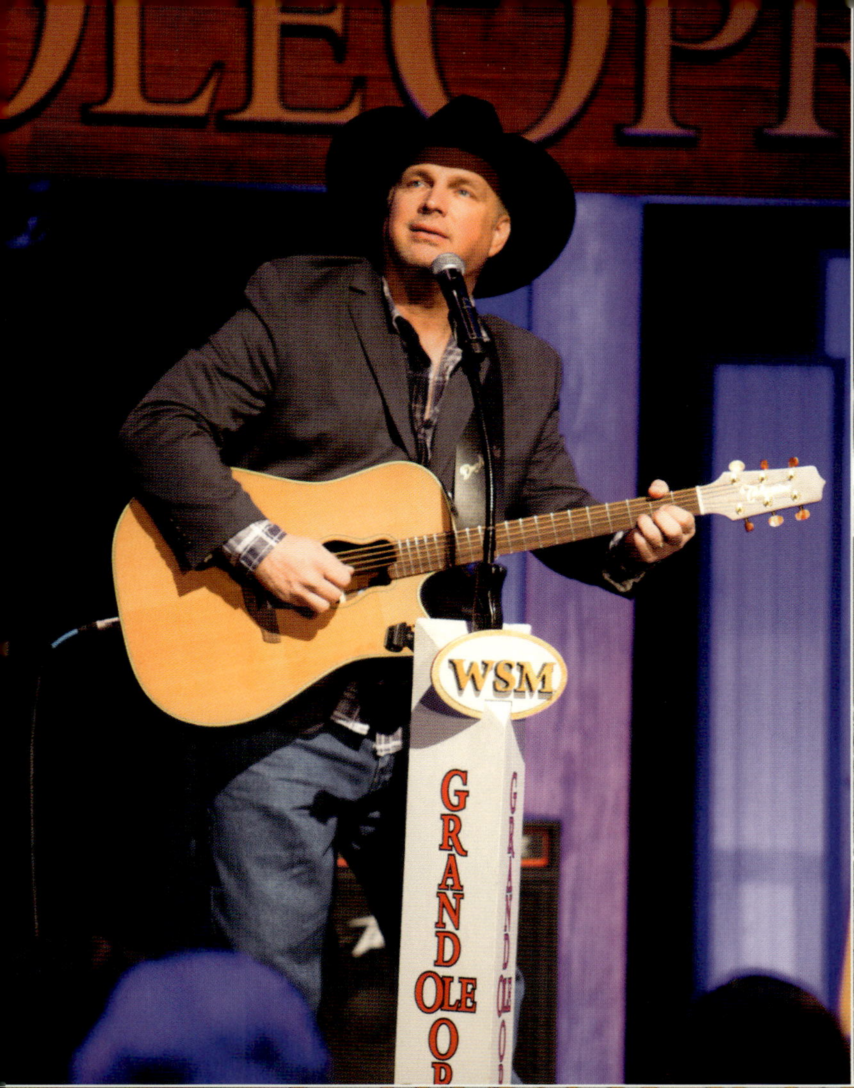
WSM
GRAND OLE OPRY

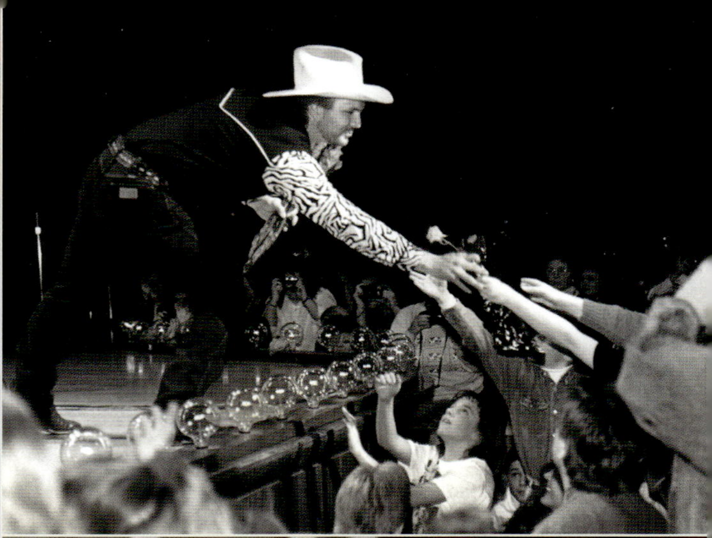

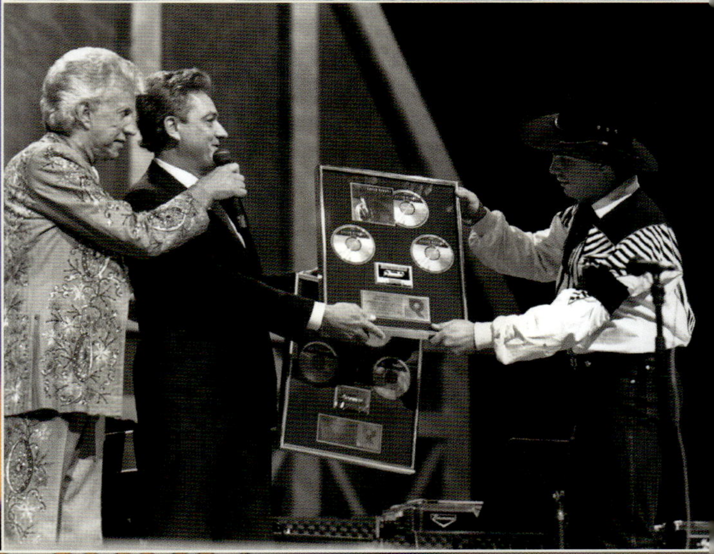

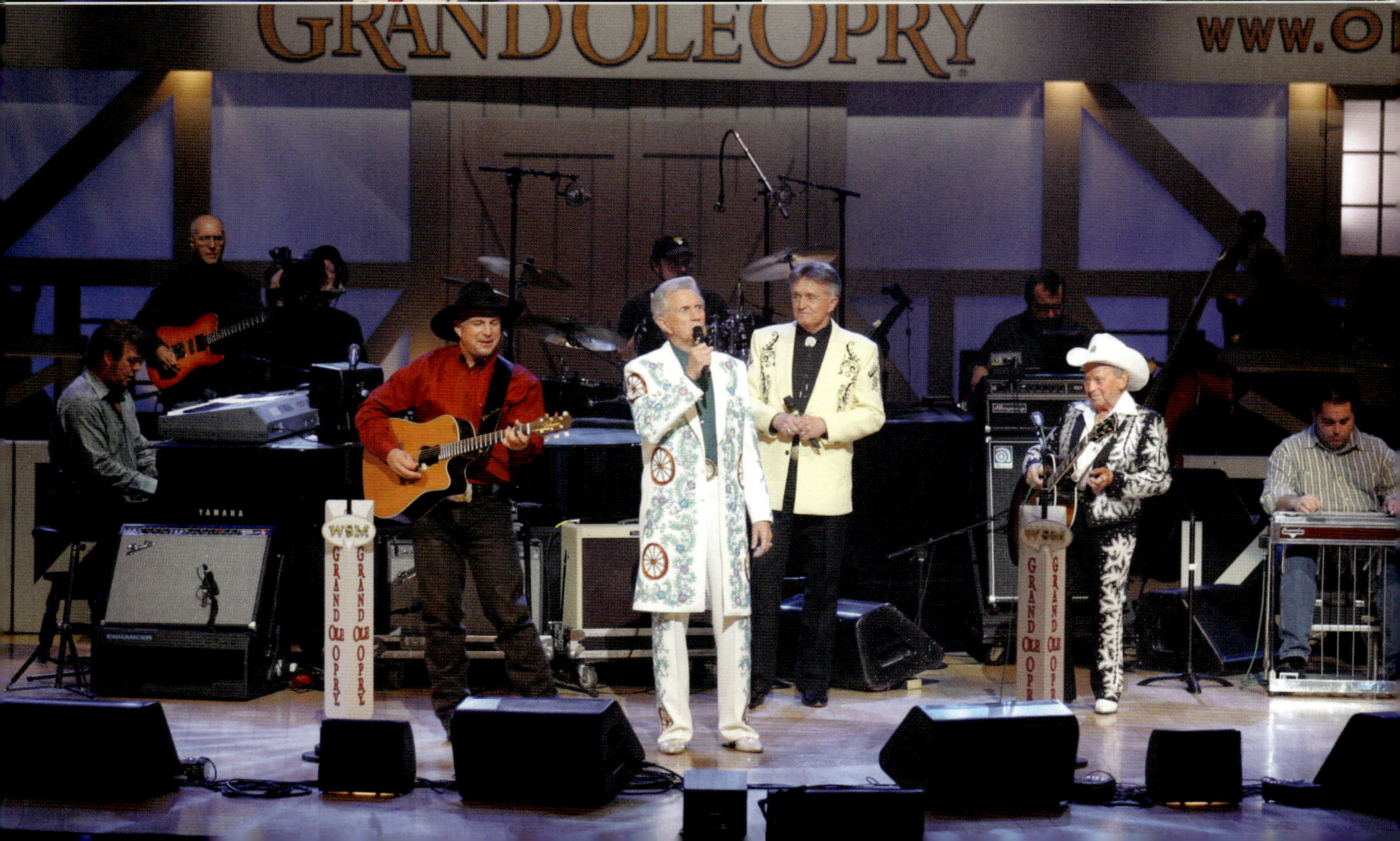
GRANDOLEOPRY
WSM
GRAND OLE OPRY
YAMAHA

TERRI CLARK
MEMBER SINCE 2004

Equally at home performing a honky-tonk classic, a quiet acoustic ballad or a hard-driving country rocker, Terri Clark followed a solid stretch of radio-friendly records by maturing into a thoughtful yet energetic artist who continues to command the devotion of legions of critics and fans.

Raised in Medicine Hat, Alberta, Terri grew up on country music — not only hearing records by contemporary artists like Reba McEntire, Ricky Skaggs, and The Judds, but learning from family members, including her grandparents.

By the time she finished high school, she was already making local appearances. Shortly after that came a trip to Nashville, where she honed her craft playing for tips at famed honky tonk Tootsie's. Signing

BIRTHPLACE: Montreal, Quebec, Canada
BIRTH DATE: August 5
OPRY INDUCTION: June 12, 2004

"WHEN WE CROSSED THE BORDER INTO THE UNITED STATES, THE GUARD AT THE BORDER SAID, 'WHERE ARE Y'ALL HEADED?' AND WE SAID, 'THE GRAND OLE OPRY!'"

---

with Mercury Records in 1994, she hit the charts in short order with four Top 10 hits ("Better Things to Do," "When Boy Meets Girl," "If I Were You" and "Poor, Poor Pitiful Me") as *Billboard* named her its Top New Female Country Artist in 1995. The following year, she picked up a Canadian Country Music Award, the first of many such awards, including eight for Entertainer of the Year.

For the remainder of the decade, Terri continued to score well at country radio with hits like "Now That I Found You," "You're Easy on the Eyes," and "Every Time I Cry." Later hits included "I Wanna Do It All" and "I Just Wanna Be Mad," which at the time was the first No. 1 country hit by a female artist in more than two years. Her stature as a major artist was confirmed in 2004 with the release of her *Greatest Hits* collection (which included another No. 1 hit, "Girls Lie Too") and when she joined the Grand Ole Opry.

"Just to be on the Opry is an honor," Terri says. "It's a tremendous responsibility, too. I feel like a lot of us who are younger members of the Opry really need to make sure that we pass down the tradition of it, and make sure that younger people who are getting into country music know what it means."

CLOCKWISE FROM TOP LEFT:
1. February 13, 2009
2. --
3. Being inducted into the Grand Ole Opry by Pete Fisher, Marty Stuart, and Connie Smith; June 12, 2004
4. March 1 2003
5. With Steve Wariner and mom, Linda, being invited to become an official Opry member; May 2004

OPRY FAMILY MEMBERS   86

WSM
GRAND OLE OPRY
GRAND OLE OPRY

WSM
GRAND OLE OPRY
WSM
GRAND OLE OPRY

GRAND OLE OPRY
WSM
GRAND OLE OPRY

WSM
GRAND OLE OPRY

LUKE COMBS
MEMBER SINCE 2019

There's a certain feeling you get backstage at the Opry, a magic that artists making their debut just can't shake. Luke Combs remembers that feeling from the first time he played the Opry in 2016.

"That night I said, 'That's it, I'm becoming a part of this, whatever it takes,'" Luke once reflected in an interview.

It's an understatement to say that Luke had a meteoric start to his career. He holds the record for having a debut album that spent the most weeks at No. 1 on *Billboard*'s Top Country Albums chart. Even with all the early success, Luke has remained anchored by a love for the Opry. This love earned him a coveted spot among the show's distinguished cast of members in 2019.

BIRTHPLACE: Charlotte, North Carolina
BIRTH DATE: March 2, 1990
OPRY INDUCTION: July 16, 2019

DID YOU KNOW? On his first trip to Nashville, Luke had breakfast with John Conlee at a Cracker Barrel. John Conlee would later ask him to become a member of the Opry.

"HOLY COW, MAN. I JUST CAN'T BELIEVE IT."
—LUKE COMBS AFTER BEING INVITED TO BECOME AN OPRY MEMBER

"If you come here and you invest in the people and this stage, you'll get back a hundredfold what you will ever give," Vince Gill told Luke at his induction ceremony.

Along with Joe Diffie, Vince was a childhood hero to Luke. Both did the honors of making him part of the Opry family. It was a full-circle moment that wasn't lost on Luke.

"Here I am on stage with people I grew up listening to and people who have shaped me as an artist. I just want to say thank you to you guys, thank you to the Grand Ole Opry, and thank you to the fans," Luke said as he held up his Opry Member Award. "Without you all, there is no country music, there is no Grand Ole Opry."

But the thank-you's didn't end there. Luke closed out his performance with his song, "This One's For You," subtly changing the final verse in a fitting tribute to those who helped him get to this famous stage. *"There's a couple of people in the Grand Ole Opry tonight that I owe a beer to…and three or four I owe more than a few."*

CLOCKWISE FROM TOP LEFT:
1. Luke makes his Opry debut on October 29, 2016.
2. In a rare acoustic set, Luke invites his friend and cowriter Ray Fulcher to sing with him on stage.
3. Luke is joined on stage by fellow members of the Opry moments after his induction.
4. John Conlee, Chris Janson, and Craig Morgan congratulate Luke on his invitation become a member of the Opry as he bends over in shock.
5. --

OPRY FAMILY MEMBERS

WSM

WSM
GRAND OLE OPRY

W S M
GRAND OLE OPRY
OPRY.COM
WSM
GRAND OLE OPRY

WSM
GRAND OLE OPRY

JOHN CONLEE
MEMBER SINCE 1981

John Conlee grew up on a 250-acre Kentucky farm, served as a licensed funeral director and embalmer, and worked as a pop music disc jockey in Nashville before settling into a career in country music during the mid-1970s. It's typical of John that he used the returns from that long string of No. 1 hits (four in 1983 and 1984 alone) to get back to farm life himself.

"I spend all of my off-time, what I have of it, with my family on our farm," John explains. "I enjoy it. There's no glamour to it. Woodworking, gunsmithing or driving a tractor requires getting grease or varnish all over you. It's dirty work, but I like it."

John joined the Grand Ole Opry cast in 1981. "Back when I joined the Opry, there was not a great big hoopla about a new member coming

BIRTHPLACE: Versailles, Kentucky
BIRTH DATE: August 11
OPRY INDUCTION: February 7, 1981

DEFINITIVE JOHN CONLEE:
"Rose Colored Glasses"
"Lady Lay Down"
"Backside Of Thirty"
"Friday Night Blues"
"Common Man"

"THE OPRY IS, HAS ALWAYS BEEN AND REMAINS A LIVE RADIO SHOW, AND THAT'S THE WAY I THINK OF IT. … IT'S STILL A LIVE RADIO SHOW TO ME."

---

on board," he says. "But now, we make a big deal out of it for the people that join. It really doesn't matter to me. I mean officially becoming a member made it a great night."

Three decades later, John still stirs the hall to the rafters with his biggest hits, as well as his more recent offerings such as a salute to the families of American fighting troops, "They Also Serve."

In addition to an active touring schedule and recording new music, John has spent much time and energy on philanthropic work. He raised more than $250,000 — one dollar at a time — for Feed the Children from the dollar bills tossed on the stage when he sang his 1983 hit "Busted." He still collects donations from fans during that song's performance, currently channeling the money to the benefit of Wounded Warriors. John was instrumental in the formation of the Family Farm Defense Fund. He helped Willie Nelson, Neil Young, and John Mellencamp organize and entertain at Farm Aid concerts that raised more than $13 million in grants.

CLOCKWISE FROM TOP LEFT:
1. October 27, 2001
2. Backstage with Bill Carlisle and Connie Smith
3. Circa 1990s
4. February 6, 2014
5. --

OPRY FAMILY MEMBERS **90**

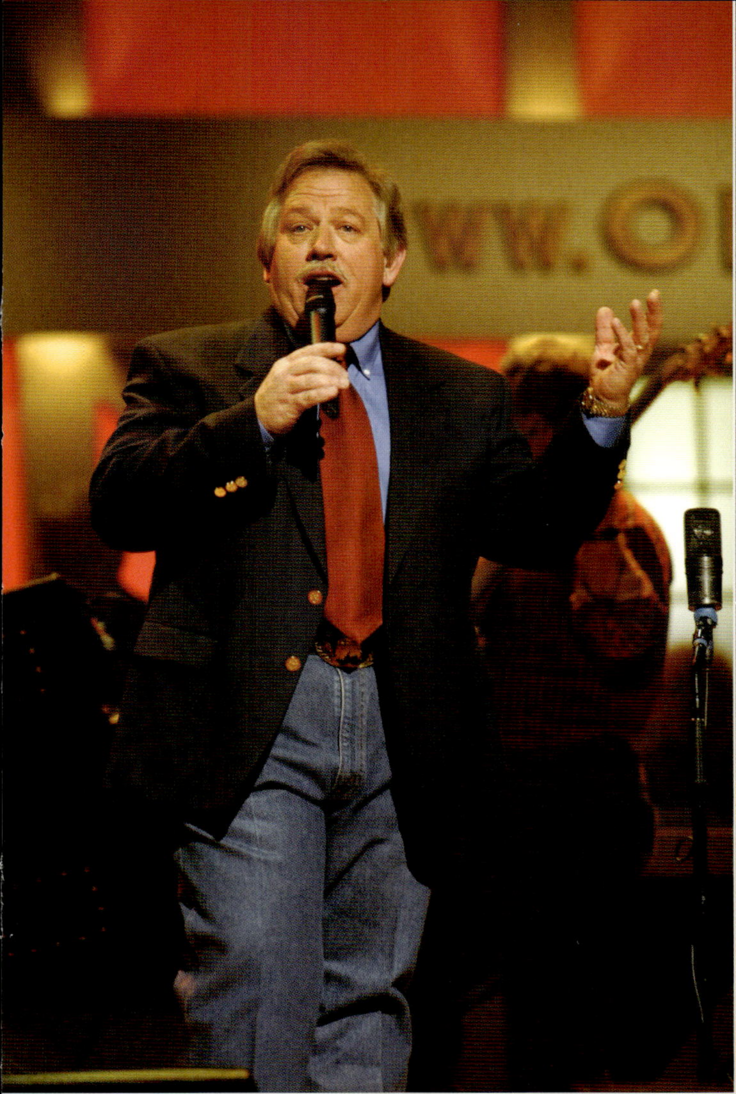

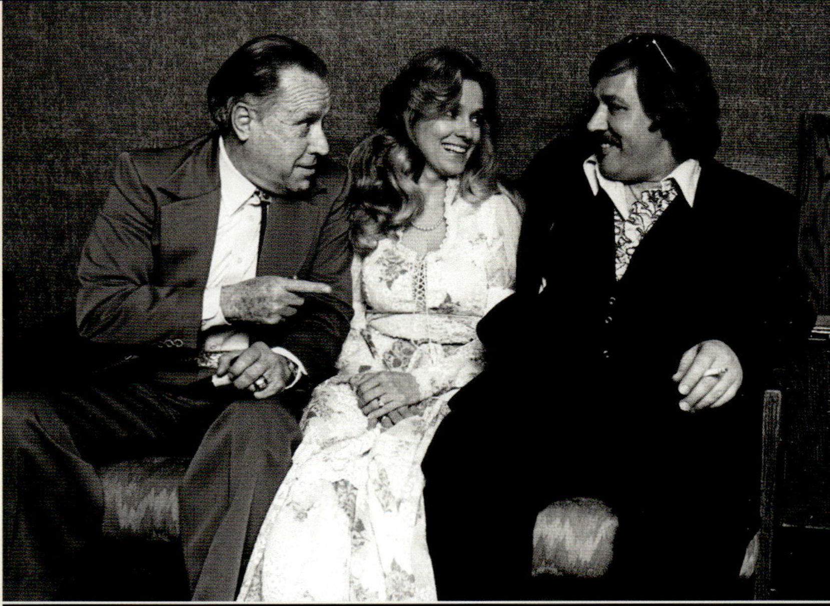

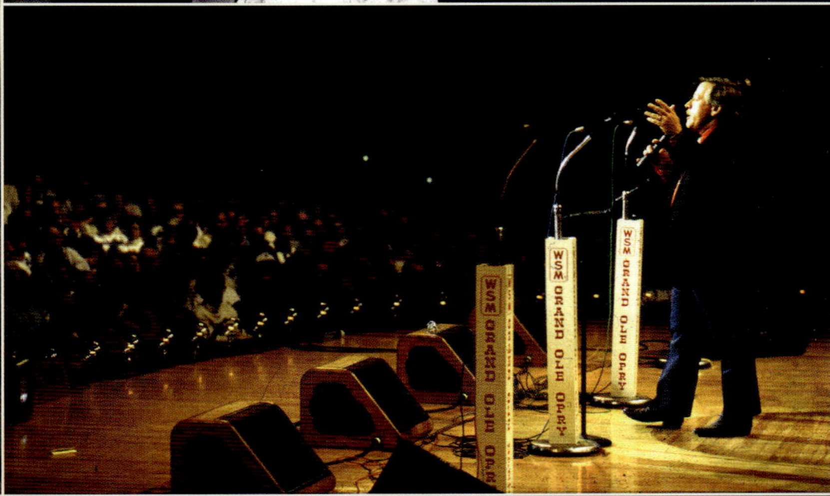
WSM GRAND OLE OPRY

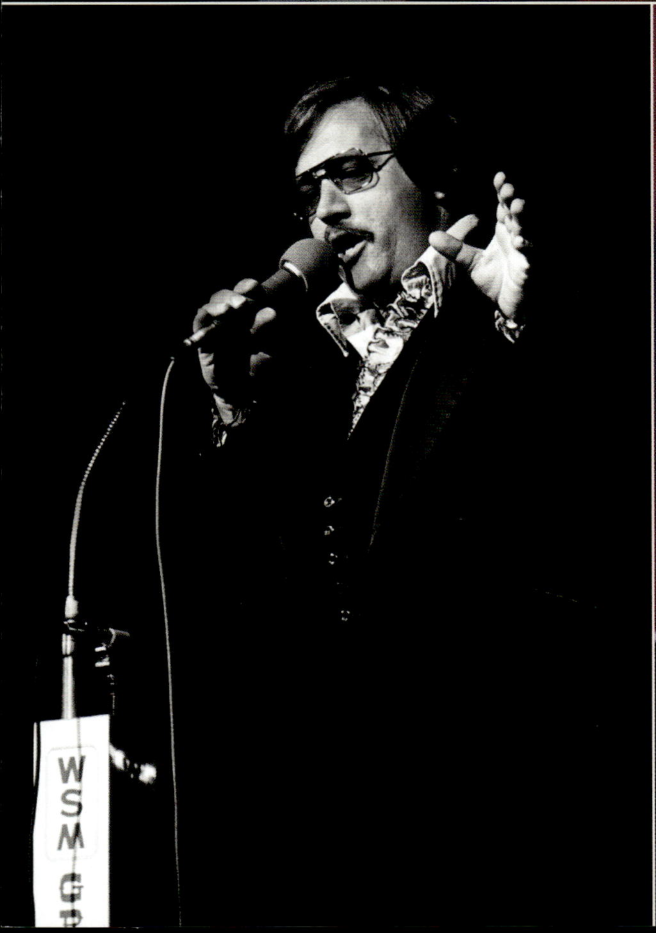
WSM

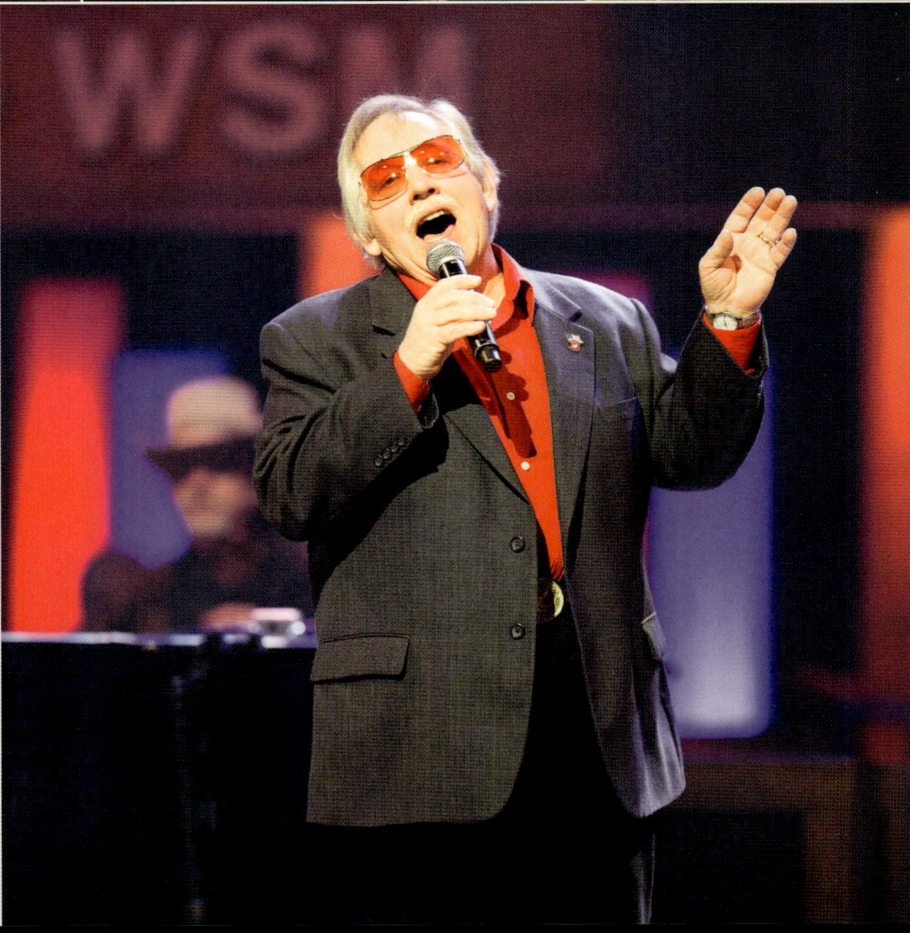
WSM

DAILEY & VINCENT
MEMBER SINCE 2017

Jamie Dailey and Darrin Vincent are bluegrass music veterans. A combined 20 years experience includes seasoned tenures with legends Doyle Lawson and Ricky Skaggs, among others. In 2007, the longtime friends decided to form a new band. The bluegrass duo Dailey & Vincent was born, making its stage debut on the Grand Ole Opry.

At the dawn of the group's 10th anniversary and in the midst of award wins, hit records, and a dynamic live show, the friends returned for their 100th Opry guest appearance in December 2016. Surprising the duo with an invitation to become official Opry members, Marty Stuart shared with them, "Country music needs you. Country music loves you. And the Grand Ole Opry welcomes you."

JAMIE DAILEY
Birthplace: Corbin, Kentucky
Birth Date: June 9

DARRIN VINCENT
Birthplace: Kirksville, Missouri
Birth Date: December 27

OPRY INDUCTION: March 11, 2017

"COUNTRY MUSIC NEEDS YOU. COUNTRY MUSIC LOVES YOU. AND THE GRAND OLE OPRY WELCOMES YOU." —MARTY STUART TO DAILEY & VINCENT AFTER HAVING INVITED THE DUO TO BECOME OPRY MEMBERS.

Jamie grew up singing and playing with family and gained national attention when he joined Doyle Lawson & Quicksilver in 1998 as lead, baritone and tenor singer. During Jamie's tenure, the band won 13 IBMA Awards, earned four Grammy Awards, and secured five Dove Award nominations. Jamie has recorded with Dolly Parton, appeared on five of Bill Gaither's Homecoming Hymns DVDs, was a guest on Ricky Skaggs' Grammy-winning *Brand New Strings* album, appeared with Meryl Streep and John C. Reilly at the Hollywood Bowl, and has dozens of other guest performances and collaborations to his credit.

Darrin started singing at age three and playing music at age six as part of his family band, The Sally Mountain Show. As a member of Ricky Skaggs & Kentucky Thunder for more than 10 years, Darrin has won five Grammy Awards and eight IBMA Awards for Instrumental Group of the Year. He has performance and recording credits with Dolly Parton, Norah Jones, Emmylou Harris, Earl Scruggs, Bruce Hornsby, Vince Gill, John Hartford, and more.

Together, Dailey & Vincent have racked up three IBMA Entertainer of the Year awards and Grammy nominations for three music genres: country, bluegrass, and gospel.

CLOCKWISE FROM TOP LEFT:
1. May 23, 2017
2. Being invited to become official Opry members by Marty Stuart, December 30, 2016
3. May 25, 2017 with Jimmy Fortune
4. Opry Induction, Opry Member Gallery, March 11, 2017

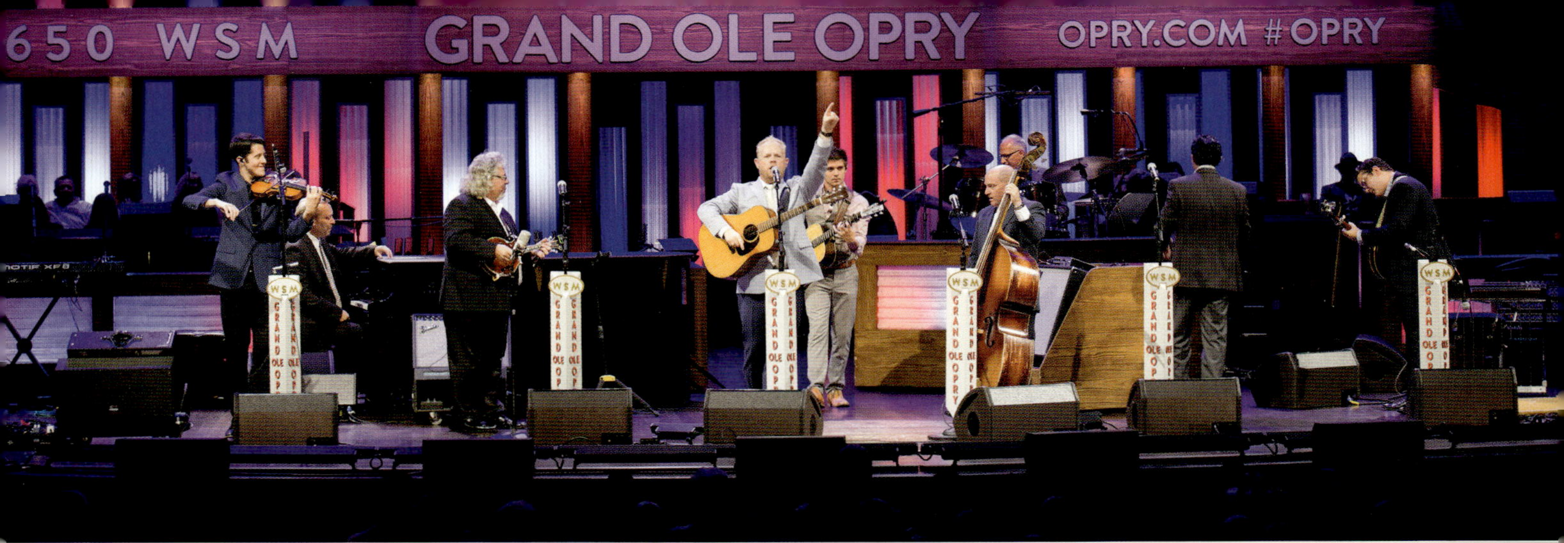
650 WSM
GRAND OLE OPRY
OPRY.COM #OPRY

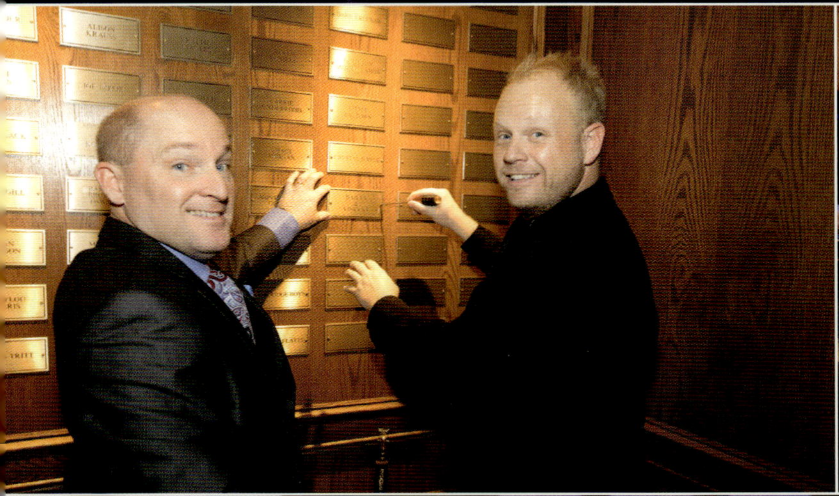

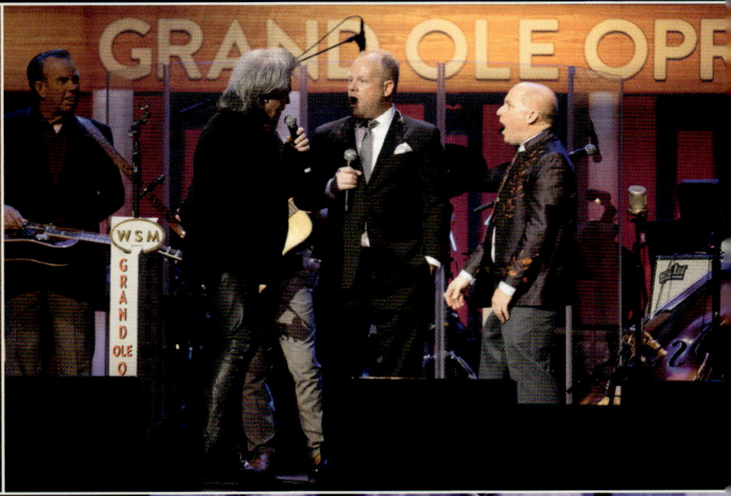
WSM

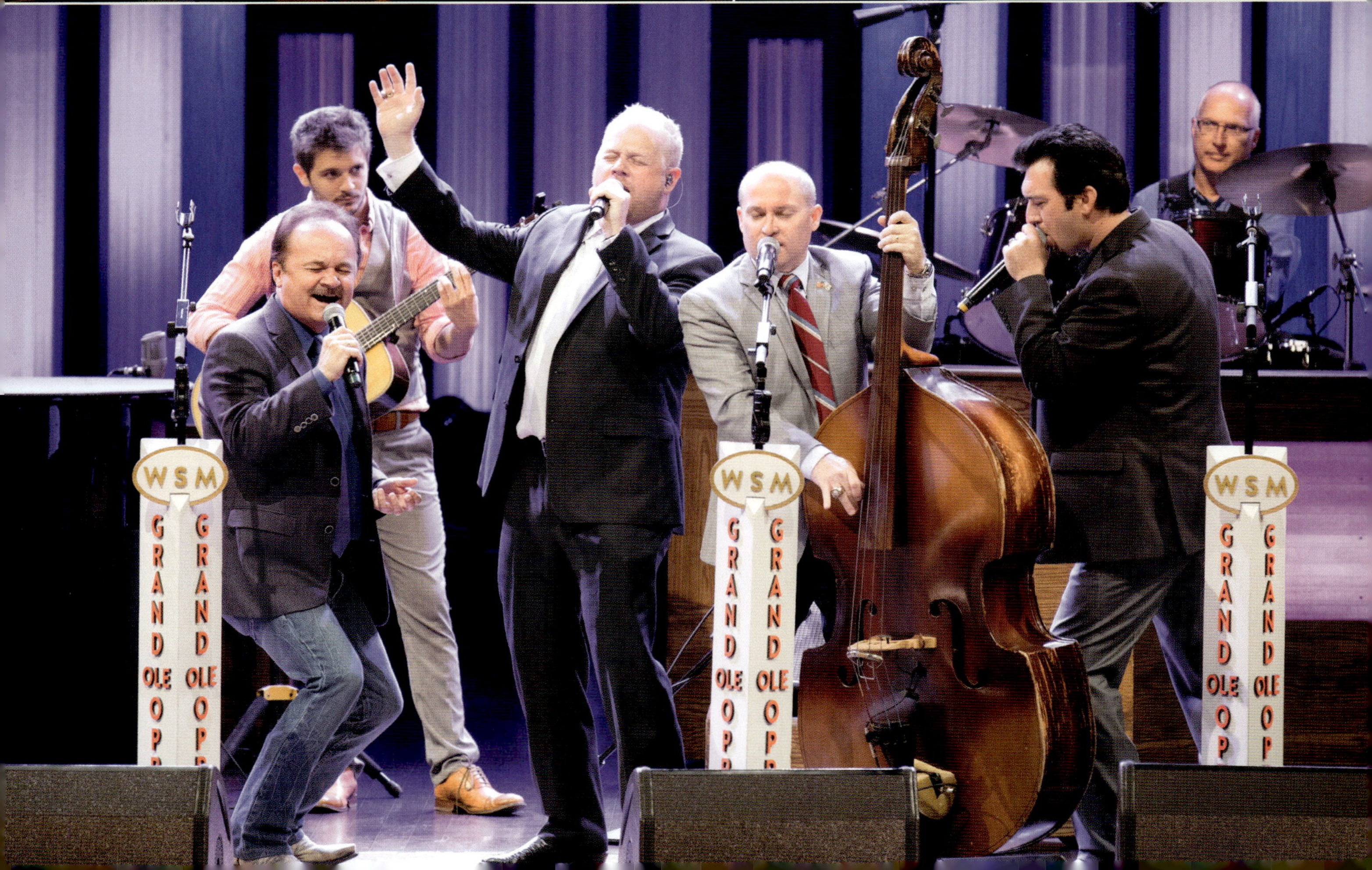
WSM
WSM
WSM

DIAMOND RIO
MEMBER SINCE 1998

Diamond Rio made its first Opry appearance in October 1991, and in 1998 became the first group since The Whites, who joined in 1984, to receive Opry membership. With their lighter-than-air harmonies and intricately woven instrumentation, this six-man group has been turning songs into standards since its 1991 debut album helped define the "young country" movement. Diamond Rio has been awarded Top Vocal Group honors a total of six times from the Academy of Country Music and the Country Music Association. The group has sold more than 10 million records, earning five gold and three platinum albums in the process.

Diamond Rio evolved from the Tennessee River Boys, a band that performed at the former Opryland theme park. Singer Marty Roe, guitarist Jimmy Olander and keyboardist Dan Truman left that group to form their own in 1986. Drummer Brian Prout and mandolin player Gene Johnson joined the new band in 1987. Bassist Dana Williams — a nephew of Opry members Sonny Osborne and Bobby Osborne — came on board two years later.

In 1991, Diamond Rio's first single, "Meet in the Middle," went to No. 1 — the first group in country music history to top the charts with its debut. The band followed "Meet in the Middle" with the hits "Mirror, Mirror" and "Mama Don't Forget to Pray for Me." In all,

MARTY ROE:
Birthplace, Lebanon, Ohio
Birth Date: December 28

JIMMY OLANDER:
Birthplace: Minneapolis, Minnesota
Birth Date: August 26

GENE JOHNSON:
Birthplace: Jamestown, New York
Birth Date: August 10

DAN TRUMAN:
Birthplace: Flagstaff, Arizona
Birth Date: August 29

DANA WILLIAMS:
Birthplace: Dayton, Ohio
Birth Date: May 22

BRIAN PROUT:
Birthplace: Troy, New York
Birth Date: December 4

OPRY INDUCTION: April 18, 1998

> "I HAVE ALL THESE MEMORIES OF THE OPRY AND THEN TO THINK THAT WE'VE BECOME MEMBERS OF THIS INSTITUTION, IT'S OVERWHELMING. IT STILL IS TO THIS DAY."
> —DANA WILLIAMS

Diamond Rio has placed more than 30 singles on *Billboard* magazine's country charts, including such chart-toppers as "How Your Love Makes Me Feel," "Beautiful Mess," and "I Believe." The 2001 hit ballad "One More Day" became a key song of healing after the September 11 terrorist attacks.

The group's members told their story in an autobiography titled after one of their most popular hits — "A Beautiful Mess."

CLOCKWISE FROM TOP LEFT:
1. Opry induction night, April 18, 1998
2. 2014
3. November 13, 2012
4. Celebrating the group's 10th Opry Anniversary, April 18, 2008

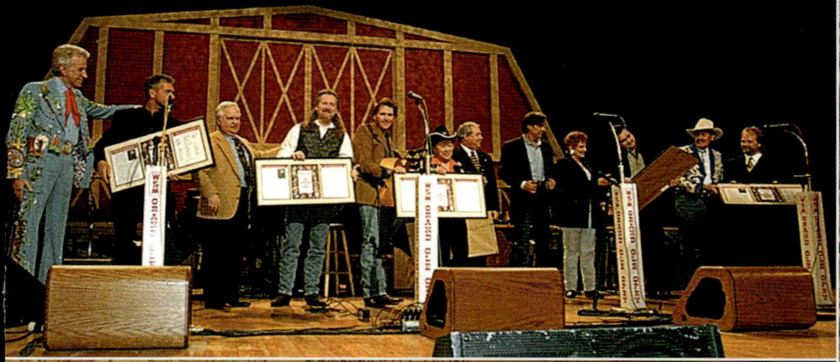

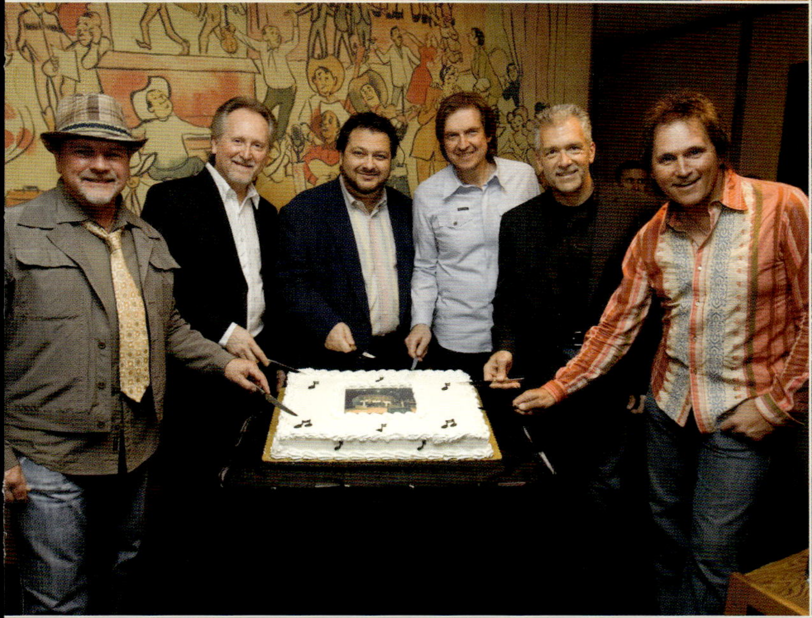

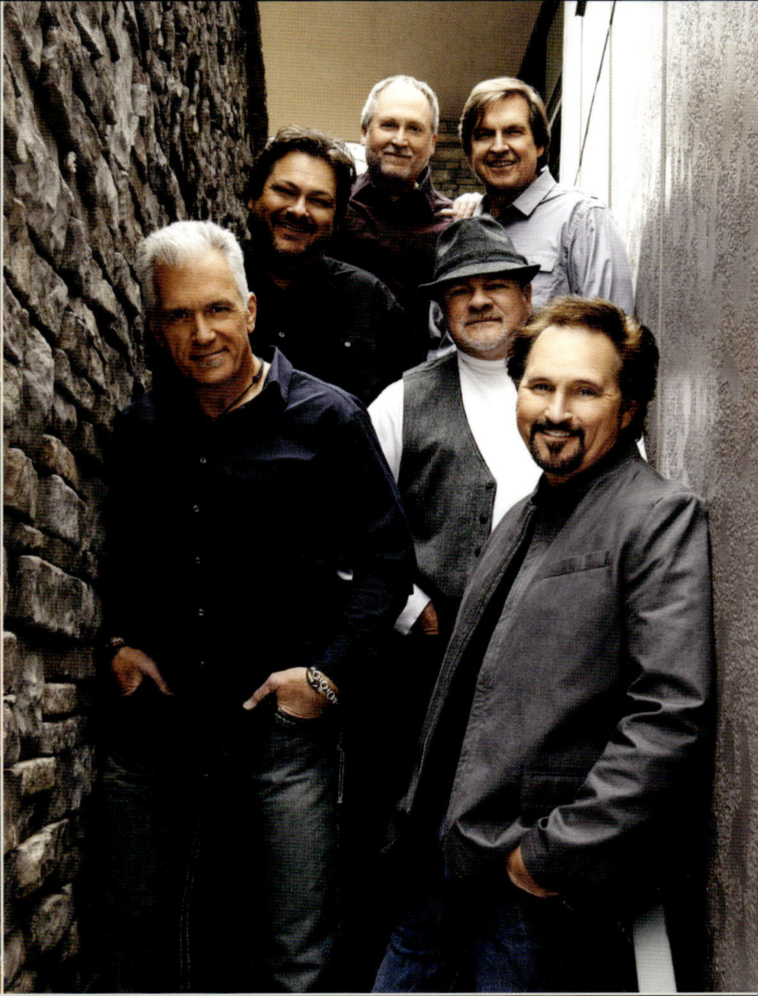

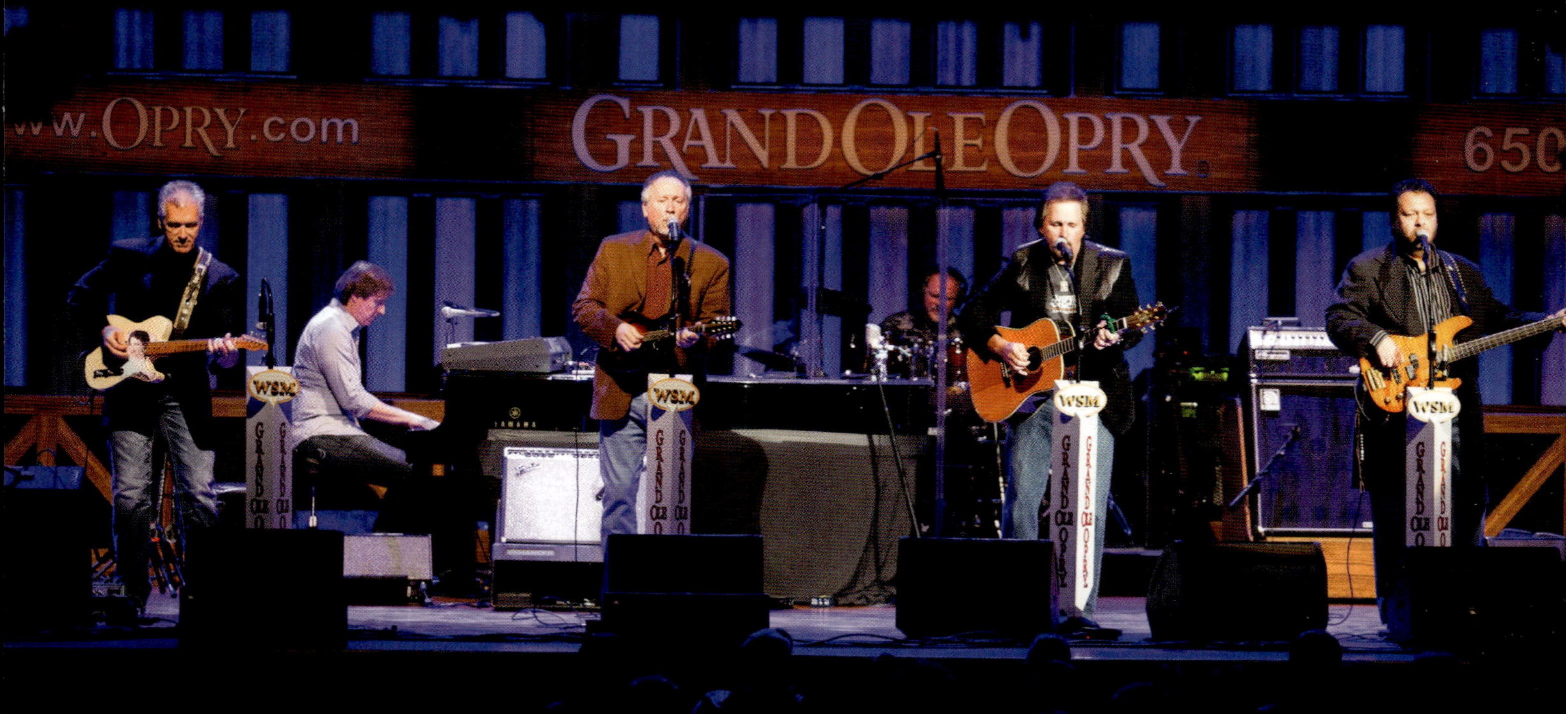
GRANDOLEOPRY
WSM

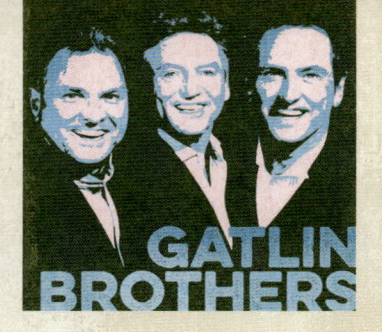

THE GATLIN BROTHERS
MEMBER SINCE 1976

Few singing groups can sound quite so harmonious as family singing groups. The Gatlin Brothers have been at it, quite harmoniously, for more than 40 years. A popular Opry attraction since their induction on Christmas Day 1976, the Gatlins have always loved to sing as a unit. They won their first talent contest at home in Texas in 1954 at a Hardin-Simmons University talent show in Abilene. Larry was six, Steve four, and Rudy only two.

They began performing gospel patterned after the Blackwood Brothers and the Statesmen on Slim Willets' radio and TV shows in Abilene that same year — dressed in cowboy outfits.

During the mid-'70s, the Gatlins became consistent hit-makers at Monument Records. Initially, Larry was signed on his own, following

LARRY GATLIN
Birthplace: Seminole, Texas
Birth Date: May 2

STEVE GATLIN
Birthplace: Olney, Texas
Birth Date: April 4

RUDY GATLIN
Birthplace: Olney, Texas
Birth Date: August 20

OPRY INDUCTION: December 25, 1976

> "THE GRAND OLE OPRY IS NOT A BUILDING. THE GRAND OLE OPRY IS A SHOW, AND IT'S PEOPLE WITH HEART AND SOUL AND TALENT."

---

his success as a songwriter, but the Gatlins wanted to perform their music together. So Larry wrote a song specifically for the three of them — in 15 minutes. "Broken Lady" went to No. 1 and won the Gatlins a Grammy the same year that they joined the Opry cast.

"I Just Wish You Were Someone I Love" climbed to the top of the charts in 1977, and "All The Gold In California" followed two years later. The Gatlins enjoyed other hits through the years, including "Sure Feels Like Love" and the chart-topping "Houston (Means I'm One Day Closer to You)."

Larry's songwriting career had begun when the Opry's Dottie West spotted him singing in Las Vegas in 1971, encouraged him to write, and even provided him a ticket to Nashville. Dottie would record two of Larry's songs; others were performed by Johnny Cash, Kris Kristofferson, and Elvis Presley.

The Brothers embarked on what they called their 60th Anniversary Tour in 2015. "We're not calling it a farewell or a final tour. We're calling it the 60th Anniversary Celebration. By no means are we retiring, but after this tour, we are going to slow down a little bit. The promoters are going to have to want us about three times more than they want us right now," he laughs.

Q: What is your most memorable Opry Moment?
A: Our most memorable moment has to be when Dottie West brought us to the Ryman to sing back up harmony with her one hot August night. Inside the Ryman it was warm–no, it was hot–as we walked in to hear Bill Anderson on stage singing one of his many hits. We also remember going into a small dressing room and listening to Grandpa Jones and Stringbean tell stories.

CLOCKWISE FROM TOP LEFT:
1. Opry 65th Birthday Special
2. Appearing with fellow cast members on the Opry's 65th Anniversary TV special
3. The Opry's 55th Birthday. October 13, 1980
4. Circa 1980s
5. Circa 2015

OPRY FAMILY MEMBERS

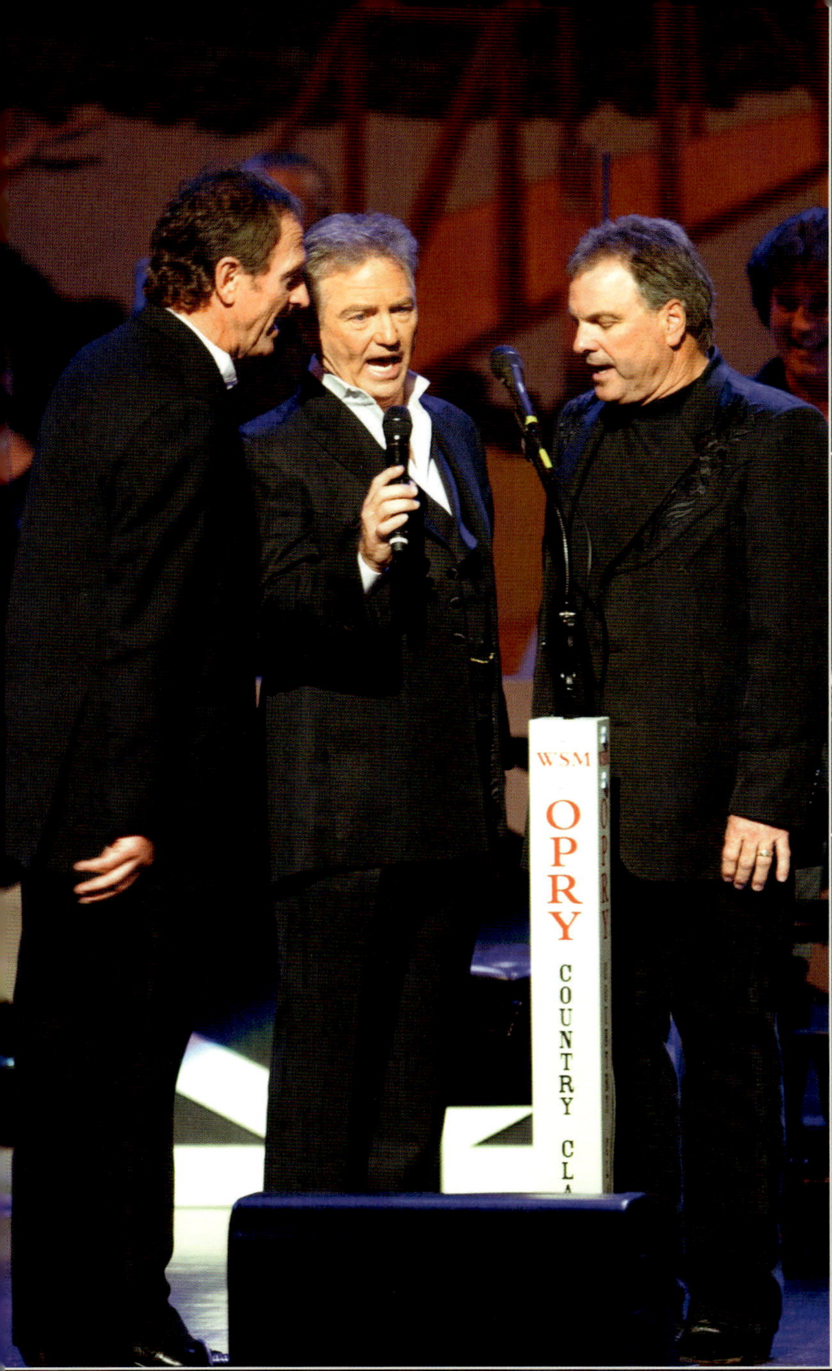
WSM
OPRY
COUNTRY

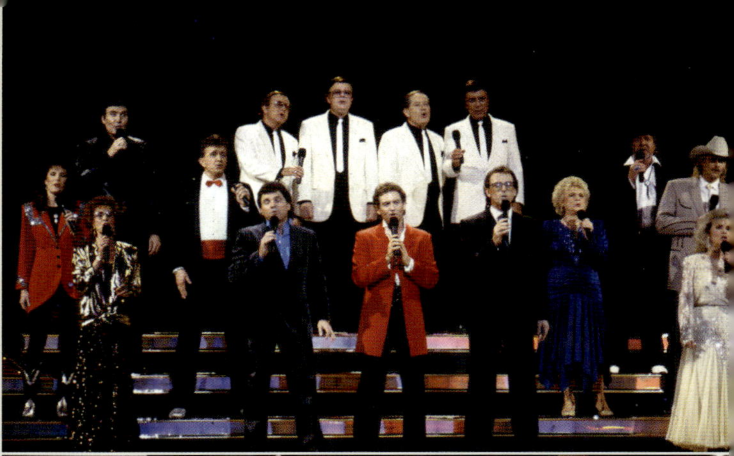

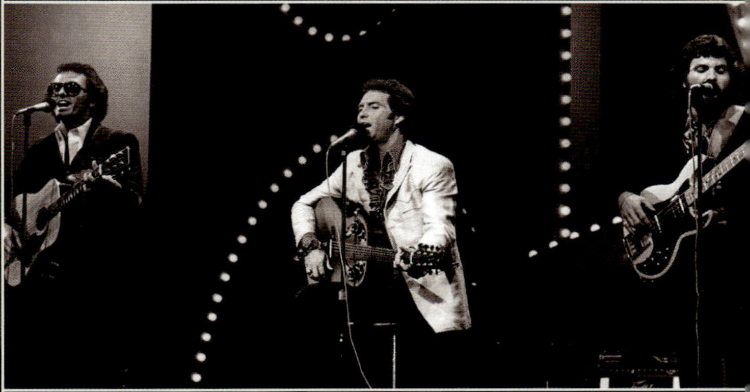

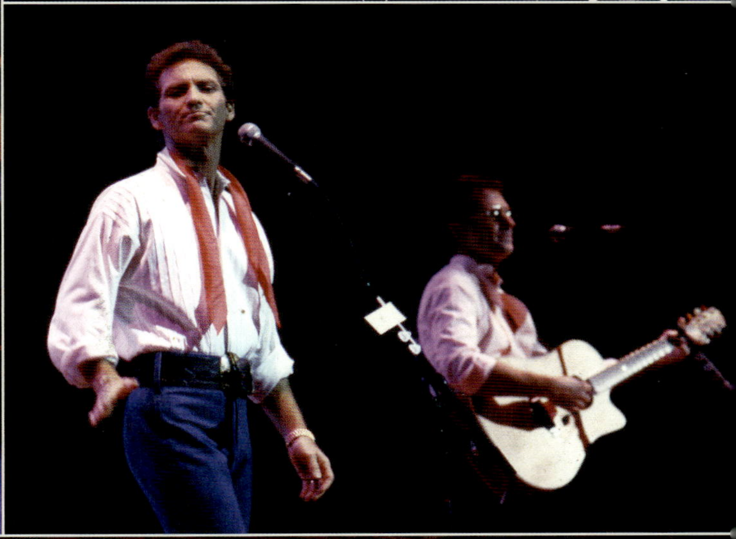

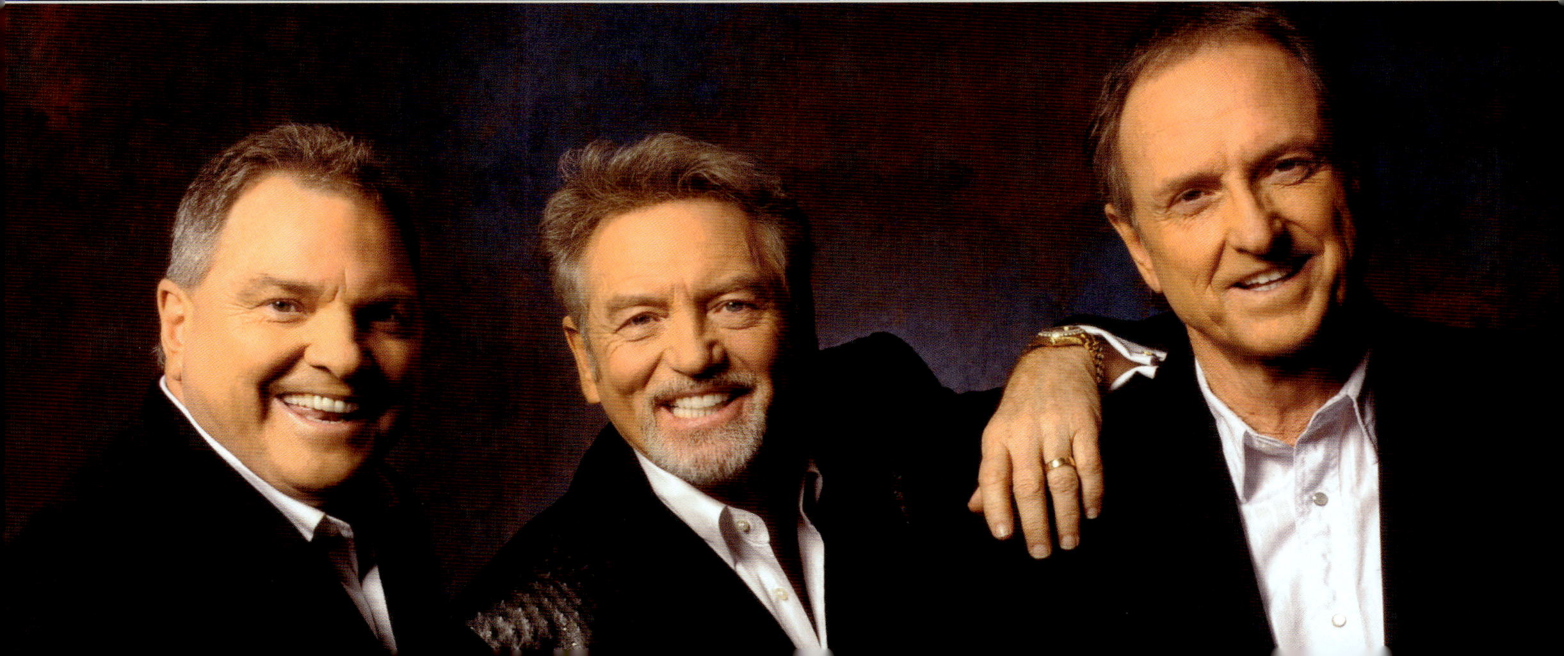

CRYSTAL GAYLE
MEMBER SINCE 2017

Crystal Gayle was born Brenda Gail Webb in Paintsville, Kentucky. Her older sister was future country music superstar and Grand Ole Opry member Loretta Lynn, though Loretta had already left home by the time Brenda was born.

The Grand Ole Opry has held a special place in Crystal's heart since even before she made her Opry debut on stage at the Ryman Auditorium at age 16. "My first time to perform on the Opry, Loretta was sick and she talked them into letting me perform in her spot," she recalls. "I remember singing 'Ribbon of Darkness' in my little shiny dress my mother made me."

Both that dress and sister Loretta were on hand on January 21, 2017, when Crystal took her rightful place as a member of the Grand Ole Opry. It was a capstone for a career full of hits, honors, and awards.

BIRTHPLACE: Paintsville, Kentucky
BIRTH DATE: January 9
OPRY INDUCTION: January 21, 2017

"I REMEMBER SINGING 'RIBBON OF DARKNESS' IN MY LITTLE SHINY DRESS MY MOTHER MADE ME."

To escape constant comparison to her sister in the early days of her recording career, Crystal developed her own vocal and musical style. She had 20 No. 1 country singles, beginning with "I'll Get Over You" and including her signature "Don't It Make My Brown Eyes Blue," which earned her a Grammy® for Best Female Country Vocal Performance and also propelled her album *We Must Believe In Magic* to become the first by a female country artist to go platinum. Among her many other chart successes are "Talking In Your Sleep," "Why Have You Left The One You Left Me For," "Half The Way," "Wrong Road Again," "When I Dream," and "Ready For the Times To Get Better."

In 2008, Crystal was inducted into the Kentucky Music Hall of Fame. She received a star on the Hollywood Walk of Fame in 2009, and the honors kept coming in 2015, as she received the Academy of Country Music's Cliffie Stone Pioneer Award.

CLOCKWISE FROM TOP LEFT:
1. Circa 1976
2. Circa 1982
3. Opry induction with Loretta Lynn, January 21, 2017
4. Circa 1978
5. Being invited to become an official Opry member by Carrie Underwood, November 15, 2016

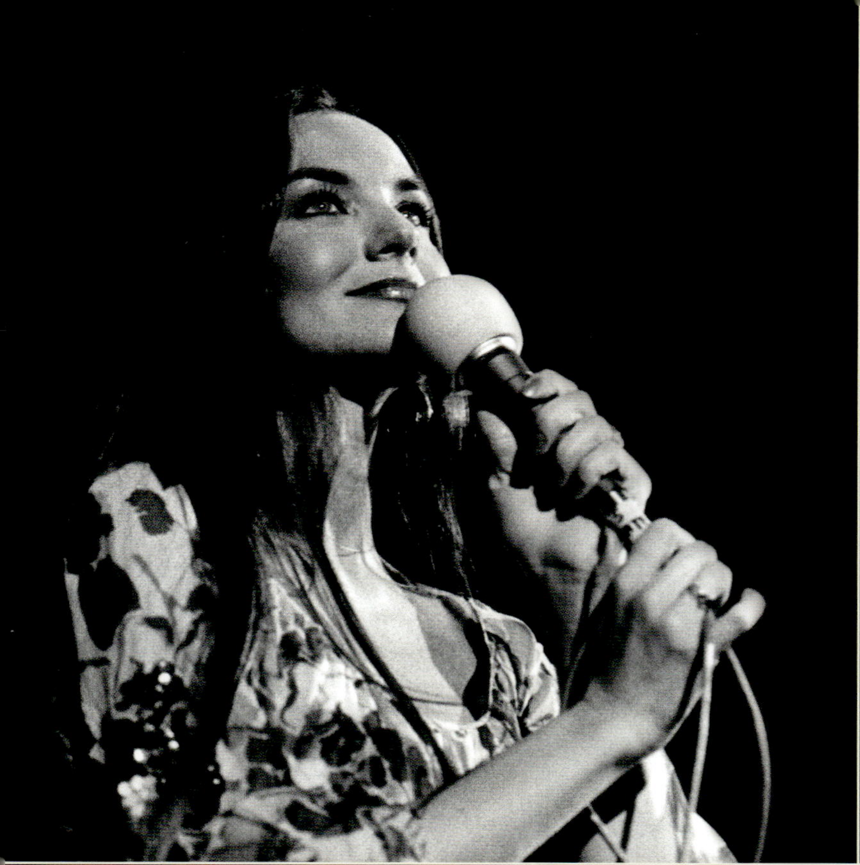

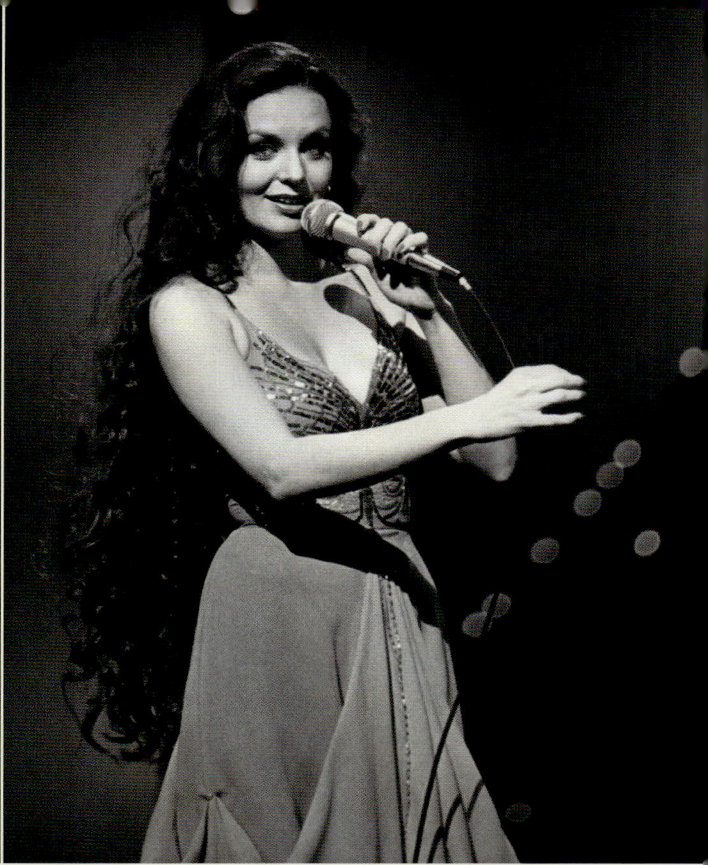

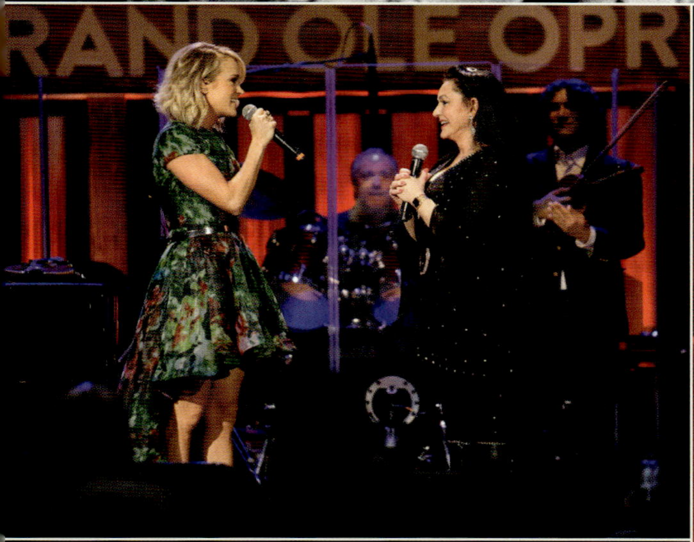
RAND OLE OPR

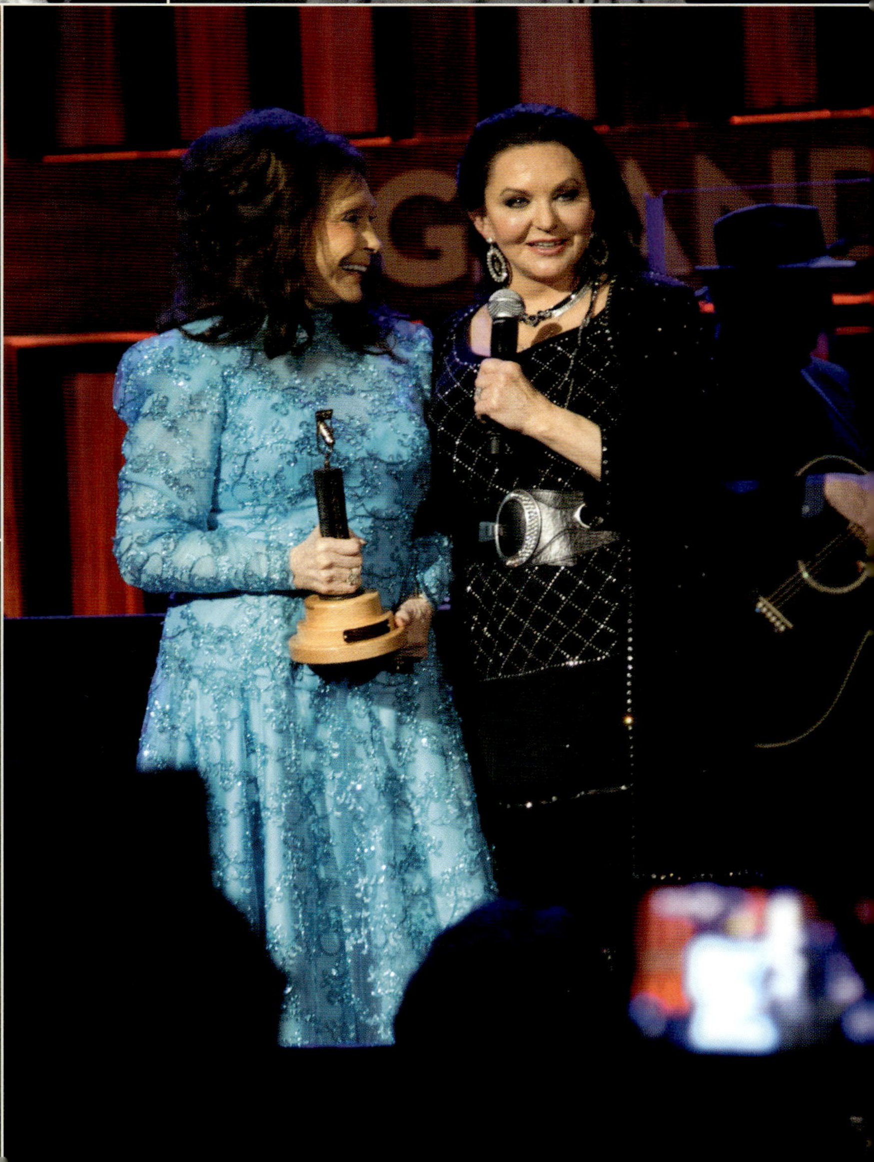

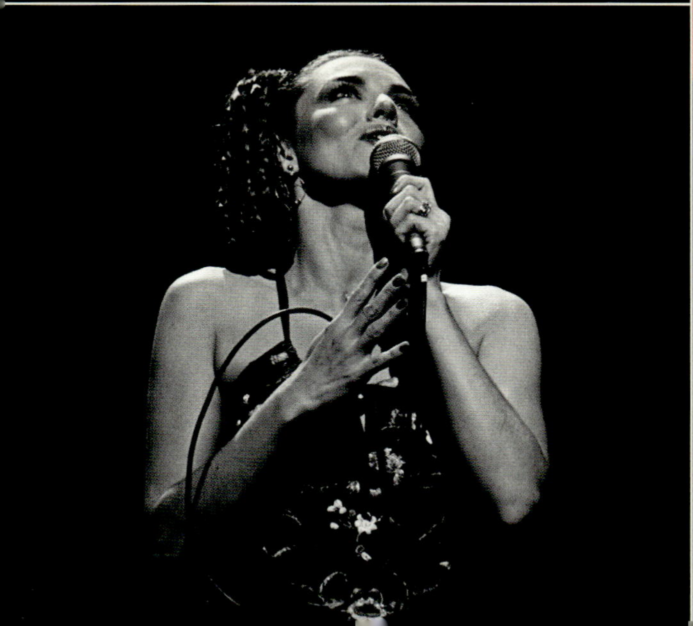

VINCE GILL
MEMBER SINCE 1991

Combining unequaled musicianship and creativity with a strong sense of tradition — and a personality that has won him a reputation as one of the nicest people in country music — Vince Gill is one of the most honored artists in the music's history.

A talented guitar and dobro picker by the time he was in his teens, Vince began his career playing with bluegrass bands — first in his native Oklahoma, then in Kentucky with the Bluegrass Alliance and, briefly, Ricky Skaggs' Boone Creek. Moving to Los Angeles, he signed on with fiddler Byron Berline's Sundance before joining the pop-country-rock Pure Prairie League. He followed that with a stint in the Cherry Bombs with Rodney Crowell and work backing Rosanne Cash. In 1984, he moved to Nashville and signed his first recording contract as a solo artist, occupying himself with work as a sideman in studios.

BIRTHPLACE: Norman, Oklahoma
BIRTH DATE: April 12
OPRY INDUCTION: August 10, 1991

> "... I'M ALWAYS LEANING A LOT COUNTRIER AT THE OPRY THAN ANYWHERE ELSE."

Vince's real breakthrough came in 1990, with the release of the now-classic "When I Call Your Name." In the years that followed, he was a steady presence in the Top 10, racking up several dozen hits that ranged from country ballads ("I Still Believe in You," "Tryin' To Get Over You") to feel-good country-rockers like "Liza Jane" and "What the Cowgirls Do" to gems such as "Go Rest High On That Mountain." Rewarded by his peers with a long list of Country Music Association awards and Grammy trophies (the most for a male country artist), Vince was a critical and commercial success, too, selling more than 25 million albums while being hailed as a soulful singer, innovative instrumentalist, and award-winning songwriter with a strong grasp of country traditions from bluegrass to honky tonk.

In more recent years, Vince has settled into a unique role as one of country music's youngest "elder statesmen." An eloquent spokesman for the Opry and for the Country Music Foundation, he has headed all-star casts at prestigious venues around the country, hosted the CMA Awards show multiple years, made guest appearances on stage and recordings with artists ranging from the world-famous to the obscure, and toured extensively. In 2007, Vince was inducted into the Country Music Hall of Fame.

CLOCKWISE FROM TOP LEFT:
1. October 17, 2014
2. Circa 1993
3. With Emmylou Harris
4. Vince and his fellow members of the Grammy-nominated Time Jumpers
5. With Amy Grant

OPRY FAMILY MEMBERS

WSM
GRAND OLE OPRY

WSM

WSM
GRAND OLE OPRY

650 WSM
GRAND OLE OPRY

EMMYLOU HARRIS
MEMBER SINCE 1992

BIRTHPLACE: Birmingham, Alabama
BIRTH DATE: April 2
OPRY INDUCTION: January 25, 1992

God didn't make honky tonk angels, but if he had, he would have broken the mold with Emmylou Harris. With her crystal-clear soprano, lissome beauty, impeccable instincts, and uncompromising integrity, Emmylou redefined the image and role of women in country music. Few if any artists have so successfully erased boundaries between country, folk, and rock and roll.

Born in Birmingham, Alabama, Emmylou spent her youth in North Carolina and Virginia. As the daughter of a career Marine, her upbringing was not particularly musical. But during the '60s she fell in love with folk music — especially Bob Dylan and Joan Baez — and began performing while studying drama at the University of North Carolina. She moved to Greenwich Village in 1967 to join the

> "MUSIC IS LIKE FOOD, SUSTENANCE. YOU CERTAINLY DON'T DO IT FOR THE SPOTLIGHT. YOU DO IT FOR THE AMAZING EXHILARATION OF SINGING, THE FEELING OF THE MUSIC GOING THROUGH YOU."

burgeoning folk revival, sharing stages with Jerry Jeff Walker and David Bromberg, and released her first record in 1969.

On the East Coast club circuit, she met Gram Parsons, and both her career and life changed forever. Gram, formerly of the Byrds and the Flying Burrito Brothers, became her mentor and singing partner, drawing her into the '70s country rock movement and strengthening her ties to traditional country music. Emmylou toured and recorded with Gram until his death in 1973.

In 1975 she recorded her first major album, *Pieces of the Sky*, introducing her Hot Band, which, over the years, included such world-class players as James Burton, Albert Lee, Rodney Crowell and Ricky Skaggs. Emmylou has enjoyed seven No. 1 hits and 27 Top 10 songs including "If I Could Only Win Your Love," "Together Again," "Sweet Dreams," "Making Believe," "To Daddy" and "Heartbreak Hill."

The 2008 Country Music Hall of Fame inductee has 10 gold albums and 12 Grammy Awards, including one for her 1987 Trio album with Linda Ronstadt and Dolly Parton as well as one for her work on the soundtrack to the motion picture *O Brother, Where Art Thou?*

CLOCKWISE FROM TOP LEFT:
1. July 2, 2010
2. With Bill Monroe
3. With The Nash Ramblers
4. An all-star jam celebrates Emmylou's 20th Opry Anniversary

WSM
GRAND OLE OPRY

WSM

WSM GRAND OLE OPRY

www.OPRY.com
WSM
GRAND OLE OPRY

THE ISAACS
MEMBER SINCE 2021

The harmonies of family-based gospel group The Isaacs, comprised of siblings Ben, Sonya, and Rebecca, and their mother Lily, enchanted Grand Ole Opry audiences for over 30 years before they received an invitation to join the Opry family.

"They are the kind of people we need at the Grand Ole Opry," Ricky Skaggs said during their induction. "The Opry is a family, and to bring a family in, is just the greatest thing, when we already have a family, to graft more into our hearts."

The Isaacs, founded in 1971 by Joe and Lily Isaacs, were inducted into the Gospel Music Hall of Fame in 2020. They have taken their unique blend of bluegrass, folk, country, and gospel across the world and have performed at top awards shows including the Doves and the Grammys. The group has performed at Carnegie Hall, and have wowed fans at NFL, MLB, NBA, and NHL games. They have won numerous Dove Awards and are multi-Grammy nominated.

LILY ISAACS
Resides in Hendersonville, Tennessee
Birth Date: September 20

BEN ISAACS
Resides in Hendersonville, Tennessee
Birth Date: July 25

SONYA ISAACS
Resides in Hendersonville, Tennessee
Birth Date: July 22

BECKY ISAACS
Resides in Hendersonville, Tennessee
Birth Date: August 2

OPRY INDUCTION: September 14, 2021

> "WE'RE HONORED TO BE ASKED TO BE MEMEERS OF THE GRAND OLE OPRY—
> I CAN'T BELIEVE I JUST SAID THAT OUT LOUD, THAT'S LIKE A DREAM COME TRUE."
> —SONYA ISAACS UPON BEING INVITED TO JOIN THE OPRY FAMILY

Their family's mission, according to Lily, is to spread the gospel of hope. The Isaacs Foundation actively raises funds to support Israeli Holocaust survivors, orphans, and lone soldiers. They also help feed America's homeless and less fortunate.

CLOCKWISE FROM TOP LEFT:
1. The Isaacs harmonize on stage during an Opry performance.
2. The Isaacs perform on the Grand Ole Opry in 2022.
3. The Isaacs perform during their induction on September 14, 2022.
4. The Isaacs take the Grand Ole Opry stage in May of 2022.
5. The Isaacs harmonize on stage during an Opry performance.

DID YOU KNOW? Lily Isaacs, the group's matriarch, is the daughter of two Polish Jewish Holocaust survivors. She was born in Germany post-war, and her family moved to America and became U.S. citizens in 1955, residing in the Bronx, New York. Ben, Sonya, and Becky reside in Hendersonville, Tennessee and are grateful for the opportunity to live the American dream, which has brought them all the way to the Grand Ole Opry stage.

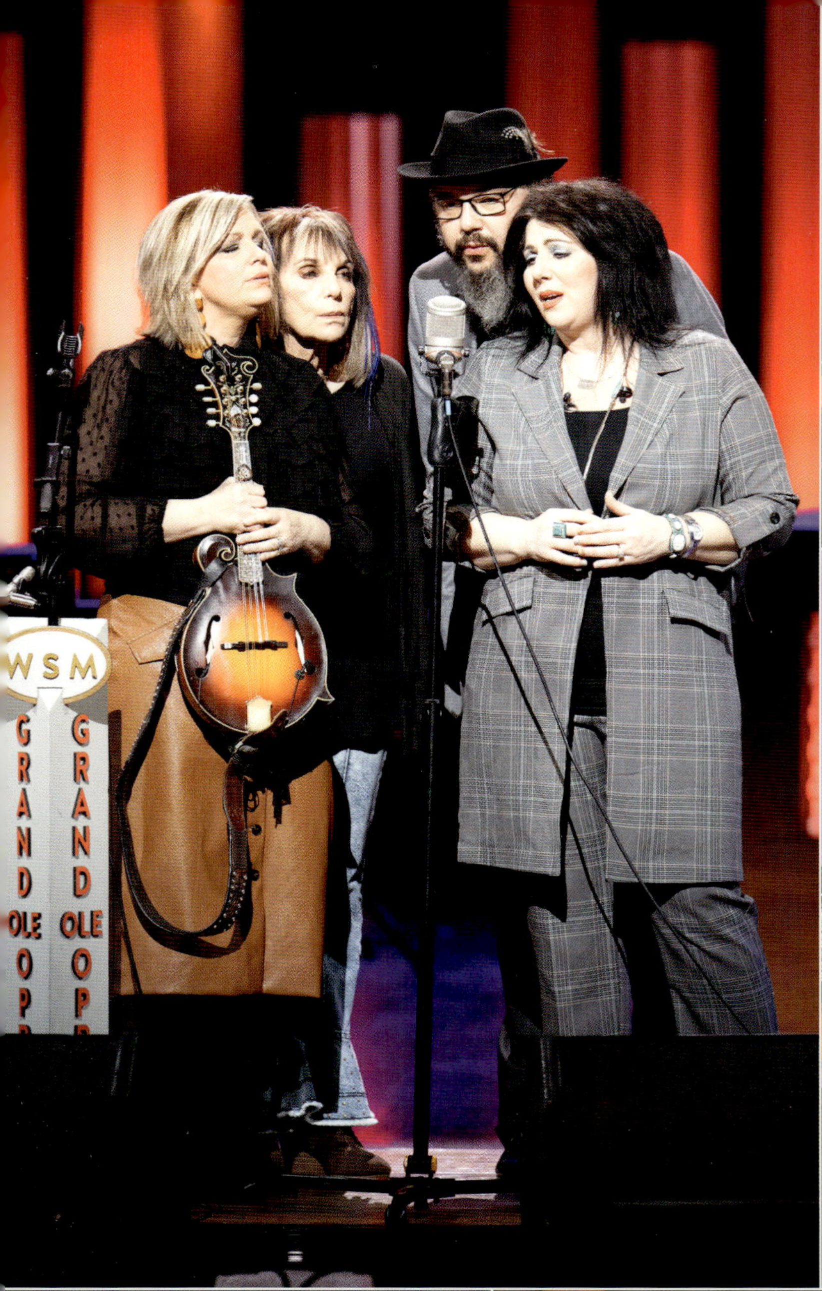
WSM
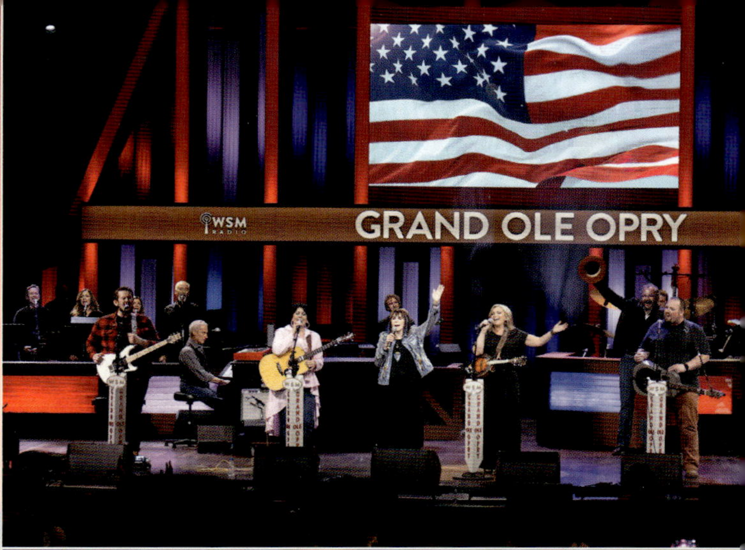
WSM RADIO
GRAND OLE OPRY
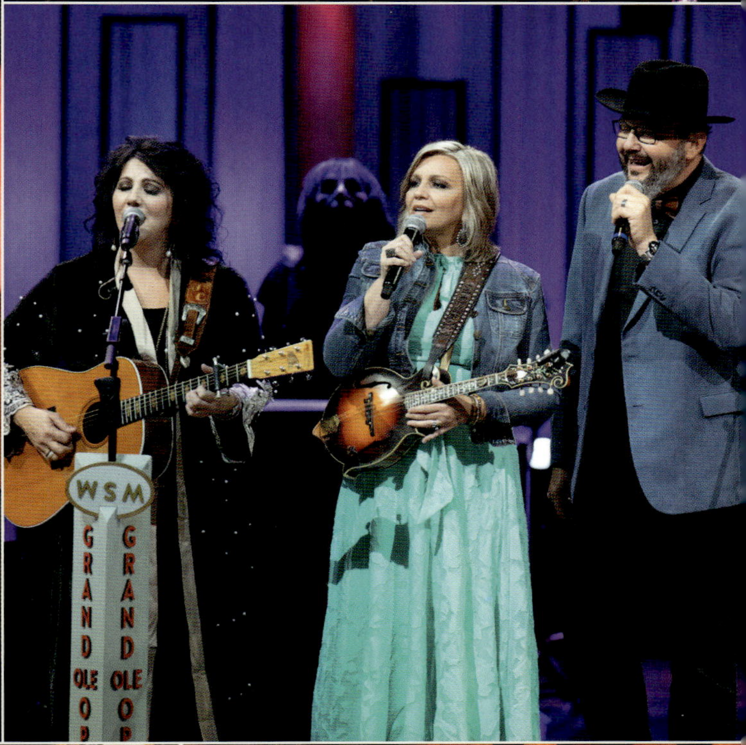
WSM
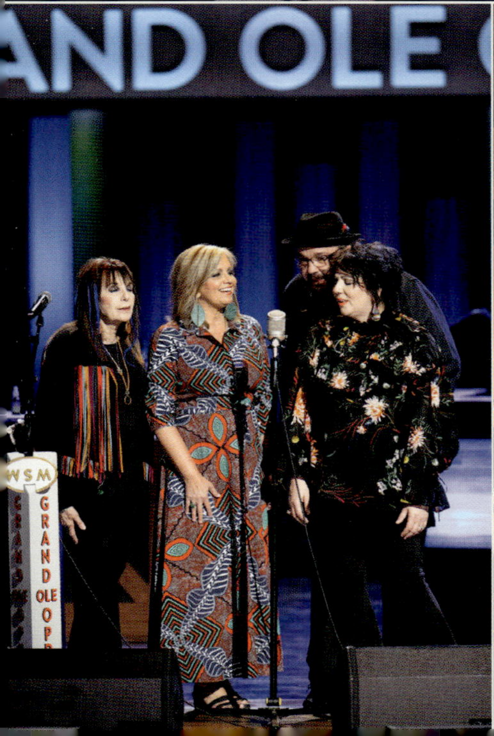
WSM
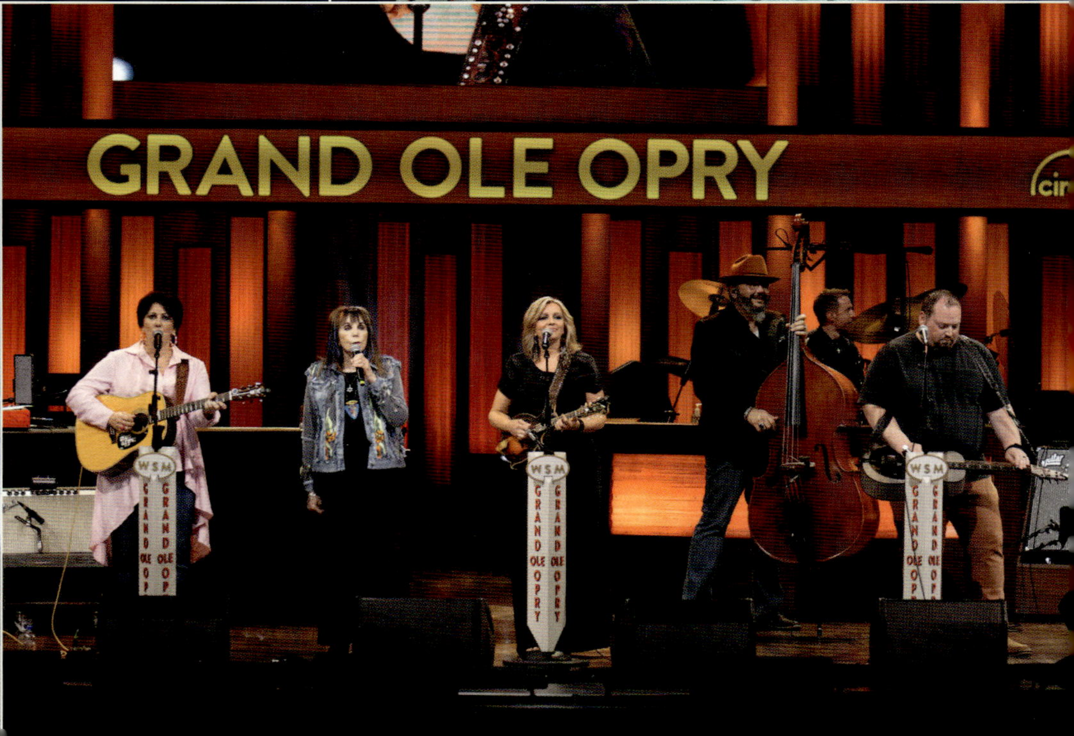
GRAND OLE OPRY
WSM

ALAN JACKSON
MEMBER SINCE 1991

Alan Jackson has sold nearly 60 million albums and has had 35 No. 1 hits. He's the rare superstar as highly regarded for his songwriting as his performing. His self-penned smashes range from "Here in the Real World," his first Top 10 hit in 1990, to standards as poignantly reflective as "Remember When" to unforgettable musical statements such as "Where Were You (When the World Stopped Turning)."

BIRTHPLACE: Newnan, Goergia
BIRTH DATE: October 17
OPRY INDUCTION: June 7, 1991

DID YOU KNOW? Alan Jackson delivered mail on the Grand Ole Opry complex before earning an Opry member mailbox in the Grand Ole Opry House Post Office.

> "THE ULTIMATE DREAM WHEN YOU'RE IN COUNTRY MUSIC IS TO BE ASKED TO JOIN THE GRAND OLE OPRY."

After high school, Alan began making the kind of traditional country music he'd grown up enjoying. By 1990, he was on the charts with the first of many hits that earned him a reputation as one of traditional country's most consistent and beloved hit-makers.

The legend of his integrity grew when he spontaneously added a snippet of George Jones' "Choices" to his performance at the 1999 Country Music Association Awards, tipping his hat to the Possum, who'd stayed home rather than accept an offer to play only a portion of his nominated song. Alan and the CMAs have been a news-making combination in general — and not just because he won Entertainer of the Year three times. He made history at the 2001 CMAs by premiering "Where Were You," the September 11 ballad embraced even by Americans who'd never paid attention to a country song before.

"Everybody wanted to put me up on a pedestal after that," Alan says. "A lot of people were emotionally affected by that song. But I'm still playing the same old kind of honky tonk songs I played 20 years ago in the bars."

Humble as his aspirations sound, when it comes to who his heroes are, it's clear Alan couldn't aim higher. "If I was gonna say somebody I wanted to be like, the two singer/songwriters in country music that stick out to me are Hank Williams and Merle Haggard," he says. "I don't know that there's two any better that have written songs."

CLOCKWISE FROM TOP LEFT:
1. International Country Music Fan Fair, 1997
2. March 22, 2013
3. September 27, 2005
4. Opry Induction, 1991
5. With George Jones on the Opry's 75th Anniversary television special

OPRY FAMILY MEMBERS

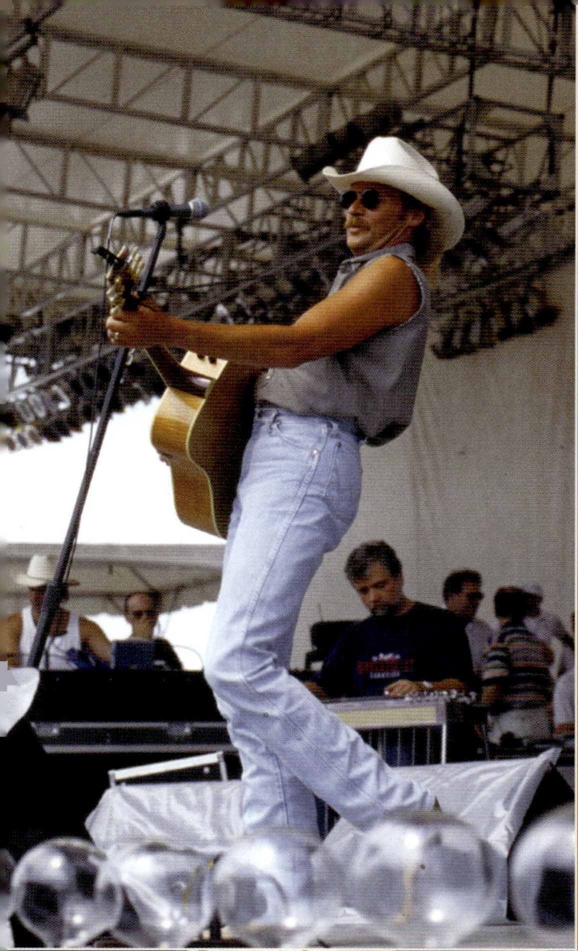

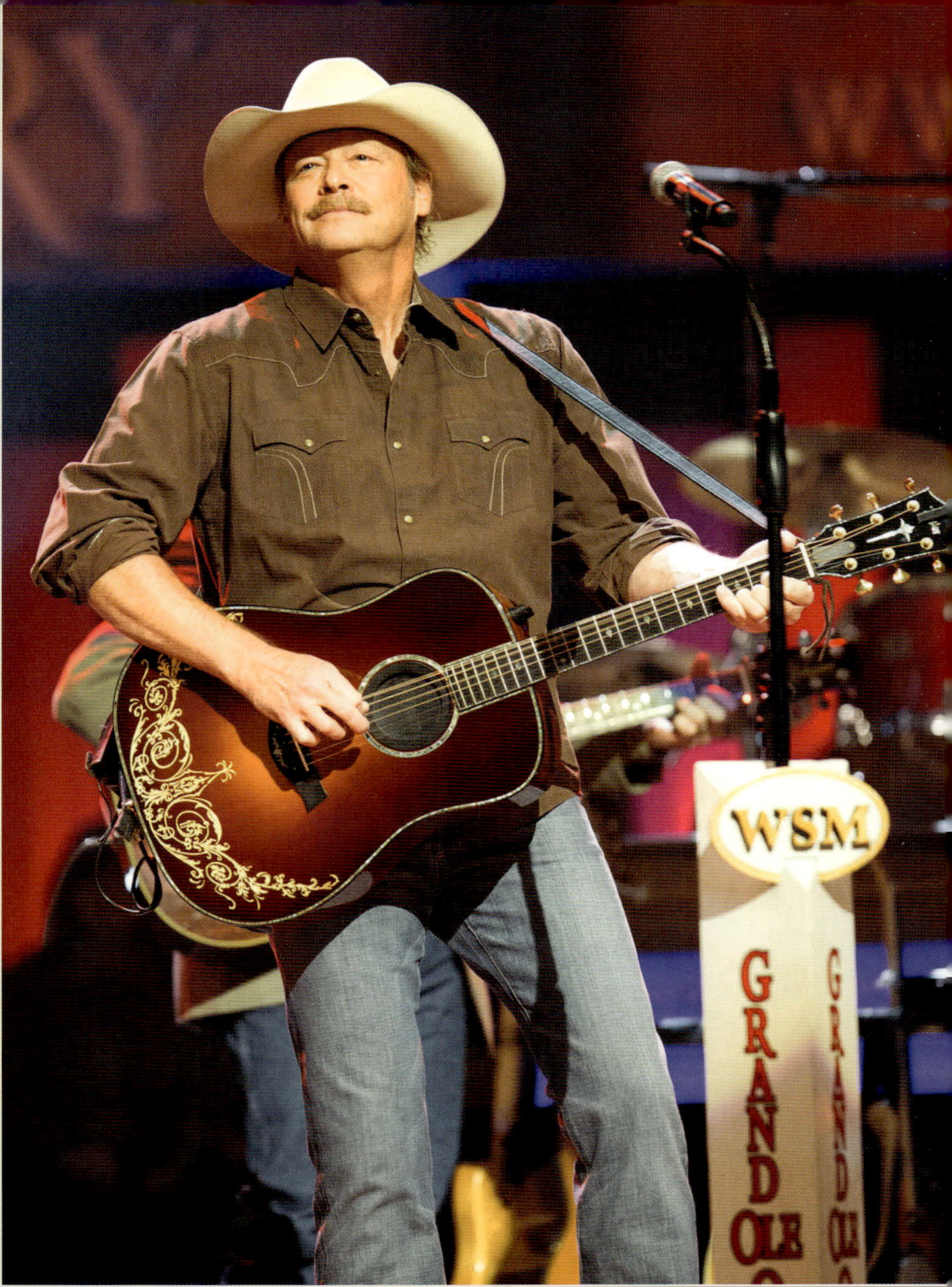
WSM

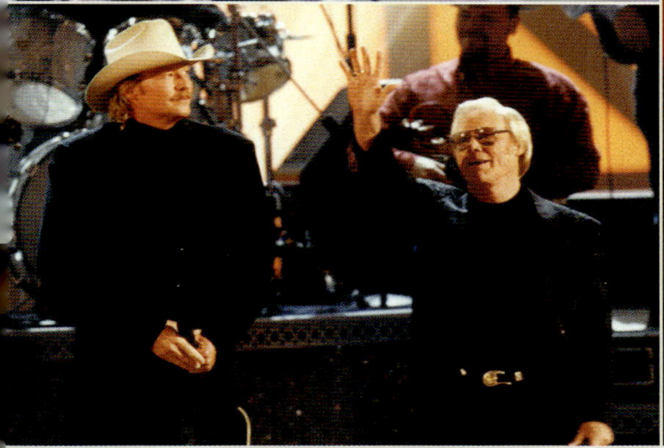

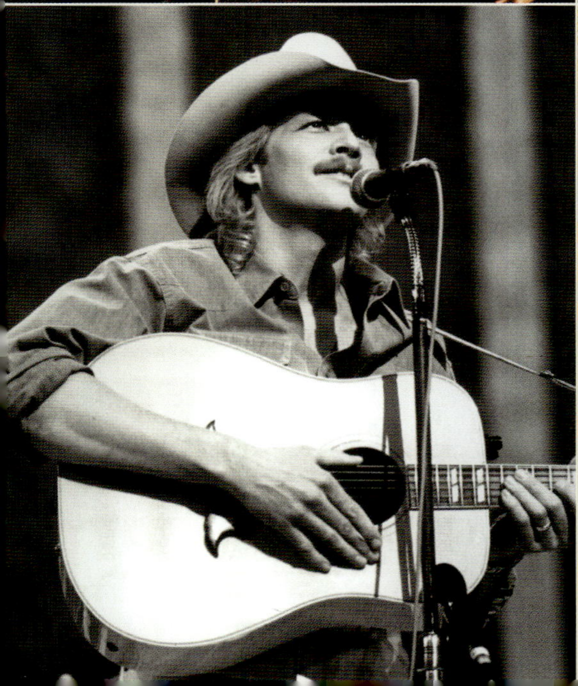

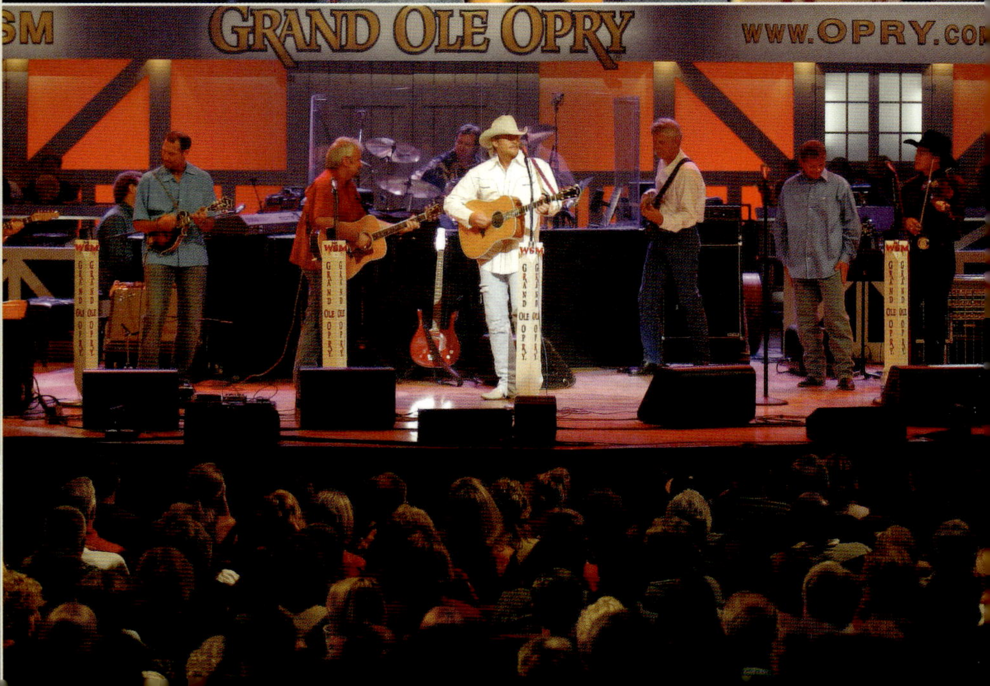
GRAND OLE OPRY

CHRIS JANSON
MEMBER SINCE 2018

Chris Janson always had two dreams: getting on the radio and playing the Grand Ole Opry. Fresh out of high school in 2004, he packed his bags for Nashville. As soon as he arrived, Chris parked his car in the alleyway behind Ryman Auditorium, hoping to get some shut-eye in the shadow of an institution where influences Johnny Cash and Hank Williams became country music greats. Things didn't go quite according to plan — he was told to move his car that night — but 14 years later, he'd find himself on the Mother Church's stage, getting a surprise invitation from Keith Urban to join the Opry family.

BIRTHPLACE: Perryville, Missouri
BIRTH DATE: April 2
OPRY INDUCTION: March 20, 2018

> "COUNTRY MUSIC WAS MADE FAMOUS WITH THE GRAND OLE OPRY, AND COUNTRY MUSIC WILL DIE WITH THE GRAND OLE OPRY WHEN THE WORLD ENDS. THAT'S JUST THE WAY IT IS."

Make no mistake, it took a lot of grit to get here. For the better part of his first year in Nashville, Chris spent every night playing at the iconic Tootsie's Orchid Lounge, living off tips that floated his way. The crowds took to him, and Chris didn't know it at first, but Music Row had, too. In the years that followed, Chris honed his skills as a songwriter, eventually penning hits like Tim McGraw's "Truck Yeah" and "How I'll Always Be" as well as LOCASH's "I Love This Life."

After making his Opry debut on February 15, 2013, Chris quickly became a regular on the show, introducing audiences to his own songs like "Buy Me a Boat" and "Fix a Drink" through high-energy performances. Whether giving an impassioned harmonica solo or belting out a chorus, Chris deeply understands the magic of the Opry, and that magic was not lost on him when he was officially inducted as a member by Garth Brooks on March 20, 2018.

Overwhelmed and elated after being handed his Opry Member Award, Chris paused a few moments to reflect. "How do you not cry during this? To know me is to know I really, truly love the Grand Ole Opry … This will be a moment I will never forget," he said before addressing the fans. "Thanks for making my dreams come true, and thanks for buying a ticket to the Opry to see it happen! I hope you come back a million times! I'll buy a ticket for ya — I don't even care. I love you that much!"

CLOCKWISE FROM TOP LEFT:
1. Feet in the air, an enthusiastic Chris knows how to get the audiences on theirs.
2. At his sold-out Ryman show, Chris is on Cloud 9 after a surprise invitation from Keith Urban to become an Opry member.
3. Chris performs with LOCASH, for whom he wrote "I Love This Life."
4. Chris makes his Opry debut on February 15, 2013.
5. Garth Brooks hands Chris his Opry Member Award.
6. A talented instrumentalist, Chris often takes a seat at the piano or performs on a harmonica during his segment.

WSM

CHRIS JANSON
WSM
GRAND OLE OPRY

WSM
GRAND OLE OPRY

WSM
GRAND OLE OPRY

WSM
GRAND

JAMEY JOHNSON
MEMBER SINCE 2022

Raised on the southern rock band Alabama and serving in the U.S. Marine Corps Reserves, a young and restless Jamey Johnson began performing at bars in Montgomery, Alabama. In 2000, he headed to Nashville to pursue music and within a few years, he was making a living recording demos for some of country music's biggest names.

Jamey quickly became a critically acclaimed songwriter, helping pen Trace Adkin's 2005 hit song, "Honky Tonk Badonkadonk," and winning the Academy of Country Music and Country Music Association's Song of the Year in 2007 as a co-writer on George Strait's "Give It Away." But he was also cooking up some chart-toppers of his own. In 2009, Jamey won the ACM and CMA's Song of the Year again, this time for his own Grammy-nominated song "In Color."

BIRTHPLACE: Enterprise, Alabama
BIRTH DATE: July 14
OPRY INDUCTION: May 14, 2022

DID YOU KNOW? When Jamey was in Montgomery, after his shows, he would sometimes go sing at country legend Hank William's gravesite. He said artists would perform there to "pay their respects."

> "I DON'T HAVE TO TELL Y'ALL WHAT THIS MEANS TO ME. IF YOU KNOW ME, YOU KNOW I'VE BEEN TALKING ABOUT THIS SINCE I WAS A KID. AND I AIN'T A KID ANYMORE."
> —JAMEY ON THE EVENING OF HIS OPRY INDUCTION.

Jamey had been playing on the Opry stage for 17 years before he was invited to join the family. When Jamey's writing partner Bill Anderson invited him to become a member of the Grand Ole Opry, he said, "You'll never perform as a guest here again." Jamey responded, "Well, I've been kicked out of a lot of places." Bill replied, "We're not kicking you out, buddy. We're welcoming you in! The next time you're on this stage, you're going to be inducted as a member of the Grand Ole Opry."

CLOCKWISE FROM TOP LEFT:
1. Jamey performs with Alison Krauss on the Grand Ole Opry.
2. Jamey performs "In Color" during his induction on May 14, 2022.
3. Jamey performs at the Opry on September 15, 2021.
4. Opry member and friend Bill Anderson helps induct Jamey Johnson into the family.
5. The Opry House audience gives Jamey a standing ovation on his induction night.

OPRY FAMILY MEMBERS

WSM
GRAND OLE OPRY

WSM
GRAND OLE OPRY

GRAND OLE OPRY
GRAND OLE OPRY

WSM
GRAND OLE OPRY

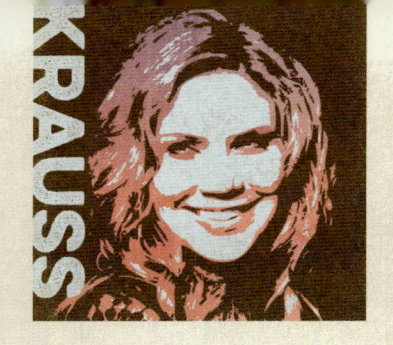

ALISON KRAUSS
MEMBER SINCE 1993

By the time 17-year-old Alison Krauss first played the Grand Ole Opry in 1989 with her band Union Station, she'd already been gracing stages across the country for a decade, winning fiddle contests and impressing audiences with her subtle, captivating singing voice. Since then she has distinguished herself as one of the world's most respected musicians and an accomplished record producer.

At 14, Alison recorded her first album, *Too Late To Cry*. By age 18, she earned a Grammy nomination for her 1989 release *Two Highways*. The following year, Alison won the Grammy for Best Bluegrass Recording for *I've Got That Old Feeling*. When she joined the Opry at 21, she became the first bluegrass artist in 29 years to be inducted and the youngest cast member at the time.

BIRTHPLACE: Decatur, Illinois
BIRTH DATE: July 24
OPRY INDUCTION: July 3, 1993

DID YOU KNOW? Alison was five years old when she got her first fiddle.

> "I THINK THAT PEOPLE RESPOND TO HONESTY IN MUSIC, SO I ONLY CHOOSE SONGS THAT ARE THE TRUTH FOR ME."

Since her first win, Alison has become the most awarded female artist in Grammys history, picking up five trophies for the 2008 album *Raising Sand* with the legendary Robert Plant among her many statuettes.

Collaboration is one of Alison's great musical loves. In addition to performing on the Opry stage with fellow members including Brad Paisley, Patty Loveless, and The Whites, she has also sung and played with guests ranging from bluegrass musicians Tony Rice, Rhonda Vincent and Dale Ann Bradley to rock singer John Waite, whom she joined on his '80s pop smash "Missing You." Alison continues to release albums with Union Station and solo projects from time to time as well as guest on the albums of many other artists in a number of genres. And she still loves watching other Opry performers as often as possible.

"I used to come here and sit in the audience and watch Ricky Skaggs, Porter Wagoner, and John Conlee," Alison says. "The amount of talent that wanders around backstage is shocking, and it sounds so beautiful out front. I love the way everybody watches everybody else play."

CLOCKWISE FROM TOP LEFT:
1. April 2007
2. With Union Station
3. With Vince Gill, Ricky Skaggs, and Marty Stuart
4. With Brad Paisley at Carnegie Hall, November 2005
5. Celebrating 20 years of Opry membership backstage

WSM
GRAND
OLE

GRAND OLE OPRY
WWW.OPRY.

ALISON
KRAUSS

GRAND OLE OPRY

WSM
GRAND OLE OPRY
WSM
YAMAHA

LADY A
MEMBER SINCE 2021

Lady A's nine-time platinum hit, "Need You Now," is the highest certified song by a Country group of all time, they have earned CMA "Vocal Group of the Year" trophies three years in a row and countless other honors, including numerous Grammy awards, *Billboard* Music Awards, People's Choice Awards, Teen Choice Awards, and even a Tony Award nod.

The trio's harmonic blend, masterful songwriting, and undeniable chemistry brought them here, and have placed them at the top of country charts for over a decade.

The magic remains because they have kept the focus on the music. They started as songwriters, and in addition to writing most of their own hits, Dave and Charles co-authored Luke Bryan's breakthrough hit, "Do I"; and Hillary was a co-writer of Sara Evans' No. 1 single "A Little Bit Stronger."

HILLARY SCOTT
Birthplace: Nashville, Tennessee
Birth Date: April 1

CHARLES KELLEY
Birthplace: Augusta, Georgia
Birth Date: September 11

DAVE HAYWOOD
Birthplace: Augusta, Georgia
Birth Date: July 5

OPRY INDUCTION: January 21, 2021

"HAVING THIS MOMENT FEELS LIKE ONE OF THOSE STAMPS OF APPROVAL LIKE YOU'VE MADE IT AND YOU'RE GOING TO BE HERE FOR A LONG TIME AND YOU'RE PART OF THE CLUB, WHICH IS REALLY COOL."

Both of Hillary's parents, country artist Linda Davis and musician Lang Scott, performed on the Opry stage.

"I grew up in these halls," Hillary said.

So, the band said they received a warm welcome at the Grand Ole Opry well before they were part of the family. But during the filming of NBC's 2021 special, *Grand Ole Opry: 95 Years of Country Music*, in January of 2021, friend and Opry member Darius Rucker surprised Hillary, Charles, and Dave on the Opry stage and announced their membership would be effective immediately.

"Playing at the Opry is one of the best feelings in the world," Charles said. "There's no place on earth like it. As a country artist, you would feel honored that they would ask you to play here time and time again."

CLOCKWISE FROM TOP LEFT:
1. Lady A performs during their induction on January 20, 2021.
2. Opry member Darius Rucker joins Lady A behind the famous wooden circle on their induction night.
3. Lady A with Opry member Rhonda Vincent backstage at the Opry House
4. Lady A performs with Ryan Hurd on the Grand Ole Opry on May 15, 2021.

OPRY FAMILY MEMBERS

OPRY.C
OPRY
WSM
GRAND OLE OPRY

GRAND OLE OPRY
OPRY.COM

GRAND OLE
OPRY
95 YEARS OF COUNTRY MUSIC
WSM
OLE OPRY
OPRY.COM

LITTLE BIG TOWN
MEMBER SINCE 2014

The four voices of bandmates Karen Fairchild, Kimberly Schlapman, Jimi Westbrook and Phillip Sweet combine to create Little Big Town. The group's members can truly say that for them, it all began at the Grand Ole Opry. For it was on the Opry stage in 1999 that Little Big Town made its very first public appearance as a band, having gained recognition from executives in the Nashville music industry who were convinced the group was ready for country's most famous stage.

Fast forward a few years, and the band was enjoying success with albums as well as singles including "Boondocks," "Bring It On Home," "A Little More You," and "Little White Church." Along the way came numerous Opry guest appearances and Vocal Group of the Year nominations from the Country Music Association, the Academy of Country Music, and others.

Then came a song about kicking back on a "Pontoon," and the band's career was forever changed. The song went to No.1, earned a Grammy, CMA Single of the Year and other honors, and propelled the group to its first-ever CMA Vocal Group win.

Throughout the group's history, its pitch-perfect harmonies and infectious songs have become favorites of fans and fellow artists alike.

KAREN FAIRCHILD
Birthplace: Gary, Indiana
Birth Date: September 28

KIMBERLY SCHLAPMAN
Birthplace: Cornelia, Georgia
Birth Date: October 15

PHILLIP SWEET
Birthplace: Cherokee Village, Arkansas
Birth Date: March 18

JIMI WESTBROOK
Birthplace: Sumiton, Alabama
Birth Date: October 20

OPRY INDUCTION: October 17, 2014

Q: What artist throughout the Opry's history would you have been most interested to meet?
A: Minnie Pearl

"THERE'S NOTHING LIKE THE OPRY ANYWHERE IN THE WORLD. IT HONORS WHAT NEEDS TO BE HONORED AND IT PROTECTS AND PRESERVES THE GREAT HISTORY OF COUNTRY MUSIC. AND PLUS, IT'S JUST REALLY COOL!"

It was Opry member and friend Reba McEntire who invited Little Big Town to join the Grand Ole Opry in 2014. As the group finished a three-song set with "Pontoon," Reba appeared from the side of the stage, improvising on the song's last few words and asking the question Karen, Kimberly, Jimi, and Phillip had been hoping to hear. "I know the Grand Ole Opry is very important to y'all, because this is the first place you guys played together as a group in 1999. I have been asked to ask y'all, Little Big Town, would y'all like to be a member of the Grand Ole Opry?"

After hugs with Reba and between the members as well as a collective "yes" from the group, Karen cheered, "Thank you, Grand Ole Opry! We will try to make you proud!"

CLOCKWISE FROM TOP LEFT:
1. March 31, 2007
2. 2014
3. With Vince Gill on Opry induction night, October 3, 2014
4. March 15, 2008
5. May 3, 2014

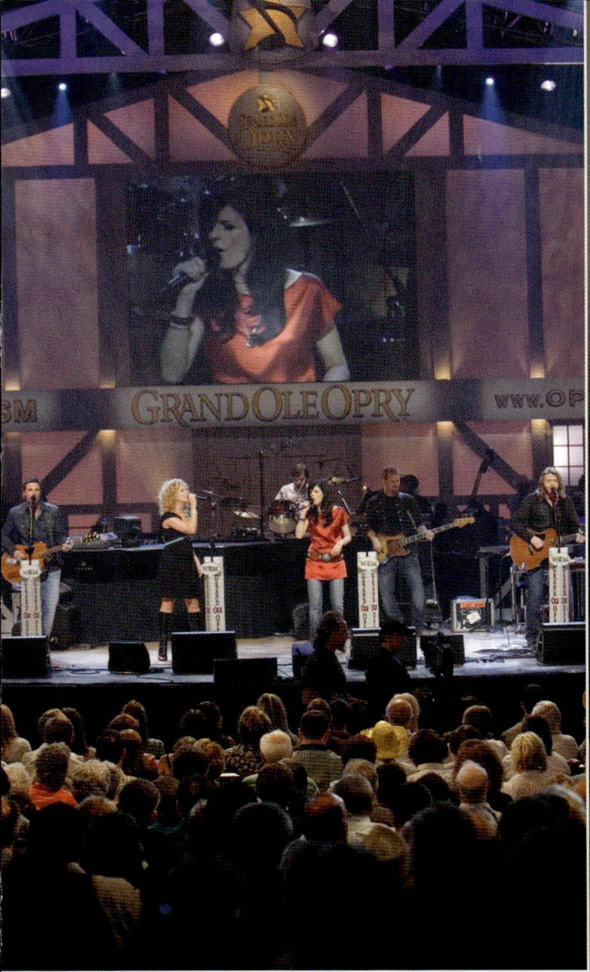
GRANDOLEOPRY

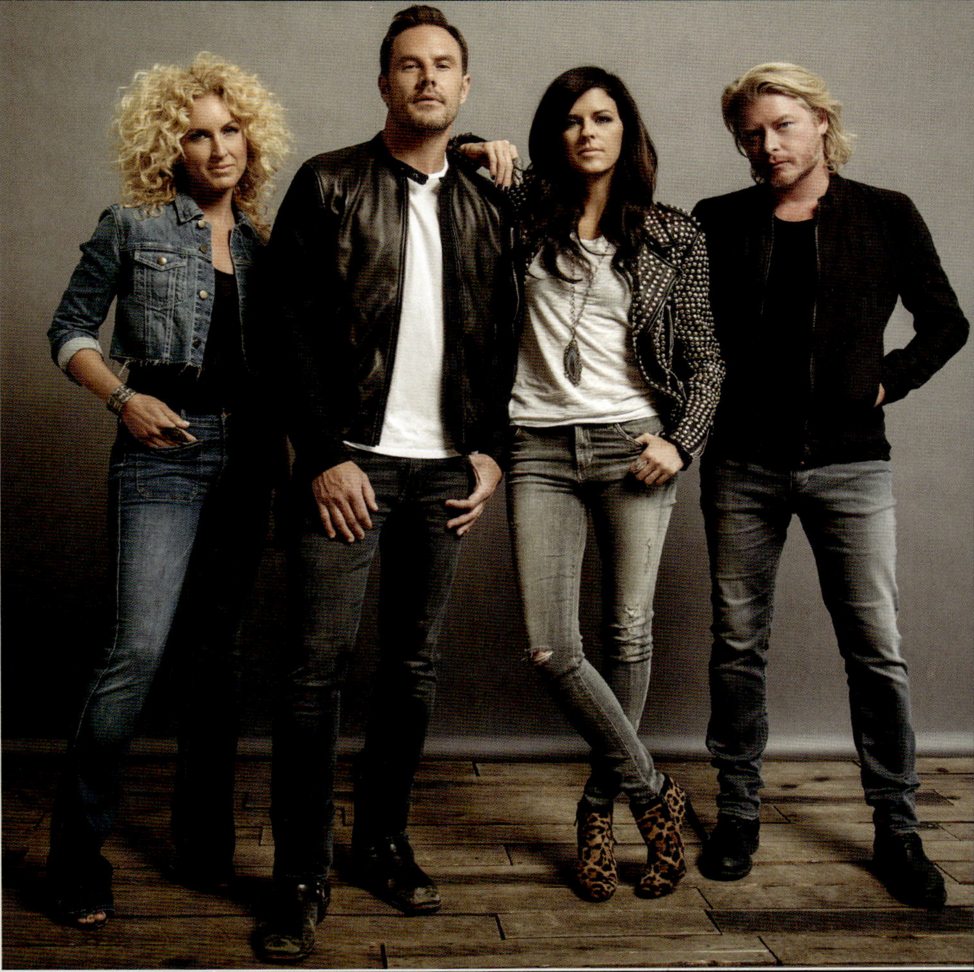

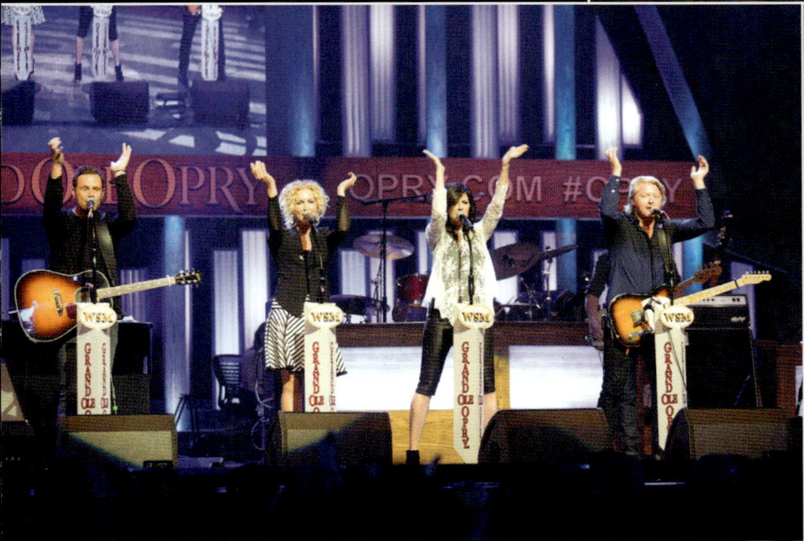
OPRY.COM

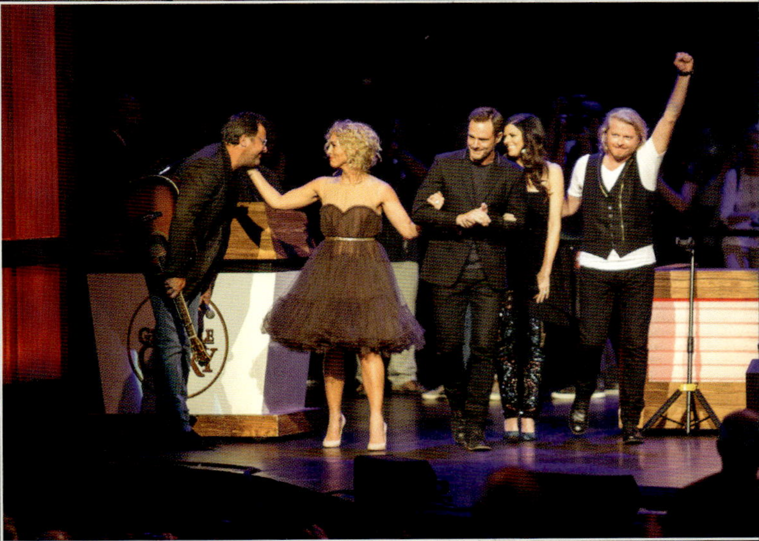

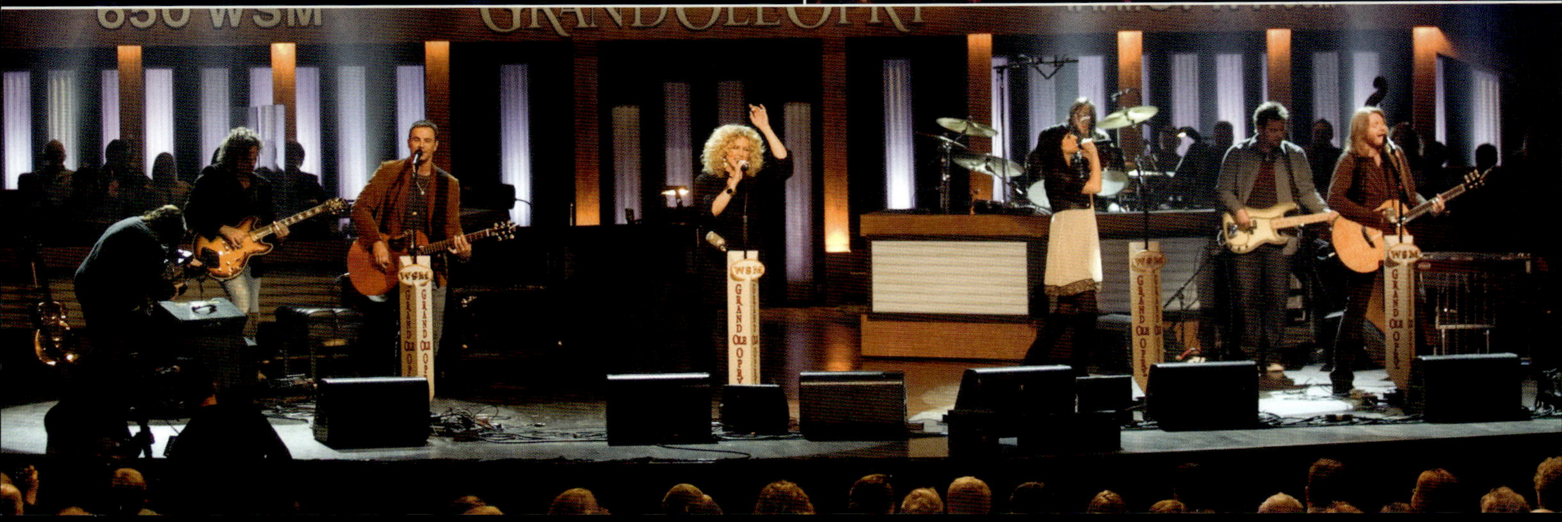
650 WSM

PATTY LOVELESS
MEMBER SINCE 1988

If any contemporary country star seemed born to be a Grand Ole Opry member, it was Patty Loveless. Growing up as one of seven children born to a Kentucky coal miner, Patty has distinct memories of singing along to the Opry on Friday and Saturday nights — at age three — while her mom mopped floors.

"My first visit to the Opry was when I was 14 years old; it was at the Ryman," she recalls. "I went as the guest of Dolly and Porter. It was the very first time I really got to visit backstage, and I felt like I was just in hillbilly heaven."

A couple of years after that, back home in Kentucky, the girl then known as Patty Ramey was drafted to fill in at a traveling Opry

BIRTHPLACE: Pikeville, Kentucky
BIRTH DATE: January 4
OPRY INDUCTION: June 11, 1988

DEFINITIVE PATTY LOVELESS
"If My Heart Had Windows"
"Timber, I'm Falling In Love"
"Blame It On Your Heart"
"Lonely Too Long"
"The Boys Are Back In Town"

"IT'S KIND OF LIKE YOUR FAMILY HAVING A REUNION." —PATTY ON THE OPRY

concert on a bill that included the Wilburn Brothers, who, like Porter before them, was struck by this teen-aged prodigy with the voice beyond her years. She eventually became the Wilburns' full-time female singer out on the road, following in the footsteps of her distant cousin Loretta Lynn.

During the mid-'80s, Patty, managed by her brother Roger, began a hailed solo career that produced a long streak of Top 10 hits and quickly led her back to the Opry, this time as a celebrated young inductee. She's still as enthralled by the behind-the-scenes aura of the Opry as she was as a young guest. "It's very family-oriented backstage," she says, "whether you're a stranger that's in town and just coming to visit, or whether you might be a visitor of one of the artists that's an Opry member. It's kind of like your family having a reunion. That's the way they always treat us, every weekend."

Patty's hits and critical successes have come from both songs that lean on a more contemporary style to those that borrow from her Appalachian roots and make her "feel like I was connecting to my father's heart."

CLOCKWISE FROM TOP LEFT:
1. December 7, 2002 at Ryman Auditorium
2. 70th Anniversary show, 1996
3. With Porter Wagoner on Opry induction night, June 11, 1988
4. July 29, 2005
5. With Loretta Lynn and Connie Smith

OPRY FAMILY MEMBERS 118

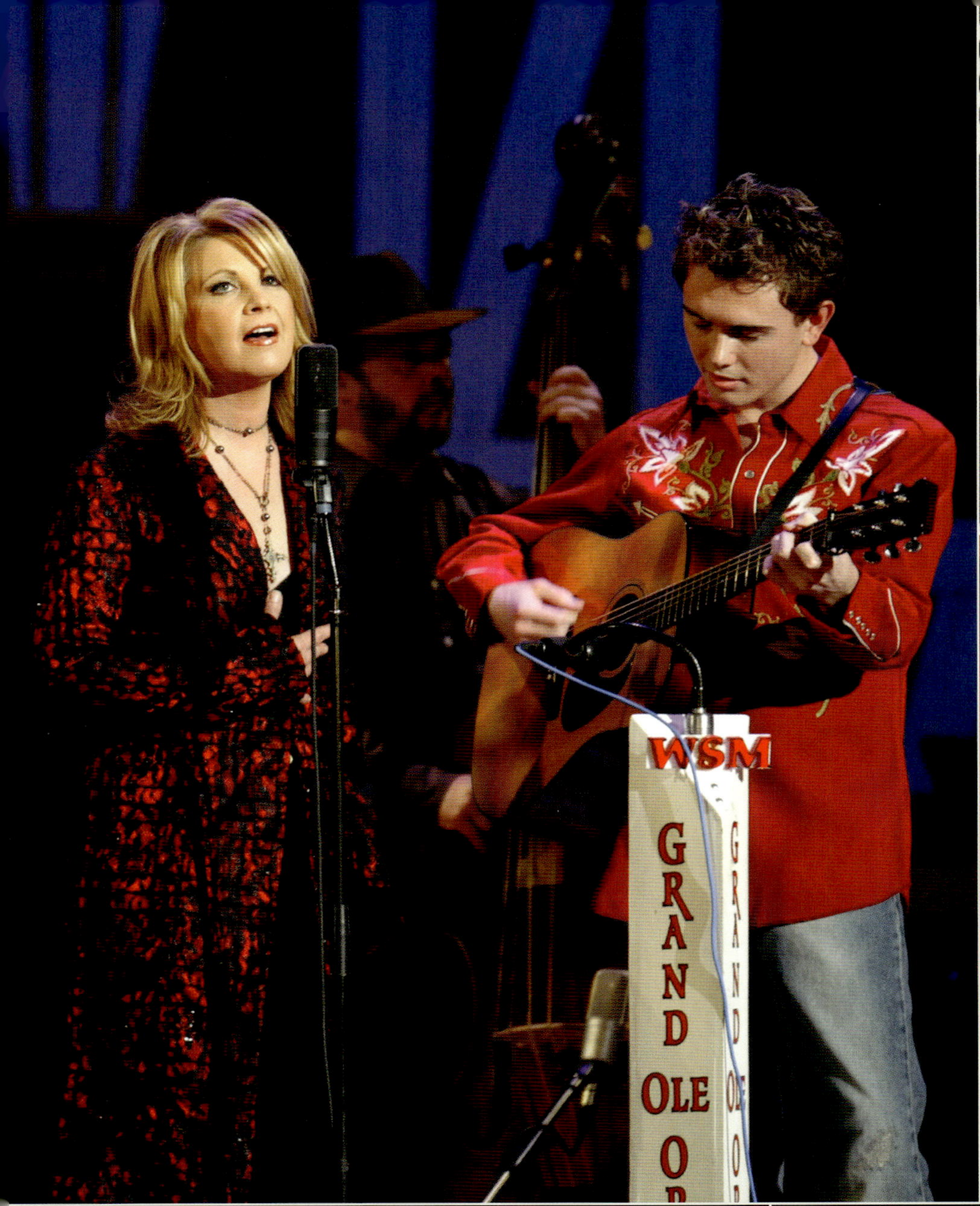
WSM
GRAND
OLE
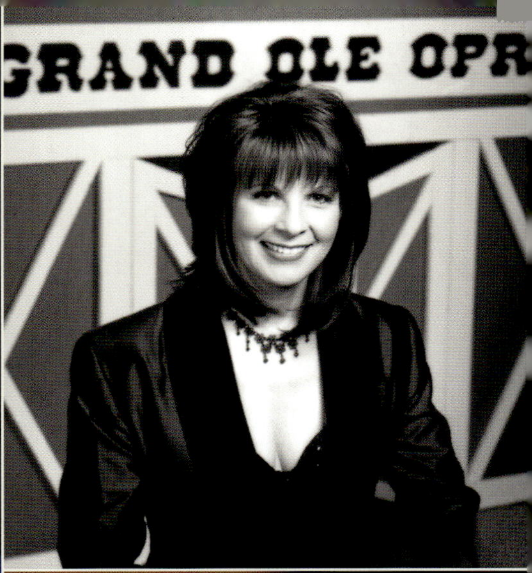
GRAND OLE
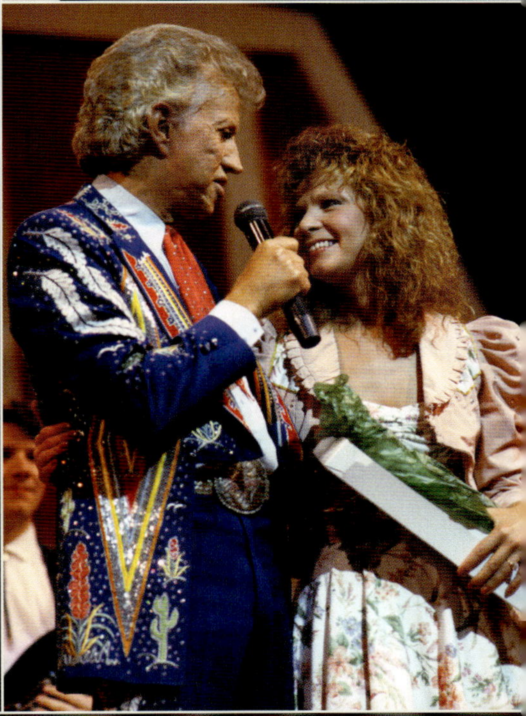
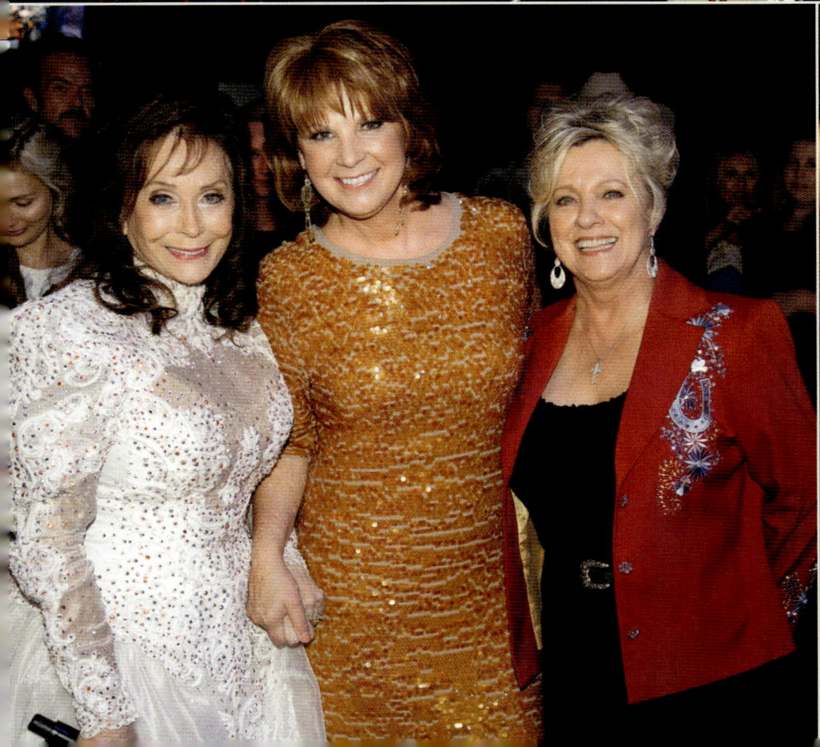
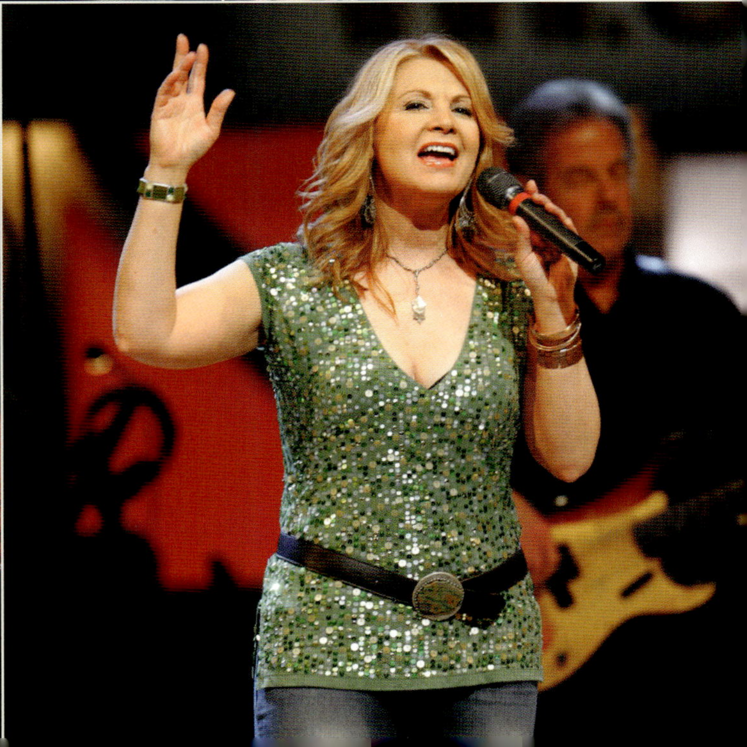

DUSTIN LYNCH
MEMBER SINCE 2019

Growing up an hour away from the bright lights of Nashville, Dustin Lynch fell in love with neotraditional country music of the '90s. When it came time for college, he packed his bags for Music City, renting an apartment behind The Bluebird Cafe. Dustin visited the reputed listening room regularly, learning from those behind the mic before he'd then get the opportunity to perform there himself.

Dustin has seen a lot of stages since those formative days, but few mean as much to him as the one he stands on at the Grand Ole Opry. He made his debut on March 2, 2012, leading off his set with a performance of his debut single "Cowboys and Angels."

Six years later, just as Dustin wrapped his performance of that same song at a 2018 Opry appearance, Trace Adkins joined him on stage, unbeknownst to Dustin.

BIRTHPLACE: Tullahoma, Tennessee
BIRTH DATE: May 14
OPRY INDUCTION: September 18, 2018

DID YOU KNOW? Before Dustin became a performer himself, the first country artist he ever met was Trace Adkins. In a twist of fate, Trace Adkins would become the person to formally invite Dustin to become an Opry member in 2018.

> "THE OPRY IS ONE OF THE MOST HALLOWED STAGES IN THE WORLD OF MUSIC BECAUSE OF ITS HISTORY AND TRADITION. GROWING UP, I WATCHED MY IDOLS GRACE THE STAGE AND I DREAMED OF PLAYING THAT STAGE."

"This is my 15th anniversary [as an Opry member], so I can do whatever I want," Trace joked to the crowd. Trace cut right to the chase: Dustin's passion for the Opry has been clear from the start, so would he like to become the institution's newest member?

Dustin's signature smile went from 1,000 watts to a million as he accepted the invitation from Trace, who was the first country artist he met long before becoming one himself.

"I wish you weren't so big. I wanted to pick you up, but I couldn't," Dustin quipped to Trace, who stands at 6 feet 6 inches tall.

A month later on September 18, 2018, Dustin was inducted by one of his idols, Reba McEntire.

"We're paving the way like Minnie, Roy, Porter, and all the greats before us paved the way for us. Congratulations and welcome to one of the best families in the world," she said before they embraced for a hug.

An Opry induction ceremony is fleeting, but as Reba said and Dustin knows, this family is forever.

CLOCKWISE FROM TOP LEFT:
1. Dustin makes his Opry debut on March 2, 2012. Though he'd been backstage before, he did not want to step into the Opry's famed circle of wood that sits centerstage until he was performing on it.
2. Donning a Reba McEntire tour shirt, Dustin performs on August 30, 2016. Dustin has often said that Reba is his lifelong crush.
3. All smiles, Dustin signs a piece of memorabilia for an eager fan on May 28, 2019.
4. Moments after Reba hands Dustin his Opry Member Award, the pair embraces for a hug.
5. Trace Adkins surprises Dustin with an invitation to join the Opry on August 21, 2018.

OPRY FAMILY MEMBERS

WSM

WSM
WSM

WSM
GRAND OLE OPRY

WSM
GRAND OLE OPRY
GRAND OLE OPRY

LORETTA LYNN
MEMBER SINCE 1962

Rising from an impoverished childhood in Butcher Hollow, Kentucky, to the stage of the Grand Ole Opry, Loretta Lynn personifies the American dream in a way few other artists can. A self-made star who hit the road with her husband visiting radio stations to introduce her debut record five decades ago, Loretta has become one of the Opry's most celebrated legends. Her countless accolades include three Grammys and eight Country Music Association Awards. In 1972, she became the first female artist to win the Country Music Association's coveted Entertainer of the Year award. Now a member of the Country Music and Songwriters Halls of Fame, she received the Grammy Lifetime Achievement Award in 2010.

BIRTHPLACE: Butcher Hollow, Kentucky
BIRTH DATE: April 14
OPRY INDUCTION: September 25, 1962

DID YOU KNOW? Loretta helped her younger sister Brenda Gail Webb conceive the stage name Crystal Gayle.

> "I SUNG 'HONKY TONK GIRL,' BUT THE ONLY THING I REMEMBER WHEN I WAS ON THAT STAGE IS PATTING MY FOOT. I GOT OFF THE STAGE—I DON'T KNOW HOW I EVEN GOT OFF THE STAGE—BUT DOO SAYS I CAME OUT THE BACK OF THE BUILDING AND I WAS HOLLERING 'I'VE SUNG ON THE GRAND OLE OPRY! I'VE SUNG ON THE GRAND OLE OPRY!'"
> —LORETTA ON HER OPRY DEBUT

Married in her teens, Loretta had four children before age 20. She and husband Mooney "Doolittle" Lynn lived in Custer, Washington, when she got her first break on a Tacoma talent show that Buck Owens hosted. Zero Records founder Norm Burley soon signed her to his label in 1960. Loretta's first single, the self-penned "I'm a Honky Tonk Girl," started climbing the charts as she and Doolittle drove across the country, visiting radio stations to promote the record. Through the years, hits for the pioneering singer/songwriter included "Don't Come Home A' Drinkin' (With Lovin' on Your Mind)," "Fist City," "One's on the Way," "You Ain't Woman Enough (To Take My Man)" and "The Pill."

Along the way, she raised six children and influenced a generation of American women with songs that honestly portrayed both the joys and challenges of marriage and motherhood.

Loretta's rags-to-riches saga captured the world's attention when her autobiographical hit "Coal Miner's Daughter" became a motion picture in 1980, earning Sissy Spacek a best actress Oscar for her lead role. The film chronicled Loretta's teenage marriage, early career, and status among the most lauded artists in American music history.

CLOCKWISE FROM TOP LEFT:
1. With Vince Gill
2. Backstage with the Willis Brothers, June 9, 1962
3. With her late husband Oliver "Mooney" Lynn
4. September 17, 2005
5. With sisters Peggy Sue Wright and Crystal Gayle
6. With the Pistol Annies, Crystal Gayle, and Lee Ann Womack celebrating her 50th Opry anniversary.
7. With Ernest Tubb

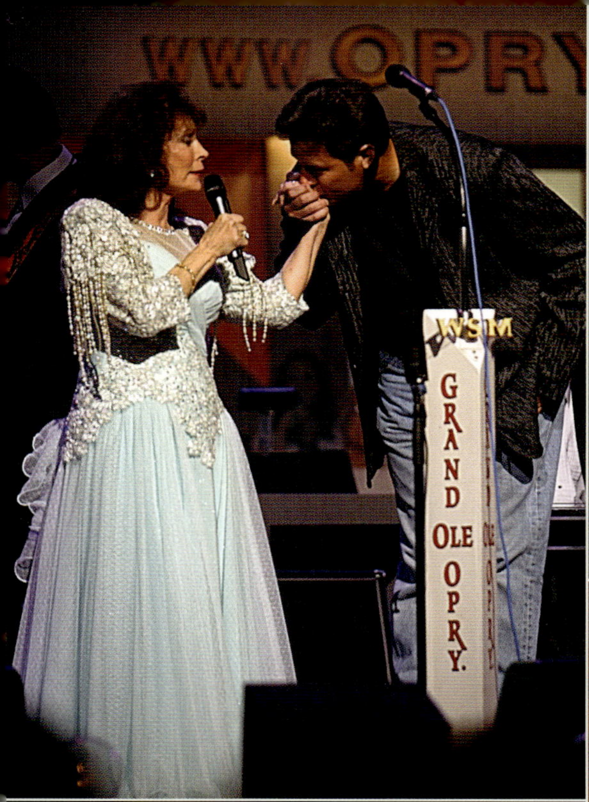
WWW.OPRY
WSM
GRAND OLE OPRY.
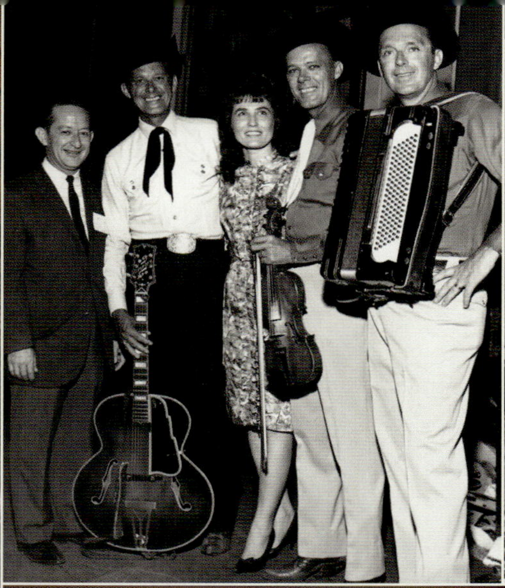
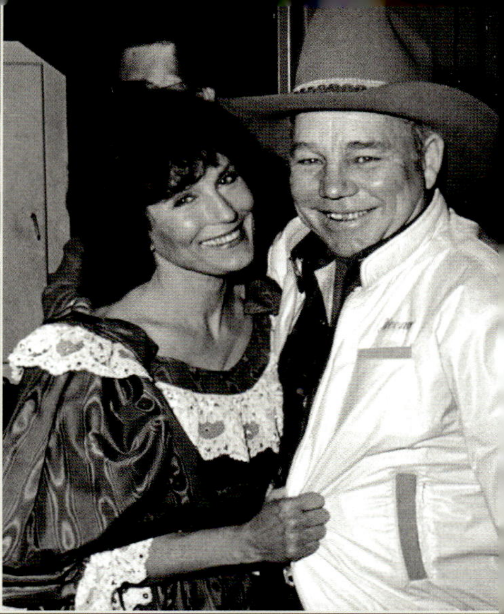
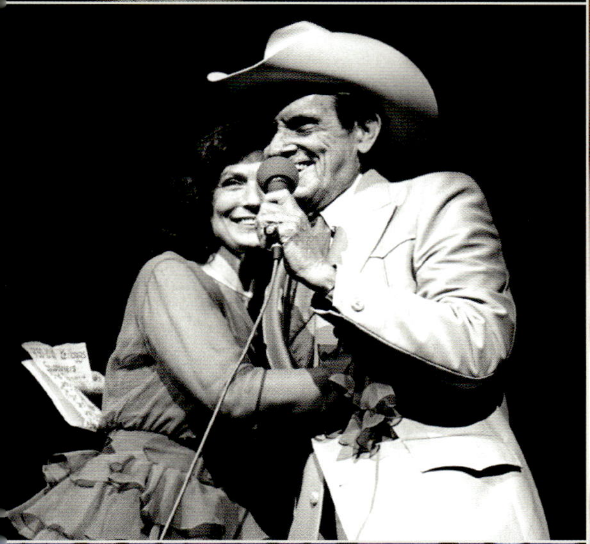
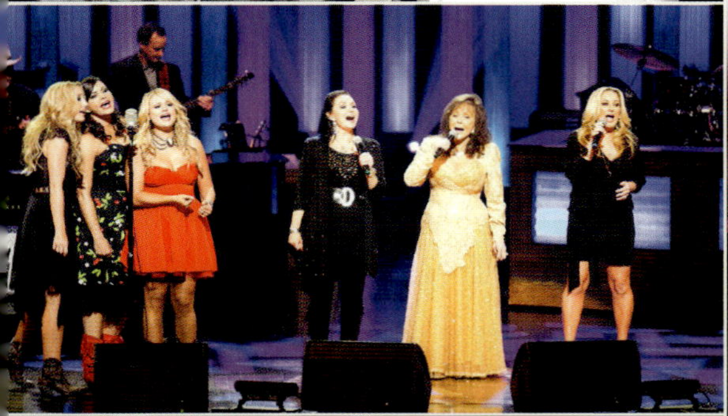
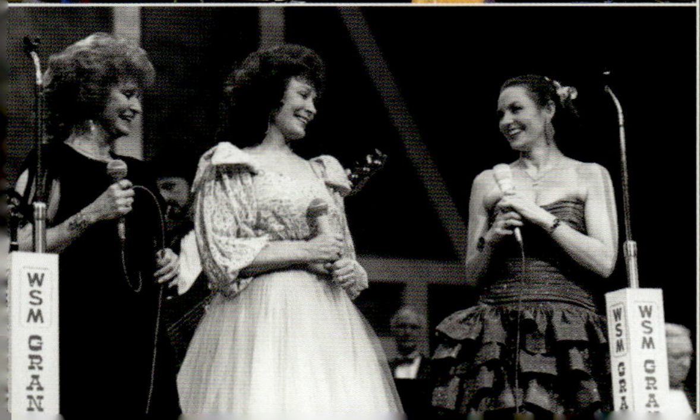
WSM GRAN
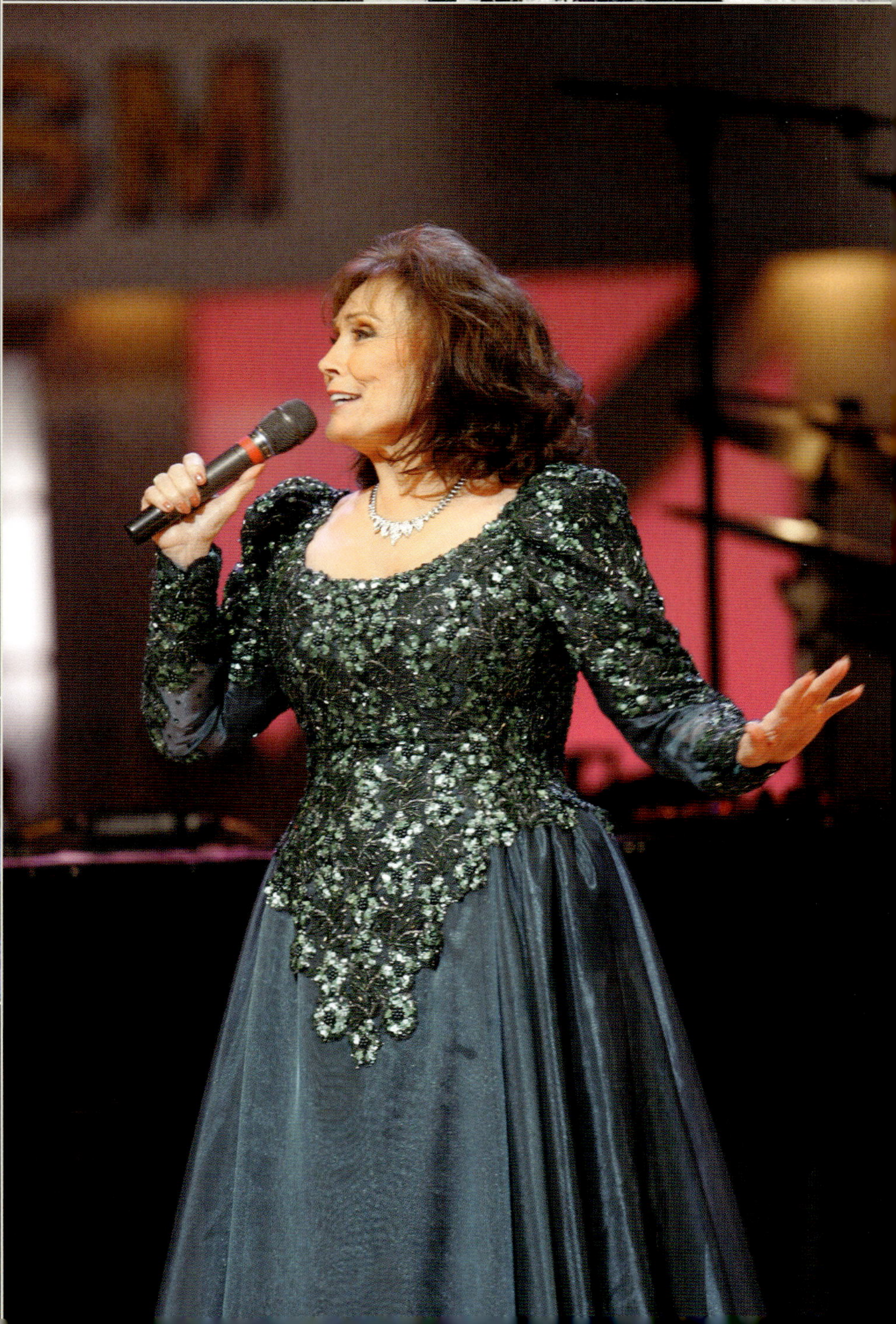
SM

BARBARA MANDRELL
MEMBER SINCE 1972

Barbara Mandrell's first visit to the Grand Ole Opry was a career-defining moment. She had been in country music for nine years, touring with the Mandrell Family Band, but had decided to take time off to enjoy her marriage to the band's drummer, Ken Dudney.

"I had never been to Nashville when we went to the Opry," she remembers. "We had front-row seats in the balcony, and Dolly Parton was onstage at the moment I made that decision [to return to music]. I was watching her and thinking, 'I can do this stuff. I love this stuff.' I turned to my dad and said, 'Dad, if you will manage me, I want to get back into the country music business.' And he said, 'Well, okay, I'd bet my last penny on you.'"

BIRTHPLACE: Houston, Texas
BIRTH DATE: December 25
OPRY INDUCTION: July 29, 1972

DID YOU KNOW? Barbara Mandrell was the first person to win CMA Entertainer of the Year honors twice.

> "I REALIZE WE'RE NOT PROMISED TOMORROW. BELIEVE ME, I REALIZE THAT. BUT IF GOD BLESSES ME AND LETS ME STAY, I LOVE MY LIFE SO MUCH, IT IS SUCH A GOOD LIFE. I AM EAGER TO THROW MYSELF AT HIS FEET, BUT I DON'T WANT TO GET ON THE FIRST BUSLOAD THAT IS GOING."

Barbara wasted no time in signing with major label Columbia Records in 1969 after she brought her father on as manager. She released "I've Been Loving You Too Long" under the tutelage of producer Billy Sherrill. While working with Sherrill she had several Top 40 hits and a duet with Opry member David Houston. In 1978, the singer moved to ABC/Dot, where producer Tom Collins brought Barbara her first No. 1, "Sleeping Single in a Double Bed." That team produced multiple hit singles and albums, including the pop crossover single "(If Loving You Is Wrong) I Don't Want To Be Right."

It was a brilliant move for the petite blonde; her father managed her throughout a career with numerous hit singles, multiple best-selling albums, a television variety series featuring her sisters, several movie roles, and an autobiography.

Barbara received the Country Music Association's Entertainer of the Year and Female Vocalist honors twice. In 2009, she was inducted into the Country Music Hall of Fame.

CLOCKWISE FROM TOP LEFT:
1. First night as Opry member
2. October 28, 2006
3. With Minnie Pearl being presented the Minnie Pearl Award, 1991
4. With Ricky Skaggs
5. With Roy Acuff

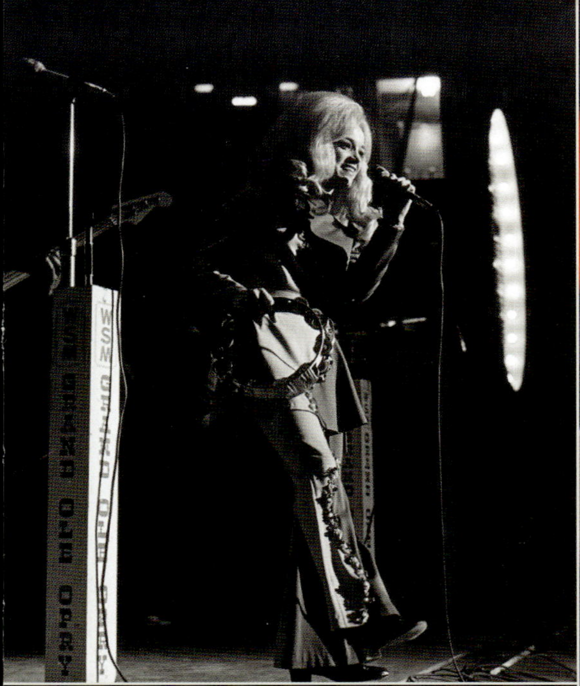
WSM GRAND OLE OPRY

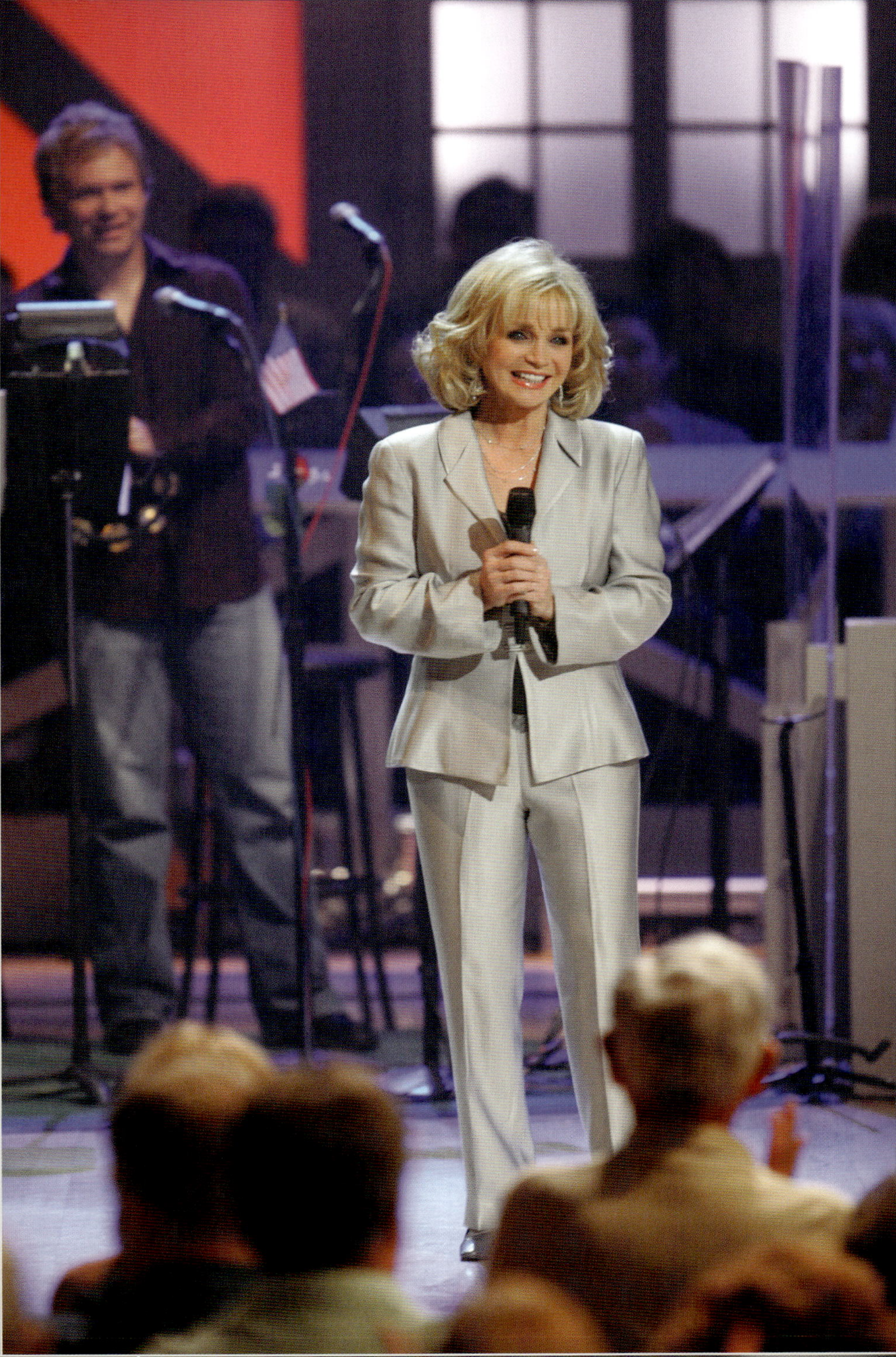

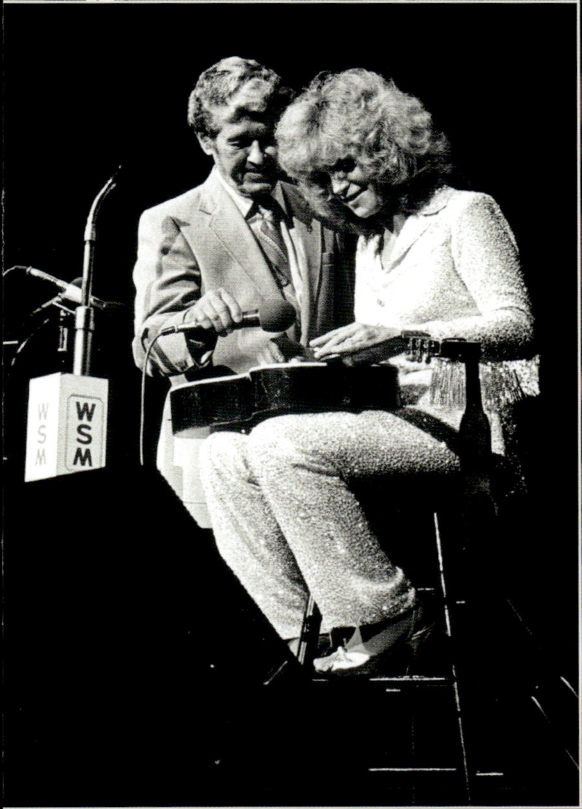
WSM
WSM

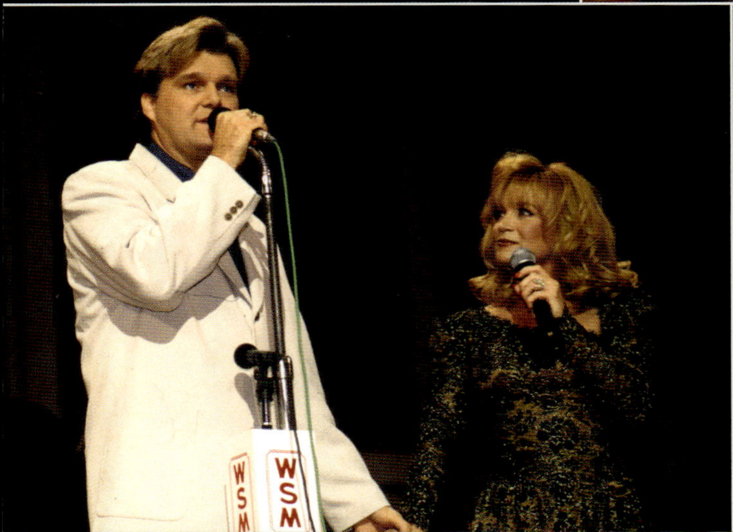
WSM

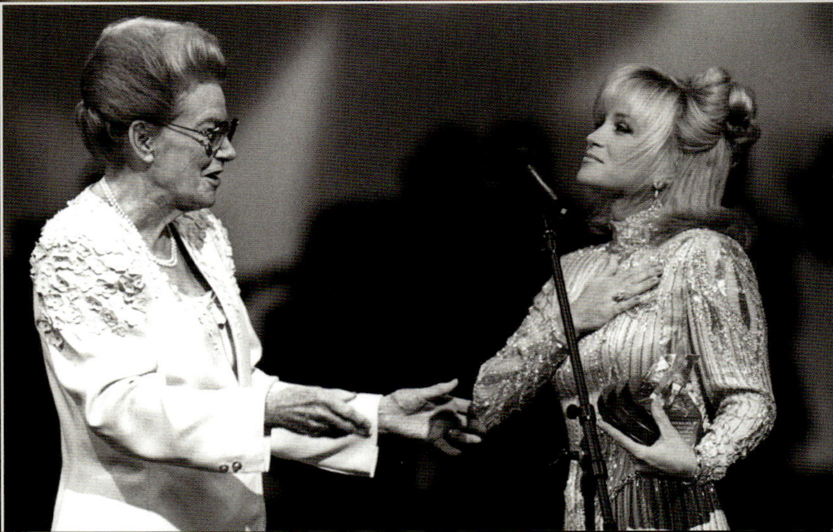

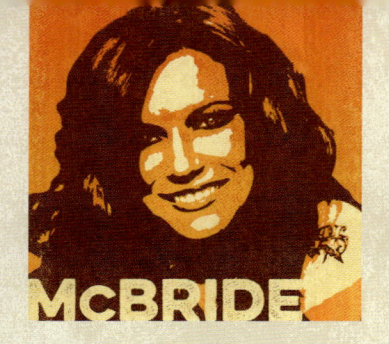

MARTINA McBRIDE
MEMBER SINCE 1995

Martina McBride has won the Top Female Vocalist trophy four times at the Country Music Association Awards and three times from the Academy of Country Music. Eight of her albums have gone platinum. Through 2010, 20 of her singles had reached the Top 10, from 1993's breakthrough "My Baby Loves Me" to, most recently, "Wrong Baby Wrong." It's a voice — and career — you'd be hard-pressed not to consider "Blessed," to cite one of her No. 1 hits.

Martina feels blessed to be a part of country music's most storied tradition. "It's one of the highest honors of my career, to be inducted into the Grand Ole Opry," she says proudly. "I love when I see new artists coming out to the Opry, because I think that it's such an interesting combination of respecting our heritage and tradition with

BIRTHPLACE: Sharon, Kansas
BIRTH DATE: July 29
OPRY INDUCTION: November 30, 1995

DEFINITIVE MARTINA McBRIDE:
"Independence Day"
"Wild Angels"
"A Broken Wing"
"I Love You"
"This One's For The Girls"

> "WHENEVER I DO THE OPRY IT STILL FEELS LIKE THE FIRST TIME. I STILL GET NERVOUS. THE OPRY'S GOING TO BE HERE FOR HUNDREDS OF YEARS, AND I'M JUST PROUD MY NAME IS ON THAT LIST. IT'S A HIGHLIGHT OF MY LIFE."

younger artists coming and performing, which brings new fans to the Opry. So it's a real give and take."

Martina's own career is a fine example of that balance. She's had a couple of crossover hits over the years, like "This One's for the Girls" and "In My Daughter's Eyes," both of which were smashes on adult-contemporary as well as country radio. "I'm known for more contemporary country music" than for being a traditionalist, she acknowledges. Yet few modern country artists have done as much to draw attention to the music's history as Martina did when she released *Timeless*, an album of classic covers.

Martina started singing with her father's group at age seven, while her mom ran the soundboard. After high school, Martina went to the "big city" — Hutchinson, Kansas — to try fronting her own bands, at which point she met a sound engineer named John McBride, who became her husband in 1988. Following a 1990 move to Nashville, she went from selling T-shirts for Garth Brooks to becoming his opening act. By the time she was inducted into the Opry in 1995, Martina had become one of the queens of country music.

CLOCKWISE FROM TOP LEFT:
1. With Loretta Lynn, Opry induction, November 30, 1995
2. With Carrie Underwood and Julianne Hough
3. Opry Goes Pink, October 22, 2011
4. With her father, Daryl Schiff
5. August 24, 2013

GRAND OLE OPRY

WSM
YAMAHA

WSM
GRAND OLE OPRY
GRAND OLE OPRY

WSM

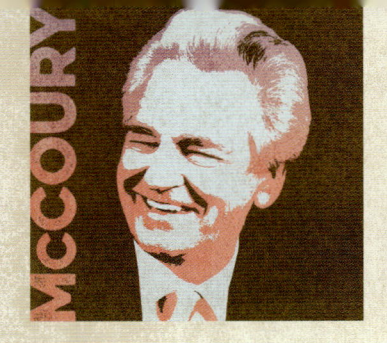

DEL McCOURY
MEMBER SINCE 2003

Del McCoury grew up in York County, Pennsylvania. At age 11, Del's older brother, G.C., introduced him to bluegrass through the music of Flatt & Scruggs. Before long, he had taken up the banjo, and by the early 1960s he was playing bluegrass in the honky tonks of the Baltimore-Washington, D.C., area. In 1963, Del made his first Grand Ole Opry appearances when he was recruited by Bill Monroe to join his Blue Grass Boys. Though he was hired as a banjo player, Bill soon made him into a guitar player and lead singer.

When Del left the band the following year, he continued as a lead singer — first during a brief stint in California with the Golden State Boys, and then back in Pennsylvania with his own band, the Dixie Pals. For the next quarter of a century, Del was a part-time musician,

BIRTHPLACE: York County, Pennsylvania
BIRTH DATE: February 1
OPRY INDUCTION: October 25, 2003

DID YOU KNOW? Del was invited to join the Grand Ole Opry while accepting the International Bluegrass Music Association's Entertainer of the Year Award.

> "I'VE PLAYED CARNEGIE HALL. I'VE PLAYED THE BIG HALL AND I'VE PLAYED THE SMALL HALL UP THERE IN NEW YORK, BUT IT NEVER EXCITES ME LIKE PLAYING ON THIS GRAND OLE OPRY STAGE."

working as a logging truck driver to support his growing family while playing at bluegrass festivals on the weekends. Though he couldn't devote himself entirely to music, his reputation as a singer of unsurpassed intensity grew steadily.

Del's son Ronnie began playing with the band on a part-time basis in 1981 at age 14. Six years later, Robbie McCoury made his debut with the band. At the beginning of the '90s, Del and his family moved to Nashville to pursue music full-time as The Del McCoury Band. By the end of the decade, the band had become the top winner at the International Bluegrass Music Association's annual awards, eventually taking home nine IBMA Entertainer of the Year trophies. The Grand Ole Opry came calling in 2003 fulfilling Del's lifelong dream of becoming a member.

Today, the Del McCoury Band enjoys the praise of traditional bluegrass lovers and tie-dyed clad "Del-Heads" alike. The band's tour dates range from performing arts centers to hardcore bluegrass festivals. After years of playing hip, youth-oriented jamfests such as Bonnaroo and High Sierra, Del launched his own in 2008 — the popular four-day DelFest in Cumberland, Maryland. Three years later, Del was elected to the International Bluegrass Music Hall of Fame.

CLOCKWISE FROM TOP LEFT:
1. --
2. --
3. With Dierks Bentley
4. Being invited to join the Opry by Ricky Skaggs and Sonny Osborne at the International Bluegrass Music Awards, 2003
5. August 30, 2005

OPRY FAMILY MEMBERS

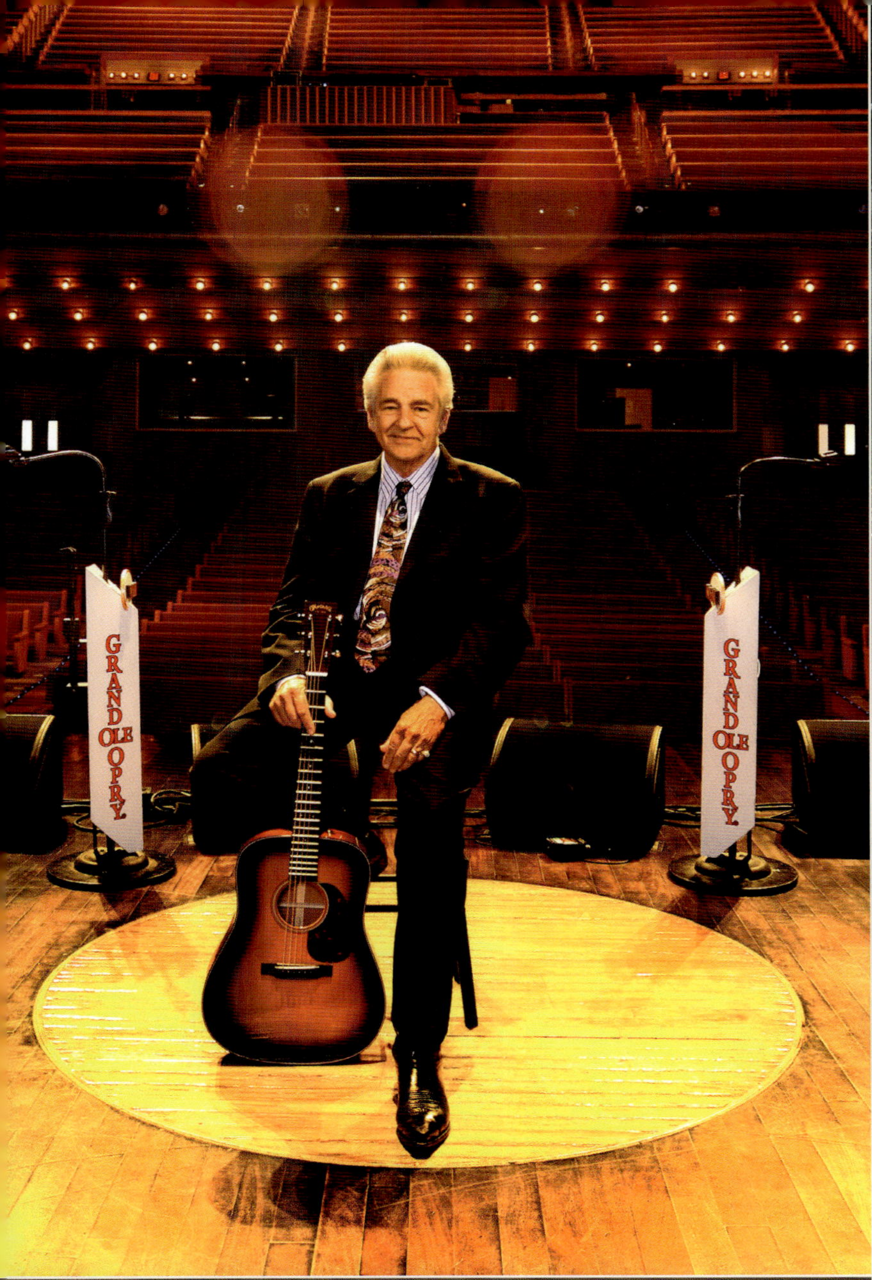
GRAND OLE OPRY
GRAND OLE OPRY

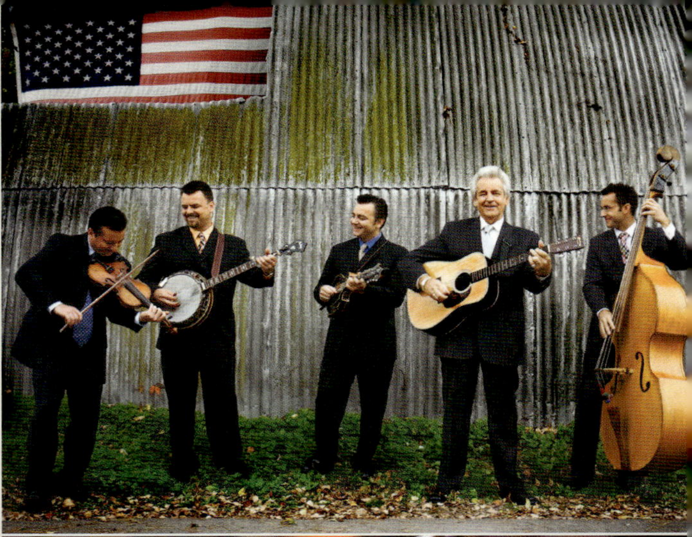

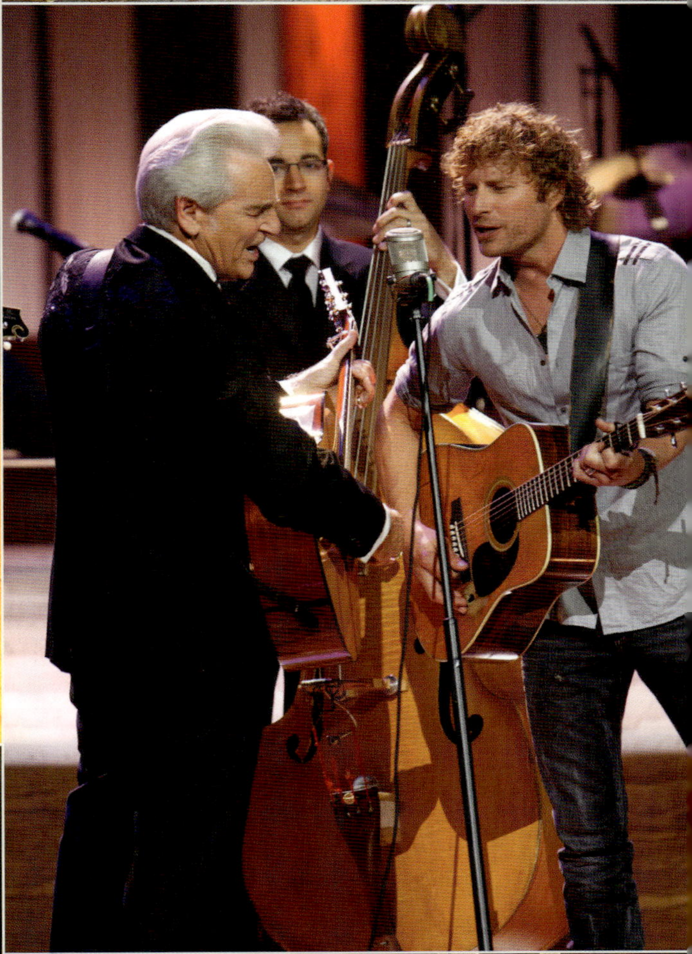

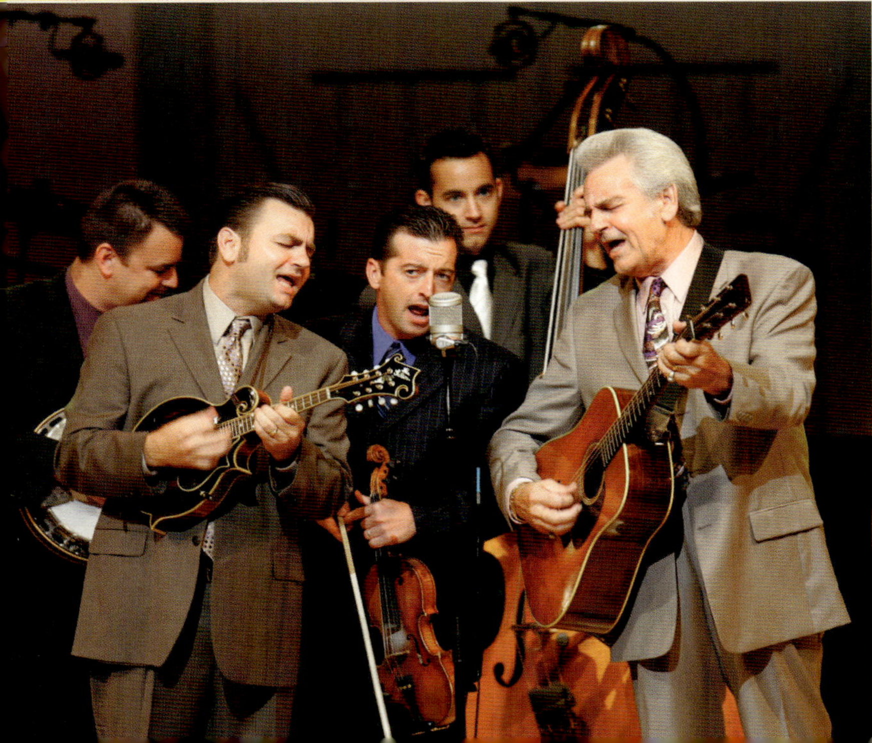

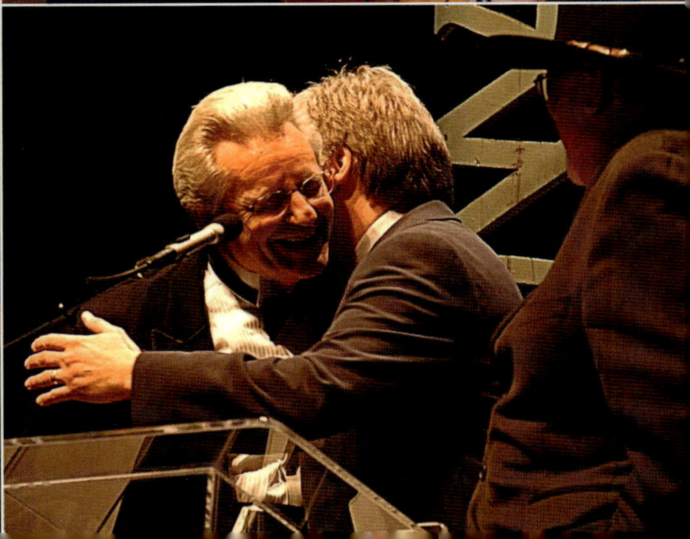

CHARLIE MCCOY
MEMBER SINCE 2022

In 1961, Charlie McCoy was paid $49 to play harmonica on Roy Orbison's record, Candy Man, one of his first of many studio sessions and the song that launched his career as a super-session musician in Nashville.

"It got Roy another hit and me a career," he said of the track.

Charlie went on to become a mainstay on records from icons like Bob Dylan, Elvis Presley, Tanya Tucker, and more. He's performed on songs with Dolly Parton, Waylon Jennings, Jerry Lee Lewis, Willie Nelson, and George Jones.

BIRTHPLACE: Oak Hill, West Virginia
BIRTH DATE: March 28
OPRY INDUCTION: July 13, 2022

DID YOU KNOW? Each of Charlie's two children and five grandchildren is credited on one of his albums in some way, through either cover artwork, singing, or playing an instrument.

"I LOVE IT HERE, IT'S THE BEST AUDIENCE IN THE WORLD."

With over 12,000 sessions and several Country Music Association and Academy of Country Music Awards under his belt – as well as a Grammy in 1972 for his album, The Real McCoy – Charlie is one of the most critically acclaimed and enduring studio musicians in Nashville. He is a member of the Country Music Hall of Fame and has been a beloved guest on the Grand Ole Opry for over 50 years.

"What a great ride it's been," he said while performing on the Opry stage on June 11, 2022. "I look back on my career and it's like a fairy tale. I've been so blessed."

That night, Opry member Vince Gill invited Charlie to become part of the Opry family, a family he was already deeply entwined with.

"I've had so many amazing things happen," Charlie said. "But I want to tell you what, this is the icing on my cake."

CLOCKWISE FROM TOP LEFT:
1. Charlie addresses the crowd at the Opry House in 2019.
2. Charlie plays harmonica on the Grand Ole Opry in 2020.
3. Charlie performs with Opry member Mandy Barnett on the Grand Ole Opry in 2018.
4. Charlie is asked to join the Opry family by Opry member Vince Gill in 2022.

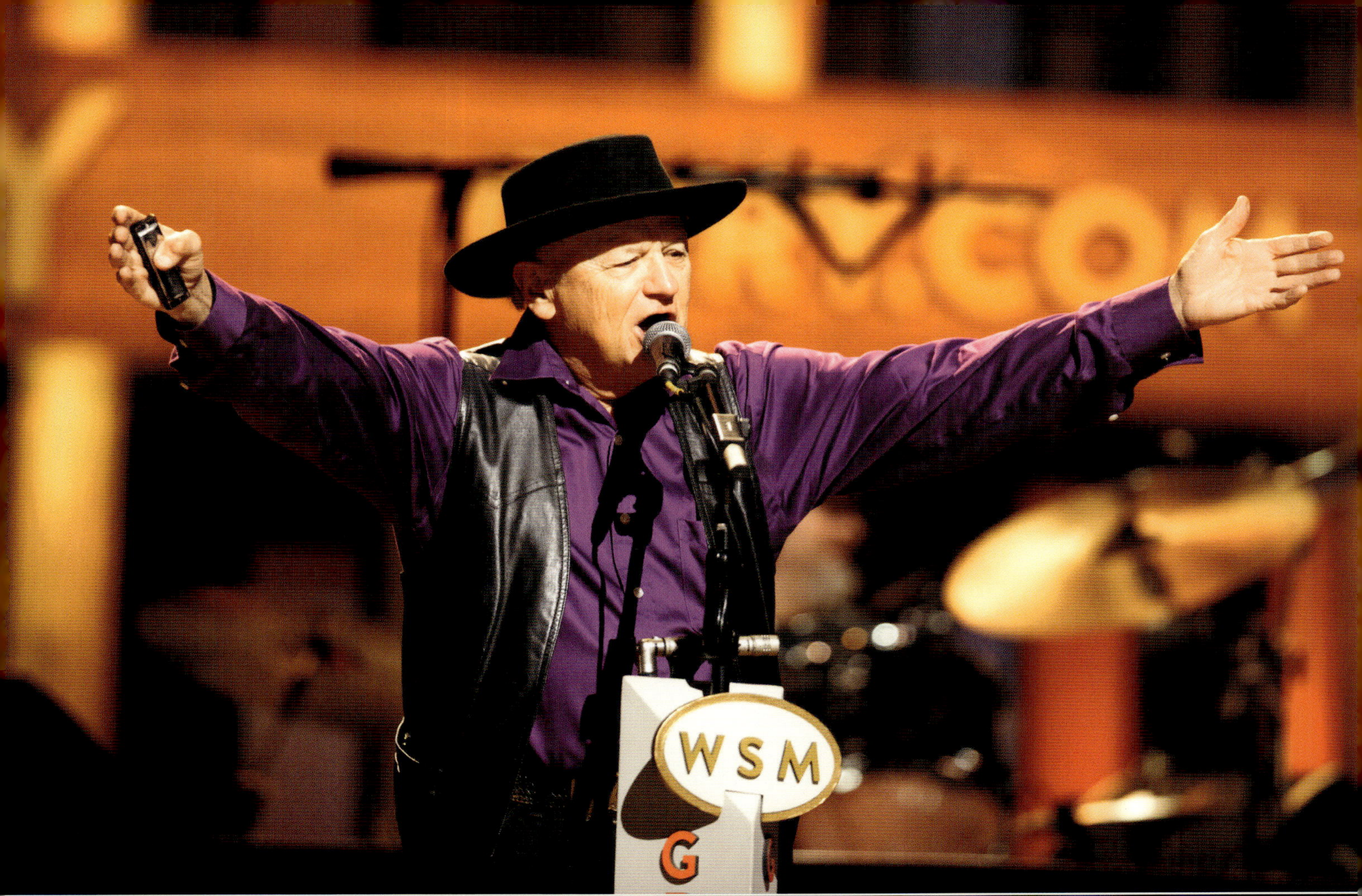
WSM

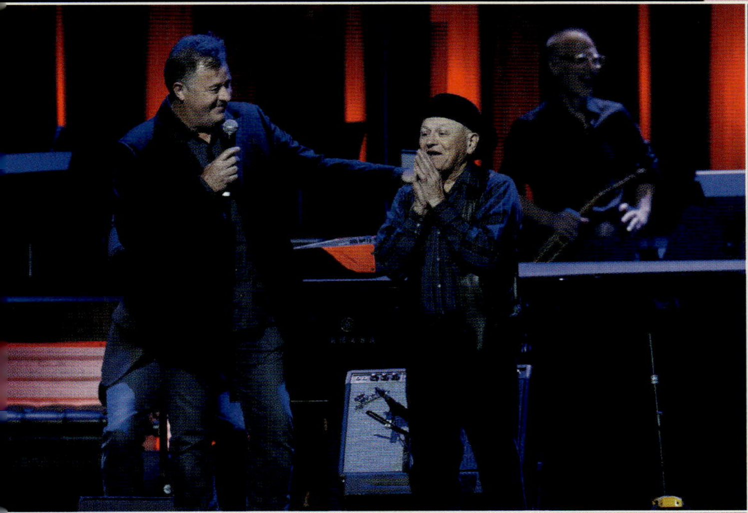

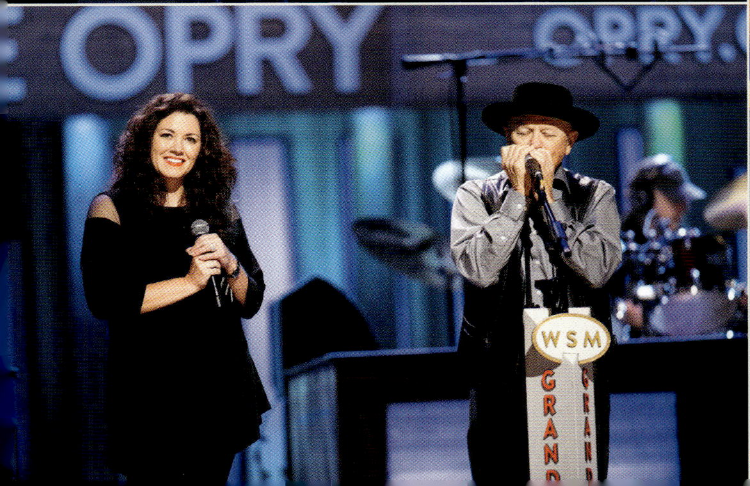
OPRY
WSM

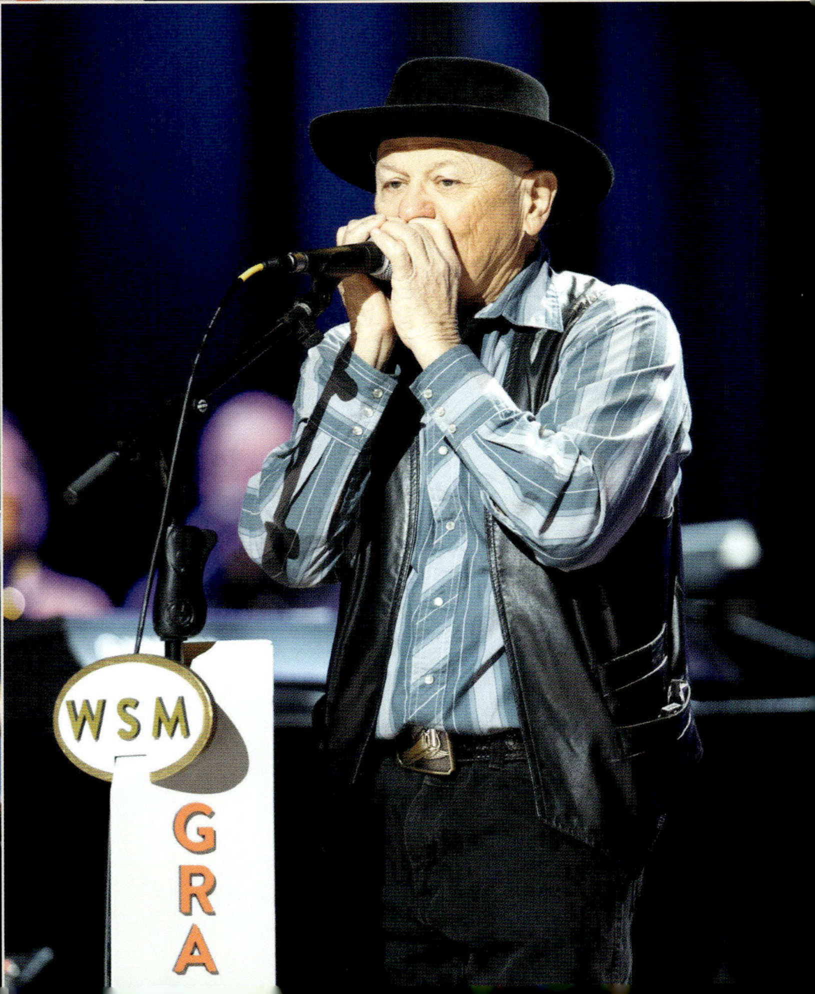
WSM

REBA McENTIRE
MEMBER SINCE 1985

When Reba McEntire made her Grand Ole Opry debut in 1977, she almost didn't make it in the door after a guard at the Opry gate missed her name on the night's list of performers. Reba found a nearby phone and called her booking agent, who arranged for her to get past security. Her parents and older sister, Alice, drove 1,400 miles round trip from their Oklahoma home to see what turned out to be Reba's three-minute performance that night. Her act was cut from two songs to just one — "Invitation to the Blues" — because of a surprise appearance from Dolly Parton.

Despite those issues, that evening still turned out better than the first time Reba came to the Opry as a fan. She was seven years old

BIRTHPLACE: McAlester, Oklahoma
BIRTH DATE: March 28
OPRY INDUCTION: November 21, 1985

> "THE GRAND OLE OPRY IS A HOME. IT'S LIKE A FAMILY REUNION WHEN YOU COME BACK AND GET TO SEE EVERYBODY."

and visiting the Opry as an audience member. She got sick during the show, ran outside and promptly threw up on the front steps.

Western singer Red Steagall discovered Reba at the National Finals Rodeo in 1974 singing the national anthem. She signed her first record deal the following year and charted her first single in 1976. Four years passed before Reba landed her first Top 10 hit with "(You Lift Me) Up to Heaven." It took another two years for Reba to get her first No. 1, "Can't Even Get the Blues." Since then, the hits have consistently kept coming for four decades. She is the only female artist to have scored No. 1 singles in each decade from the 1980s through the current one.

Reba, who received a star on the Hollywood Walk of Fame in 1998, has sold more than 55 million albums and earned two Grammy Awards. She is the most nominated female artist in the history of the Country Music Association Awards, which named her its Entertainer of the Year in 1986. She also has found success in film, television, books, fashion, and even on the Broadway stage as the star of *Annie Get Your Gun*.

CLOCKWISE FROM TOP LEFT:
1. With The Whites
2. May 9, 2009
3. Circa late 1980s
4. Circa early 1980s
5. With Vince Gill

OPRY FAMILY MEMBERS

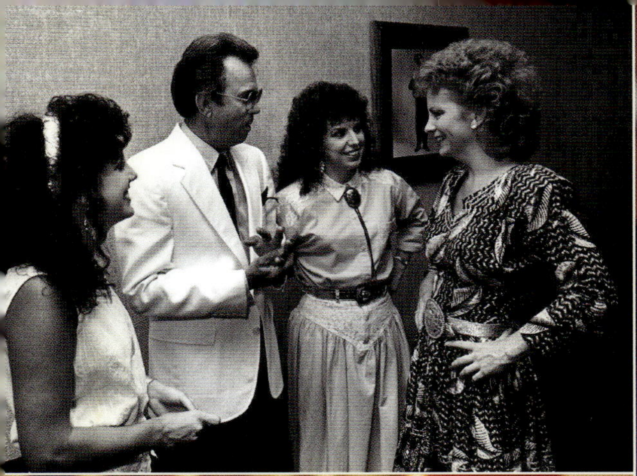

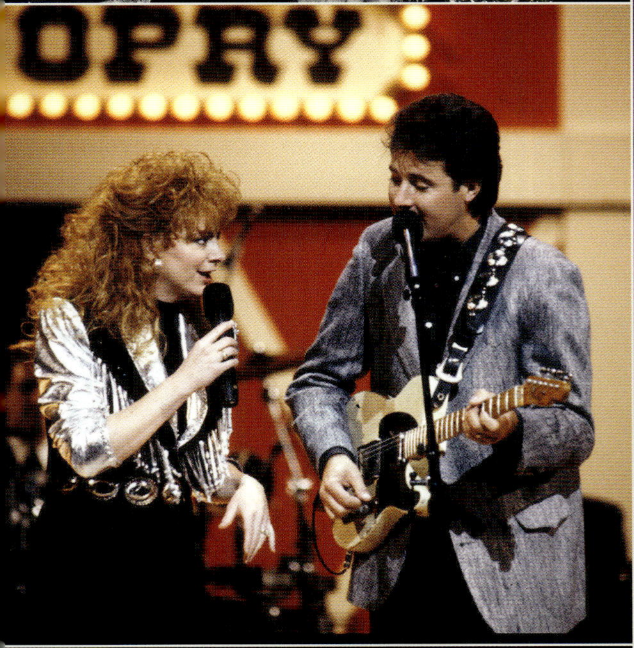
OPRY

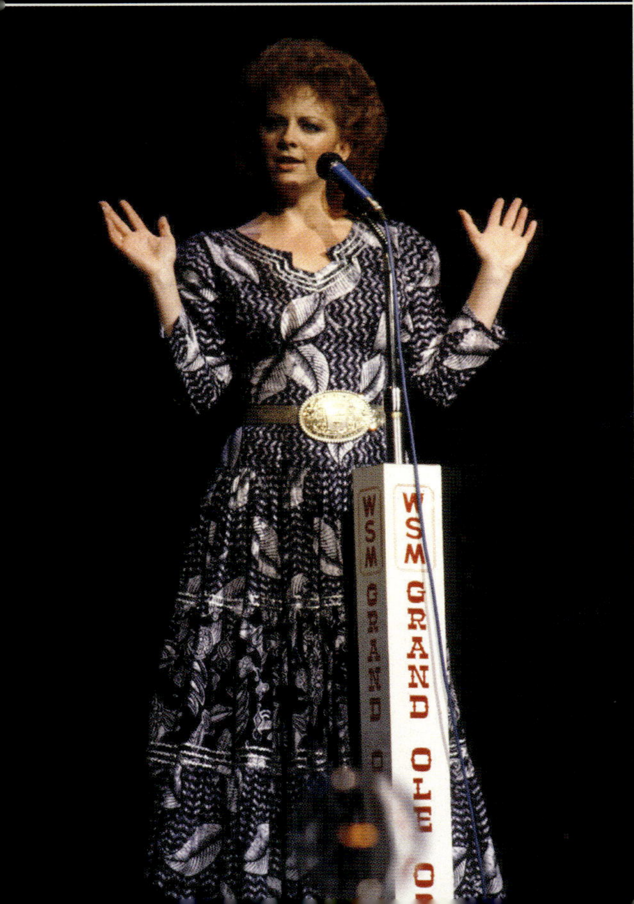
WSM
WSM GRAND OLE

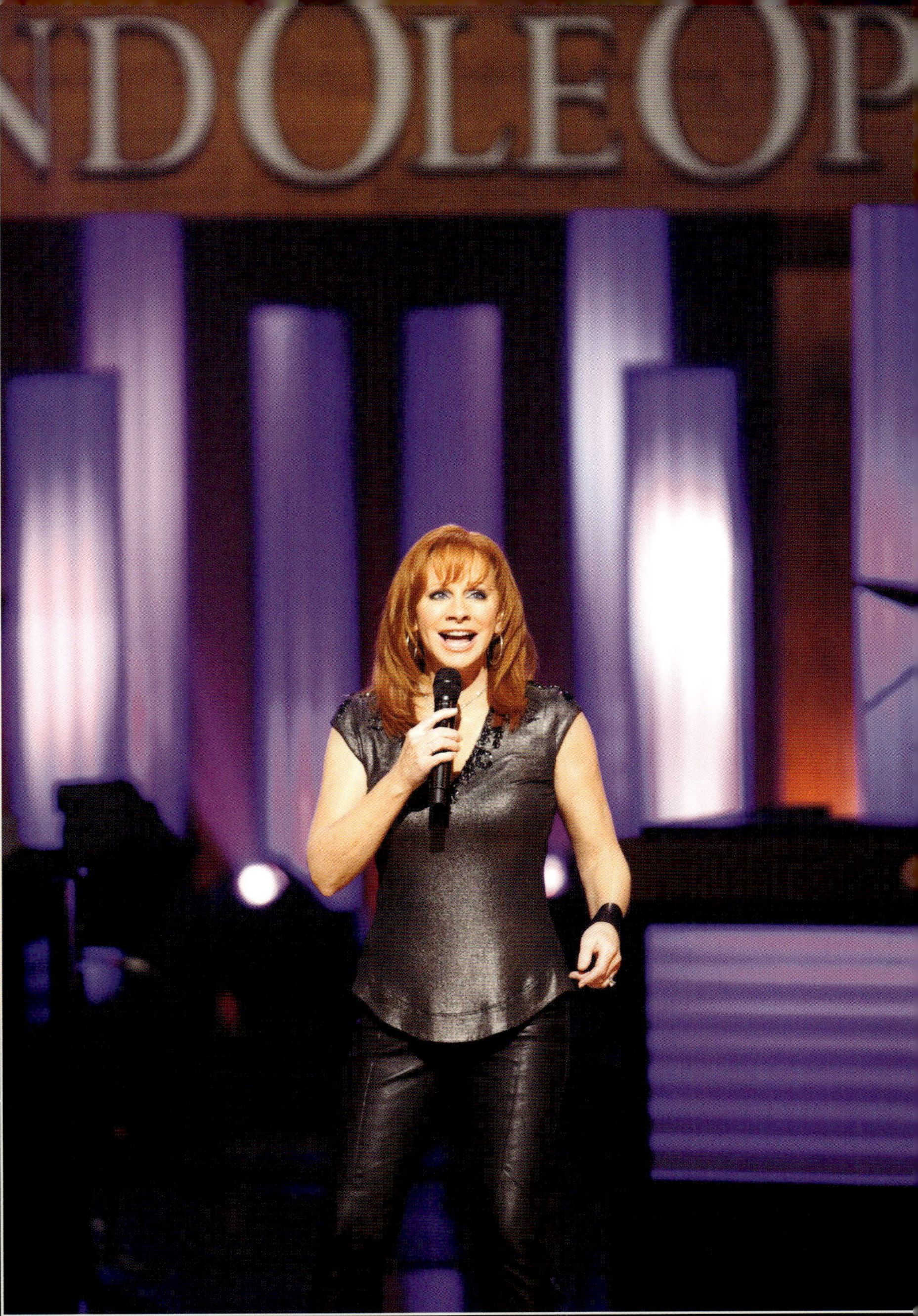

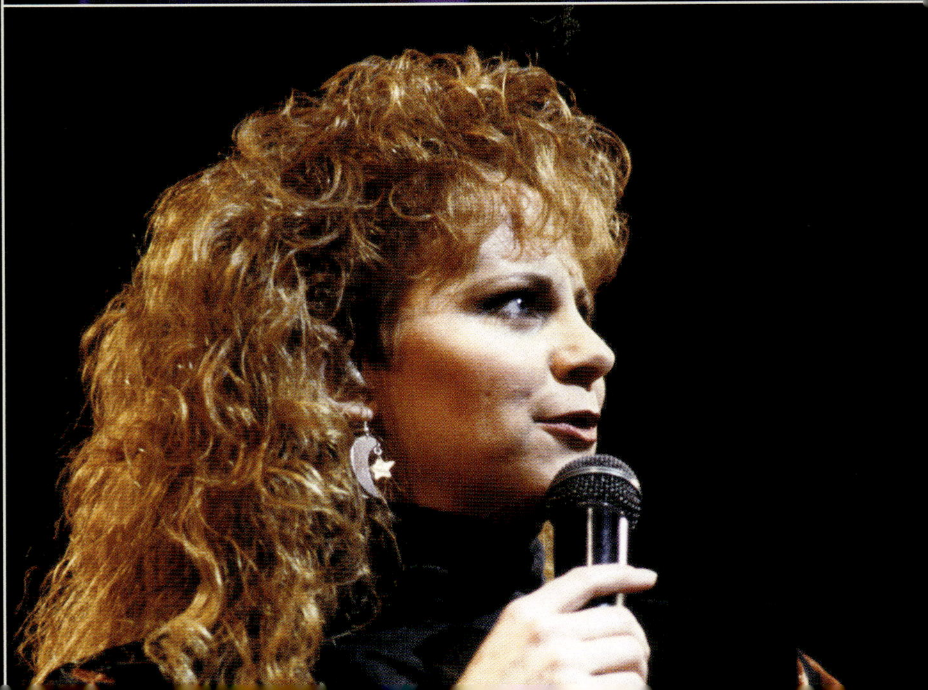

JESSE McREYNOLDS
MEMBER SINCE 1964

Jesse McReynolds forged his singing and mandolin-playing reputation as one-half of Jim and Jesse, one of the most talented and acclaimed acts in bluegrass music. Since brother Jim died late in 2002, Jesse has continued to fill listener demands for that McReynolds sound, while also striking out in new musical directions. Inspired by the five-string banjo playing of Hoke Jenkins, Jesse originated the complex "cross-picking" style of mandolin playing. His music combines bluegrass, mainstream country, rock, folk, pop, Spanish, and other styles. Even though he's best known as a bluegrasser, Jesse has shown himself to be one of the most innovative and prolific mandolin players around.

BIRTHPLACE: Coeburn, Virginia
BIRTH DATE: July 9
OPRY INDUCTION: March 2, 1964

> "I WENT OUT AND SAT IN THE AUDIENCE ONE NIGHT—WENT UP IN THE BALCONY AND WATCHED THE SHOW—AND I THOUGHT, 'IF I WASN'T ON THE OPRY, WHAT WOULD I GIVE JUST TO WALK OUT ON STAGE AND DO ONE SONG?' I'M HONORED TO DO ONE SONG ANYTIME."

Raised near Coeburn, Virginia, Jesse McReynolds grew up in a family steeped in traditional mountain music. That background made it natural for him to follow the footsteps of his grandfather, Charlie McReynolds, who was one of the first musicians to record for Victor (later known as RCA) in Bristol, Virginia, in 1927.

In 1952, Jim and Jesse made their major-label debut on Capitol Records. In 1967, three years after joining the Opry, the duo had a country hit with "Diesel on My Tail." The brother act recorded for several other labels, including their own Old Dominion Records, releasing such classics as "The Flame of Love," "Cotton Mill Man," and John Prine's "Paradise." They were inducted into the International Bluegrass Music Association's Hall of Honor in 1993.

Working with or without Jim, Jesse has performed in musical settings that cross a variety of genres. While working with banjoist Eddie Adcock, fiddler Kenny Baker and Dobro player Josh Graves, Jesse recorded during the late '80s and early '90s as part of the Masters supergroup.

Having spent more than 60 years in music, Jesse still tours with his Virginia Boys, performing frequently at bluegrass festivals, in addition to their regular Opry appearances.

CLOCKWISE FROM TOP LEFT:
1. 2014
2. May 25, 2013
3. Jim & Jesse, 1950s
4. 2014
5. Circa 1960s promoting Martha White Flour

WHITE
CORN MEAL MIX
Hot Rize
MARTHA WHITE
FLOUR

NBC
WSM
GRAND
OLE
OPR

RONNIE MILSAP
MEMBER SINCE 1976

With a catchy, danceable country pop sound, Ronnie Milsap dominated radio during the '70s and '80s and pushed the genre beyond its rural roots and into mainstream entertainment. Born blind in a poor region of North Carolina, Ronnie lived with his grandmother until he was six years old. He attended Morehead State School for the Blind in Raleigh, where he was given strict Classical training. But late at night he listened to his favorite country, gospel, and R&B broadcasts. The music reminded him of home.

Ronnie studied pre-law at Young Harris Junior College near Atlanta, eventually earning a scholarship to Emory. Instead of continuing with law, he threw himself into music, forming his own

BIRTHPLACE: Robbinsville, North Carolina
BIRTH DATE: January 16
OPRY INDUCTION: February 6, 1976

Q: How does being backstage at the Opry differ from being backstage elsewhere on tour?
A: The Grand Ole Opry is the mother church of country music. It is always more special than being backstage anywhere else. Just the fact that you're backstage at the Opry, that means more to me than anything.

> "THE NIGHT ROY ACUFF INDUCTED ME INTO THE GRAND OLE OPRY, HE SAID, 'YOU KNOW, HE PLAYS THE PIANO, AND IT WON'T BE BUT A TIME OR TWO COMING OUT HERE ON THE GRAND OLE OPRY STAGE, AND HE'LL BE ABLE TO FIND HIS PIANO EVERY TIME.' THE PROBLEM IS THEY KEEP MOVING THE DAMN THING."

band. During the mid-'60s, he landed session work, notably on Elvis Presley's "Kentucky Rain" and "Don't Cry Daddy."

In 1973, Ronnie moved from Memphis to Nashville. Before one could say "overnight success," he was signed by RCA and released the two-sided hit, "All Together Now (Let's Fall Apart)" and "I Hate You." He followed with "That Girl Who Waits on Tables" and "Pure Love." A year later, he had three No. 1 songs. The flood of hits made for quite the country music catalog: "Daydreams About Night Things," "(I'm A) Stand by My Woman Man," "Smoky Mountain Rain," "Lost in the Fifties Tonight (In the Still of the Night)," "How Do I Turn You On," and "Don't You Ever Get Tired of Hurting Me" all stormed the charts.

Along with his multiple gold and platinum albums, Ronnie has earned six Grammys and shelves of other awards, including CMAs and ACMs. In 2014, he was elected to the Country Music Hall of Fame.

CLOCKWISE FROM TOP LEFT:
1. With Roy Acuff
2. --
3. August 23, 2003
4. June 3, 2006
5. March 4, 1978

OPRY FAMILY MEMBERS 136

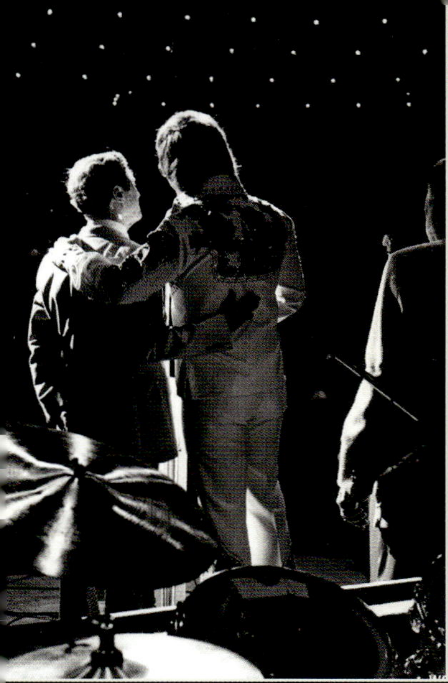
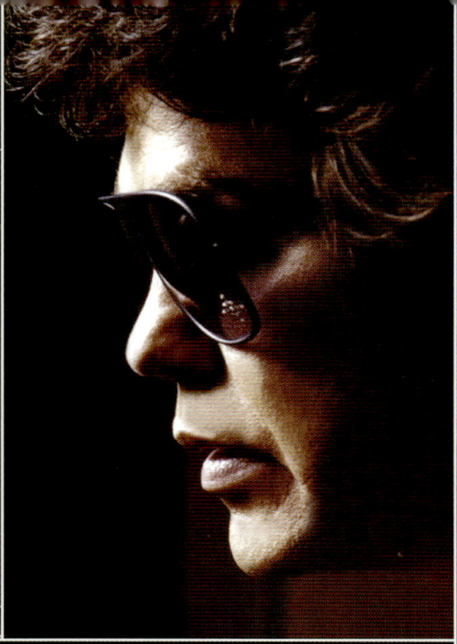
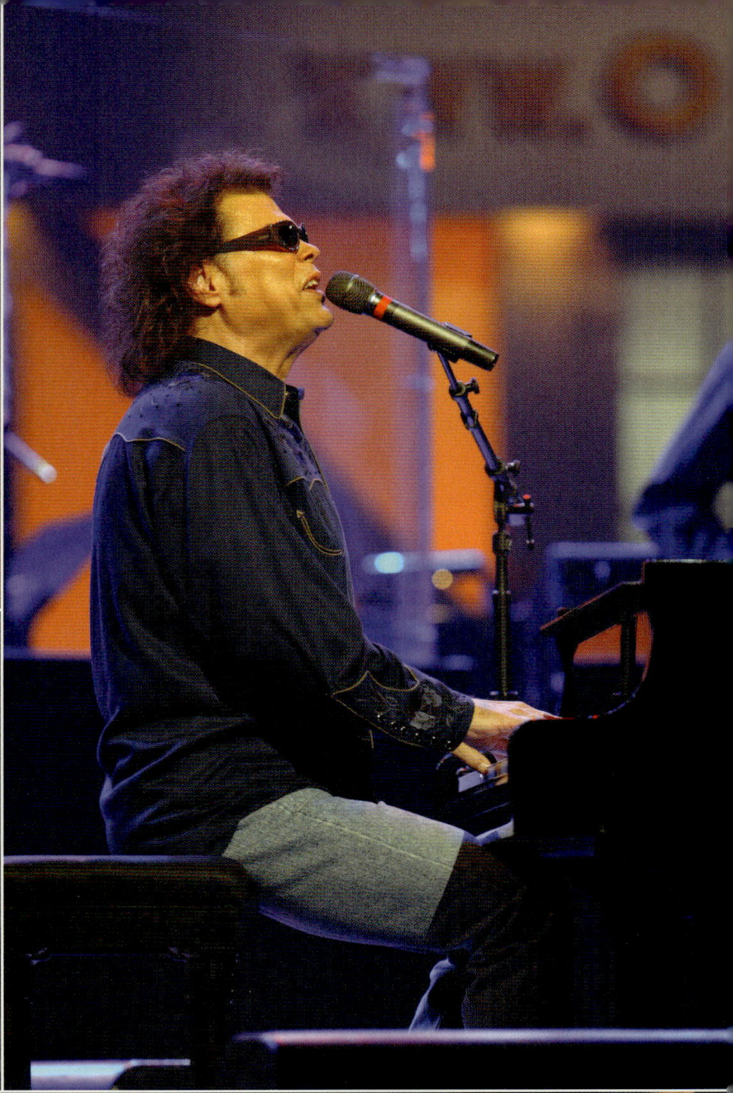
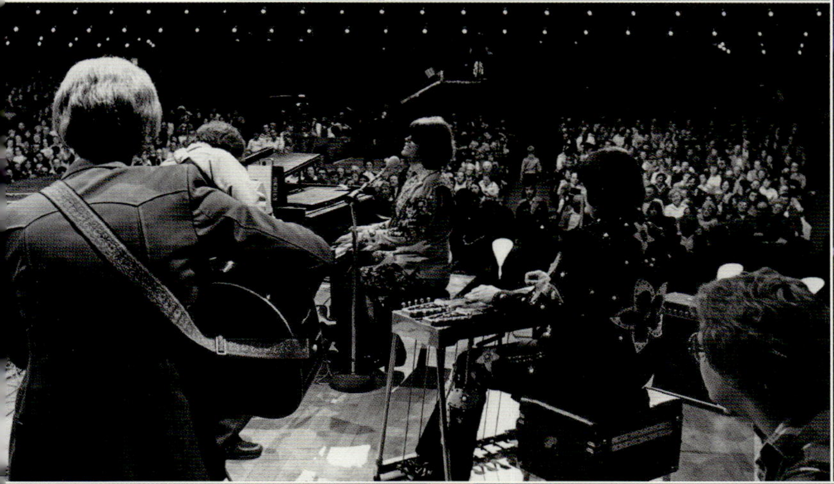
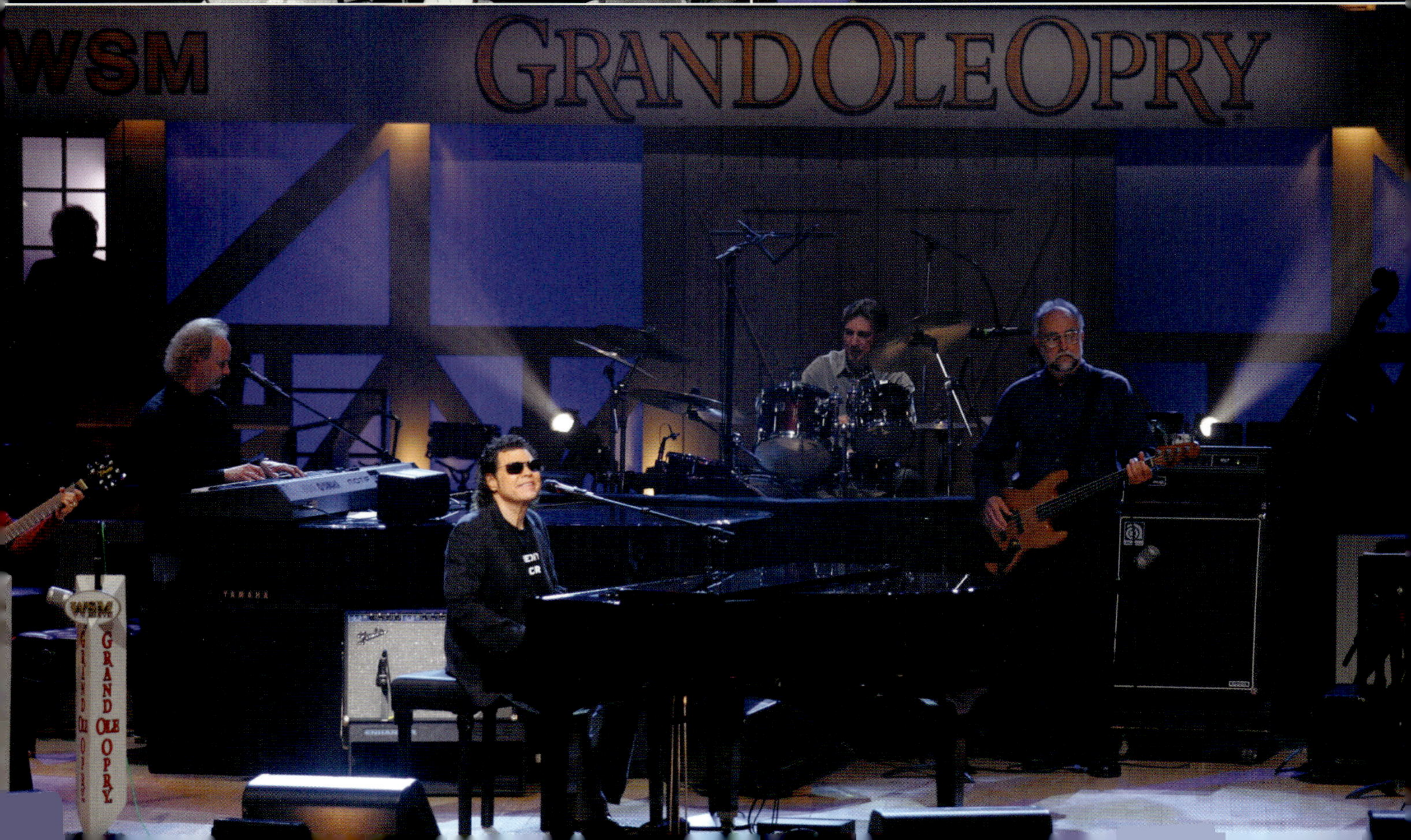
WSM
GRAND OLE OPRY

CRAIG MORGAN
MEMBER SINCE 2008

Craig Morgan received his invitation to become a Grand Ole Opry member during a special concert for U.S. troops at Fort Bragg in Fayetteville, North Carolina, on September 18, 2008. That evening represented a homecoming for the singer: He was stationed at Fort Bragg from 1990 to 1992 during his 10-year active-duty tenure in the U.S. Army's 82nd Airborne Division.

Opry member John Conlee surprised Craig with the invitation onstage during his performance of "Rose Colored Glasses," a song popularized by John in 1978 and often found on Craig's set list. When John invited Craig to become the newest member of the Opry, Craig responded quickly: "Oh, God, yes! I do love the Grand Ole Opry, and, I gotta tell you, it's cool to be invited right here."

BIRTHPLACE: Kingston Springs, Tennessee
BIRTH DATE: July 17
OPRY INDUCTION: October 25, 2008

Q: To what do you attribute the Opry's longevity over the past nine decades?
A: I attribute the Opry's longevity to one word: integrity. The Opry is truth in country music. The Opry is the moral gauge of our format and the cornerstone on which all country music careers are built. The Opry is a family I'm very proud to be a part of.

"THERE'S NO SUCH THING AS A BAD NIGHT... EVERY NIGHT'S A GOOD NIGHT TO BE AT THE OPRY."

Craig has made a name for himself as the host of *Craig Morgan All Access Outdoors* on the Outdoor Channel in addition to massive radio airplay of his signature hits, among them "Almost Home," (which *Music Row* magazine named its song of the year for 2003); "That's What I Love About Sunday," which spent four weeks at No. 1 and was *Billboard* magazine's most-played country song of 2005; and regular-guy singles including "Redneck Yacht Club," "Bonfire," and "International Harvester." He also knows his way around a heartbreaking ballad, as his 2013 hit "Wake Up Lovin' You" proves.

Since making his Opry debut on April 21, 2000, he has performed on the Opry stage countless times and often plays in excess of 200 concerts a year. The TV host and Army veteran also frequently performs at military bases, both at home and abroad; he received the USO Merit Award for his musical contributions to the troops.

CLOCKWISE FROM TOP LEFT:
1. November 26, 2013
2. 2014
3. Being invited to join the Opry by John Conlee, September 18, 2008
4. Opry induction with John Conlee, October 25, 2008
5. With George Jones

WSM
GRAND OLE OPRY
GRAND OLE OPRY

BUCK
KNIVES

HAMMOND

OPRY.COM
WSM
GRAND OLE OPRY

WWW.OPRY.CO
WSM
GRAND OLE

LORRIE MORGAN
MEMBER SINCE 1984

"You can't imagine how it felt the night I became a member of the Opry," Lorrie Morgan says. "The first time I could really call this place home. I couldn't stop shaking or trembling or crying."

That Saturday night more than 30 years ago might have been Lorrie's first night as an official member, but it certainly wasn't her first night at the Grand Ole Opry. Lorrie grew up backstage at the Opry, the daughter of Country Music Hall of Famer George Morgan, a 26-year member known everywhere for his smash 1949 hit "Candy Kisses."

Born in 1959, Lorrie made her Opry stage debut early, introduced at the Ryman Auditorium by her proud father. "My little 13-year-old knees were absolutely knocking," she recalls. "But Dad was standing there

BIRTHPLACE: Hendersonville, Tennessee
BIRTH DATE: June 27
OPRY INDUCTION: June 9, 1984

DEFINITIVE LORRIE MORGAN:
"Dear Me"
"'Til a Tear Becomes A Rose" (with Keith Whitley)
"Something In Red"
"What Part Of No"
"Good As I Was To You"

> "ALL THESE PEOPLE I IDOLIZED HAVE VERY FORTUNATELY BECOME SOME OF MY VERY GOOD FRIENDS. I'VE BEEN BLESSED BY BEING EMBRACED IN THE ARMS OF THIS GREAT INSTITUTION."

right beside me with big tears in his eyes, and those people gave me a standing ovation. I thought, 'This is what I'm doing the rest of my life.'"

"This was a dream of my dad's long before it was my dream," Lorrie says. "I have all of this because of Dad. We're very blessed to be a musical family here at the Grand Ole Opry. What more could you ask for?"

George Morgan died when Lorrie was 16, but she still carries in her heart two pieces of advice he left her: "Never say, 'I can't,'" and "Always remember your manners."

Morgan's vocal style, combining country sincerity and pop sophistication, really took off in 1989 with the emotion-filled hit "Dear Me." She won a CMA award in 1990 for her work with her late husband, Keith Whitley, the great country traditionalist who had died the year before. Subsequent albums *Leave the Light On*, *Something in Red*, and *Watch Me* all sold more than a million copies.

Throughout her career, Morgan says, she has thought of the Opry as home. "The Opry gave me my start in country music," she says. "It's a place we all need to go from time to time to remember why we're here and what gave us the opportunity to be here."

CLOCKWISE FROM TOP LEFT:
1. Making her Opry debut at the Ryman Auditorium while father George Morgan looks on
2. October 28, 2006
3. With son Jesse Keith Whitley, June 6, 2014
4. With Bill Anderson on Opry induction night, June 9, 1984
5. With Patti Page

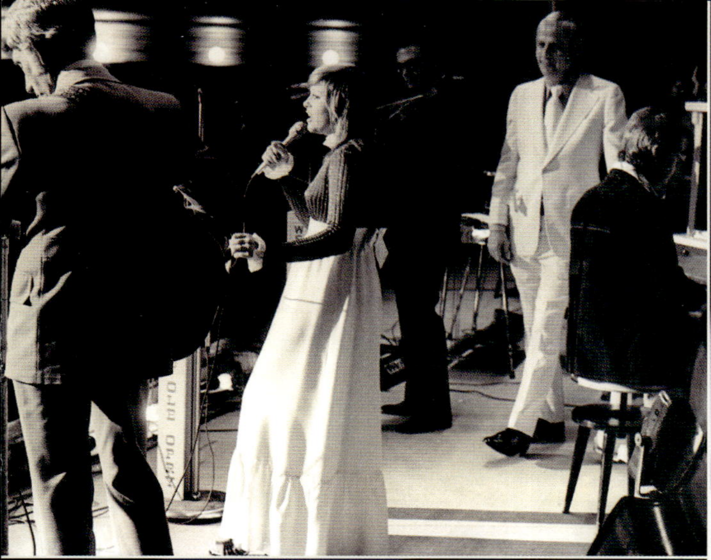

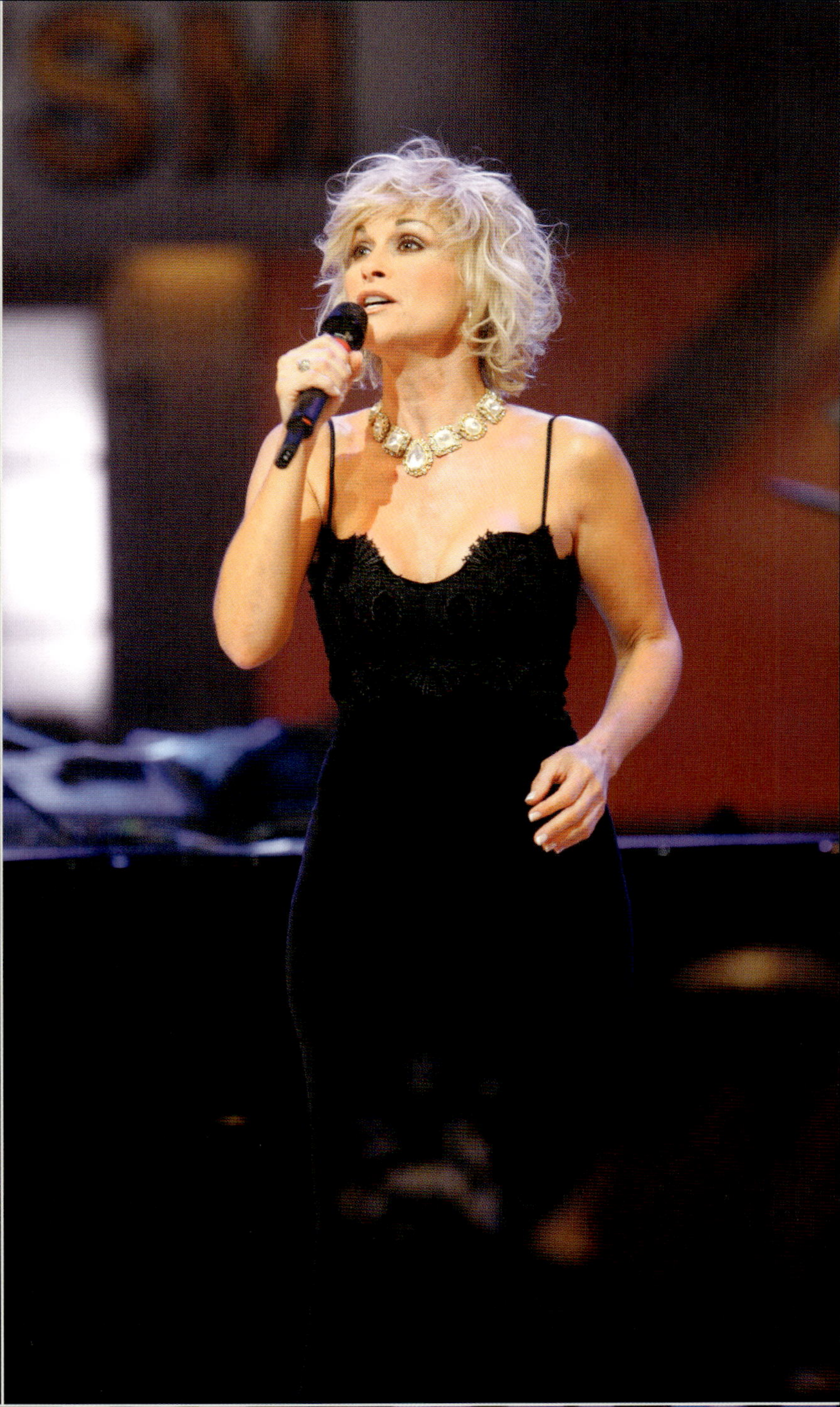

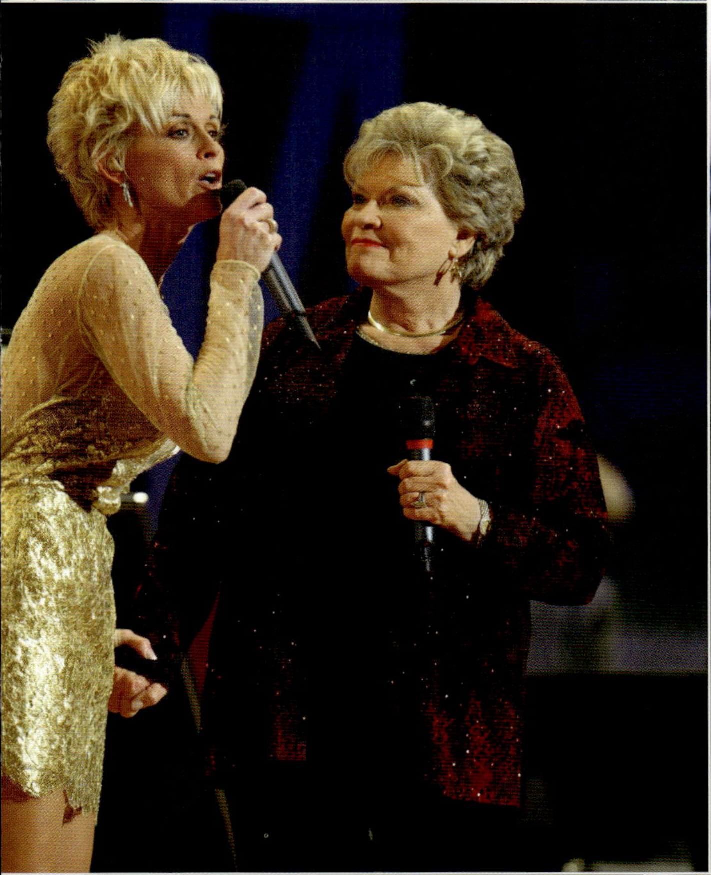

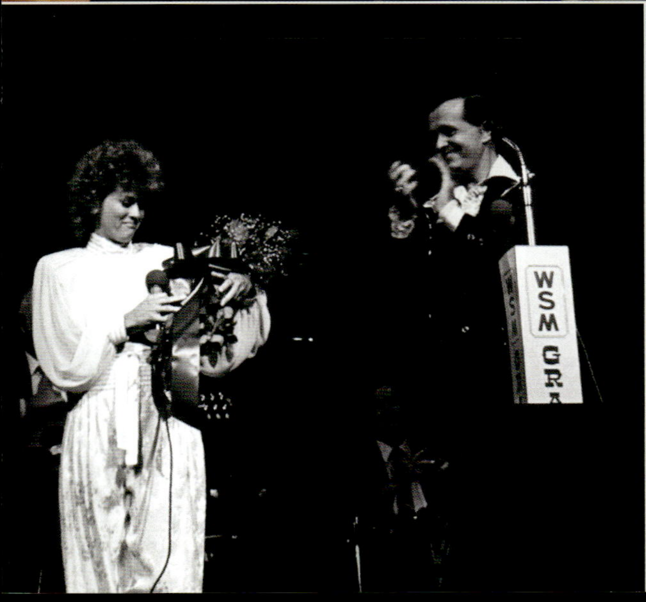
WSM

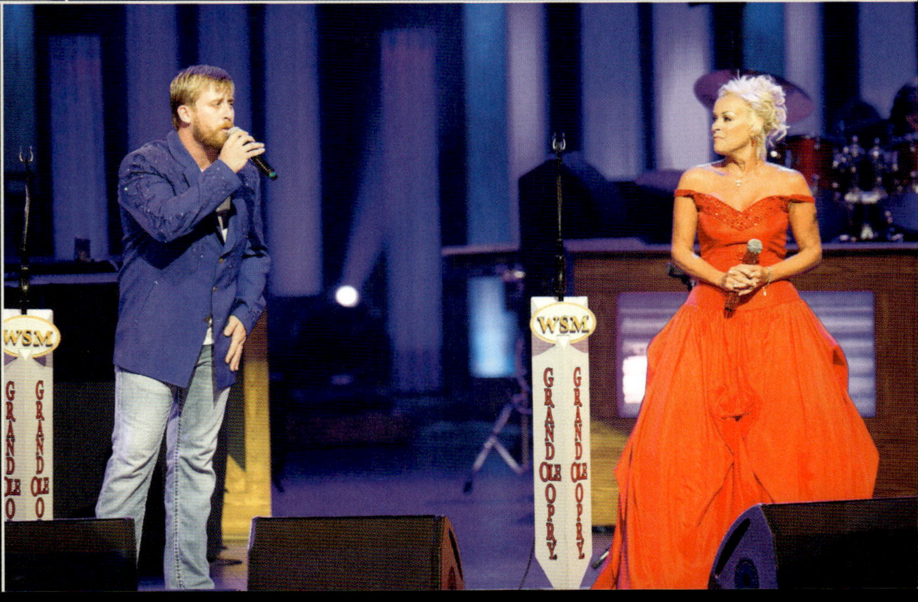
WSM
GRAND OLE OPRY

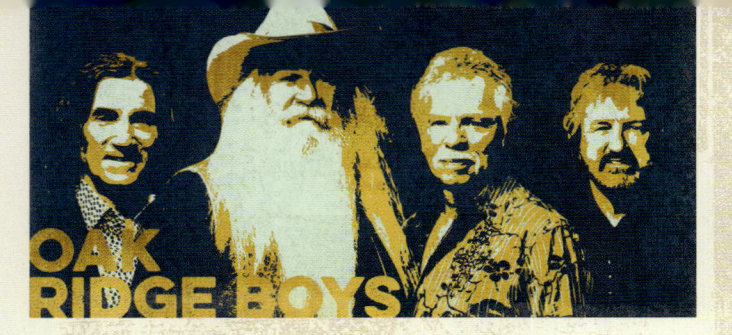

OAK RIDGE BOYS
MEMBER SINCE 2011

One of the longest running groups in country music, The Oak Ridge Boys were first nationally known as a gospel quartet. After moving onto the country charts, they took hit after hit to the top in the 1970s, '80s and '90s, their sound remaining deeply rooted in country gospel harmony.

The Oaks' existence dates back to World War II, circa 1942-1943, when a Knoxville, Tennessee, group began performing gospel songs in nearby Oak Ridge, the home of an atomic bomb research facility. Originally dubbed the Oak Ridge Quartet, they initially appeared at the Grand Ole Opry in 1945 and made their first recordings in 1947.

In the years between 1943 and 1973, the group evolved through a number of personnel changes, moved to Nashville, and became known as The Oak Ridge Boys. William Lee Golden joined in 1965, Duane Allen in 1966, Richard Sterban in 1972, and Joe Bonsall came onboard in 1973.

JOE BONSALL
Birthplace: Philadelphia, Pennsylvania
Birth Date: May 18

DUANE ALLEN
Birthplace: Taylortown, Texas
Birth Date: April 29

RICHARD STERBAN
Birthplace: Camden, New Jersey
Birth Date: April 24

WILLIAM LEE GOLDEN
Birthplace: Brewton, Alabama
Birthdate: January 12

OPRY INDUCTION: August 6, 2011

> "WE'VE ALWAYS BELIEVED IN THE OPRY AND LOVED AND RESPECTED EVERY MEMBER TO THIS BROTHERHOOD AND SISTERHOOD OF COUNTRY MUSIC." —JOE BONSALL

The group scored a breakout hit in 1977 with "Y'all Come Back Saloon," the title song from their MCA label debut album. During the next twenty years they scored nearly 20 chart-toppers and more than 30 Top 10 hits—including a double-platinum single about a girl named "Elvira"—and won countless Grammy, CMA, ACM, and other awards. The Oak Ridge Boys have sold more than 30 million records and continue to tour, performing more than 150 shows across the U.S. and Canada each year.

After decades of Grand Ole Opry visits, The Oak Ridge Boys officially joined the Opry family on August 6, 2011. The group was surprised on stage that night by a video greeting from President George H.W. Bush. "I cannot think of any group or any person who deserve this honor more," President Bush said. "I think of the Opry and the Oaks both as American icons—beloved from coast to coast and known around the world. I can't think of a better union."

In 2015, the Oak Ridge Boys were elected to the Country Music Hall of Fame.

Q: To what do you attribute the Opry's longevity over the past nine decades?
A: The Opry knows what works for the vast and varied country audience out there. They have mixed the classic country and the new kids singing today quite well over the years, and the constant growth and magic of "the circle" reflects that. An evening at the Opry is a family affair and there is always something there for everyone. The Oak Ridge Boys are honored beyond words to be a part of this legendary family!

CLOCKWISE FROM TOP LEFT:
1. February 6, 2010
2. With Little Jimmy Dickens, who became an "itty bitty Oak Ridge Boy" in order to invite the group to become the Opry's newest member; July 8, 2011
3. 2014
4. At the Opry Member Gallery on induction night, August 8, 2011
5. February 20, 1981

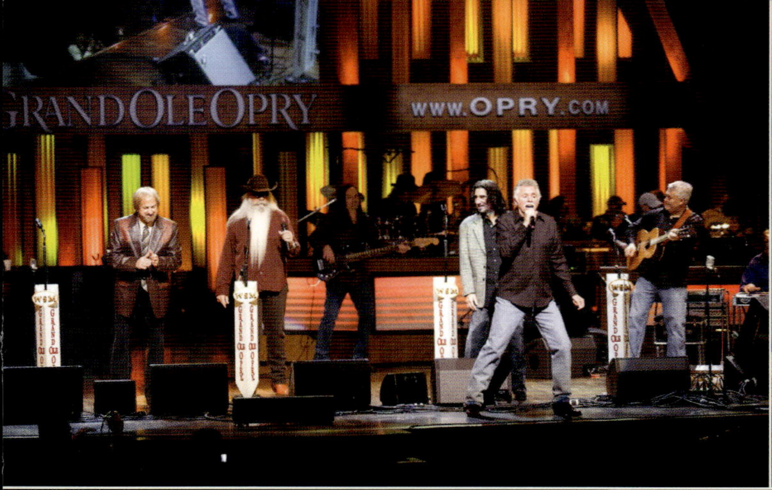
GRAND OLE OPRY
www.OPRY.com

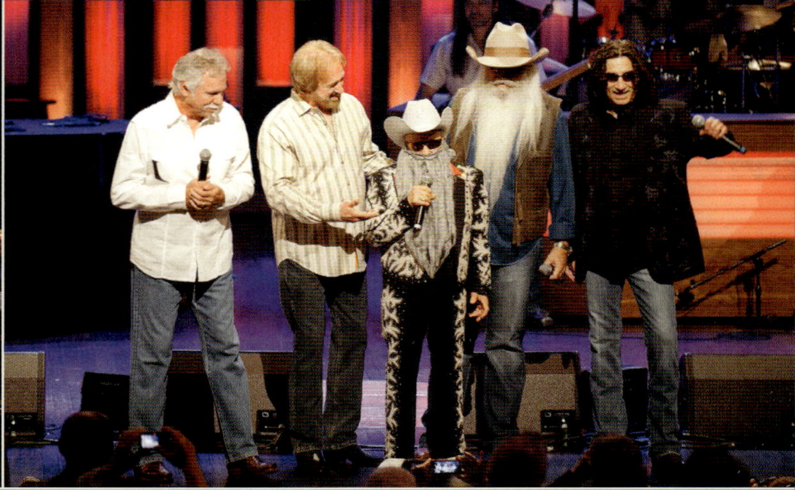

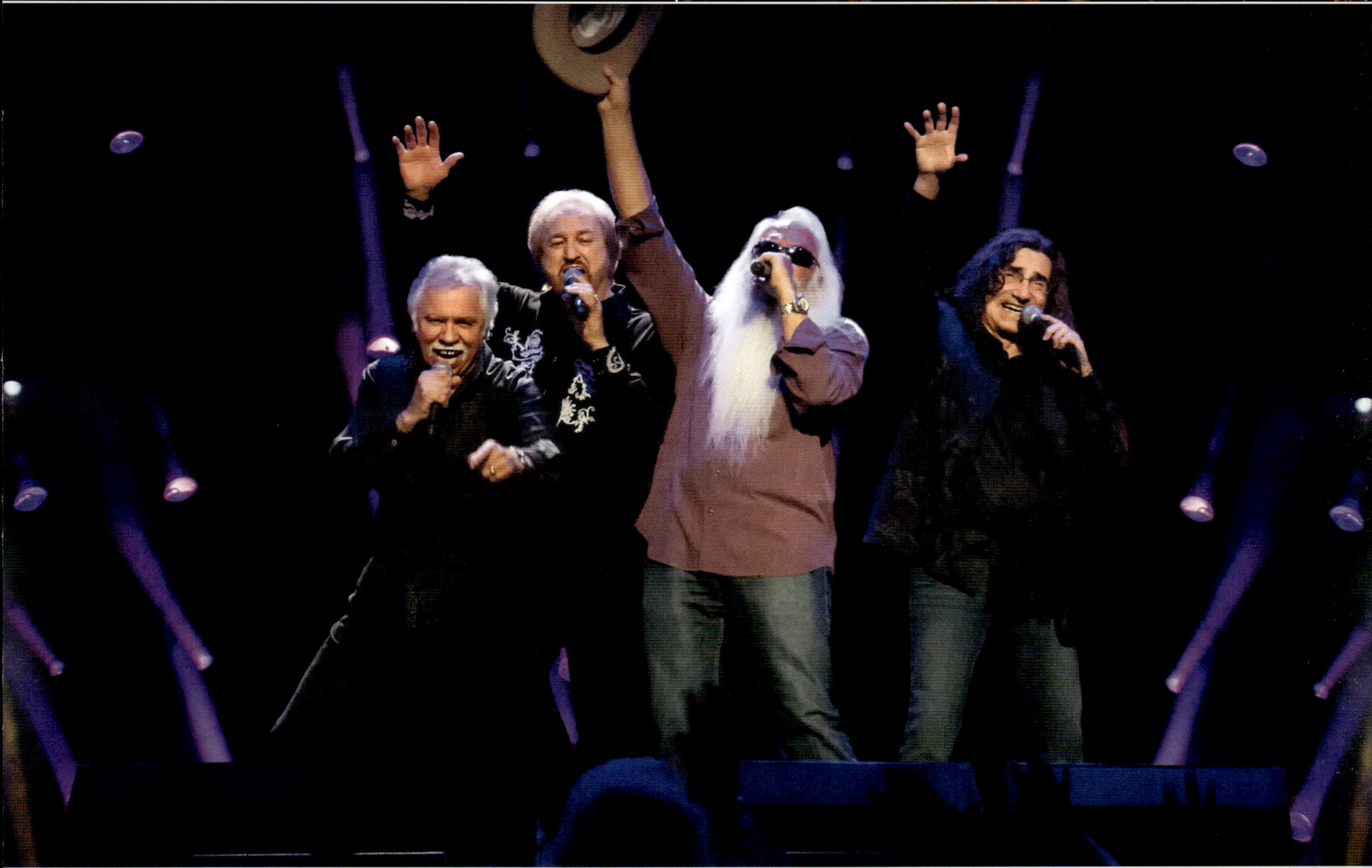

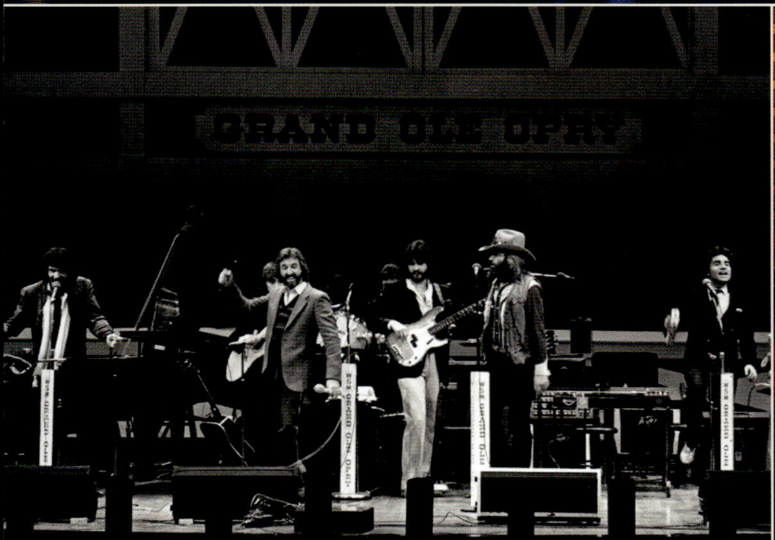

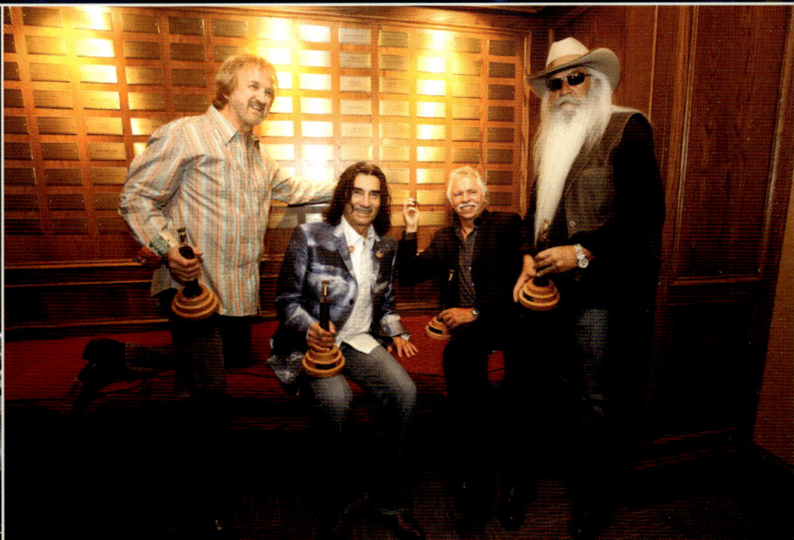

OLD CROW MEDICINE SHOW
MEMBER SINCE 2013

Some of the award-winning group Old Crow Medicine Show's first performances in Nashville were on the sidewalks outside the Opry House in summer 2000, playing for fans entering and exiting Opry performances. The band graduated to the Opry stage for its official Opry debut on Jan. 13, 2001 and quickly became a fan favorite during dozens of Opry performances that followed. Marty Stuart invited the group to join the Opry on Aug. 16, 2013 in Cleveland, Ohio.

When the band officially became part of the Opry family a month later, it wasn't lost on the band or on the Grand Ole Opry itself that both entities were quite poetically coming full circle. Old Crow had officially graduated from the Opry Plaza it had played week after week all those years earlier to center stage. The Opry, meanwhile, was adding to its ranks, nearly nine decades into its life, a band with a sound much like groups such as Roy Acuff and his Smoky Mountain Boys from the show's very early days.

Old Crow Medicine Show got its start busking on street corners in New York state and through Canada, winning audiences along the way with its boundless energy and spirit. The band members eventually found themselves in Boone, North Carolina where they caught the attention of legendary folk icon Doc Watson, who invited them to play at his Merlefest, helping to launch the band's career. Shortly afterward, the band relocated to Nashville and began its fateful residency on the Opry Plaza.

KETCH SECOR
Birthplace: Denville, New Jersey
Birth Date: May 14

CRITTER FUQUA
Birthplace: Austin, Texas
Birth Date: March 16

MORGAN JAHNIG
Birthplace: Chattanooga, Tennessee
Birth Date: November 29

KEVIN HAYES
Birthplace: Malden, Massachusetts
Birth Date: December 27

CHANCE MCCOY
Birthplace: Washington, DC
Birth Date: May 1

CORY YOUNTS
Birthplace: Nashville, Tennessee
Birth Date: September 3, 1979

GILL LANDRY
Birthplace: Lake Charles, Louisiana
Birth Date: December 10, 1975

OPRY INDUCTION: September 17, 2013

"WE THE OLD CROWS ARE JUST SO PROUD TO BE ENTRUSTED TO CARRY ON THE TRADITIONS OF THE GRAND OLE OPRY'S GOOD-NATURED RIOT."

More than a decade later, the band has toured the world, sold hundreds of thousand of albums, and performed at renowned festivals like Bonnaroo, Coachella, and The Hardly Strictly Bluegrass Festival.

Speaking on behalf of the group on its induction evening, Ketch Secor related that years ago members of the band asked themselves if they'd ever make it big in TV. Secor recalled having said, "I don't know about TV, but we might make something of ourselves on radio." Fast forwarding to the present, Secor concluded, "We're standing out here on the most beloved broadcast anywhere on earth. I think we made it big on radio!"

CLOCKWISE FROM TOP LEFT:
1. June 10, 2000
2. Affixing Old Crow's Member Gallery plaque, September 17, 2013
3. --
4. Marty Stuart invites Old Crow to join the Opry in Cleveland, Ohio; August 16, 2013.
5. February 19, 2014

OPRY FAMILY MEMBERS

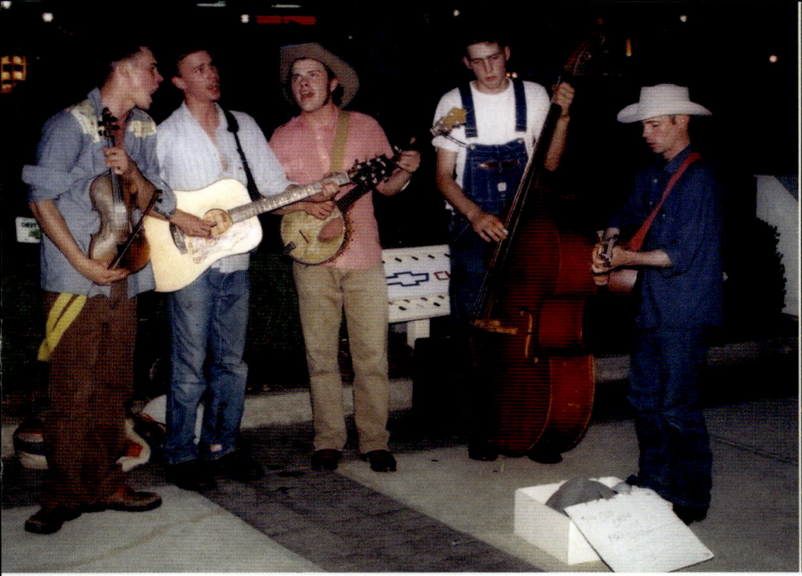

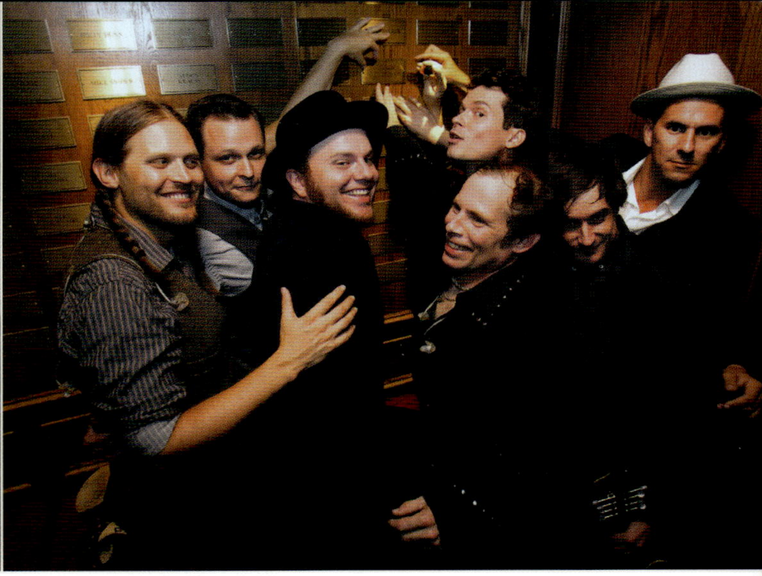

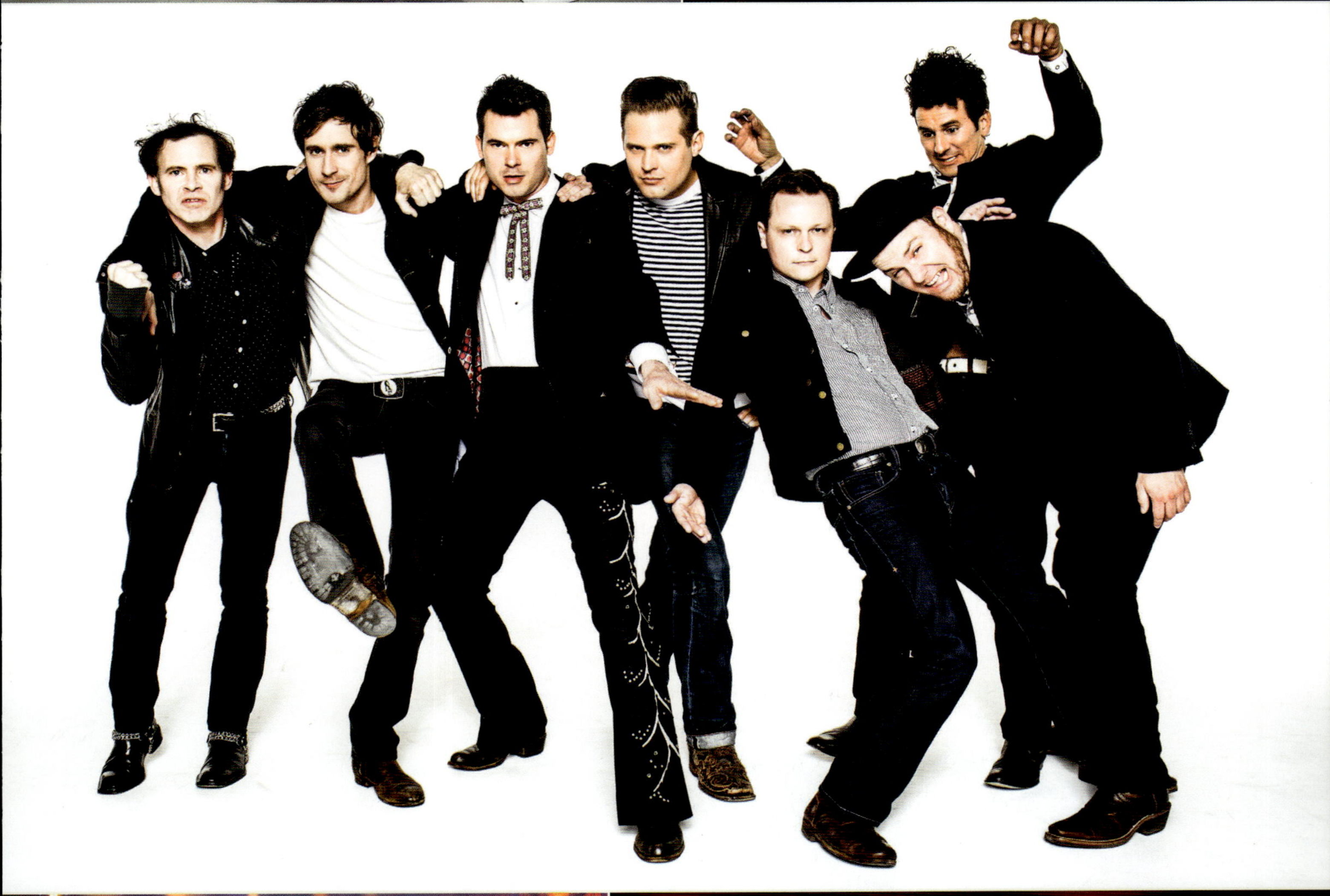

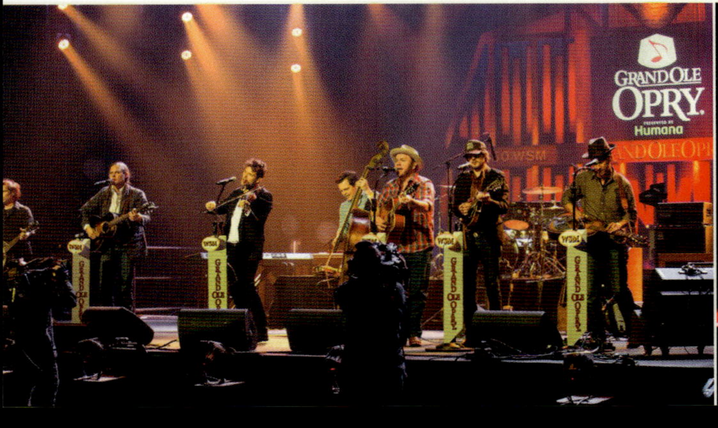
GRAND OLE OPRY
Humana

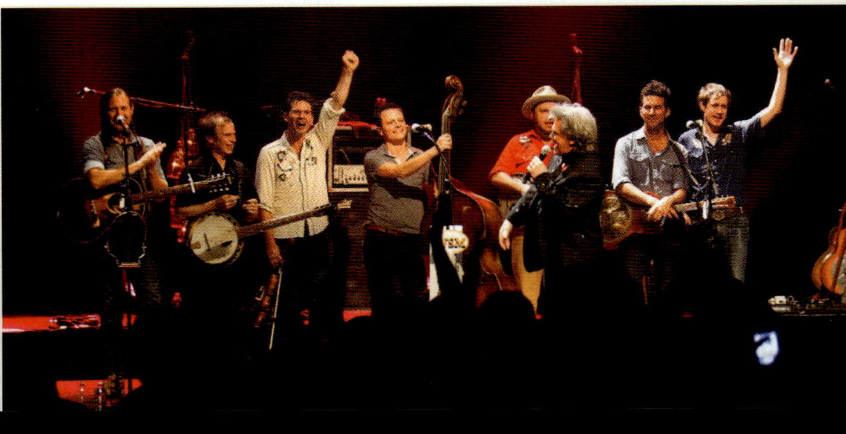

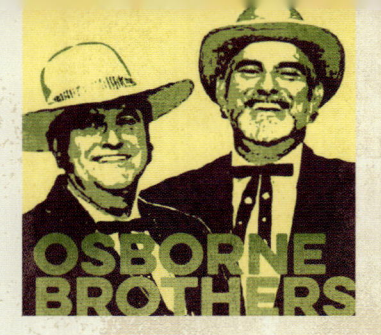

THE OSBORNE BROTHERS
MEMBER SINCE 1964

Born in the coal mining region of Southeastern Kentucky, Bobby and Sonny Osborne grew up immersed in tunes like "Nine Pound Hammer" and "The Knoxville Girl," as well as other mining songs and folk ballads of the Appalachian Mountains. Because of a six-year age difference, they didn't start out working together professionally. Mandolinist Bobby worked with bluegrass greats including Jimmy Martin and the Stanley Brothers, while a teen-aged Sonny played banjo with the great Bill Monroe.

The brothers formed a duo in 1953 following Bobby's discharge from the U.S. Marine Corps. Based on a rich harmony blend that usually included a third singer and masterful, distinctive picking from both brothers, The Osborne Brothers' sound became one of the most distinctive and most imitated in bluegrass music. Their recording debut came in 1956 with tracks that continue to rank among the

BOBBY OSBORNE
Birthplace: Roark, Kentucky
Birth Date: December 7

SONNY OSBORNE
Birthplace: Roark, Kentucky
Birth Date: October 29

OPRY INDUCTION: August 8, 1964

Q: What is your most memorable "Opry Moment"?
A: My most memorable moment would have to be the night that Sonny and I were signed as members of the Grand Ole Opry on August 8th, 1964.

"SO IT'S JUST BEEN MY LIFE. BLUEGRASS MUSIC HAS BEEN MY LIFE."

classic examples of Osborne Brother style. It was on these recordings that they changed the customary arrangement of trio harmony parts in bluegrass. Their sound featured Bobby singing lead in a high tenor, with two harmony parts arranged below.

In 1963, The Osbornes signed with Decca Records and continued to make waves with adventuresome arrangements sometimes involving non-traditional instruments such as drums and electric guitar.

In addition to the brothers' beloved signature song "Rocky Top" (an official Tennessee state song), their other hit records include "Making Plans," "Up This Hill and Down," "Midnight Flyer," "Take Me Home, Country Roads," "Tennessee Hound Dog," and "Ruby." Plus, the Osbornes haven't limited themselves to just one state song. Their "Kentucky" is an official song of their home state.

The brothers headed for the White House to perform for President Richard Nixon in 1973 then back to the bluegrass state in 1994 for what is regarded as the highest honor in bluegrass, induction into the International Bluegrass Music Association's Hall of Honor. Though still a proud Opry member, Sonny retired from performing in 2005 while Bobby continues to record and perform with his band, the Rocky Top X-Press.

CLOCKWISE FROM TOP LEFT:
1. Osborne Brothers with Dottie West & Ott Devine August 8, 1964
2. Bobby Osborne August 11, 2007
3. October 19, 2001
4. 43rd Opry Anniversary
5. Circa 2010

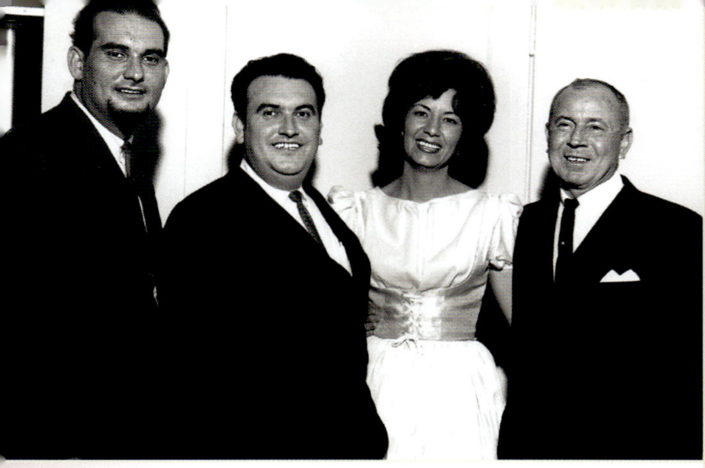

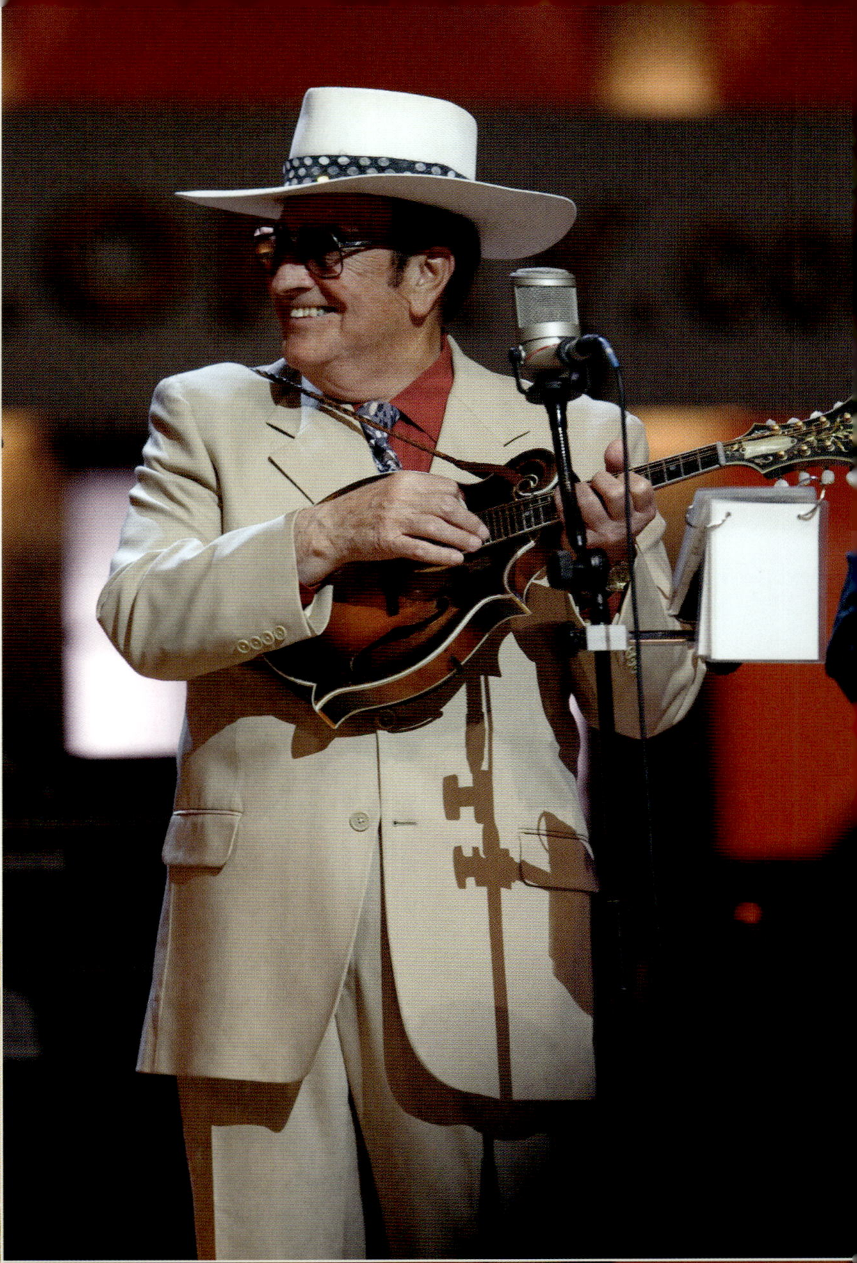

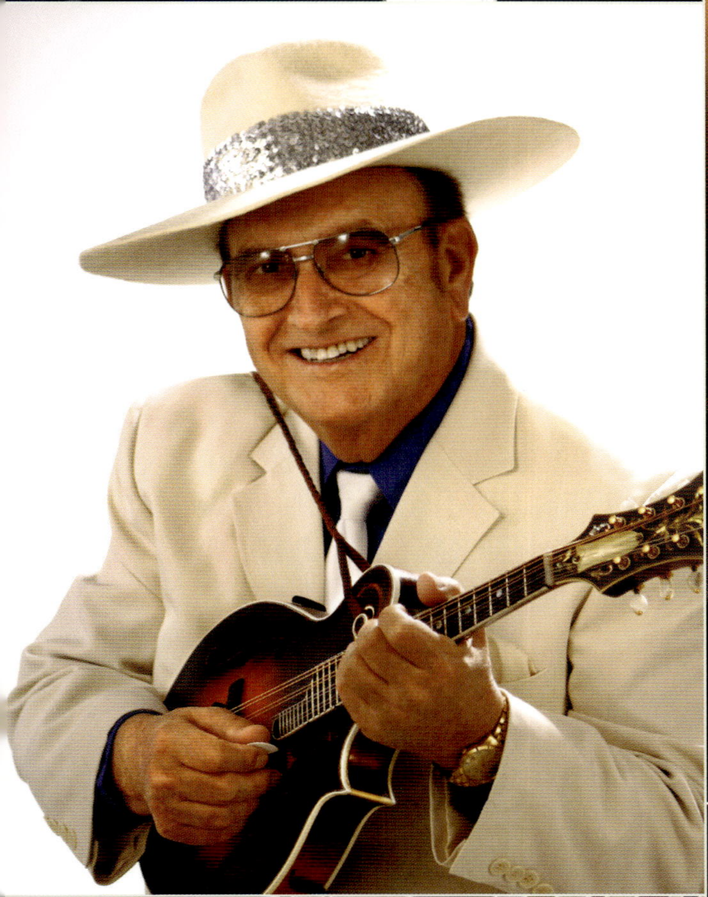

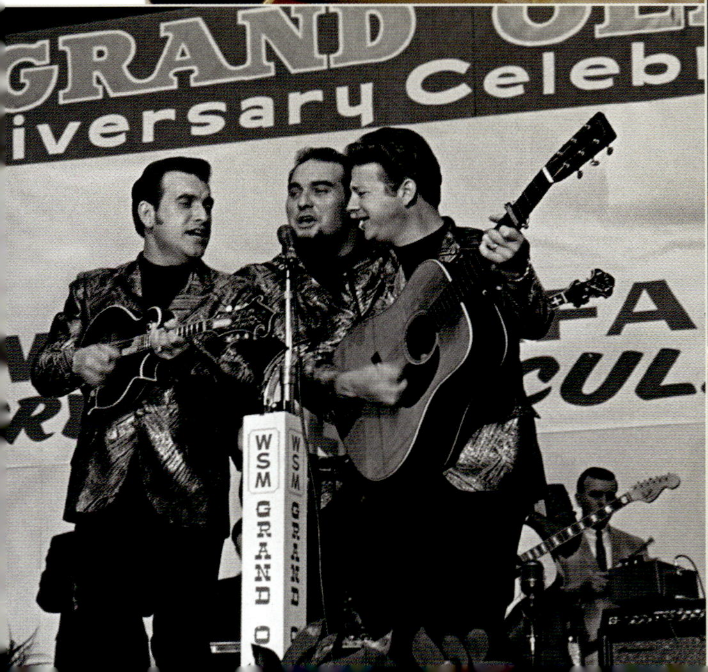

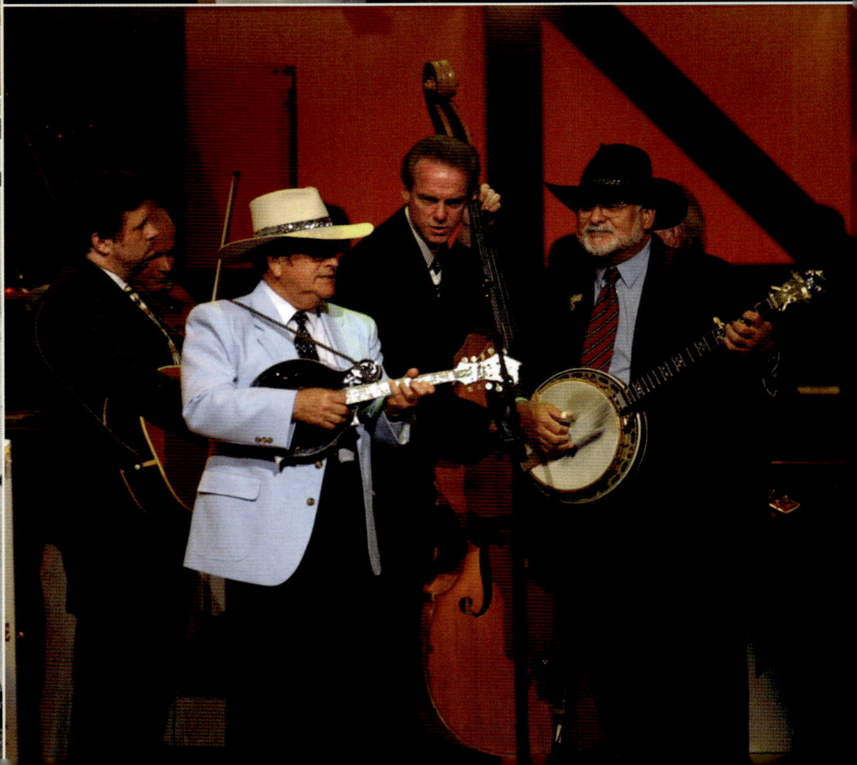

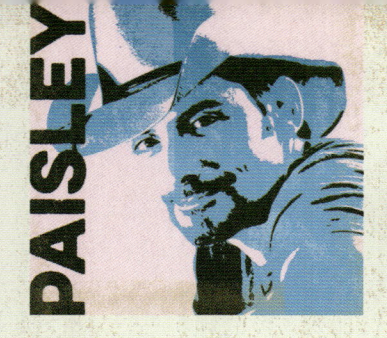

BRAD PAISLEY
MEMBER SINCE 2001

When Brad Paisley was inducted into the Opry in 2001, George Jones wrote a letter that was read to the crowd. "I am counting on you to carry on the tradition," George wrote, "and make folks sit up and listen to what good country music should sound like." It doesn't seem to matter how many modern elements Brad brings to his music — between his rock-influenced guitar-shredding skills, state-of-the-art touring visuals and topical songs like "Online" and "Welcome to the Future" — there's something about his attitude that also speaks to tradition.

"You don't last long here," Brad has said of the Opry, "if you're anything other than humble and down-to-earth." Those adjectives fit Brad to a tee, even though he's sold millions of albums and seems incapable of releasing a single that doesn't leave an indelible mark.

BIRTHPLACE: Glen Dale, West Virginia
BIRTH DATE: October 28
OPRY INDUCTION: February 17, 2001

DID YOU KNOW? Brad Paisley had opened shows for the likes of Ricky Skaggs and George Jones by age 13.

> "PILGRIMS TRAVEL TO JERUSALEM TO SEE THE HOLY LAND, AND THE FOUNDATIONS OF THEIR FAITH. PEOPLE GO TO WASHINGTON, D.C., TO SEE THE WORKINGS OF GOVERNMENT, AND THE FOUNDATION OF OUR COUNTRY. AND FANS FLOCK TO NASHVILLE TO SEE THE FOUNDATION OF COUNTRY MUSIC, THE GRAND OLE OPRY."

The small-town West Virginia native became known as a teenager on Wheeling's celebrated weekly *Jamboree USA* show. A post-collegiate songwriting deal quickly led to a record deal, and his second single, "He Didn't Have To Be," became his first No. 1 in 1999. He's won male vocalist awards multiple times from both the Academy of Country Music and the Country Music Association, for which he has also served as multiple year co-host . He's also a winner in his personal life, married to actress Kimberly Williams-Paisley, who, along with their two sons, inspires plenty of songs, be they humorous, romantic, or both.

CLOCKWISE FROM TOP LEFT:
1. May 3, 2011
2. Being invited to join the Opry by Jimmy Dickens, Bill Anderson, and Jeannie Seely
3. With Steve Martin
4. With Carrie Underwood
5. Making a surprise appearance to honor George Jones the day the legendary artist passed away

WSM
GRAND OLE OPRY
GRAND OLE OPRY

WSM
GRAND OLE OPRY
GRAND OLE OPRY

WSM
GRAND OLE OPRY
www.OPRY.com

WSM
GRAND OLE OPRY
WSM
GRAND OLE OPRY

DOLLY PARTON
MEMBER SINCE 1969

"It was always my dream to be on the Opry," Dolly Parton says. As an early starter, she didn't have to wait long. "I actually got to sing on the Grand Ole Opry when I was about 10 years old. I became a member in the late '60s. They call it the 'Mother Church,' because the old Ryman was a church, but it's sacred to me, wherever it goes — the church of my heart. For me, the Opry is like the song 'New York, New York' — if you can make it there, you can make it anywhere."

And Dolly has made it everywhere. As a worldwide icon, famous for acting as well as music, she is arguably country music's greatest global ambassador. If she has sometimes unabashedly embraced show-biz glitz, somehow that never canceled out the backwoods authenticity that still characterizes her after five decades of stardom. "I've always

BIRTHPLACE: Locust Ridge, Tennessee
BIRTH DATE: January 19
OPRY INDUCTION: January 4, 1969

DID YOU KNOW? Dolly Parton once lost a Dolly Parton look-alike contest.

> "IT MEANS A LOT TO ME TO KNOW THAT I HAVE THE ABILITY TO MAKE PEOPLE HAPPY, AND THAT PEOPLE COUNT ON IT. BY MAKING THEM HAPPY, I MAKE MYSELF HAPPY, SO IT'S AN EVEN TRADE."

thought that a certain bit of what magic I may have had in the minds of people was based on the fact that I look completely artificial," Dolly says. "But I am completely real as a human being. I'm a country girl, grew up poor and with nothing, always wanting to have things and be things. Even though my look may be phony, my heart ain't."

Dolly grew up in the foothills of the Great Smoky Mountains, near where her Dollywood theme park now attracts millions of tourists. She came to fame singing with Porter Wagoner in a partnership that lasted from 1967-74. At the same time, as a solo artist she was recording autobiographical classics including "Coat of Many Colors" ("Being made fun of as a younger child, I knew that feeling," she says) as well as bold anthems of female pride, love, and empowerment including "Just Because I'm a Woman," "Jolene," and one of the most successful songs in music history, "I Will Always Love You."

Later chart successes such as "Islands in the Stream" and "9 to 5" (for which Dolly was nominated for an Academy Award) hit both pop and country radio as the icon became one of the most recognized entertainers of all time. Dolly's lasting impact on the country genre was recognized with her 1999 election to the Country Music Hall of Fame.

CLOCKWISE FROM TOP LEFT:
1. July 2, 2002
2. Opry induction
3. --
4. September 24, 2011
5. --

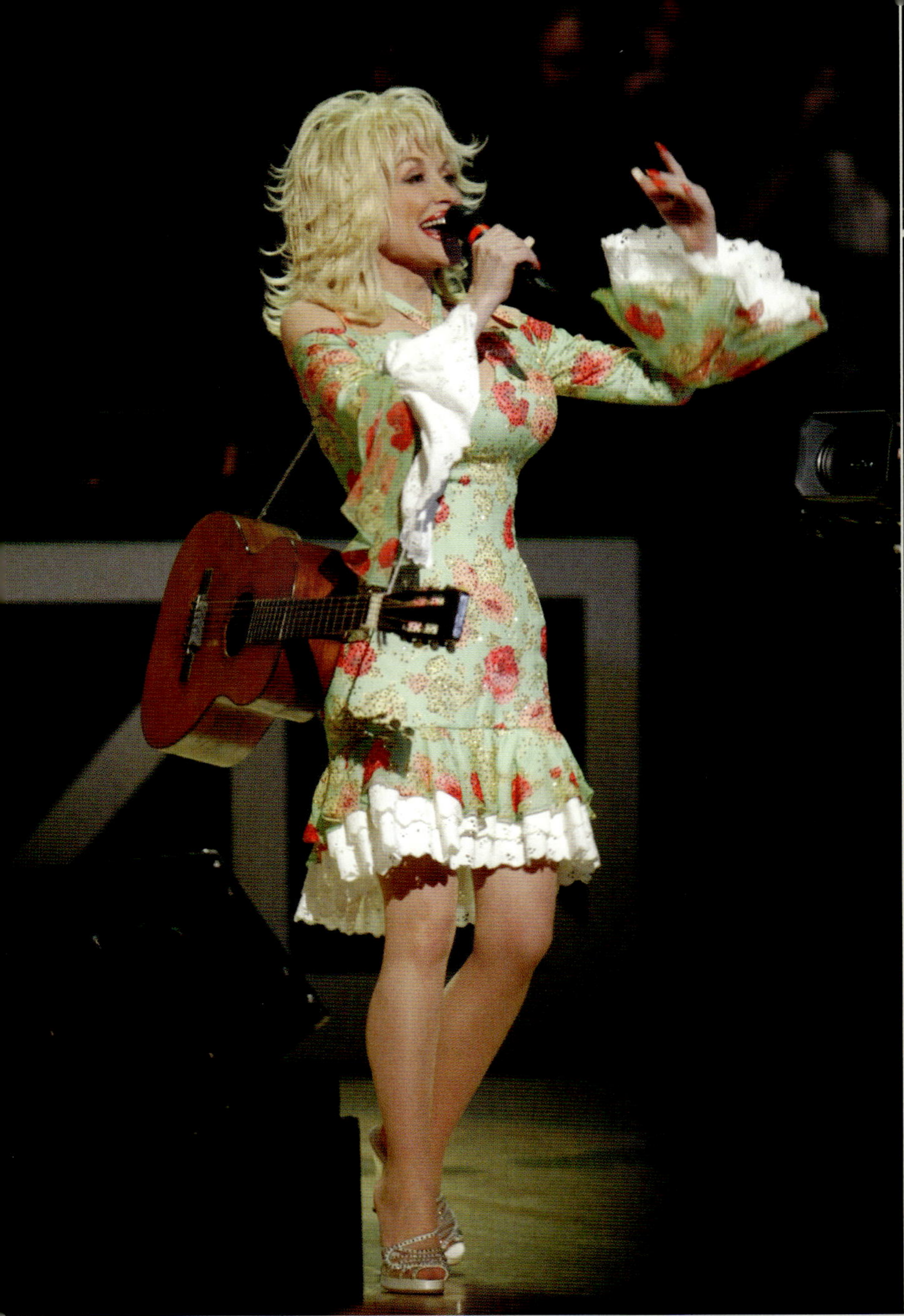

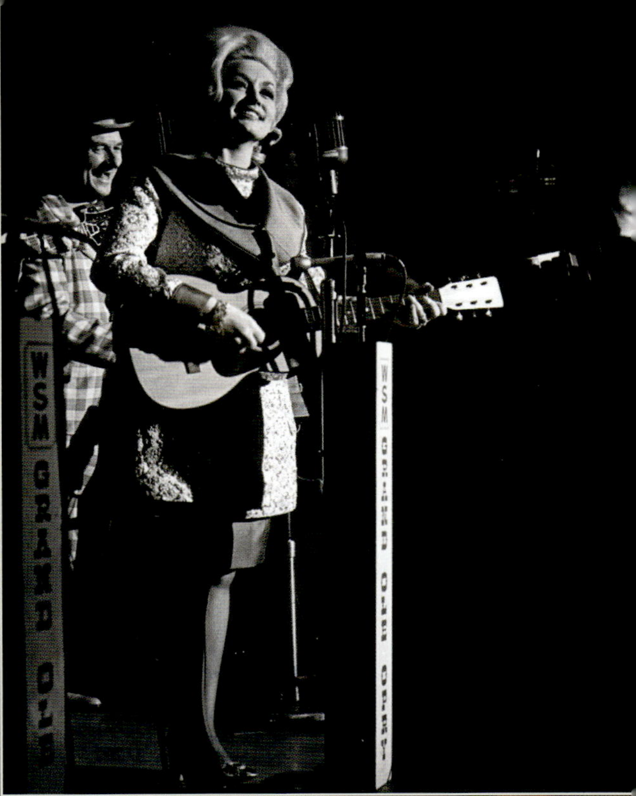
WSM GRAND OLE OPRY

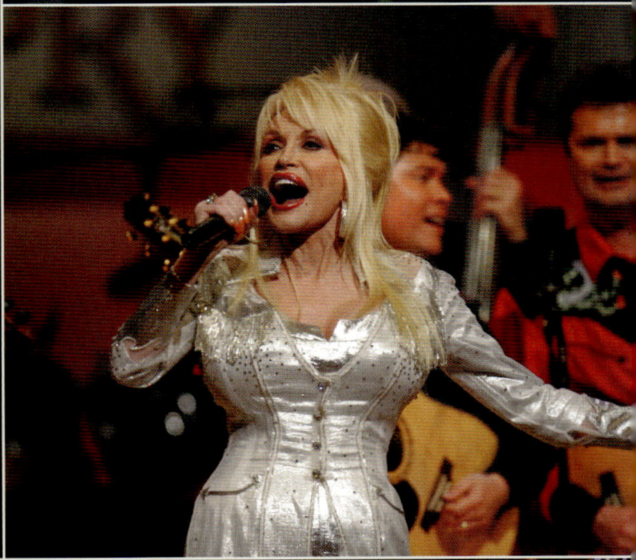

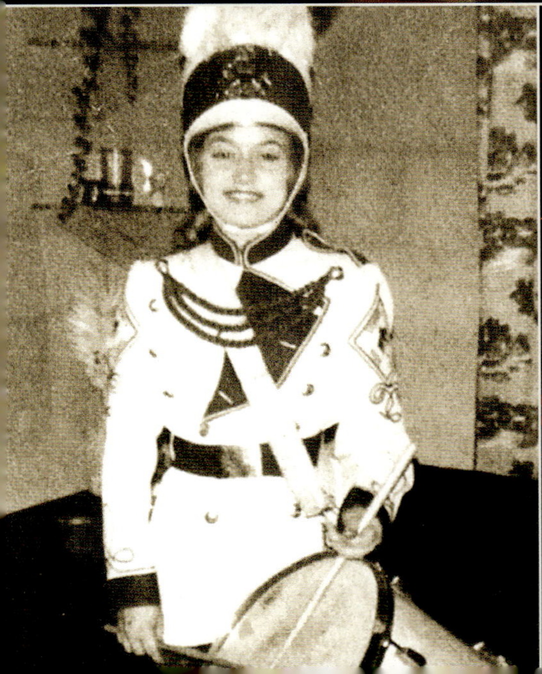

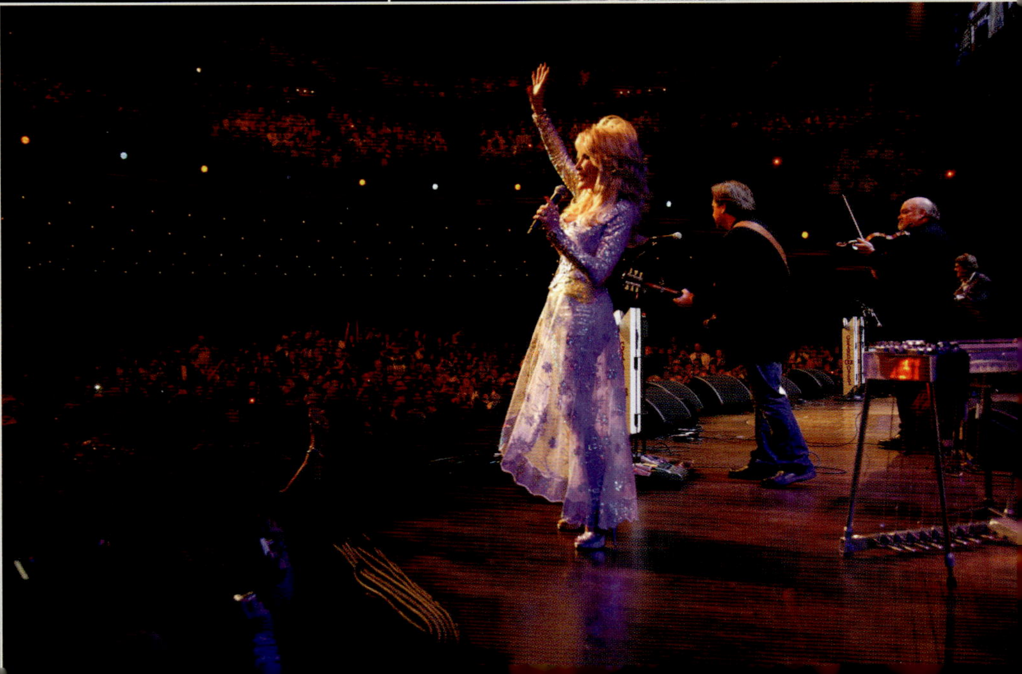

CARLY PEARCE
MEMBER SINCE 2021

Carly Pearce had her sights set on the Grand Ole Opry from the start.

"When I was a little girl, I dreamt of country music and I dreamt of singing on this stage," she said on her induction night.

She left high school and her home in Kentucky at age 16 to sing at Dollywood. Less than a decade later, in 2015, she made her Opry debut. Since, she has charted three No. 1 songs, including her platinum debut "Every Little Thing," and quickly began raking in industry awards from the Academy of Country Music, CMT, and the Country Music Association. With 2021's critic and fan-lauded 29: Written In Stone, Carly's truth fully connected. She was named CMA Female Vocalist of the Year and in 2022, ACM Female Artist of the Year.

BIRTHPLACE: Taylor Mill, Kentucky
BIRTH DATE: April 24
OPRY INDUCTION: August 3, 2021

DEFINITIVE TRACKLIST:
"Never Wanted To Be That Girl"
"What He Didn't Do"
"I Hope You're Happy Now"
"Next Girl"
"Every Little Thing"

> "GRAND OLE OPRY, THIS ISN'T JUST ANOTHER FEATHER IN MY CAP, THIS ISN'T ANOTHER ACCOLADE, THIS ISN'T ANOTHER THING TO ADD TO MY WALL. THIS IS A PROMISE TO ALL OF YOU AND TO THIS ORGANIZATION THAT I WILL DO MY DUE DILIGENCE AS A GRAND OLE OPRY MEMBER, THAT I WILL MAKE SURE THE CIRCLE IS NEVER UNBROKEN."

"A lot of other things about this career can fade," Carly said. "But what you can always go to sleep at night knowing, is that you're a part of this family and nobody can ever take that away from you."

In one of the biggest full-circle moments, Dolly Parton was the one to invite Carly to join the Opry family after more than 85 appearances.

"I feel like I'm using my pain for purpose and watching my music affect people and also having a platform that allows me to show people it's ok to go through things that are real in life," Carly said. "And I feel like the Opry has always allowed me to be real and to be me and they took a chance on a 25-year-old Airbnb cleaner and I'll never forget that."

CLOCKWISE FROM TOP LEFT:
1. Carly performs on the Grand Ole Opry stage on May 22, 2021.
2. Carly performs on the Grand Ole Opry stage on February 25, 2022.
3. Opry members Trisha Yearwood and Jeannie Seely join Carly on stage during her induction on August 3, 2021.
4. Carly on her induction night on August 3, 2021.
5. Carly performs with Matthew West on the Grand Ole Opry on April 10, 2021.

650 WSM
WSM

WSM
GRAND OLE OPRY

GRAND OL
WSM
GRAND OLE OPRY
GRAND OLE OPRY

STU PHILLIPS

MEMBER SINCE 1967

BIRTHPLACE: Montreal, Quebec, Canada
BIRTH DATE: January 19
OPRY INDUCTION: June 1, 1967

Montreal native Stu Phillips grew up in Calgary, Alberta, in the foothills of the Canadian Rockies, where he wrote many of his early songs. He grew up listening to the Grand Ole Opry on a small crystal radio set and fell in love with the show and country music in general.

Stu formed his own band at an early age, establishing a following at local events as well as working part-time for a radio station. His position as a radio announcer led to other jobs, including producer, engineer, and disc jockey.

On the air, Stu was host to a variety of shows in Canada, including *Stu for Breakfast*, *Town and Country*, and *Cowtown Jamboree*. From radio, Stu moved to television, first as host of *The Outrider*, then hosted *Red River Jamboree*, a major Saturday night show on the CBC network.

"WHENEVER I TRAVEL OVERSEAS, HOME IS TENNESSEE, WHERE I LIVE."

In addition to his TV work, Stu began to enjoy recording success with his *Echoes of the Canadian Foothills* album. After four more years with the CBC, Stu set his sights on Music City, moving to Nashville in 1965.

He started working for a local morning TV show and that year signed with RCA Records. With Chet Atkins producing, Stu began hitting the country charts with such tunes as "Bracero," "The Great El Tigre," "Vin Rose," and "Juanita Jones."

He joined the Opry in 1967 after making some 20 guest appearances. Stu has toured extensively in Asia, the Middle East, and Africa, where his records received the equivalent of gold records. In 1993, Germany's Bear Family Records released a CD featuring 35 songs from his early Canadian albums. That same year, Stu was inducted into the Canadian Country Music Hall of Fame.

A little more than 31 years after joining the Grand Ole Opry, Stu Phillips became an American citizen. Having lived in the U.S. longer than in his native Canada, Stu celebrated American citizenship with his wife, Aldona, on the Opry stage during the Fourth of July weekend in 1998.

CLOCKWISE FROM TOP LEFT:
1. 42nd Opry Anniversary, 1967
2. Circa 1990s
3. With Patti Page
4. With trumpeter Doc Severinsen and David "Stringbean" Akeman.
5. --

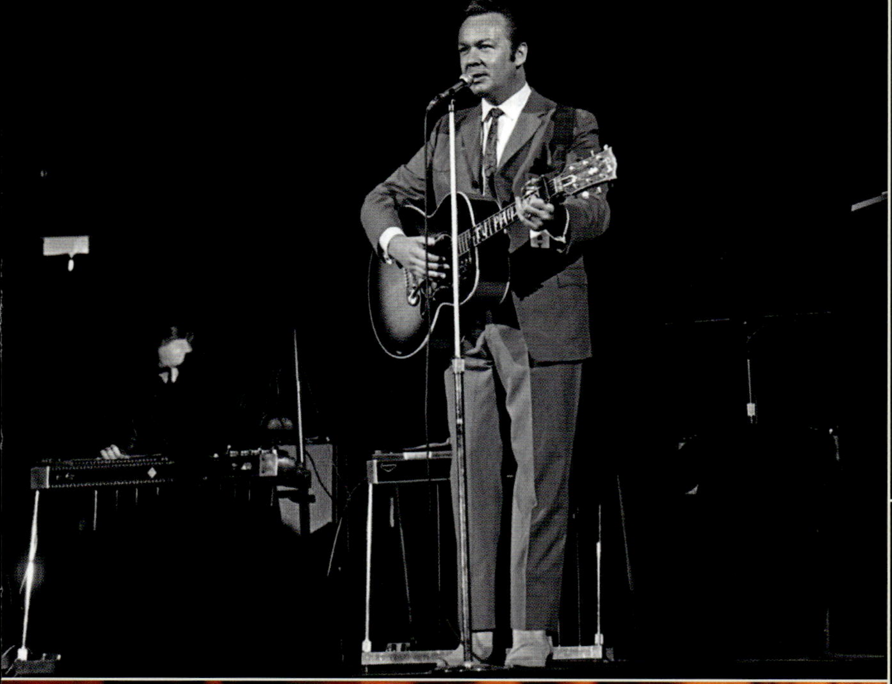

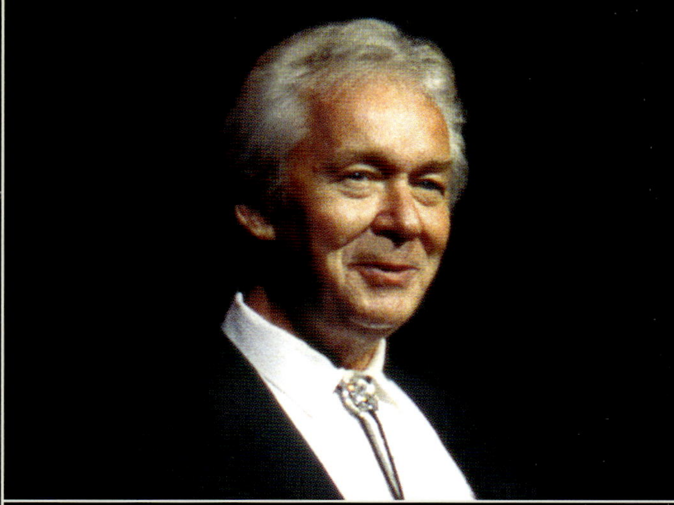

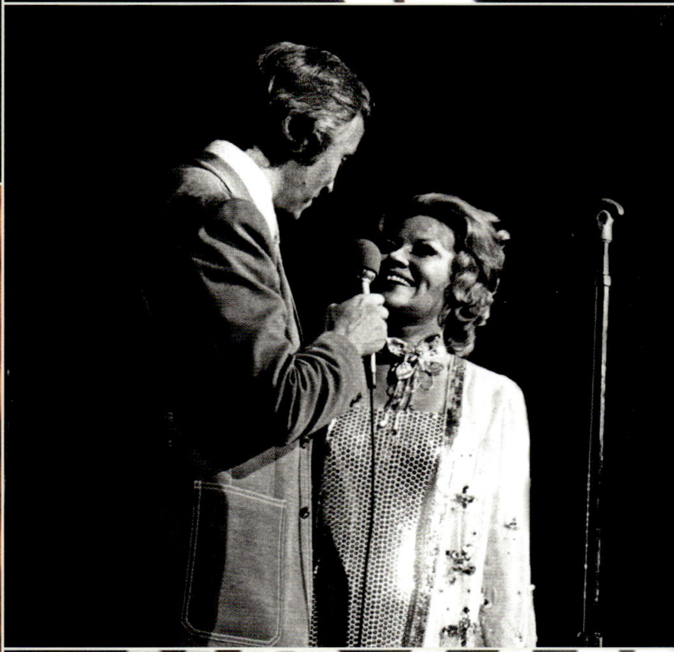

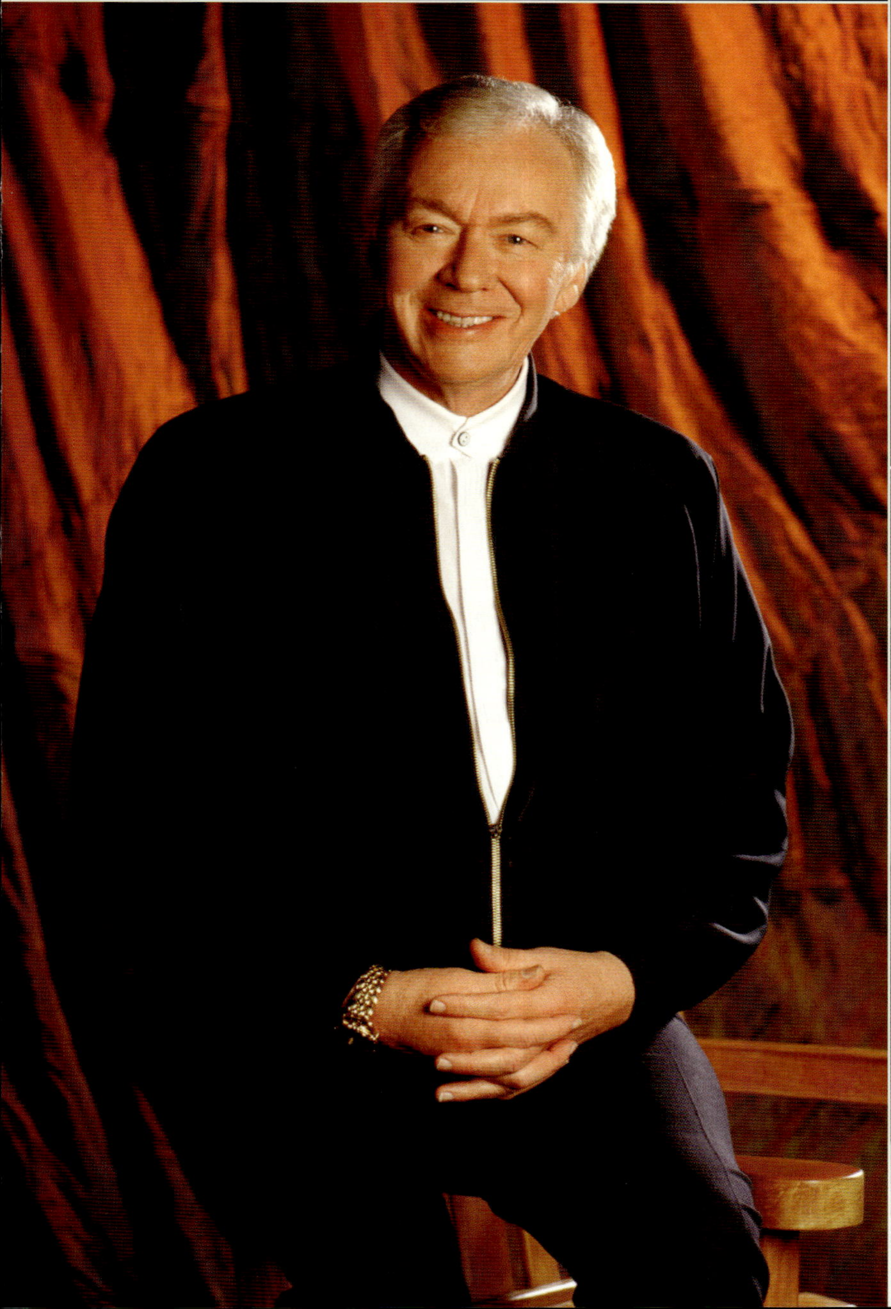

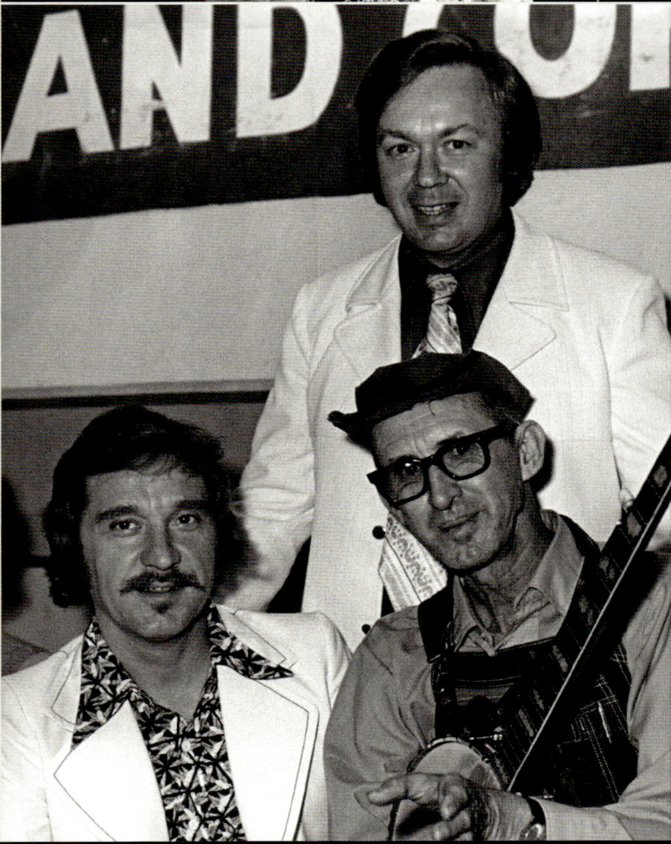
AND

RAY PILLOW
MEMBER SINCE 1966

Ray Pillow recalls it was his Uncle Roger who introduced him to music and was responsible for his first public performance. "I sort of got talked into substituting for a sick member of my uncle's band one night," Ray recalls. "When I walked out on stage to the microphone, I knew that was what I wanted to do for a lifetime! Music!"

Thirty-five years after joining the Opry, Ray got to introduce his 87-year-old uncle to the Opry stage. "I told the people that my uncle was the person that believed in me and wanted me to come to Nashville. I handed him a guitar and said Uncle Roger, you and I are going to sing." He brought the house down and got a standing ovation.

Ray came to Nashville in 1961 as a regional winner in the Pet Milk Talent Contest. He came in second in the national finals, and his performance landed him a guest spot on the Opry. That stoked his desire even more for a country music career. He soon released his first two singles, "Take Your Hands Off My Heart" and "Thank You Ma'am." In 1965 Capitol Records released his first album *Presenting Ray Pillow* and by late 1966 he was a star. That was the year he teamed with Opry star Jean Shepard on a pair of hits, the Top 10 "I'll Take the Dog" and "Mr. Do-It-Yourself." Between those two singles he became an official Opry member.

In addition to his own performing career, Ray has helped shape the professional paths of others including Lee Greenwood. His publishing company published many of Lee's hits including the 1985 Country Music Association Song of the Year "God Bless the USA." Ray is well known on Music Row as a publisher who can match the right artist with the right song and recording company.

In 1994 the state of Virginia added him to its Country Music Hall of Fame.

BIRTHPLACE: Lynchburg, Virginia
BIRTH DATE: July 4
OPRY INDUCTION: April 30, 1966

> "I'M EXCITED STILL WHEN I WALK OUT ON THAT STAGE."

CLOCKWISE FROM TOP LEFT:
1. Circa 2010
2. 43rd Opry Anniversary, 1968
3. Backstage with Merle Travis
4. Backstage with Robert Duvall
5. 52nd Opry Anniversary, 1977
6. Ray's Uncle Roger and members of Ray's early group the Western Stardusters. (l-r) Uncle Roger, Curly Garner, Curtis Wooten, and Jack Williams joined the Opry member (center) to celebrate his induction into the Virginia Country Music Hall of Fame.

OPRY FAMILY MEMBERS

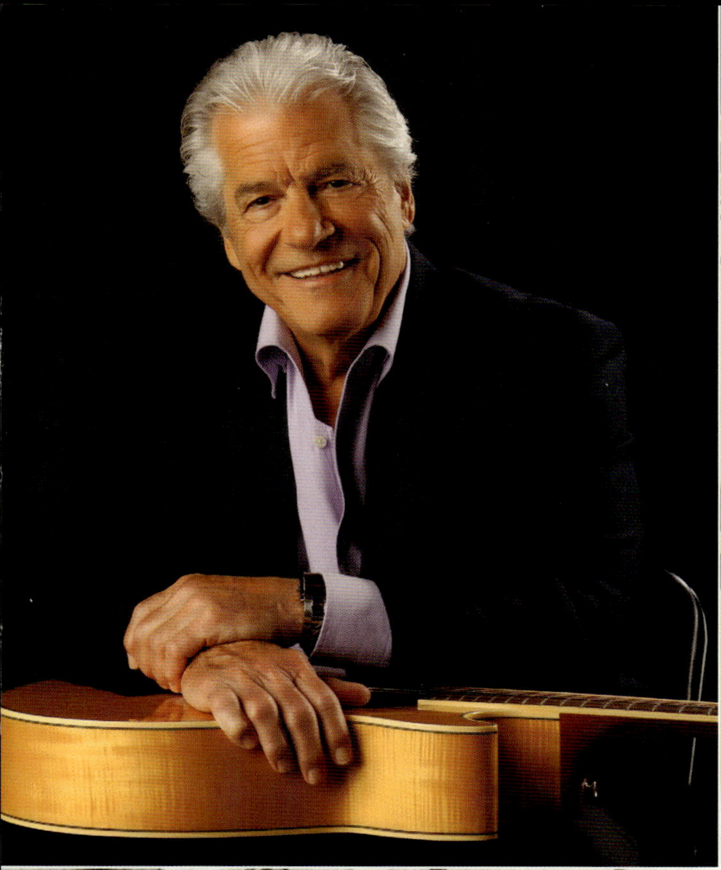

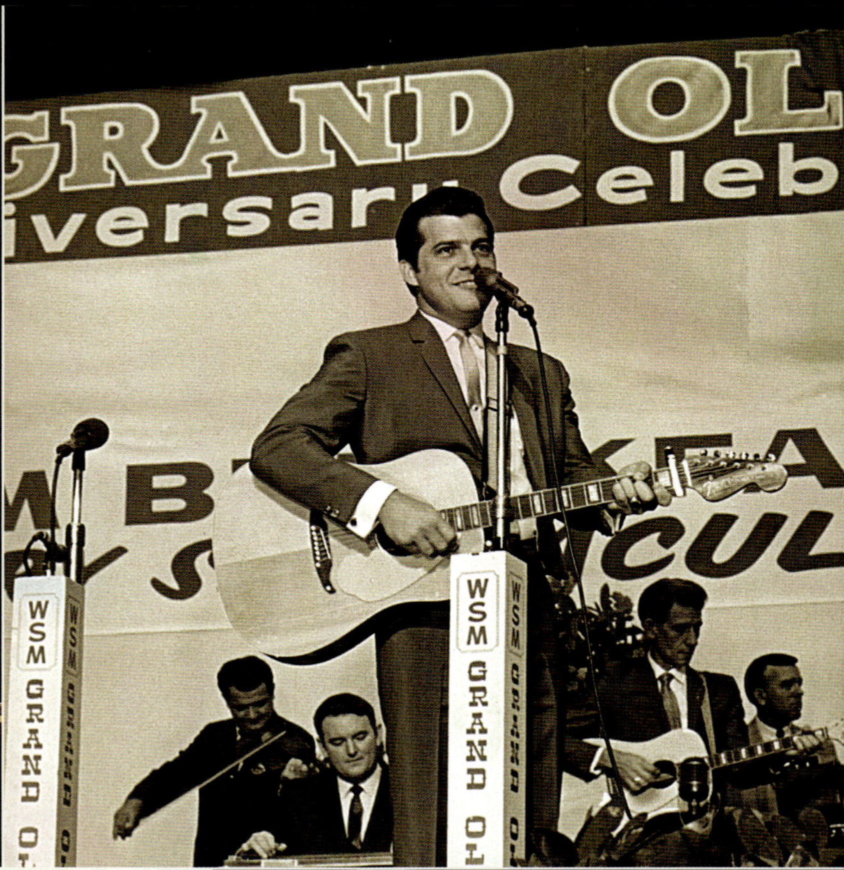
GRAND OL
iversary Celeb
WSM GRAND OL
WSM GRAND

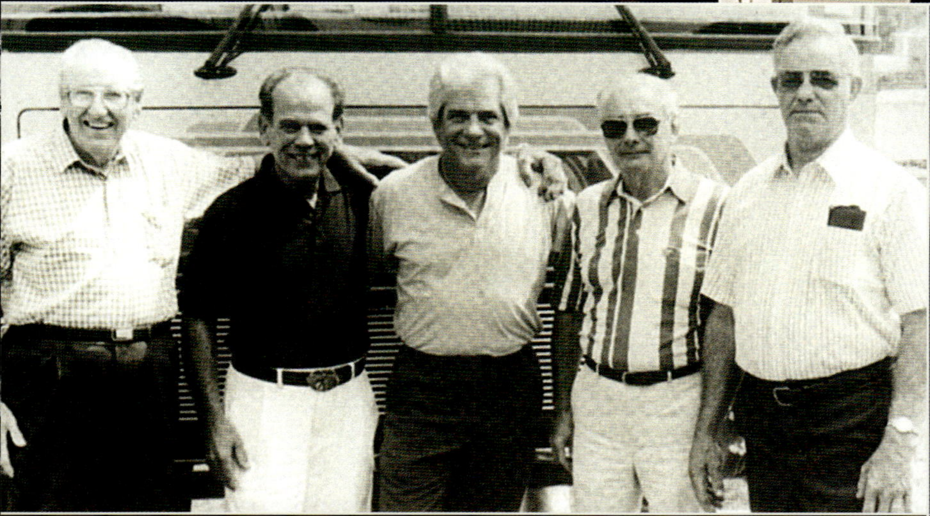

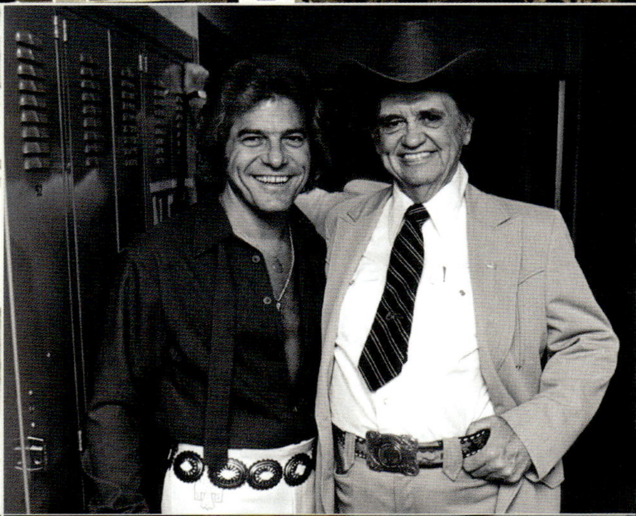

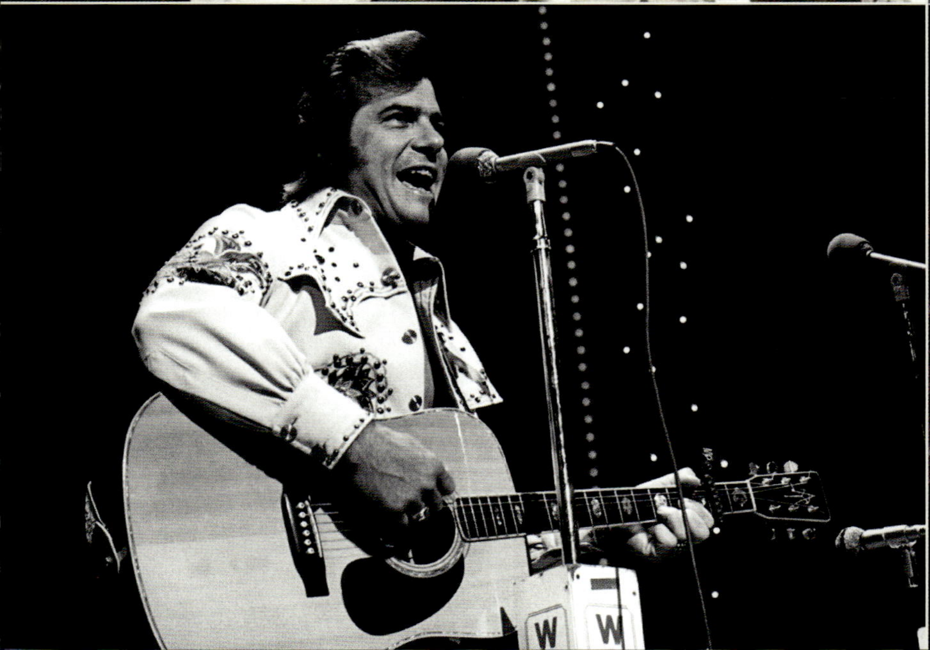

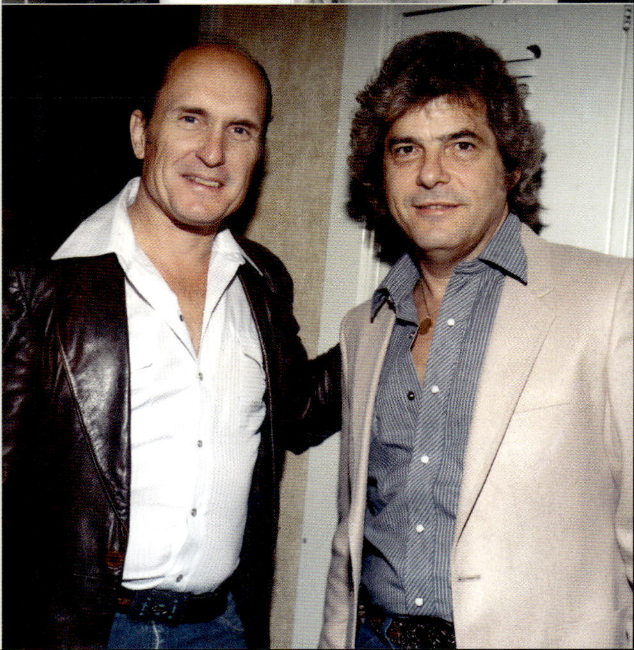

JEANNE PRUETT
MEMBER SINCE 1973

While Jeanne Pruett has enjoyed worldwide success with dozens of singles, the three-week chart-topper "Satin Sheets" earned her 1973 Song, Single, and Album of the Year nominations from the Country Music Association and continues to define her career. One of 10 children born to a full-time Alabama farmer and part-time cotton mill worker, Jeanne moved to Nashville in 1956.

Jeanne also worked as a songwriter for Marty Robbins Enterprises. Marty recorded several of Jeanne's songs, including the hits "Count Me Out" and "Love Me." Tammy Wynette, Conway Twitty and others also covered Jeanne's songs. "It is easier to be accepted in the music business by your peers as a performer after you have proven yourself as a writer," she says. "The acceptance of fans is another thing. You sell them after you have gone into the studio and come up with the best you have." She first won their acceptance in 1971 with the single "Hold to My Unchanging Love." Her own version of "Love Me" reached the Top 40 but those records just set the stage for what was to come.

"Satin Sheets" hit country radio in March 1973, aided by 1,600 pieces of pink satin fabric that Jeanne cut by hand and sent to radio programmers and music executives across the nation. The international hit topped the country charts that May. A few weeks later, Jeanne became an official Opry member — the last vocalist to join the show before it moved from the Ryman to the Grand Ole Opry House.

Jeanne's subsequent hits included "I'm Your Woman," "You Don't Need To Move a Mountain," and "Welcome to the Sunshine (Sweet Baby Jane)." In 1983 alone, she had three Top 10 hits: "Back to Back," "Temporarily Yours," and "It's Too Late."

BIRTHPLACE: Pell City, Alabama
BIRTH DATE: January 30
OPRY INDUCTION: July 21, 1973

> "I FEEL AS THOUGH I'VE STOOD SIDE BY SIDE WITH KINGS AND QUEENS OF THE GREATEST COUNTRY IN THE WORLD—THE WORLD OF COUNTRY MUSIC."

CLOCKWISE FROM TOP LEFT:
1. With Dolly Parton and Porter Wagoner on her Opry induction night
2. With Ricky Skaggs
3. Circa 1980s
4. With Bill Anderson
5. With Jeannie Seely

WSM GRAND
WSM GRAND

WSM GRAND OLE

GRAND OLE OPRY.

GRAND OLE OPRY

RASCAL FLATTS
MEMBER SINCE 2011

Rascal Flatts is made up of Gary LeVox and Jay DeMarcus—second cousins from Columbus, Ohio—and Joe Don Rooney, a Picher, Oklahoma native. The group began its musical journey at a local bar in Nashville's Printer's Alley.

After landing a record deal, the group recorded their self-titled debut album in 2000. "Prayin' for Daylight" became the group's first smash single. And so began a string of multi-platinum albums and monster singles. The band's second album, *Melt*, appeared in October 2002. By 2008, the group had amassed enough hits from multi-platinum albums to release Flatts' *Greatest Hits, Vol. 1* including favorites such as "Take Me There" and "Bless The Broken Road." Other top-selling albums and radio favorites have followed, including "Here Comes Goodbye," "Summer Nights," "Banjo," "Why Wait," "Easy," and "Rewind." Their current career accolades now boast more than 20 million albums and 25 million digital downloads sold, double digit No. 1 singles and millions of concert tickets sold.

With all the hits came millions of fans at live shows and awards to fill each group member's mantle, now totaling more than 40 awards. Among them, the seven wins as the Academy of Country

GARY LEVOX
Birthplace: Columbus, Ohio
Birth Date: July 10

JAY DEMARCUS
Birthplace: Columbus, Ohio
Birth Date: April 26

JOE DON ROONEY
Birthplace: Picher, Oklahoma
Birth Date: September 13

OPRY INDUCTION: October 8, 2011

Q: To what do you attribute the Opry's longevity over the past nine decades?
A: With the diversity in this genre, the Opry has kept up with the changes in our format and adapted and kept the music that we love in the forefront for all of us. Any tourist that comes to Music City will forever wanna go see where the legends and future legends have performed. "

"THE OPRY IS GROUND ZERO OF COUNTRY MUSIC FOR THE WORLD."

Music's Top Vocal Group award while the Country Music Association honored the group with its Horizon (Best New Artist) award in 2002 followed by six consecutive Vocal Group of the Year trophies.

Amid all their success, the guys in Rascal Flatts always made visits to the Grand Ole Opry. On September 27, 2011, the group received a coveted invitation to join the Opry family. Rascal Flatts' Opry dreams came true when the group was added to the Opry's member roster less that two weeks later on October 8.

CLOCKWISE FROM TOP LEFT:
1. At the Opry Member Gallery on the group's induction night, October 8, 2011
2. August 23, 2011
3. 2014
4. With Vince Gill and Jimmy Dickens on Opry induction night
5. Being invited to join Opry by Vince Gill, September 27, 2011

OPRY FAMILY MEMBERS

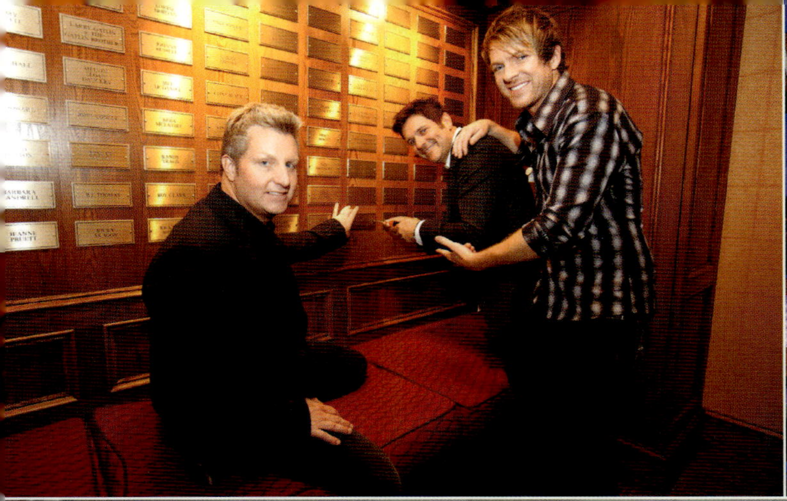

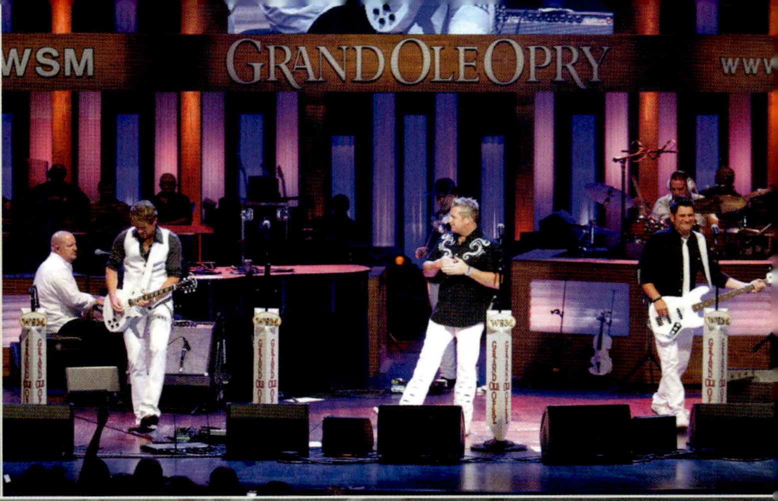
WSM
GRAND OLE OPRY

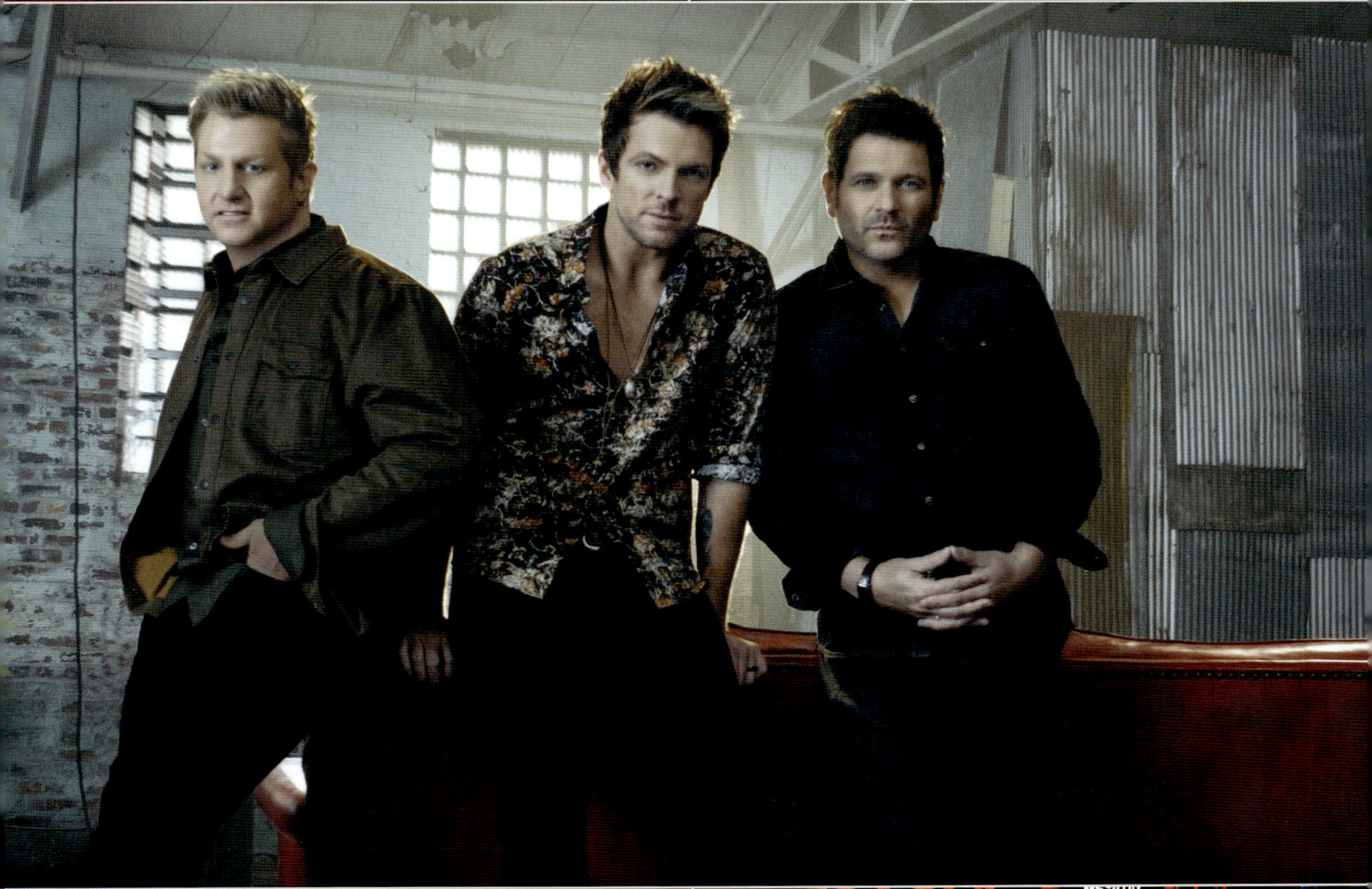

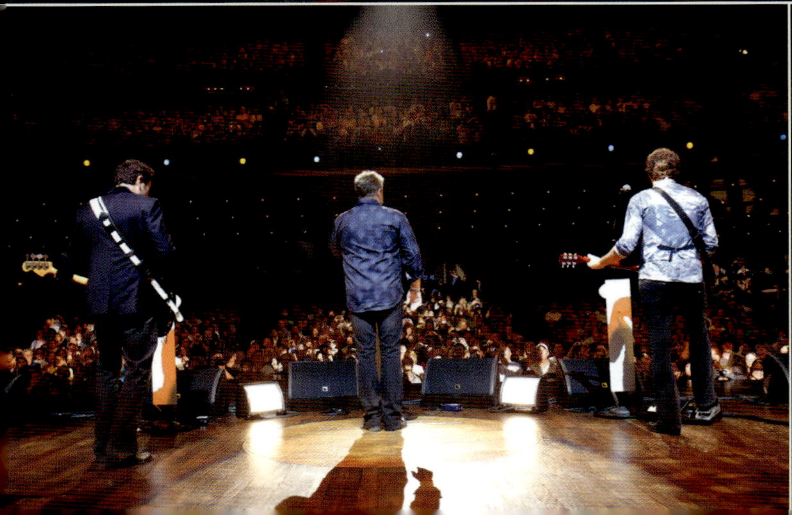

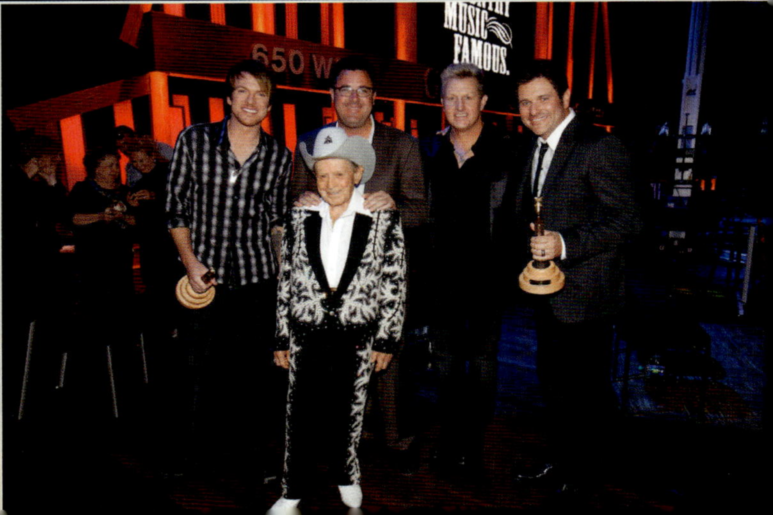
MUSIC
FAMOUS.

RIDERS IN THE SKY
MEMBER SINCE 1982

One of the Opry's most beloved groups got its start in late 1977, when guitarist Doug "Ranger Doug" Green invited bassist Fred "Too Slim" LaBour to join him for a gig at a Nashville nightclub. With Paul "Woody Paul" Chrisman on fiddle, the trio dubbed themselves Riders In The Sky. Their recorded debut, *Three on the Trail* (1979), showcased impeccable vocal and instrumental work in the mold of such Western music heroes — and Country Music Hall of Fame members — as Gene Autry, Roy Rogers, and the Sons of the Pioneers, while their live shows added a strong dose of broad, quick-witted humor that had them poking gentle fun at one another and at aspects of the movie cowboy image. This combination led to their induction into the Opry's cast in 1982.

"Zeke Clements had a cowboy routine, the Willis Brothers sang some cowboy songs, and, of course, Marty Robbins sang some cowboy songs, too, but we're the group that deliberately set about to preserve the Western tradition on this show," notes Ranger Doug. "It's a piece of country music history that we think is just as exciting and interesting as modern country, classic country, or bluegrass, and we're the guys keeping it alive."

For the Riders, who became a quartet when they "promoted" longtime accordionist Joey "The Cowpolka King" Miskulin to full membership, the mission of keeping the cowboy style alive has led to exhaustive touring, a long-running radio show (*Riders Radio Theatre*), a CBS television series, and a long string of popular recordings, including two soundtrack companion CDs that earned the group Grammy awards in 2001 and 2003.

Along the way, Riders In The Sky have earned multiple awards, including six Western Music Association Entertainer of the Year trophies and membership in the organization's Hall of Fame, the Academy of Western Artists' Western Music Group of the Year award (five times), and a presence on both the Country Music Foundation's Walkway of Stars and the Walk of Western Stars in Newhall, California.

JOEY, THE COWPOLKA KING
Birthplace: Chicago, Illinois
Birth Date: January 6

RANGER DOUG
Birthplace: Great Lakes, Illinois
Birth Date: March 20

WOODY PAUL
Birthplace: Nashville, Tennessee
Birth Date: August 23

TOO SLIM
Birthplace: Grand Rapids, Michigan
Birth Date: June 3

OPRY INDUCTION: June 19, 1982

> "...WE'RE THE GROUP THAT DELIBERATELY SET ABOUT TO PRESERVE THE WESTERN TRADITION ON THIS SHOW."

Q: What performance by another artist on the Opry do you most distinctly recall?
A: Introducing Loretta Lynn. Standing in the wings alongside Roy Acuff and Minnie. Ray Price nailing it. The love coming over the footlights for Charley Pride. Dolly singing to Porter "I Will Always Love You." Tons of new artists standing there in the circle, singing their story straight from the heart.

CLOCKWISE FROM TOP LEFT:
1. Circa 2005
2. With the Opry's Hal Durham and Ernest Tubb on the evening of the group's Opry induction
3. Roy Acuff, Gene Autry, Ranger Doug, and Too Slim
4. May 13, 2006
5. Backstage with Roy Rogers
6. With Wilford Brimley

OPRY FAMILY MEMBERS **162**

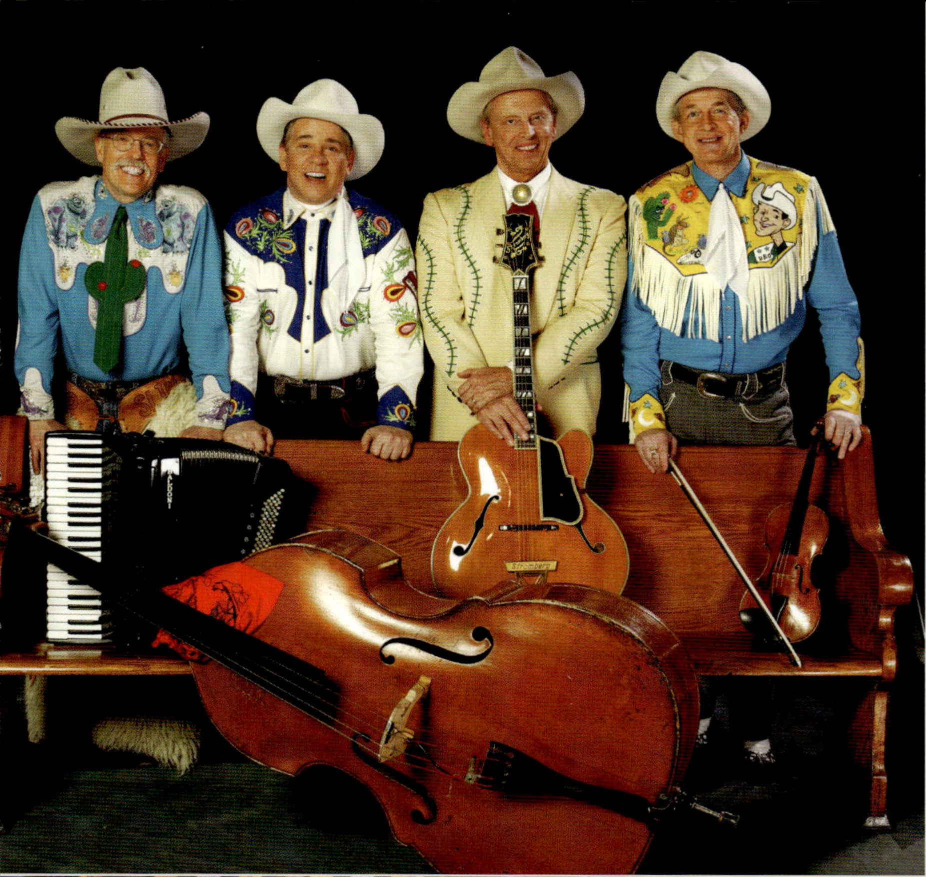

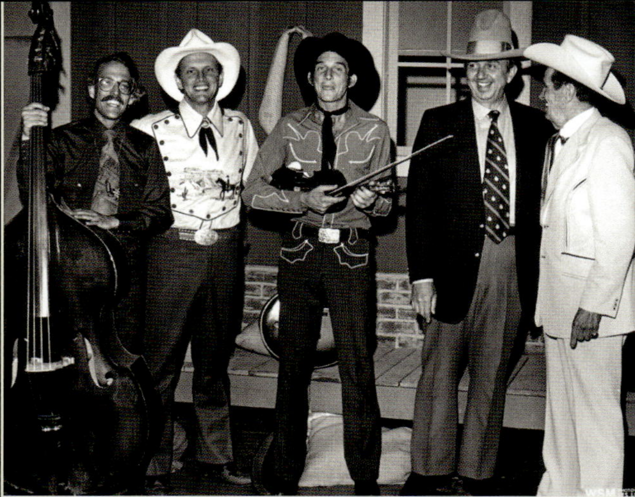

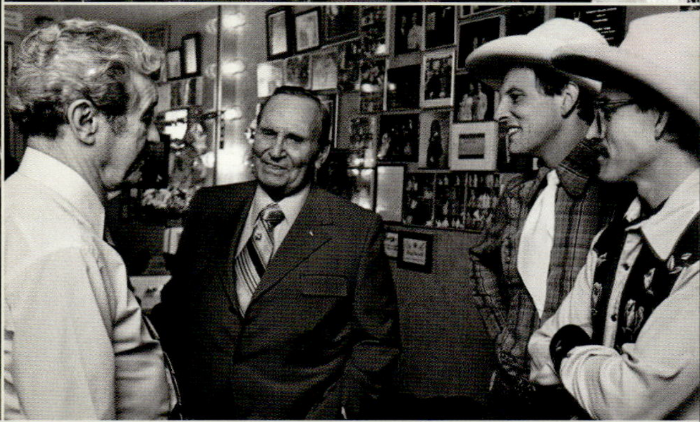

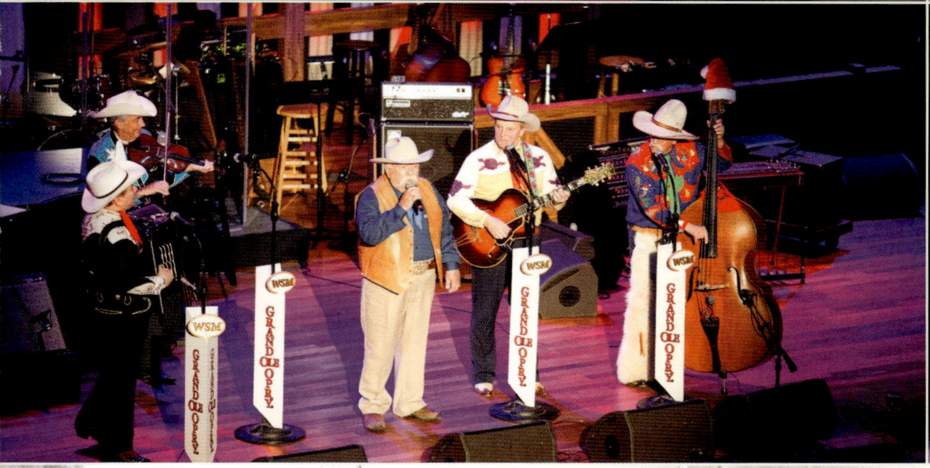
WSM
GRAND OLE OPRY

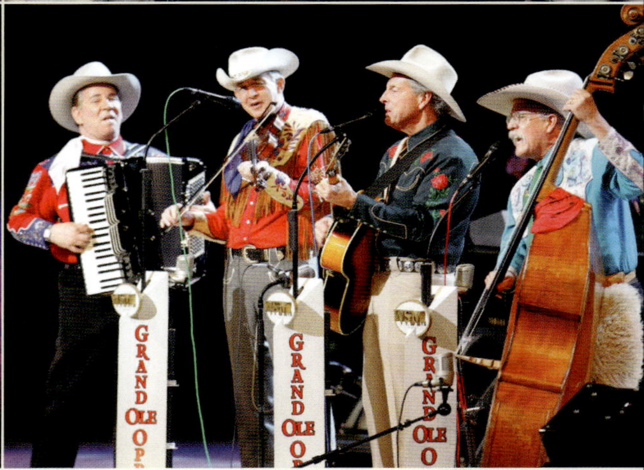
GRAND OLE OPRY

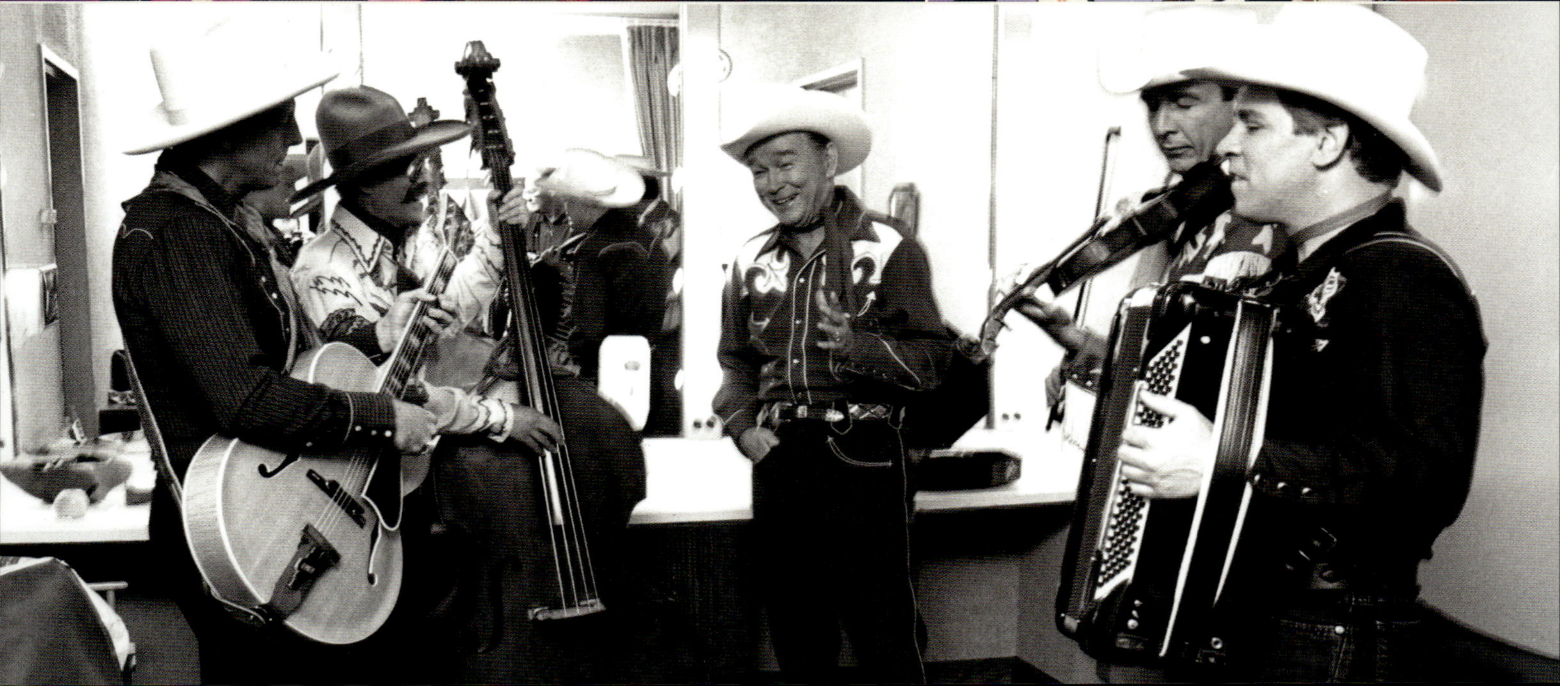

DARIUS RUCKER
MEMBER SINCE 2012

"Welcome him home, everybody! This is his new home right here," said Darius Rucker's good friend Brad Paisley to a Grand Ole Opry audience on October 2, 2012, just after Brad invited Darius to become an official member of the Opry. The invitation cemented a place in both country music and the genre's undisputed home for the soulful, rich baritone singer whose diverse career first landed him in pop music as the lead singer/co-writer for the wildly successful Hootie & the Blowfish.

Success as a solo country artist came quickly for Darius, whose first single, "Don't Think I Don't Think About It" and the album on which it was included, *Learn To Live*, became No. 1 smashes. As "Don't Think I Don't Think About It" was on its way up the charts in 2008, Darius played the Opry for the first time.

BIRTHPLACE: Charleston, South Carolina
BIRTH DATE: May 13
OPRY INDUCTION: October 16, 2012

Q: How does being backstage at the Opry differ from being backstage elsewhere on tour?
A: Being backstage at the Opry is different from being backstage anywhere else because it's the Opry. It's such a great hang with everybody back there. Whether people are playing music or practicing or getting their song together with the band—it's just a whole bunch of music back there, and it's pretty awesome.

"THANK YOU FOR OPENING YOUR ARMS AND LETTING ME IN."
OCT. 2, 2012, UPON HAVING BEEN INVITED TO JOIN THE OPRY.

"When I was asked if I wanted to perform on the Grand Ole Opry, I yelled, 'Are you kidding me?'" recalls Darius. "I've been waiting for that my whole life. To be invited where so many of the greatest country artists have performed is an honor, and I still can't believe it has been bestowed on me. Just to stand in the circle where so many greats have stood — Hank Williams, Kitty Wells, I just couldn't believe it."

In addition to his smash debut single, Darius has enjoyed other radio favorites, including "Alright," "It Won't Be Like This For Long," "This," and the Grammy-winning "Wagon Wheel," among others.

Presenting him with the Opry Member Award during his October 16, 2012, induction, Vince Gill said to Darius, "I don't think there's a more beloved guy in our music than you. ... Before you even open your mouth and sing a song you've written, everybody is really crazy about you. You will find this place right here to be one of the greatest homes you'll ever have. Thanks for wanting to be a country music singer!"

CLOCKWISE FROM TOP LEFT:
1. Being invited to join the Opry by Brad Paisley, October 2, 2012
2. Opry induction night, October 16, 2012
3. With Abbey June 7, 2011
4. With Big & Rich

WSM
GRAND OLE OPRY

WWW.OPRY.COM
WSM
GRAND OLE OPRY

WSM
GRAND OLE OPRY

WSM

DON SCHLITZ
MEMBER SINCE 2022

Country Music Hall of Famer Don Schlitz is among the most influential and beloved songwriters in the history of country music.

His chart-topping songs have become pillars of country songwriting for over 50 years. His works have been recorded by Kenny Rogers, Randy Travis, The Judds, Tanya Tucker, Keith Whitley, Alison Krauss, and so many more talented artists who resonate with how Don captures the extraordinary emotions of the human experience.

Don has had 50 top 10 singles, including 25 number one country hits. With three CMA Song of the Year awards, two Academy of Country Music Song of the Year awards, two Grammys, and many other industry accolades, he has far surpassed earning his keep as a member of the Songwriters Hall of Fame.

BIRTHPLACE: Durham, North Carolina
BIRTH DATE: August 29
OPRY INDUCTION: August, 2022

DEFINITIVE TRACKLIST:
"The Gambler"
"When You Say Nothing At All"
"Forever and Ever, Amen"
"On The Other Hand"
"I Feel Lucky"
"Strong Enough to Bend"
"Rockin' With The Rhythm Of The Rain"

"CAN I BRING MY SONGS WITH ME?"
—DON UPON BEING INVITED TO JOIN THE GRAND OLE OPRY

"The Gambler" singer Kenny Rogers perhaps said it best when he said, "Don doesn't just write songs, he writes careers."

Opry member Vince Gill invited Don, who has performed on the Grand Ole Opry over 50 times, to join the Opry family on June 11, 2022, the same night that legendary session musician Charlie McCoy was asked to join. Don's response: "Can I bring my songs with me?"

CLOCKWISE FROM TOP LEFT:
1. Don with Kenny Rogers and Randy Travis at the ACM Honors.
2. Don performing on the Grand Ole Opry in 2018.
3. Opry member and friend Vince Gill hugs Don on stage after inviting him to be part of the family.
4. During Covid Don was still asked to play, even though the house was empty

OPRY FAMILY MEMBERS

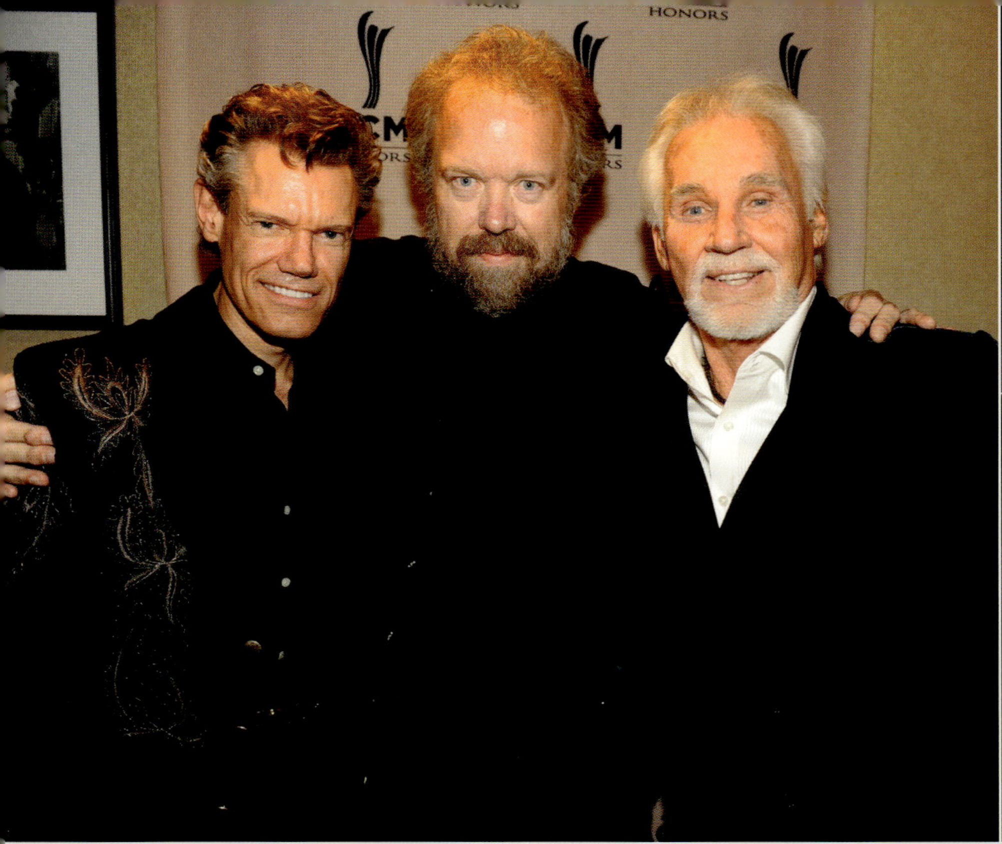
HONORS

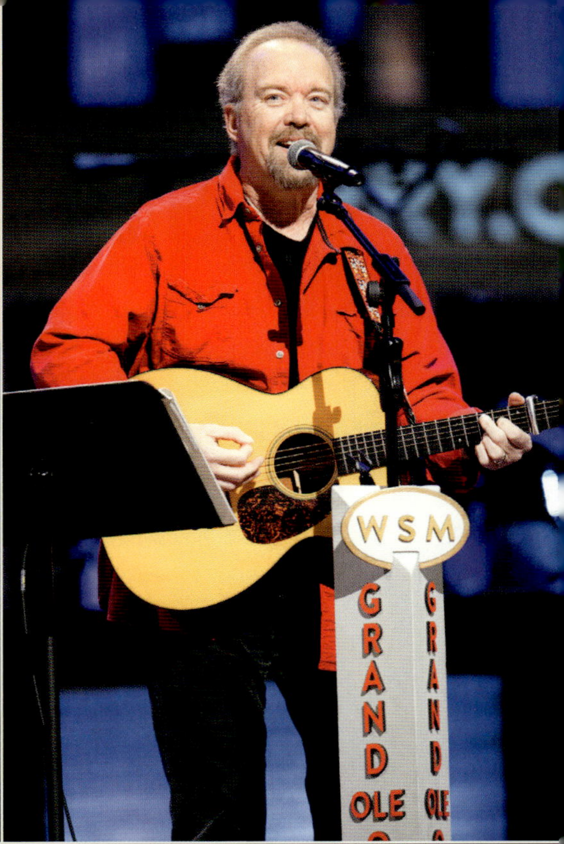
WSM
GRAND OLE

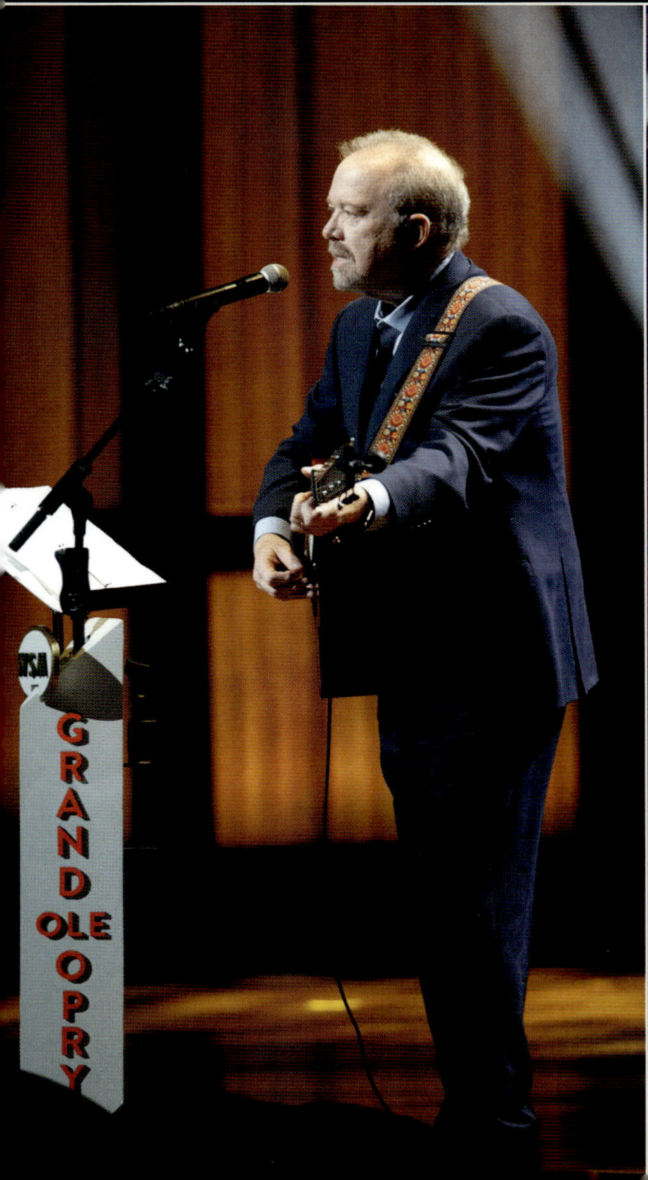
GRAND OLE OPRY

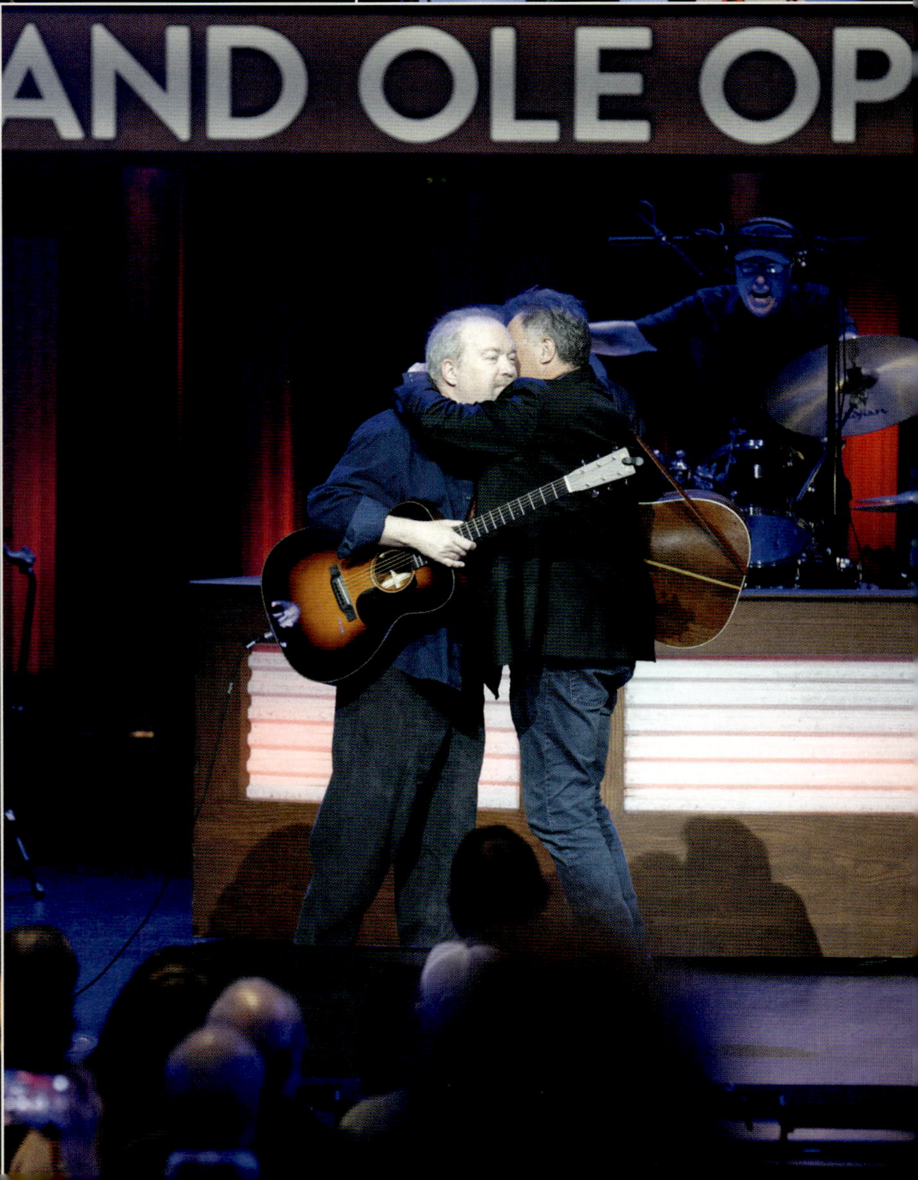
AND OLE OP

JEANNIE SEELY
MEMBER SINCE 1967

Jeannie Seely's mother said that Jeannie was just four years old when she learned to stretch up, tune the knob on her family's big console radio to 650 WSM and keep it there. Jeannie is still on the dial at 650 WSM — performing regularly on the stage of the Grand Ole Opry.

By age 11, she was performing on a weekly radio show in nearby Meadville, Pennsylvania, and a few years later was on TV in Erie. Years of playing auditoriums, small clubs, and country music parks followed. She moved to California and worked as a secretary with Liberty and Imperial Records in Hollywood before coming to Nashville in 1965 at the urging of Opry member Dottie West "I don't know enough to go there yet," Jeannie remembers telling Dottie. The more experienced singer responded, "Jeannie, that's where you go to learn."

BIRTHPLACE: Titusville, Pennsylvania
BIRTH DATE: July 6
OPRY INDUCTION: September 16, 1967

Q: What is one of your favorite nights at the Opry?
A: I loved the evening Keith Urban became a member of the Opry. I had the honor of introducing him on the night's second show, his first as a full-fledged part of the family. A member of his crew brought me a Keith Urban T-shirt, and I put it on before taking the stage. It added to what was already a very, very fun night for everyone there.

"MY HOME CONTINUES TO BE THE GRAND OLE OPRY AND THAT'S WHERE MY HEART IS."

A recording contract with Monument Records gave Jeannie her first hit in 1966 with "Don't Touch Me," which went to the top of the charts and earned her a Grammy Award. One year later, the singer who became famous as "Miss Country Soul" fulfilled her childhood dream of becoming a member of the Opry cast.

More hits followed, including "I'll Love You More (Than You Need)," "Can I Sleep in Your Arms," and "Lucky Ladies." Jeannie briefly worked as duet partner of Porter Wagoner and had a successful touring and recording partnership with fellow Opry member Jack Greene resulting in multiple award nominations and such hits as the Top 10 single "Wish I Didn't Have to Miss You." Jeannie also is a successful songwriter, having written Faron Young's No. 1 hit, "Leavin' and Sayin' Goodbye," a BMI award-winner. She also has had songs cut by Dottie West, Connie Smith, Willie Nelson, and Ray Price.

Known for her plainspoken ways and sharp sense of humor, Jeannie published a book of witticisms, *Pieces of a Puzzled Mind*, in 1989. She continues to tour, record, and work on new stage material, preferably for the Opry stage she calls home.

CLOCKWISE FROM TOP LEFT:
1. With Lorrie Morgan November 3, 2001
2. With Jack Greene, opening night at the Grand Ole Opry House, March 16, 1974
3. May 31, 2014
4. 1976
5. 2014

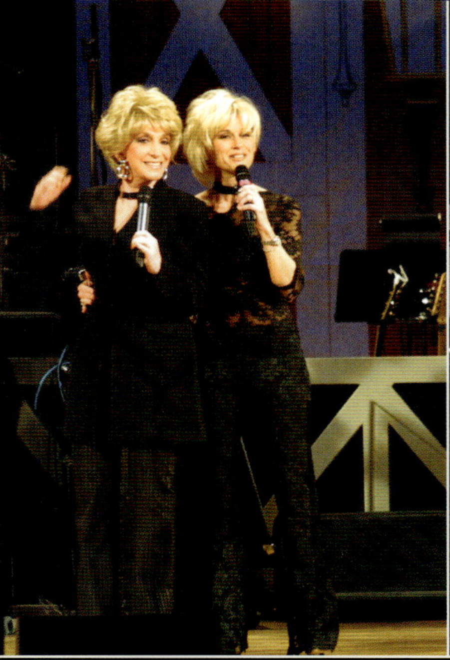

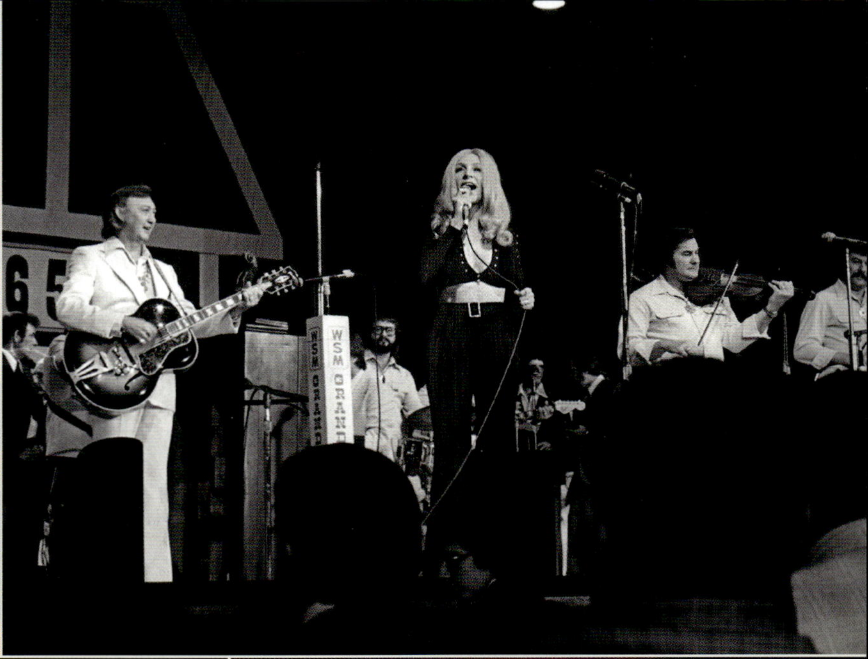
WSM GRAND

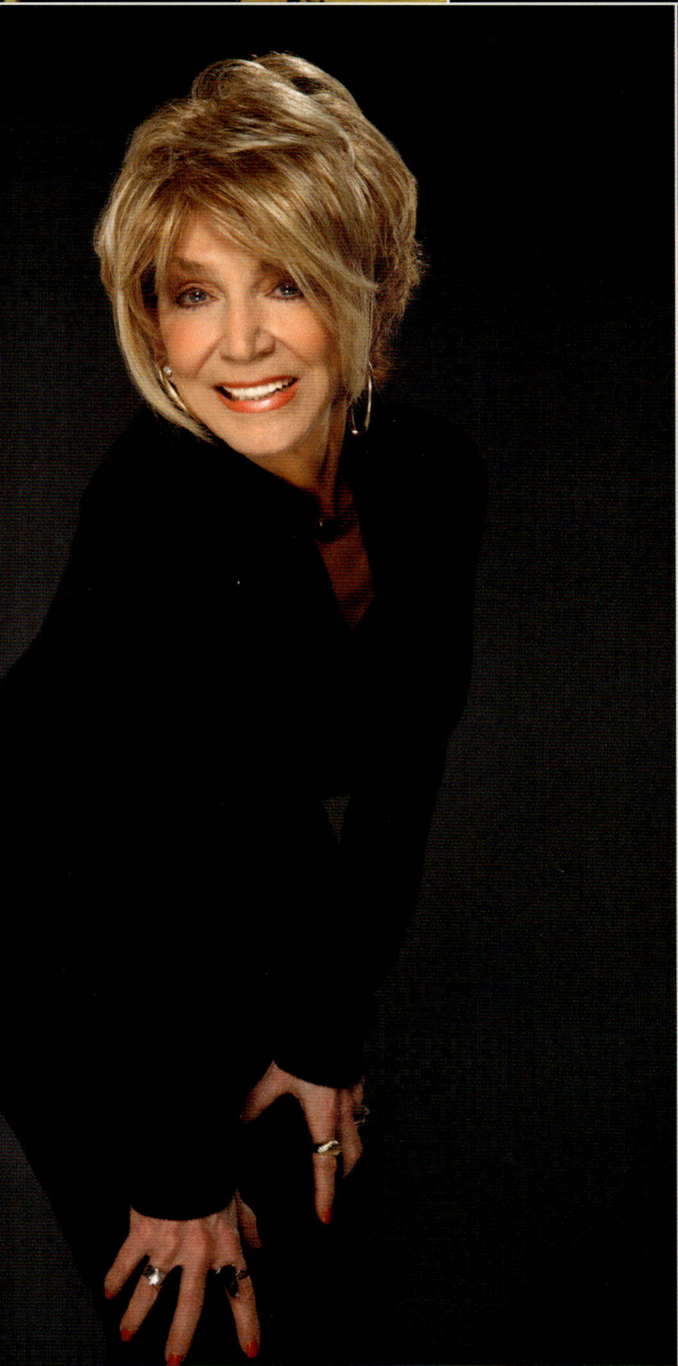

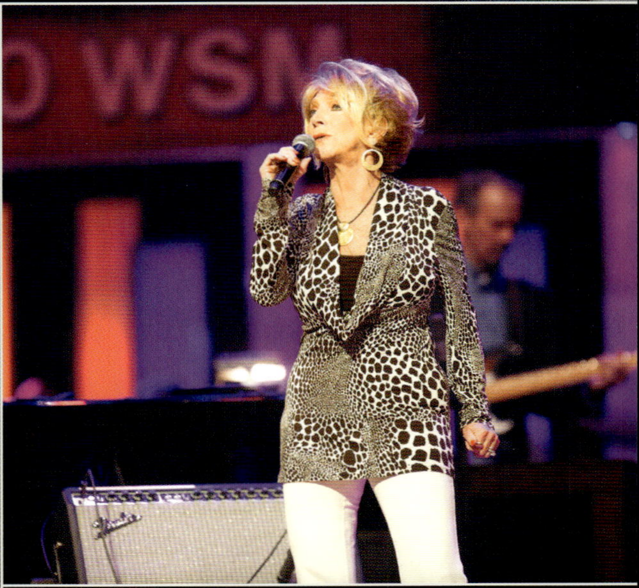
WSM

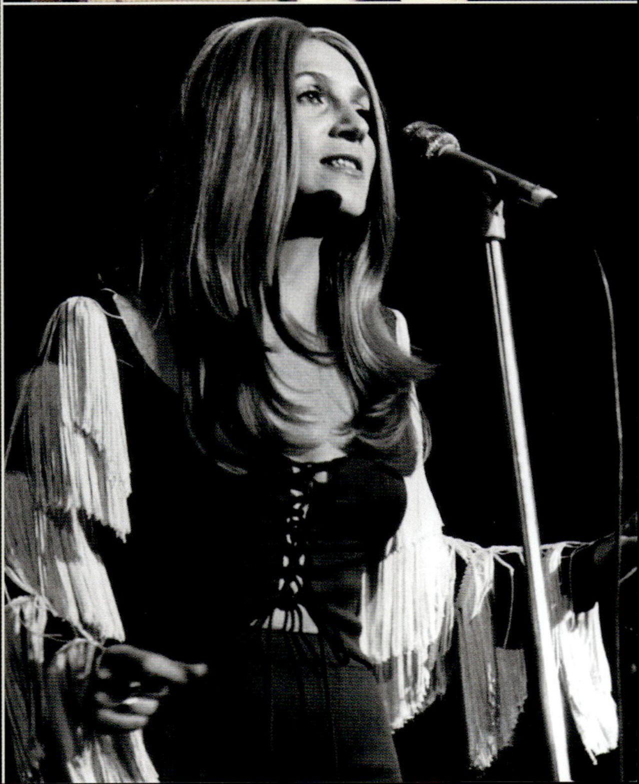

BLAKE SHELTON
MEMBER SINCE 2010

Few country artists have ever known the kind of success Blake Shelton has earned. Fewer still have done it with the openness and honesty he brings to the table. More than a decade into a career that started with his chart-topping "Austin," that transparency has helped Blake become one of the best ambassadors the country music genre has ever had, in a league with Glen Campbell and Roger Miller. His wit, intelligence and, above all, his irreverent sense of fun have endeared him to his peers on NBC's *The Voice* and to the millions of fans he is introducing to country music. He is, says wife Miranda Lambert, "the life of every party he goes to," and these days, the world is his party.

BIRTHPLACE: Ada, Oklahoma
BIRTH DATE: June 18
OPRY INDUCTION: October 23, 2010

DID YOU KNOW? Blake Shelton was invited to join the Opry via Twitter.

> "TONIGHT FOR ME IS THE NASHVILLE DREAM. TONIGHT IS THE PINNACLE. THIS IS WHAT I WANTED FROM THE BEGINNING—TO MAKE A MARK. AND TONIGHT IS THE ULTIMATE ONE." —BLAKE SHELTON ON THE EVENING OF HIS OPRY INDUCTION.

Blake has won CMA Entertainer of the Year and multiple Male Vocalist of the Year honors, and he and Miranda garnered Song of the Year honors for co-writing the platinum-selling chart-topper "Over You." He has earned a host of other awards and nominations, including multiple Grammy nominations, gold and platinum albums, and has hosted the ACM Awards repeatedly.

With songs like "All About Tonight," "Who Are You When I'm Not Looking," "Honey Bee," "God Gave Me You," "Drink on It," "Boys 'Round Here," and "Mine Would Be You," he has proven his versatility and shown himself as one of the genre's strongest and most compelling vocalists. His live show—hit-filled, high energy, unpredictable—has kept him among country's most popular touring acts.

On October 23, 2010, Blake was inducted into the Grand Ole Opry. "I get the same feeling when I come to the Opry as when I see one of my heroes," says Blake. "I am in awe. To me, the Grand Ole Opry is an artist and I'm really proud to be one of its songs."

CLOCKWISE FROM TOP LEFT:
1. --
2. Celebrating the Opry House's 40th anniversary
3. With Trace Adkins, October 23, 2010
4. October 23, 2010
5. Being invited to join the Opry via Twitter, September 28, 2010

OPRY FAMILY MEMBERS

OFFICE

WSM

WSM

WSM
GRAND OLE OPRY
GRAND OLE OPRY

GRAND OLE OPRY
WSM

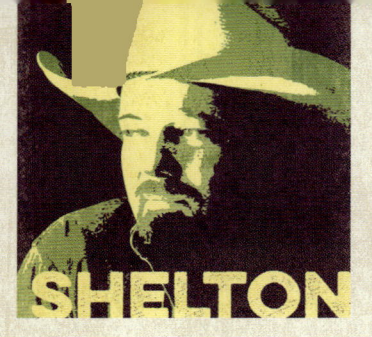

RICKY VAN SHELTON
MEMBER SINCE 1988

It took Ricky Van Shelton years of hard work — in country music and at "real jobs" — to become an overnight sensation. In 1984, he moved to Nashville with his future wife, Bettye. Then, in June 1986, CBS Records offered him a recording contract. Producers and studio musicians were startled by the high quality of the rookie's vocal performances, which he'd sharpened through years of practice.

Ricky hit the Top 40 for the first time in 1987 with the title track from his debut album *Wild Eyed Dream*. That launched a recording career that would include 10 No. 1 hits. But Ricky had worked for years as a salesman, house painter, plumber, appliance store manager, and construction worker — working days and practicing at night, waiting for his big break.

A year later, he had his first hit. In 1988, when he joined the Opry, he told the audience that he had dreamed of having a big bus and of hearing himself on the radio.

BIRTHPLACE: Danville, Virginia
BIRTH DATE: January 12
OPRY INDUCTION: June 10, 1988

Q: What is an Opry Moment you most vividly recall?
A: The first time I ever performed on the Opry was a dream come true for me. I was so emotionally moved by the opportunity, I forgot the words to my No. 1 hit, "Somebody Lied." The audience seemed to be as moved as I was and showed so much support, I finished the song and received a standing ovation. I will never forget how I was humbled and honored in the same moment.

> "BECAUSE OF THE OPRY'S COMMITMENT TO TRUE COUNTRY MUSIC, I AM CONFIDENT IT WILL BE STRONG FOR ANOTHER 90 YEARS AND LONGER. LONG LIVE COUNTRY MUSIC AND THE GRAND OLE OPRY!"

"And I dreamed about playing the Grand Ole Opry," Ricky said. "But one thing I never dreamed is that I'd be asked to join."

From his first recordings, country fans realized they were witnessing the rise of an especially gifted singer who performed in the smooth style of Eddy Arnold, Jim Reeves, and Conway Twitty.

His steady stream of No. 1 hits included "Somebody Lied," "Life Turned Her That Way," "I'll Leave This World Loving You," "I've Cried My Last Tear for You," "I Am a Simple Man," and "Keep It Between the Lines." In 1991, he teamed with fellow Opry member Dolly Parton for the smash hit duet "Rockin' Years."

He turned songs previously associated with other Opry stars — "Life Turned Her That Way" (Jimmy Dickens) and "Statue of a Fool" (Jack Greene) — into hits again.

Ricky gave his last Opry performance on July 2, 2004, and officially retired from touring in 2006, but he still manages to keep himself busy. He has distinguished himself as a painter, pilot, collector, and author.

CLOCKWISE FROM TOP LEFT:
1. May 5, 1997
2. Induction into Grand Ole Opry on June 10, 1988, with Roy Acuff
3. March 21 2000
4. --
5. 1991
6. 1990 TNN/Music City News Awards Male Vocalist & Entertainer of the Year

OPRY FAMILY MEMBERS

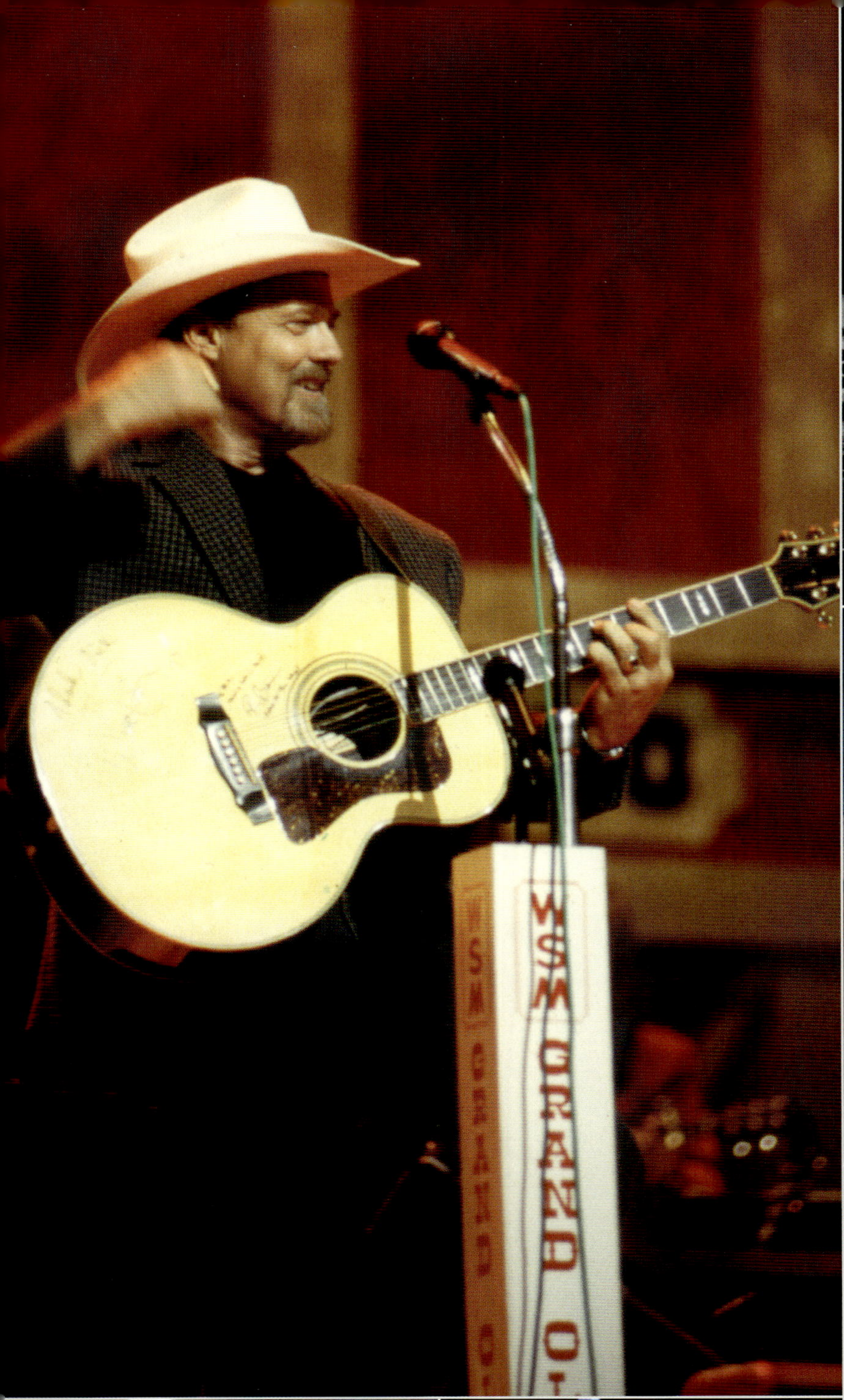
WSM GRAND
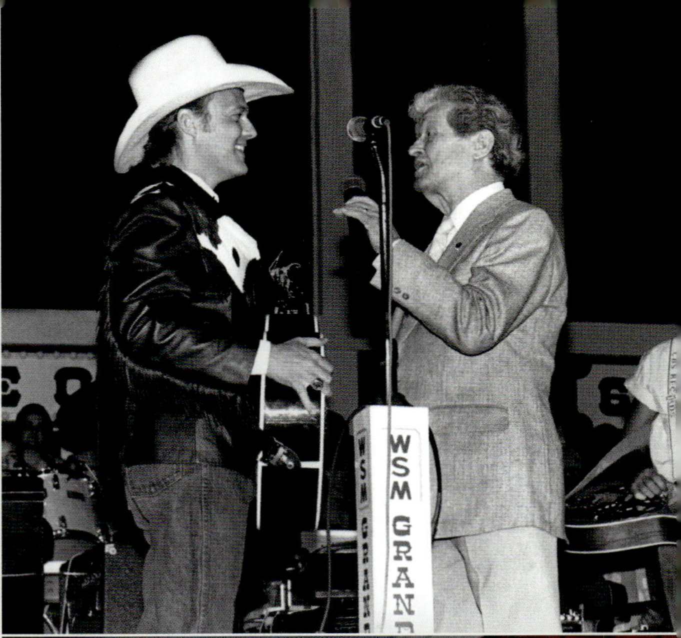
WSM GRAND
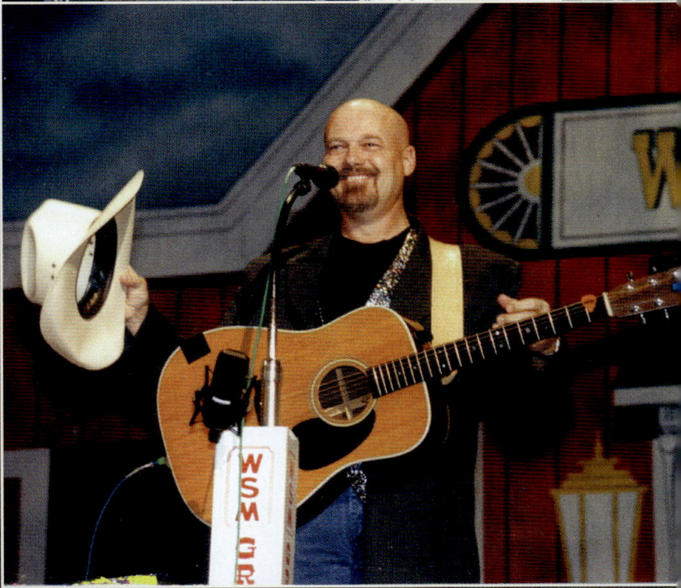
WSM
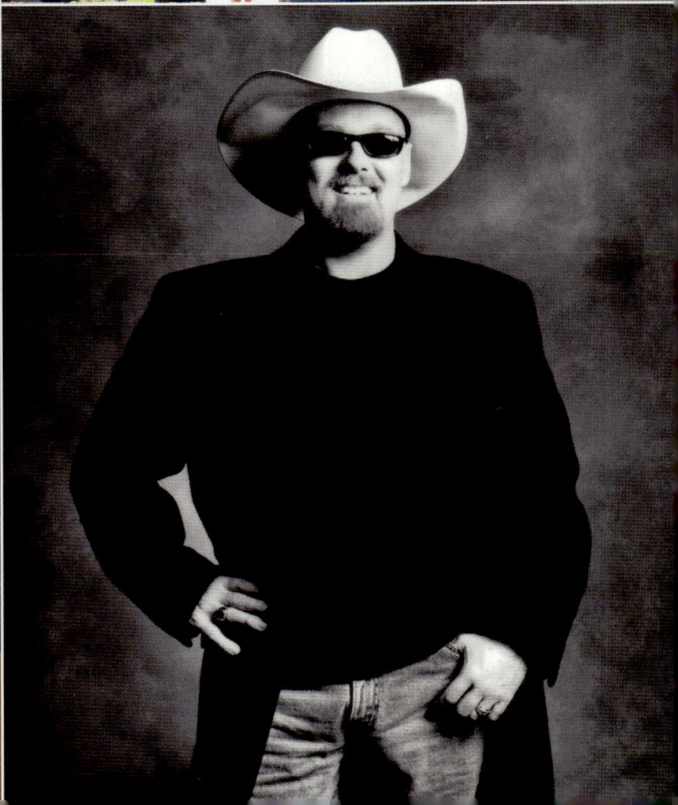
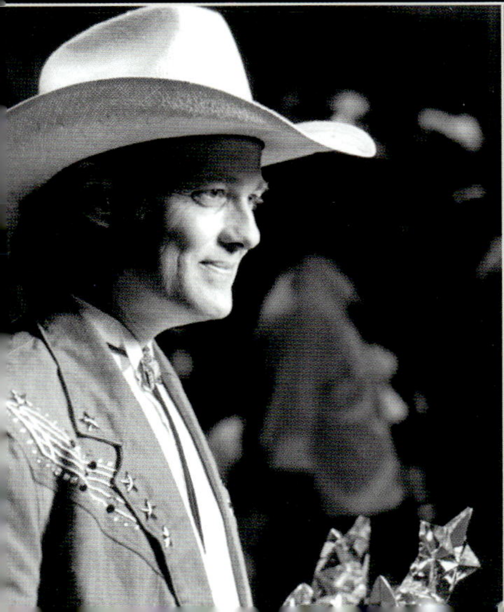
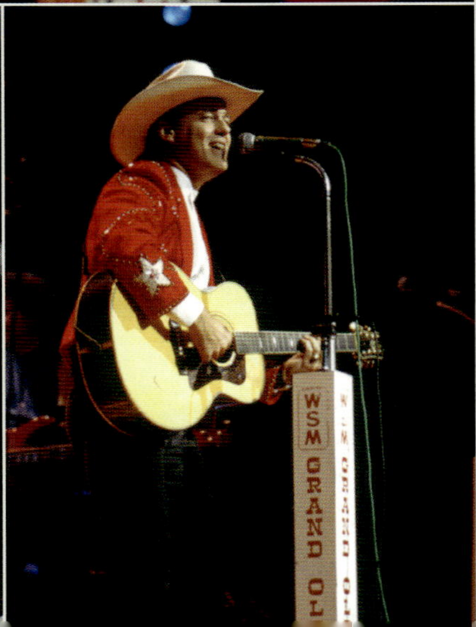
WSM GRAND

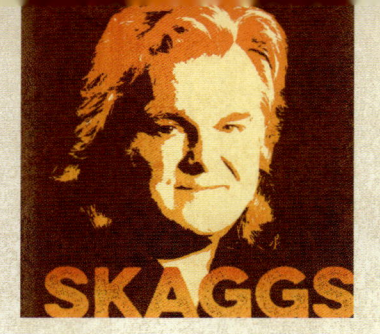

RICKY SKAGGS
MEMBER SINCE 1982

Though more than a half-century has passed since Ricky Skaggs made his television debut on Flatt & Scruggs' *Martha White* show, he's still one of the youngest Grand Ole Opry stars to legitimately qualify as an elder statesman of country and bluegrass music. Beginning with that 1961 appearance at the age of seven, Ricky has blazed an astonishing path through music, first as a sideman and then as a star, earning lasting acclaim for his signature combination of skill, passion, tradition, and creativity.

Ricky entered the world of professional music with another future star, his friend Keith Whitley, when bluegrass pioneer Ralph Stanley took the teen-aged musicians under his wing in 1971 for summer touring and recording. High-profile stints with the Country Gentlemen and J. D. Crowe's New South came after high school, followed by the

BIRTHPLACE: Cordell, Kentucky
BIRTH DATE: July 18
OPRY INDUCTION: May 15, 1982

Q: What is a performance by another artist on the Opry most distinctly recall?
A: There was a very special night I'll always remember. I had invited a 10 year old fiddler named Carson Peters to be a guest on my show. After he sang a version of the Bill Monroe classic "Blue Moon Of Kentucky" every person in the Grand Ole Opry House stood to their feet to cheer and give him a standing ovation. I don't think I've ever been so proud for someone as I was for Carson.

> "I THINK THE REASON THE OPRY HAS BEEN AROUND FOR SO LONG IS THAT ALTHOUGH THE MUSIC HAS CHANGED OVER THE YEARS, IT'S STILL A RADIO SHOW WITH A FOCUS ON BEING A RADIO SHOW, NOTHING MORE NOTHING LESS."

formation of Boone Creek, an influential band that bridged tradition and more modern sounds. Skaggs' career as a band member and sideman concluded in the late '70s with a tour of duty in Emmylou Harris' Hot Band, during which he produced several of her most admired albums.

In 1981, Ricky moved to center stage when his singles began to hit the top of the country charts. His fresh combination of traditional material and modern production, soulful singing and hot picking on hits like "Heartbroke," "Highway 40 Blues," and "Country Boy" kept him there through most of the 1980s. He was among the top 20 artists of the decade and the top 100 of the past 50 years in airplay. He also earned eight awards from the Country Music Association, including Entertainer of the Year in 1985.

Ricky's career took a new direction in the mid-'90s, when he vowed to carry on the legacy of Bill Monroe by rededicating himself to bluegrass. Beginning with 1997's *Bluegrass Rules!*, a steady stream of albums and concert, festival and television appearances with his award-winning band Kentucky Thunder have brought a new round of honors, including multiple Grammys and International Bluegrass Music Association trophies.

CLOCKWISE FROM TOP LEFT:
1. With Bill Monroe, Earl Scruggs, Jim and Jesse, The Whites, Sonny Osborne
2. May 31, 2014
3. With Ernest Tubb
4. With Peter Frampton
5. Circa 2012

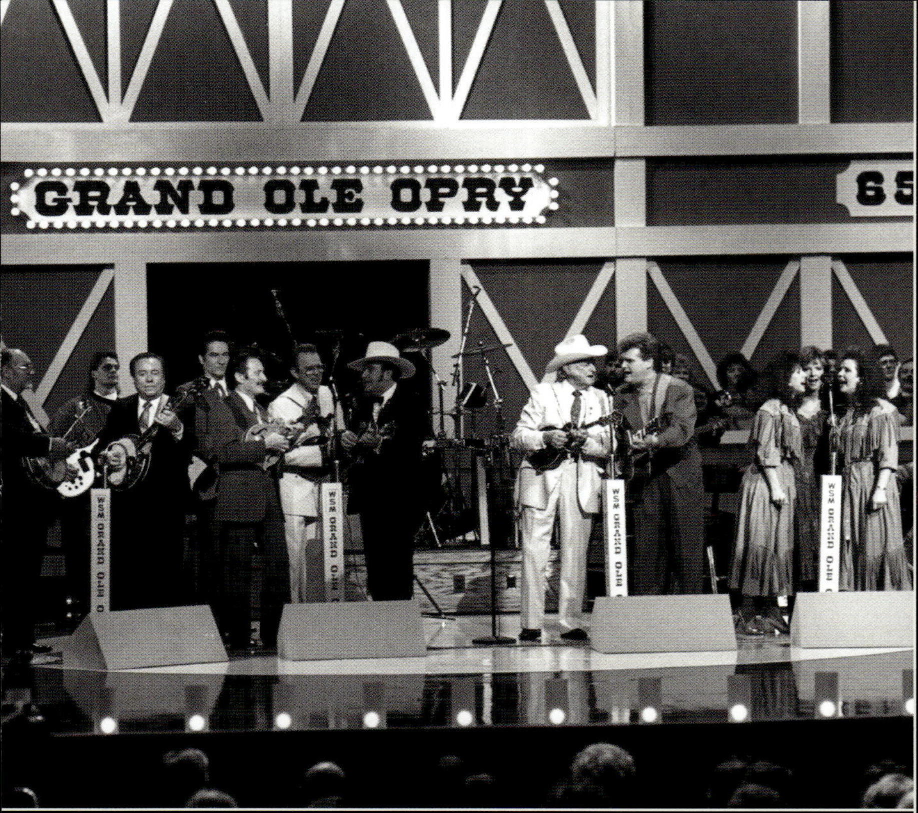
GRAND OLE OPRY
65

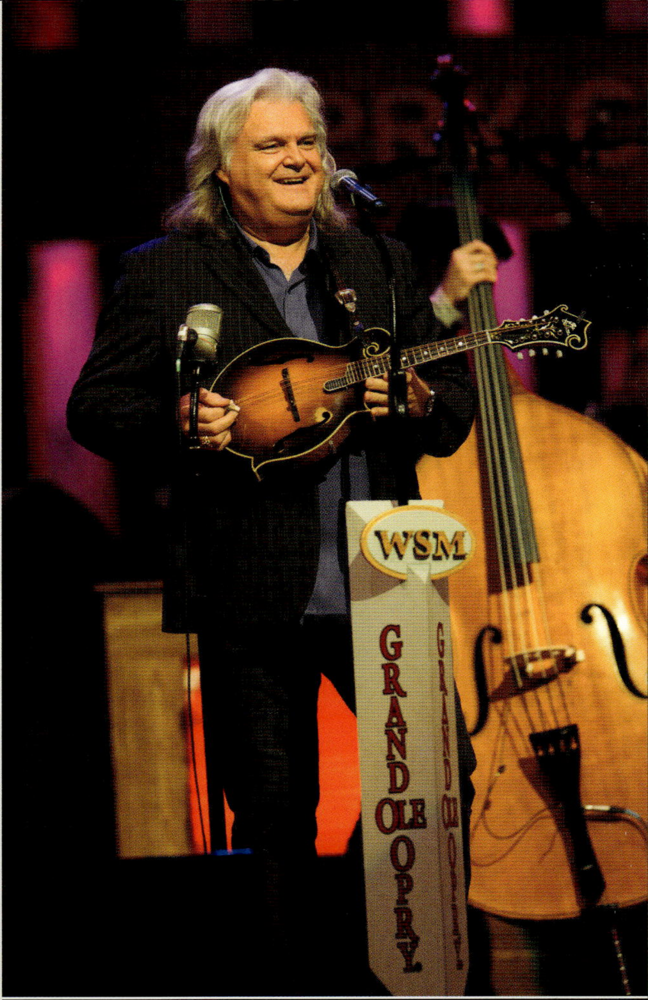
WSM
GRAND OLE OPRY

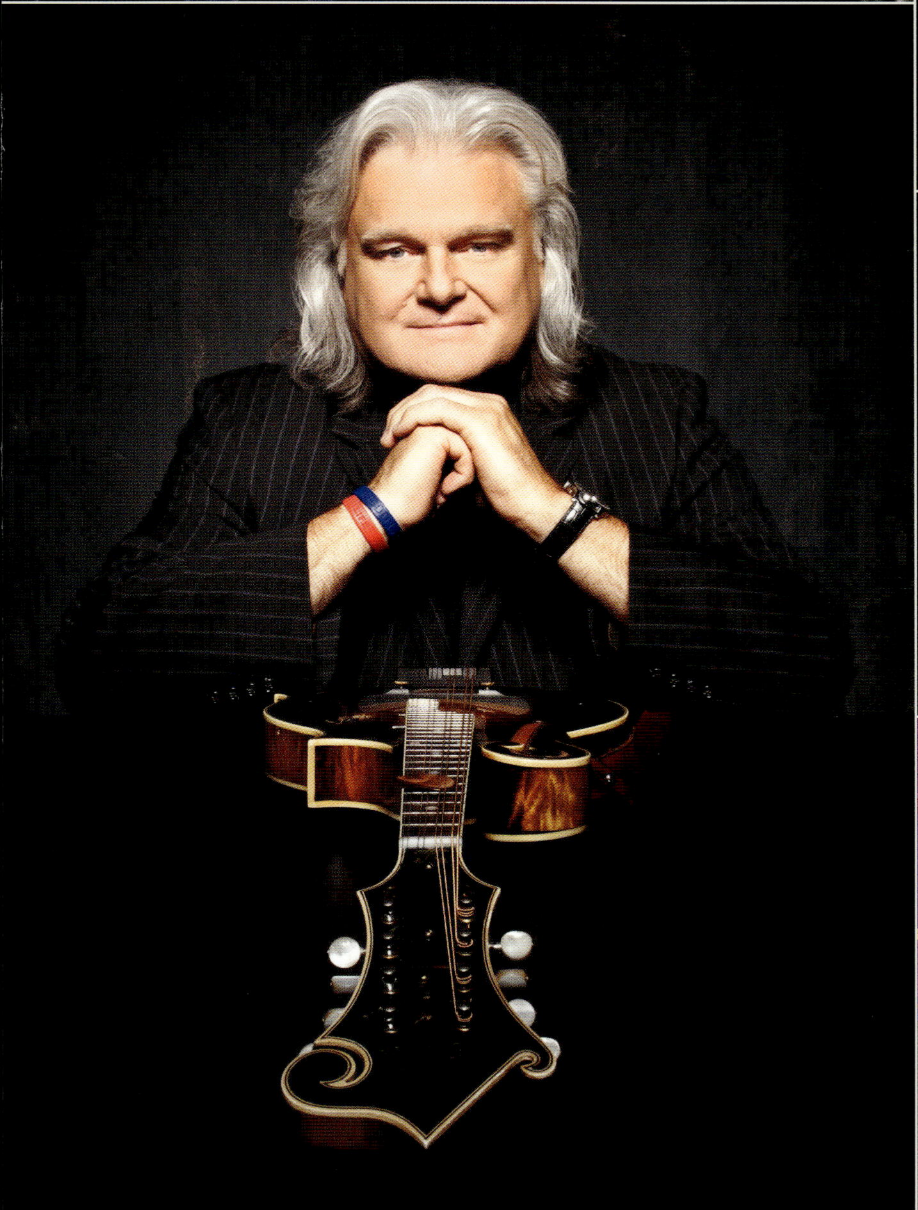

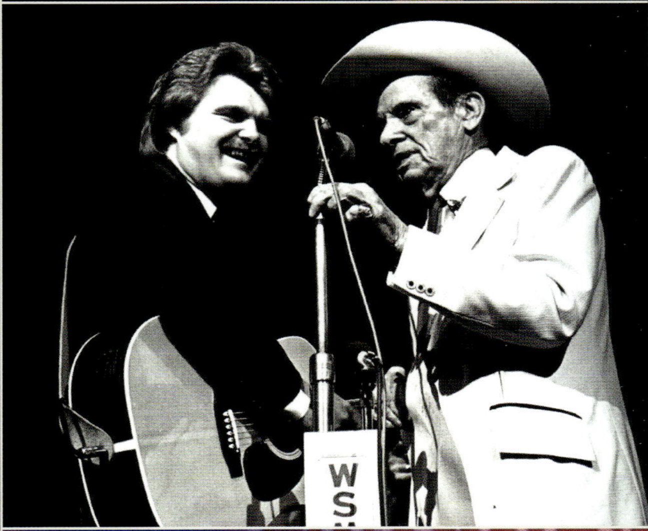

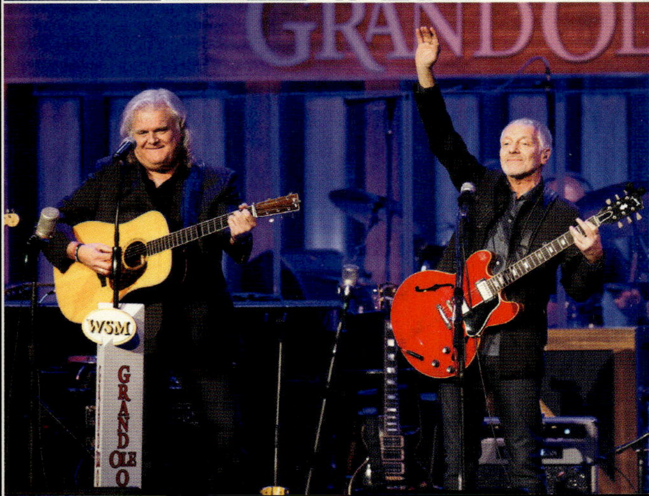
WSM

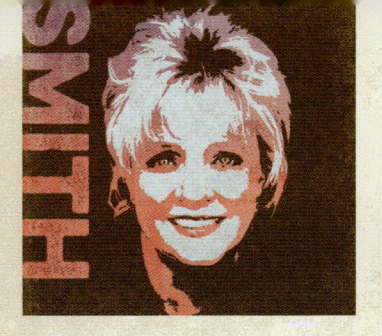

CONNIE SMITH
MEMBER SINCE 1965

As a shy five-year-old, the eighth child in a family of 14, Constance June Meador once made the prophetic proclamation, "Someday I'm gonna sing on the Grand Ole Opry!" A member of the Opry since 1965, Connie Smith's dream became a reality. Decades later, she continues to astonish audiences with a powerhouse voice that is one of the most respected and recognizable in country music.

Born in Indiana and raised in West Virginia and Ohio, Connie was a young housewife and mother with a four-month-old son in Warner, Ohio, in 1963, when she traveled to the Frontier Ranch Park in Columbus. Talked into entering a talent contest, Connie won five silver dollars and the chance to meet Opry member Bill Anderson. By the next year, Chet Atkins had signed her to RCA Records and she had recorded a song penned by Anderson, "Once a Day."

BIRTHPLACE: Elkhart, Indiana
BIRTH DATE: August 14
OPRY INDUCTION: August 21, 1965

> "THERE'S REALLY ONLY THREE FEMALE SINGERS IN THE WORLD: STREISAND, RONSTADT, AND CONNIE SMITH. THE REST OF US ARE ONLY PRETENDING." —DOLLY PARTON

Released in August, the now-classic reached the top of the charts by November and became the first-ever debut single by a female country act to reach No. 1. The song spent eight weeks at the top and also was nominated for a Grammy. Her debut album was also a chart-topper, and she followed with a host of other hits, including "I Never Once Stopped Loving You," "Nobody but a Fool," "Ain't Had No Lovin'," and "Cincinnati, Ohio." Along the way, she earned the name "Sweetheart of the Grand Ole Opry" from the King of Country Music, Roy Acuff.

A born again Christian, Connie also has enjoyed success with gospel recordings and continues to treat Opry audiences to such favorites.

In July 1997, Connie married fellow Opry member Marty Stuart. Fifteen years later, the lauded vocalist who still enjoys recording as well as performing with her band the Sundowners, was inducted into the Country Music Hall of Fame.

CLOCKWISE FROM TOP LEFT:
1. July 29, 2005
2. With baby, October 17, 1974
3. 1979
4. January 19, 2002
5. With Marty Stuart
6. Circa 1970s

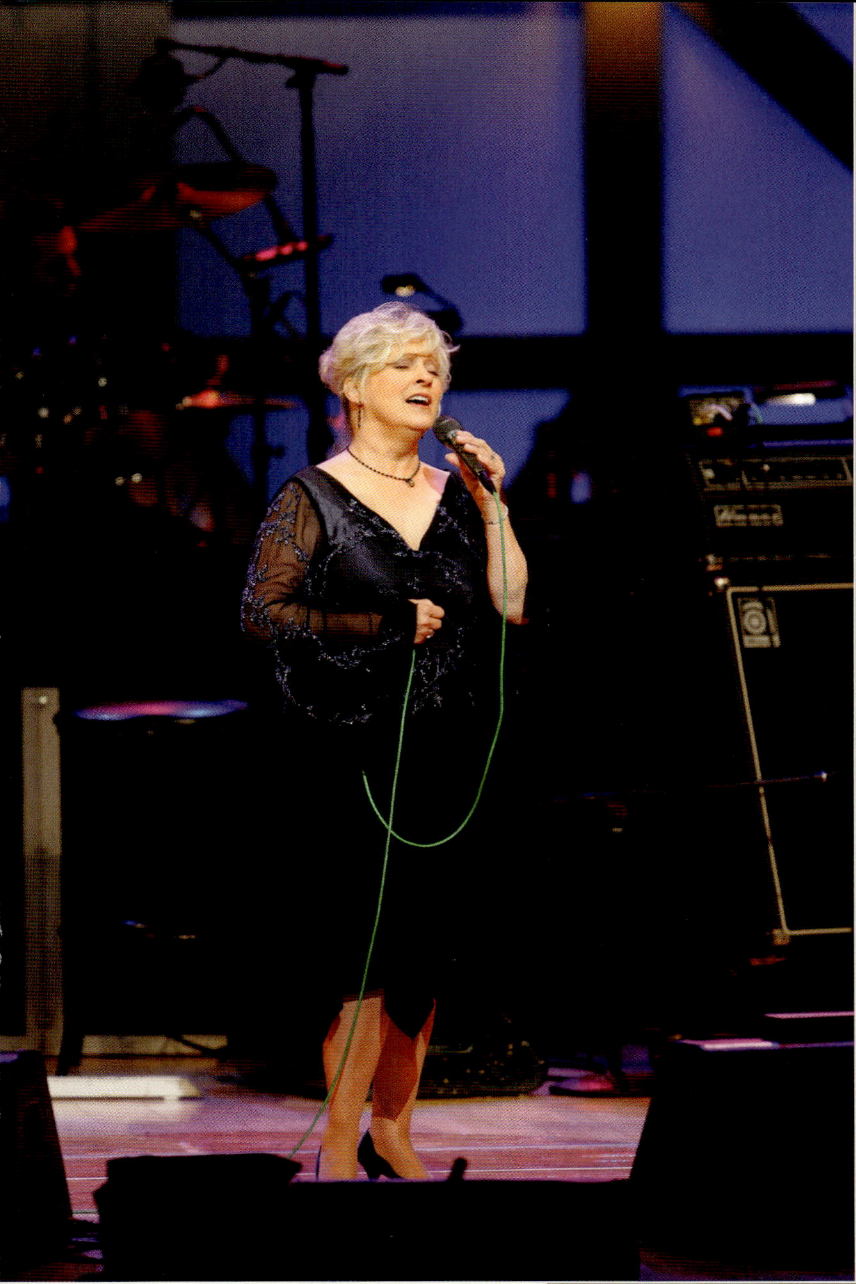

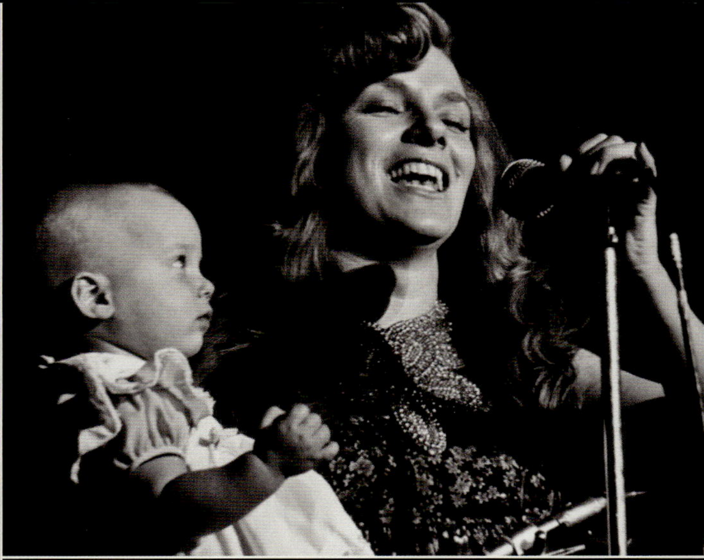

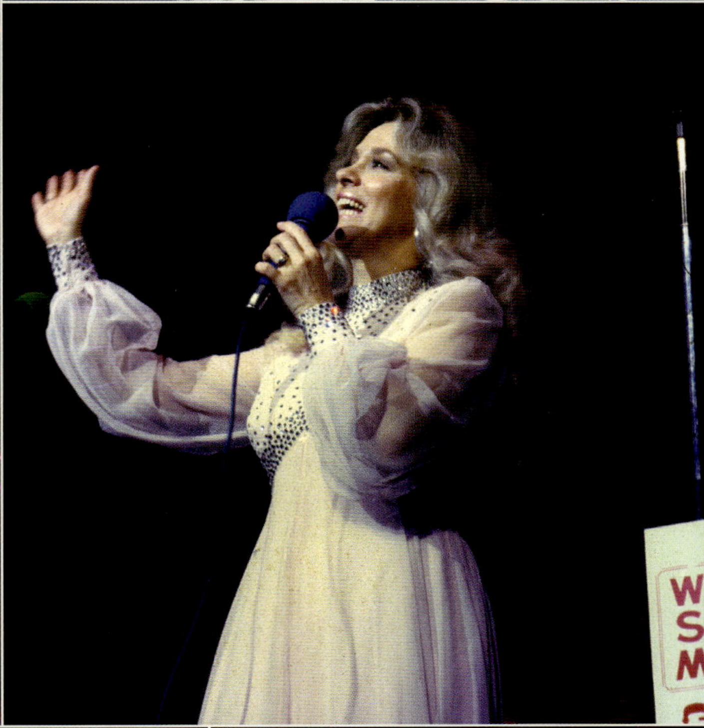

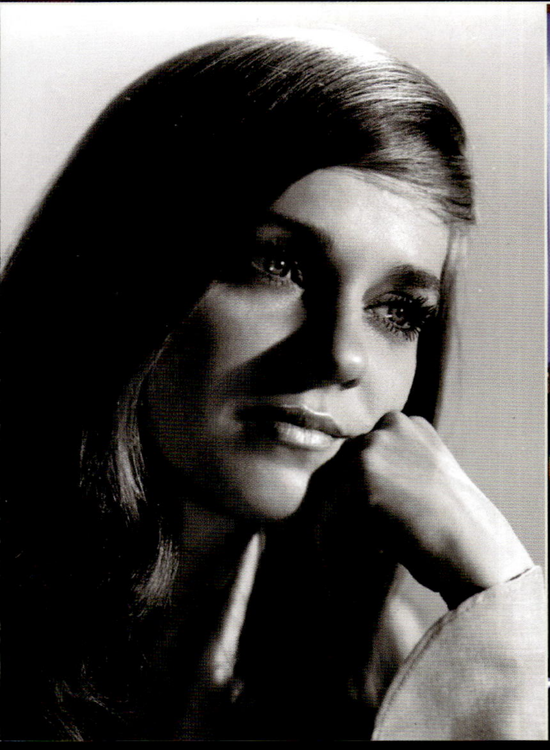

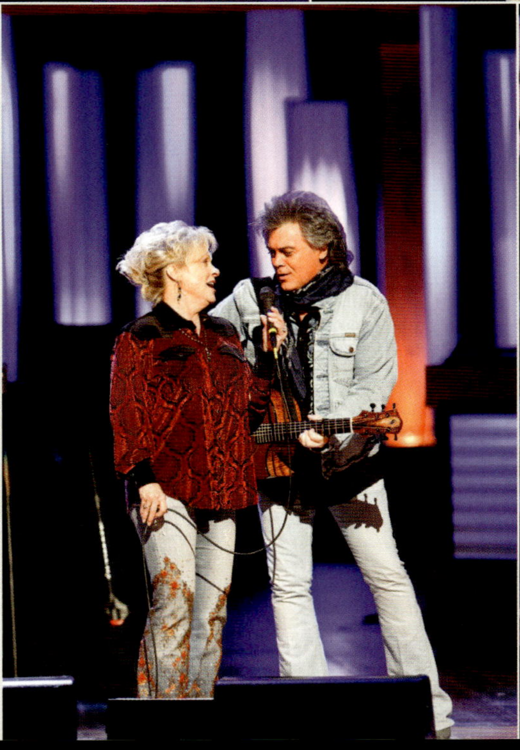

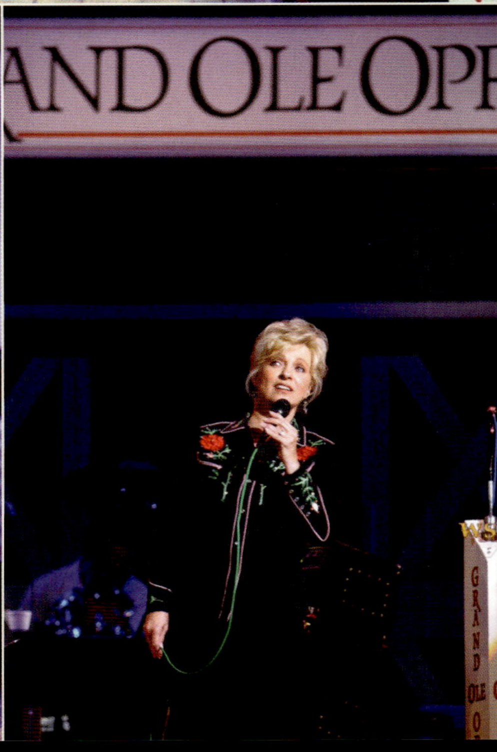
AND OLE OP

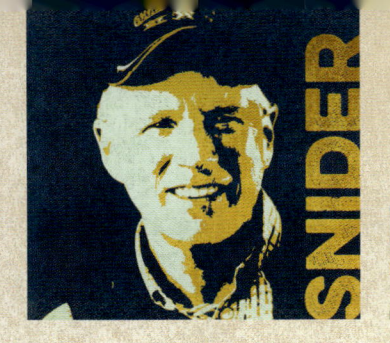

MIKE SNIDER
MEMBER SINCE 1990

When Mike Snider and his old-time string band take the stage of the Grand Ole Opry, they bring a combination of musical excellence and rural comedy that always leaves a delighted audience cheering. Mike's blend of irreverent humor and utter reverence for the old-time music tradition makes him a perennial favorite of Opry audiences and a much-respected member of the music community.

Mike began playing banjo at age 16, after hearing a Flatt & Scruggs album. In short order he became the Tennessee State Bluegrass Banjo Champion, then won the Mid-South Banjo Playing Contest. At age 23, he found himself the National Bluegrass Banjo Champion. Today, his musical accomplishments also include playing the mandolin and harmonica.

BIRTHPLACE: Gleason, Tennessee
BIRTH DATE: May 30
OPRY INDUCTION: June 2, 1990

> "I LIKE TO COME TO THE OPRY. IT'S NOT JUST TO GET OUT ON STAGE AND PLAY FOR THE AUDIENCE. I LOVE TO SEE MY FAMILY EVERY WEEKEND."

Mike's popularity grew with appearances on The Nashville Network's *Nashville Now* alongside Ralph Emery, and as a cast member of the syndicated comedy variety show *Hee Haw*, which he joined in 1987. In 1990, six years after his Opry debut, the legendary Minnie Pearl inducted Mike as a member of the Grand Ole Opry. Mike finds himself heir apparent of the country comedy mantle once worn by Minnie and her partner Rod Brasfield, Jerry Clower, and others.

A showman to the core, Mike's pronounced (and genuine) Tennessee drawl incites laughter the moment he opens his mouth. He regales the audience with tales featuring his wife, Sweetie, and an endless supply of jokes about country life.

"It don't seem like I've been at the Grand Ole Opry no 20 years, in one way and then it seems like I've been here my whole life," Mike says. "I remember the first night I walked out on the stage; I felt like I was at home."

When Mike and the band take the stage, audiences know they'll laugh, tap their toes, and hear perhaps the best string band in existence. They will be well entertained, and, for Mike Snider, that makes for a good night at the Opry.

CLOCKWISE FROM TOP LEFT:
1. December 22, 2006
2. April 28, 2012
3. Circa 1990s
4. Circa 1990s
5. With Marty Stuart
6. Circa 1990s

OPRY FAMILY MEMBERS

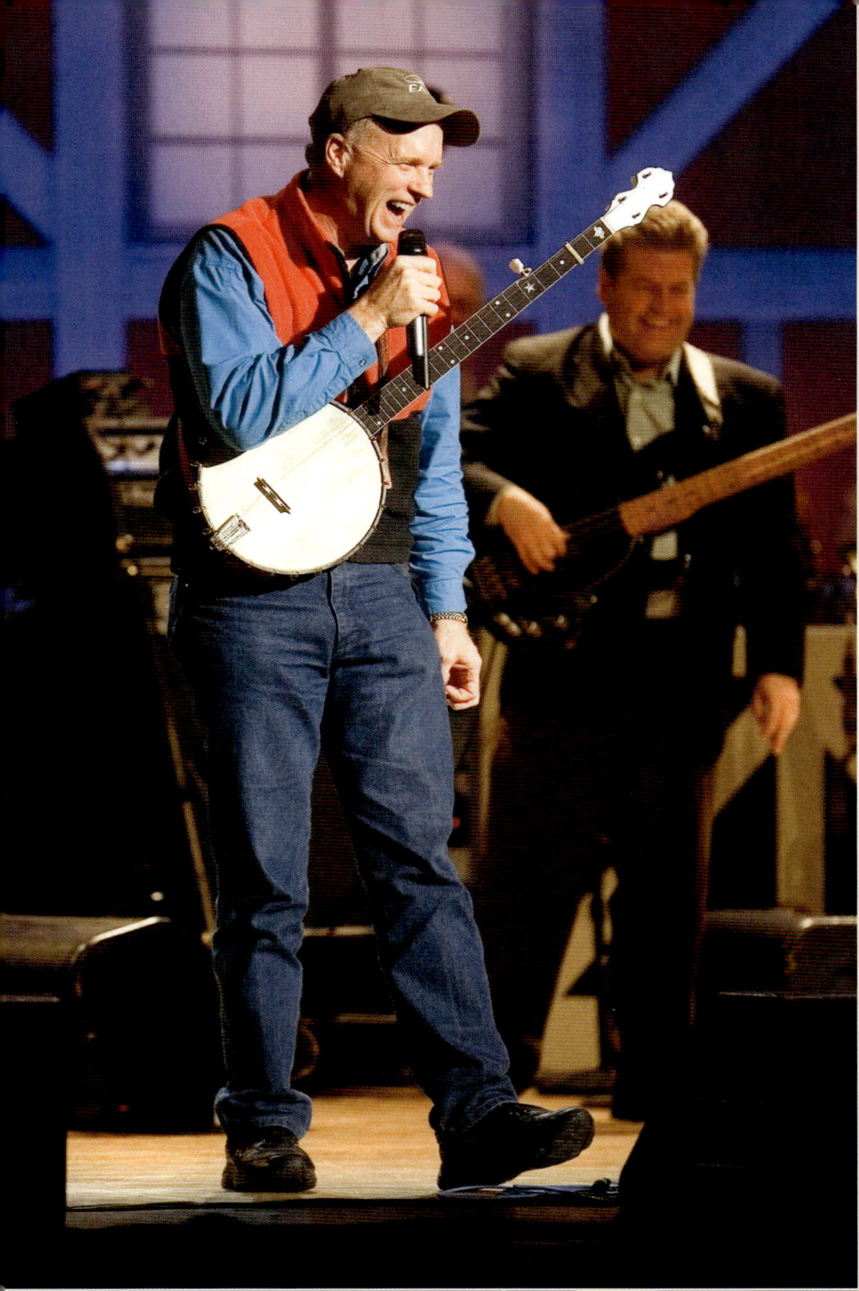

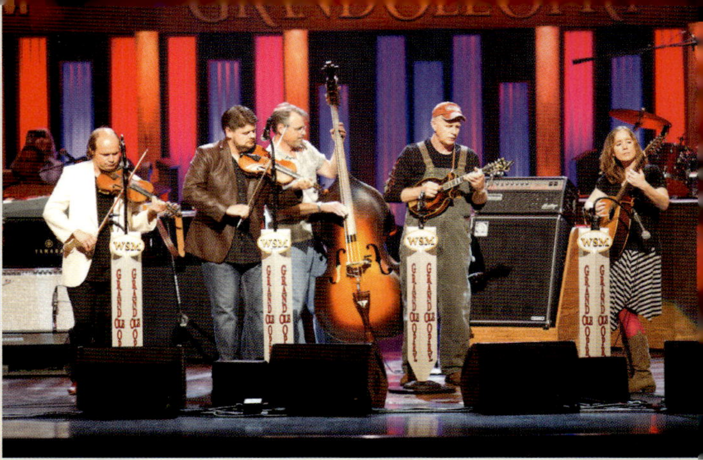
WSM

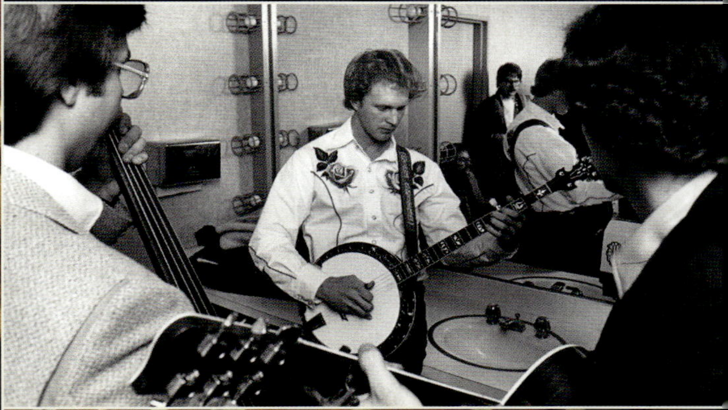

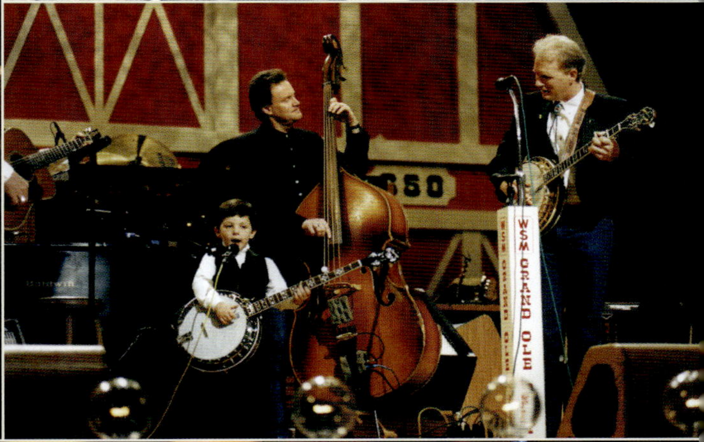
650
WSM GRAND OLE

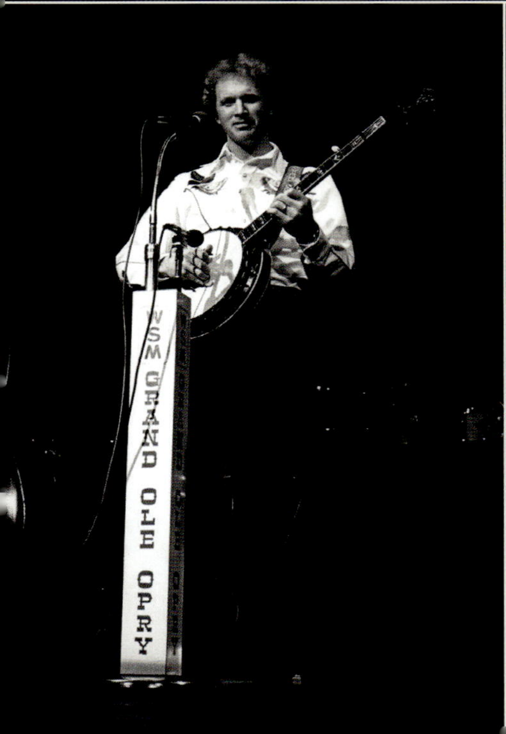
WSM GRAND OLE OPRY

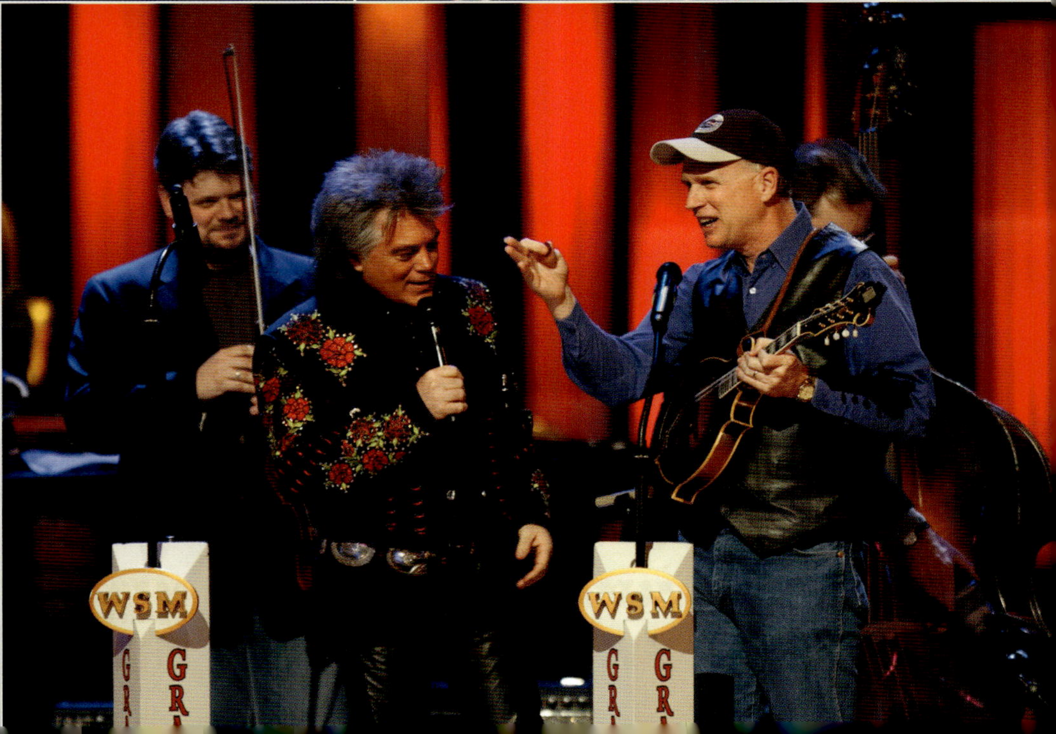
WSM
WSM

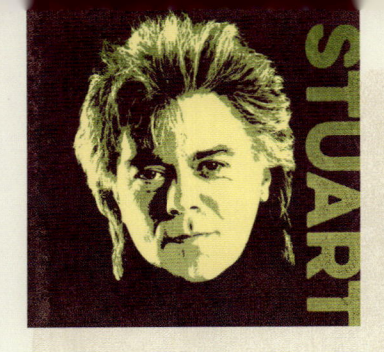

MARTY STUART
MEMBER SINCE 1992

Over the years, Marty Stuart's love of country music has found multiple avenues for expression. In addition to writing and recording such hits as "Hillbilly Rock," "Tempted," and "The Whiskey Ain't Workin," the latter a Grammy-winning duet with pal Travis Tritt, Marty has become one of country music's noted historians. *Sparkle & Twang: Marty Stuart's American Musical Odyssey*, his traveling exhibit of music memorabilia and photography, has been displayed at the Tennessee State Museum and the Rock and Roll Hall of Fame. In 2008, Marty launched *The Marty Stuart Show* on cable's RFD Network. Each program features Marty's band, The Fabulous Superlatives, as well as his wife Connie Smith, plus fellow Grand Ole Opry members and other guests.

BIRTHPLACE: Philadelphia, Mississippi
BIRTH DATE: September 20
OPRY INDUCTION: November 28, 1992

DID YOU KNOW? Marty Stuart first played the Grand Ole Opry at age 13.

"THE OPRY IS A WAY OF LIFE. IT'S AN INSTITUTION THAT GETS PASSED ON EVERY WEEKEND. IF YOU'RE GOING TO BE A COUNTRY PERFORMER, THE OPRY IS THE PLACE TO BE."

Marty's passion for country music began when he taught himself to play mandolin as a child. By the time he was 13, he had been recruited to join the legendary Lester Flatt's band. Marty has performed with some of country music's most notable musicians, including fiddler Vassar Clements and guitarist Doc Watson. He also spent several years in Johnny Cash's band before pursuing a solo career.

In 1990, he hit the Top 10 for the first time with the title track of his album *Hillbilly Rock*. In 1991, he released *Tempted*, and the title track became a Top 5 single. In the early '90s, he also teamed with Travis for such hits as "The Whiskey Ain't Workin'" and "This One's Gonna Hurt You."

Following that string of hits, Marty turned his attention to many of the other styles of music he truly loves from traditional country to gospel and several others in between. In 2010, he issued *Ghost Train*, which was recorded in RCA's famed Studio B, where Marty played on his first session with Flatt when he was 13.

Though he's seen many changes in the country music industry over the years, Marty says the Opry has remained constant. "The thing that has absolutely not changed is the Grand Ole Opry," he says. "The Mother Church of Country Music has remained, and it all revolves around it."

CLOCKWISE FROM TOP LEFT:
1. June 19, 2009
2. October 19, 2001
3. With Willard Scott
4. With Connie Smith
5. With Paul Shaffer
6. Opry induction night, November 28, 1992
7. As a young member of Lester Flatt's band

OPRY FAMILY MEMBERS

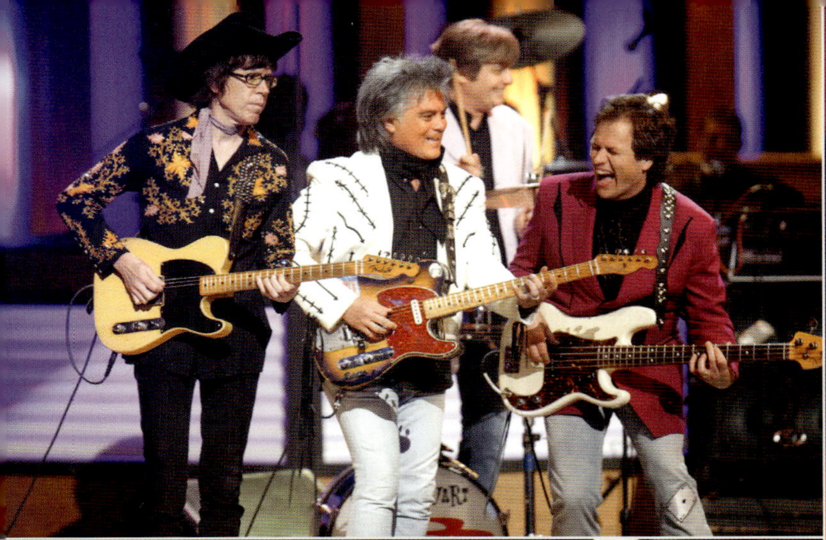

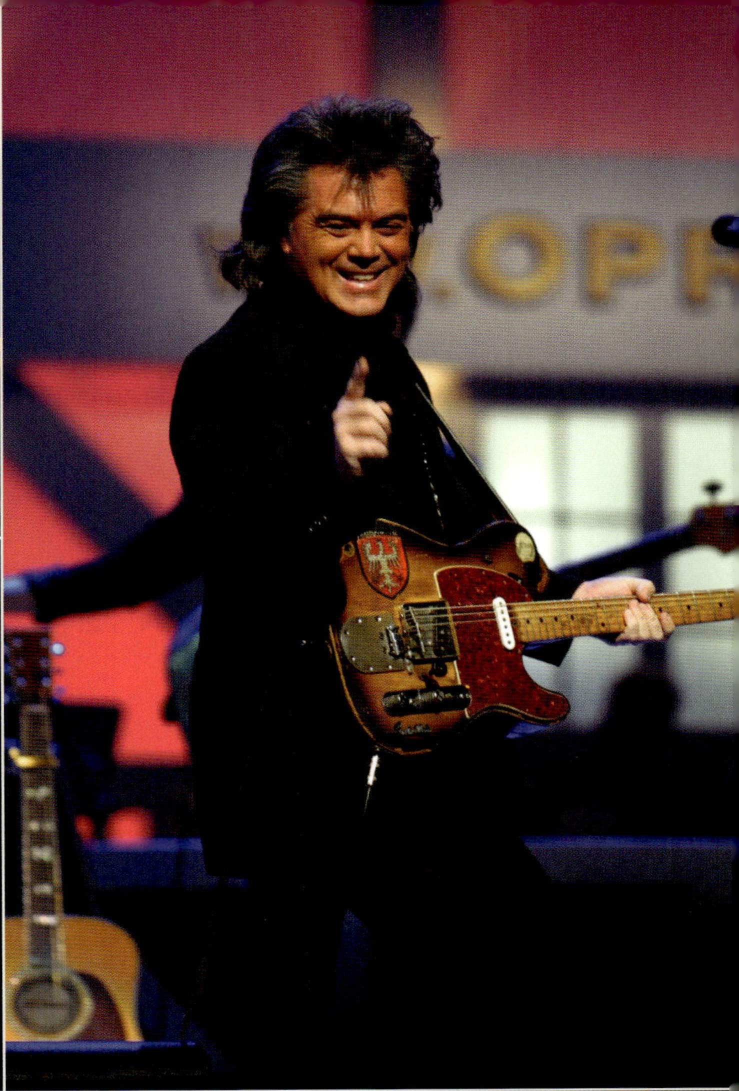

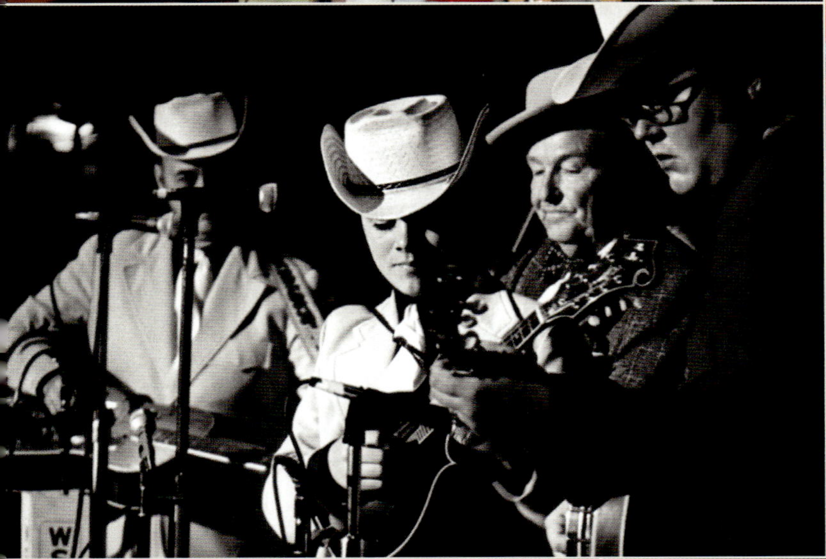

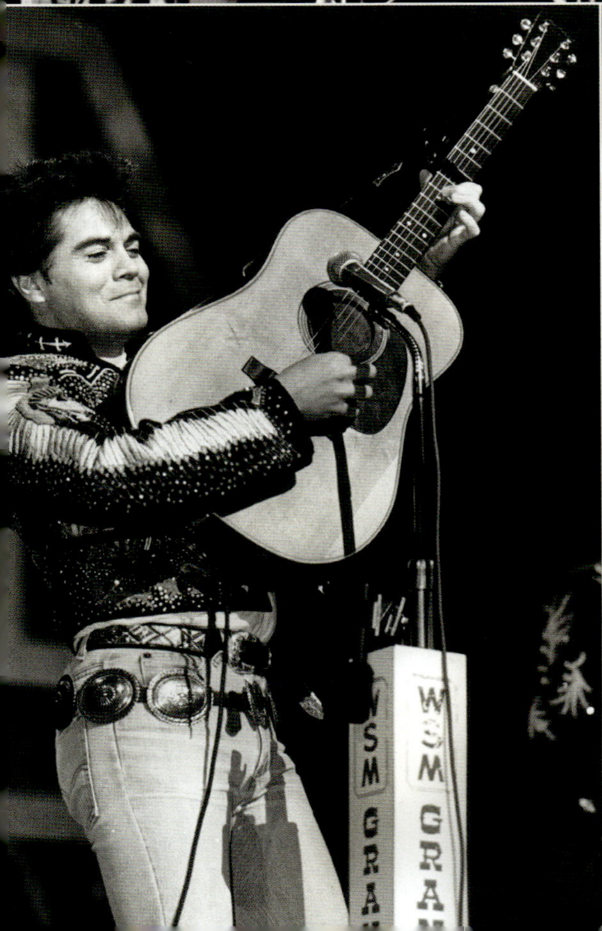
WSM

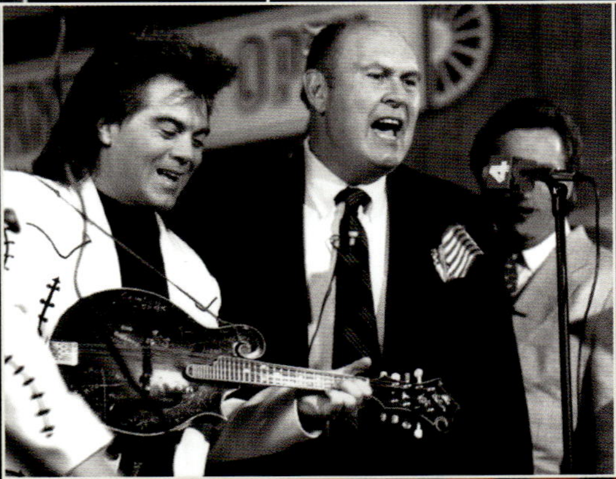

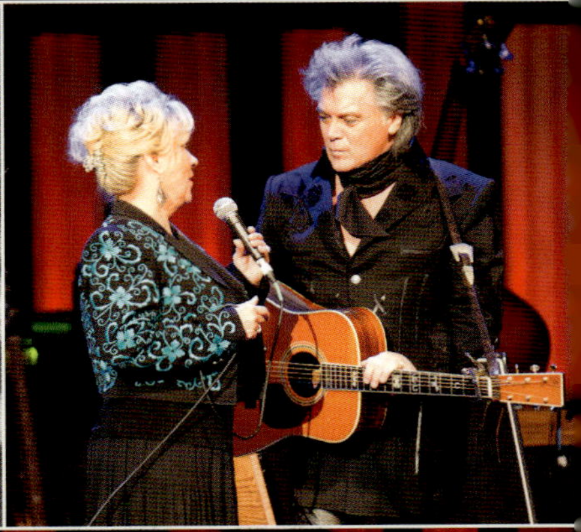

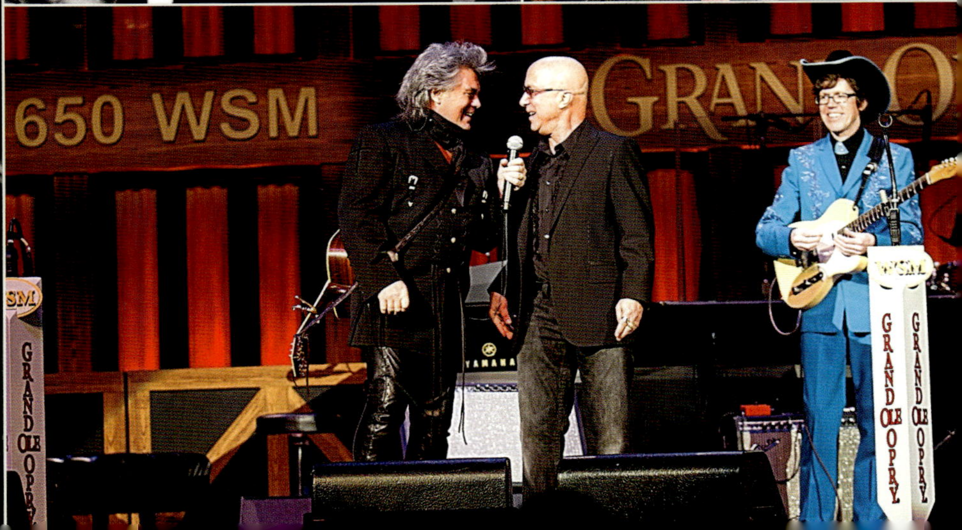
650 WSM

PAM TILLIS
MEMBER SINCE 2000

BIRTHPLACE: Plant City, Florida
BIRTH DATE: July 24
OPRY INDUCTION: August 26, 2000

Pam Tillis has enjoyed many career-defining moments on stage at the Grand Ole Opry. The daughter of singer and songwriting legend Mel Tillis, she made her Opry debut on the Ryman Auditorium stage at age eight, singing "Tom Dooley" with her dad. "It was a larger-than-life moment for me," Pam recalls. "It was sort of like he was passing me the baton. The microphone came down to me and it was in s-l-o-o-o-w motion. My little knees were knocking together. I got my knees under control and it traveled up. My lip was twitching and I was like little kiddie Elvis!"

In 2000, Pam was on the legendary stage once again, now looking down rather than up, as Little Jimmy Dickens invited her to become an Opry member. Without a moment's hesitation she said yes.

> "ONCE YOU'RE IN THAT CIRCLE [IN THE MIDDLE OF THE OPRY STAGE], YOU JUST CAN SENSE WHO STOOD THERE. YOU REALLY FEEL THAT."

Throughout her career, Pam has earned nearly 20 Top 10 singles, three Country Music Association awards — including the coveted Female Vocalist of the Year in 1994 — and two Grammys. She has experimented with pop, Broadway, and jazz, seamlessly incorporating those influences into music that remains unmistakably country at its core.

Through the '80s, Pam worked as a back-up vocalist, jingle singer, club performer, songwriter, and demo singer before her first hit single, "Don't Tell Me What to Do" reached the Top 5 in 1990. She followed with hits including "Maybe It Was Memphis," "Shake the Sugar Tree," "Mi Vida Loca," and "All The Good Ones Are Gone." Two albums were million-sellers.

"In all of my years in the music business," Pam says, "I've been very proud that I wasn't calculated, that I really did what I felt, and what I thought was honest for me to sing. Daddy always said, 'Never change who you are; let it come around to you.' So when things did happen for me, it was because what I wanted to do was what people now wanted to hear."

CLOCKWISE FROM TOP LEFT:
1. With father and fellow Opry member Mel Tillis
2. March 11, 2006
3. Circa 2006
4. With Lorrie Morgan
5. With one of the world's most famous canines, Lassie

GRAND OLE OPRY
www.OPRY.com

WSM
GRAND OLE OPRY
WSM
GRAND OLE OPRY

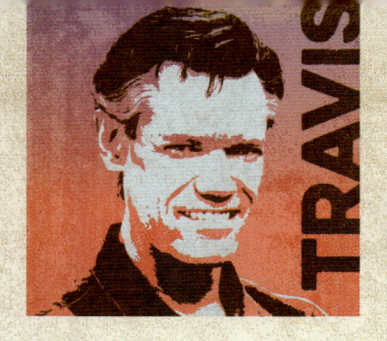

RANDY TRAVIS
MEMBER SINCE 1986

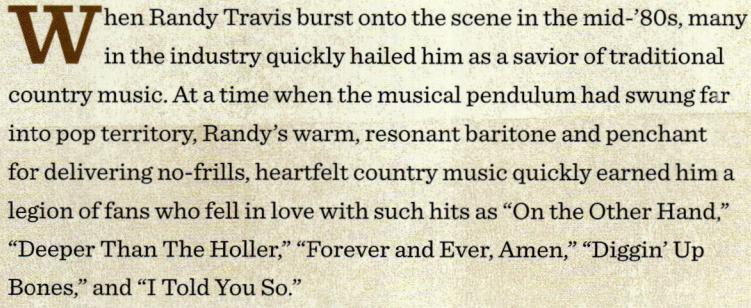

When Randy Travis burst onto the scene in the mid-'80s, many in the industry quickly hailed him as a savior of traditional country music. At a time when the musical pendulum had swung far into pop territory, Randy's warm, resonant baritone and penchant for delivering no-frills, heartfelt country music quickly earned him a legion of fans who fell in love with such hits as "On the Other Hand," "Deeper Than The Holler," "Forever and Ever, Amen," "Diggin' Up Bones," and "I Told You So."

Randy's early years in Nashville were challenging, and nearly every record label in town turned him down before he finally signed with Warner Bros. Records in 1985. His debut album the next year, *Storms of Life*, became one of the landmark albums in country music history,

BIRTHPLACE: Marshville, North Carolina
BIRTH DATE: May 4
OPRY INDUCTION: December 20, 1986

> "TO ME, COUNTRY MUSIC TELLS A STORY ABOUT, AND DEALS WITH, THE WAY PEOPLE LIVE THEIR LIVES AND WHAT THEY DO."

selling more than 4 million copies, winning the Academy of Country Music's Album of the Year award, and spawning such classic hits as "On the Other Hand" and "1982."

After a dozen years on Warner Bros., Randy signed with a different record label and served up such hits as "Out of My Bones," "Spirit of a Boy, Wisdom of Man," and "Three Wooden Crosses." In addition to his successful singing career, Randy also branched out into acting, appearing on such TV shows as *Touched by an Angel* and in numerous films, including *Black Dog* with Patrick Swayze and *The Rainmaker* with Matt Damon. In recent years, he also found success in the gospel music field, recording highly acclaimed inspirational albums and earning multiple Dove Awards.

An Opry member since 1986, Randy has earned numerous accolades, among them six CMA, 10 American Music Awards, nine ACMs, six Grammys, and a star on the Hollywood Walk of Fame. In 2008, he reunited with Warner Bros. for *Around the Bend*, a collection of traditional country gems that reminded country fans yet again why his name is frequently mentioned alongside such country legends as George Jones, Keith Whitley, and Lefty Frizzell.

CLOCKWISE FROM TOP LEFT:
1. With Carrie Underwood
2. With Roy Acuff May 1988
3. Circa 1980s
4. With Connie Smith, Joe Stampley and Gene Watson, October 4, 2011
5. October 16, 2010

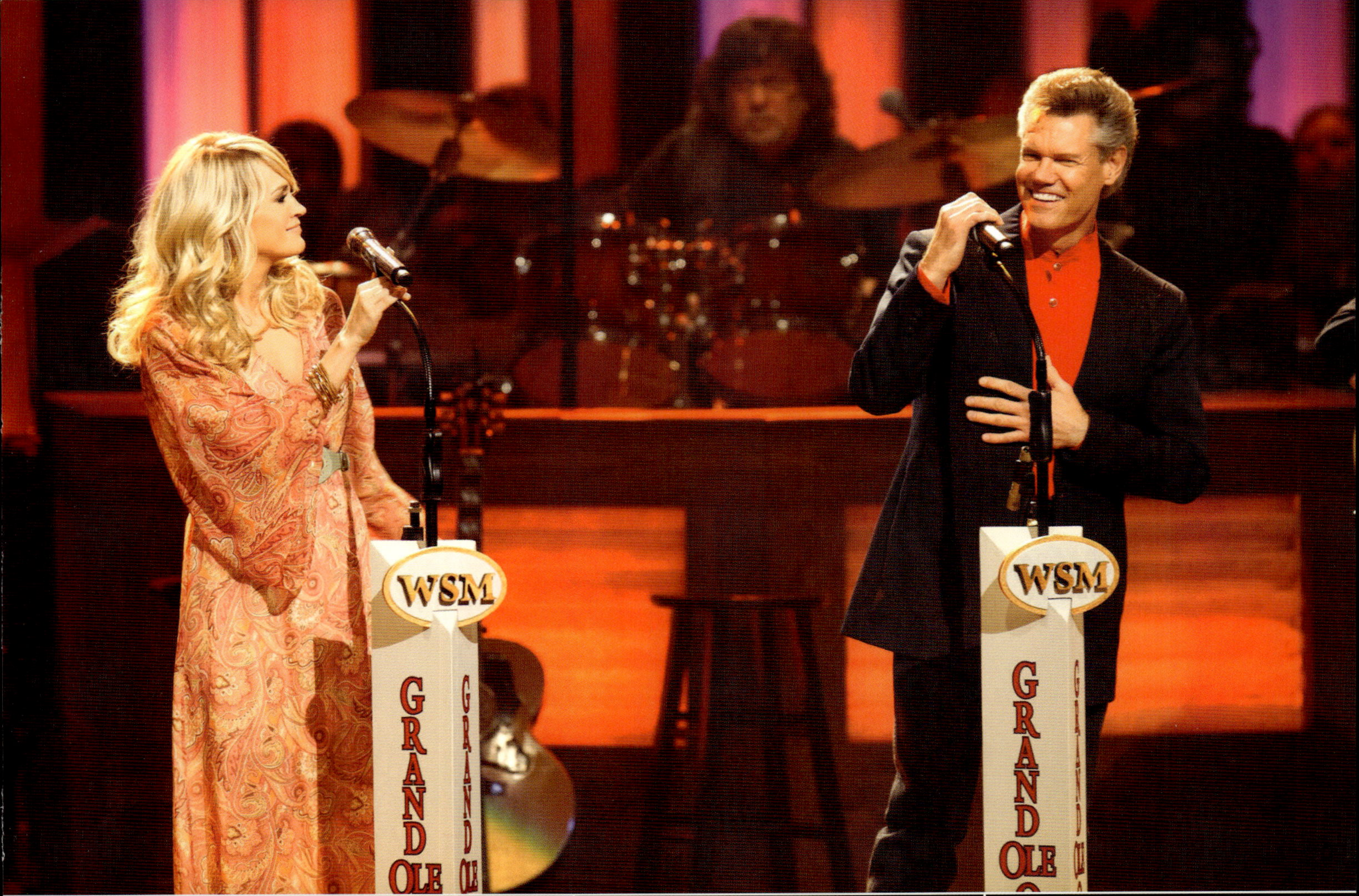
WSM
GRAND OLE
WSM
GRAND OLE

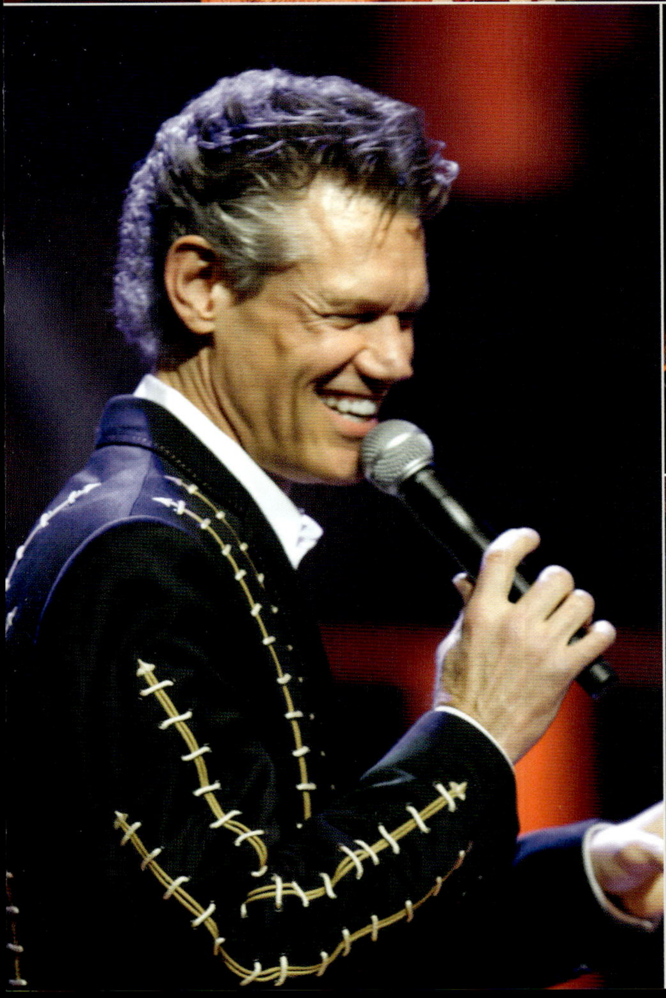

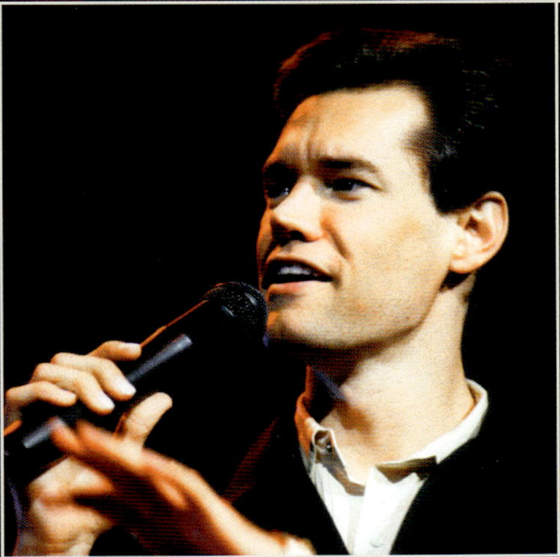

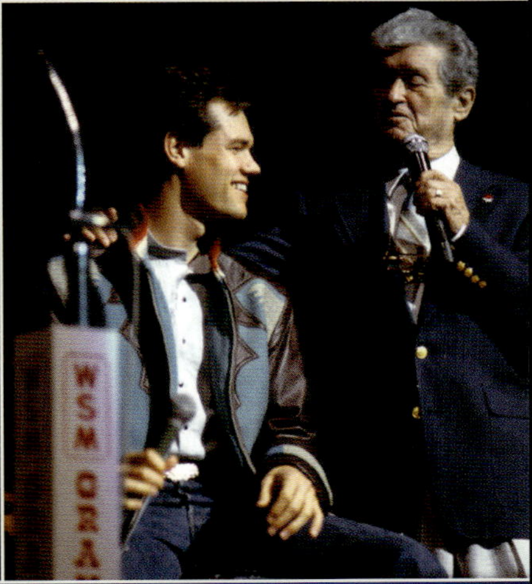
WSM

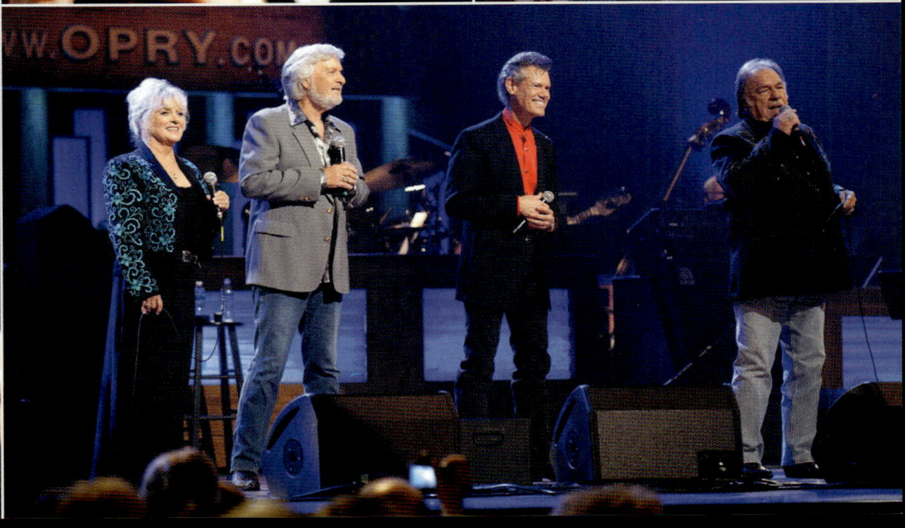
WW.OPRY.COM

TRAVIS TRITT
MEMBER SINCE 1992

A Georgia native who came up in the state's rough-and-tumble club circuit before moving to Nashville, Travis Tritt built his reputation on a blend of Southern rock swagger, honky tonk themes and songwriting craft that found favor with older stars like Roy Acuff and young fans alike.

He began his musical career as a soloist in a Marietta, Georgia, church's children's choir, teaching himself guitar at age eight and writing his first song at age 14 before plunging into Atlanta's night life as a singer and bandleader. After signing with Warner Bros. Records in 1988, he released the album *Country Club*, a strong debut that cracked the Top 10 with its title cut and then yielded three Top 5 singles ("Help Me Hold On," "I'm Gonna Be Somebody," and "Drift Off to Dream") that showed off his muscular singing and versatility.

BIRTHPLACE: Marietta, Georgia
BIRTH DATE: February 9
OPRY INDUCTION: February 29, 1992

> "I DON'T KNOW WHY TO THIS DAY," HE SAYS WITH A SMILE, "BUT ROY ACUFF SAW SOMETHING IN ME THAT HE LIKED. ... HE CAME UP AND PUT HIS ARM AROUND ME BACKSTAGE AND SAID, 'SON, WE WANT TO SEE YOU BACK HERE AT THE OPRY MORE OFTEN.'"

In recognition of his spectacular rise, *Billboard* magazine named him the top new male artist of 1990, while the Country Music Association gave Travis its Horizon Award in 1991. Then he began to make regular appearances on the Grand Ole Opry's stage. "I don't know why to this day," he says with a smile, "but Roy Acuff saw something in me that he liked. ... He came up and put his arm around me backstage and said, 'Son, we want to see you back here at the Opry more often.'" The following year Travis was invited to join the Opry cast.

For the next decade, Travis was a near-constant presence on the country charts, alternating rowdy anthems like "T-R-O-U-B-L-E" and "Ten Feet Tall and Bulletproof" with power ballads such as "Foolish Pride" and contemplative stories like "Anymore." Travis also teamed up several times with fellow Opry member Marty Stuart for songs that included the CMA and Grammy award-winning "The Whiskey Ain't Working" and Top 10 hit "This One's Gonna Hurt You (For a Long, Long Time)."

Travis announced in 2010 that he was forming his own label for future releases, starting with one to mark his 20th anniversary as a country star. "In some ways it seems like 20 minutes," Travis told *Billboard*. "In some ways it seems like forever."

CLOCKWISE FROM TOP LEFT:
1. October 21, 2006
2. With Earl Scruggs and Marty Stuart
3. May 24, 2003
4. With Porter Wagoner
5. December 8, 2001

OPRY FAMILY MEMBERS

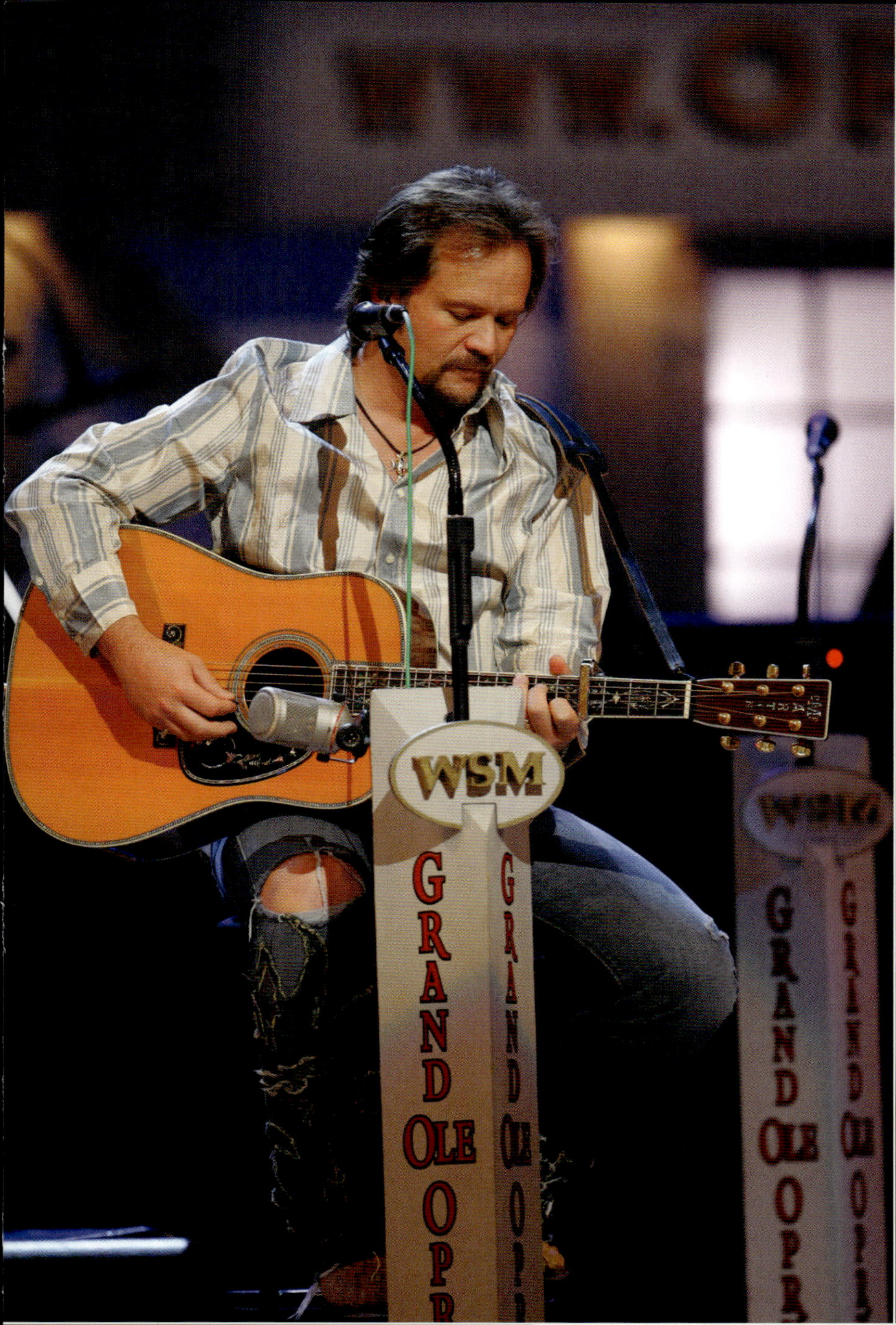
WSM
GRAND
OLE
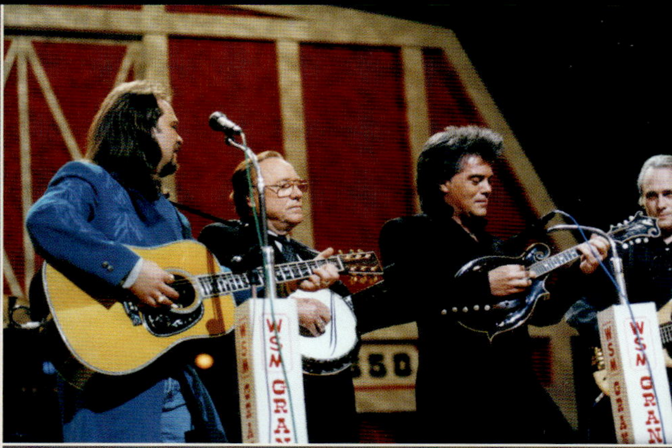
WSM
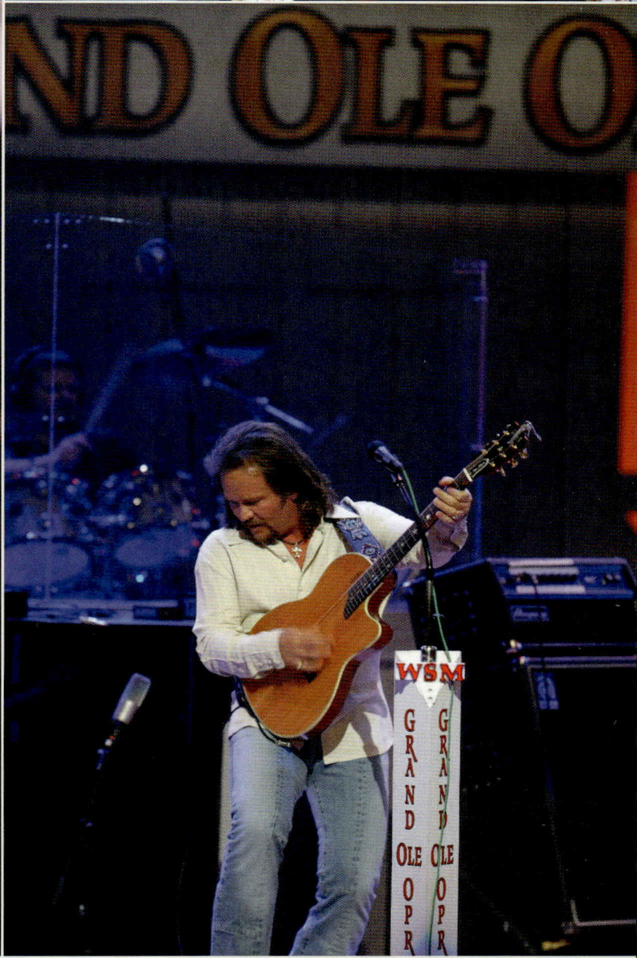
ND OLE O
WSM
GRAND
OLE
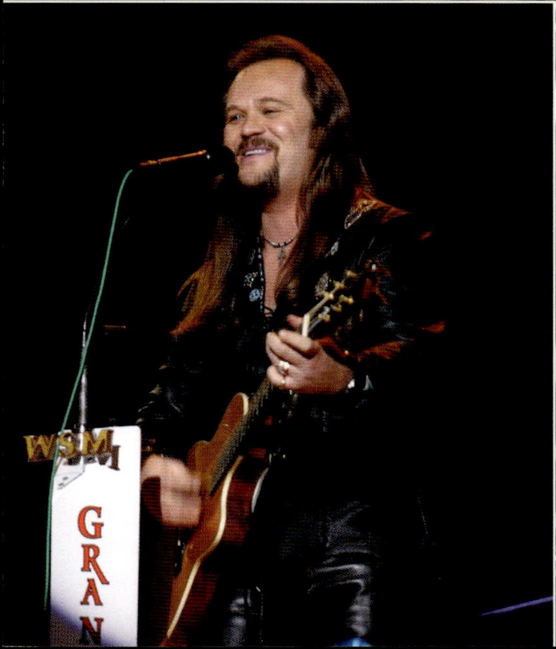
WSM
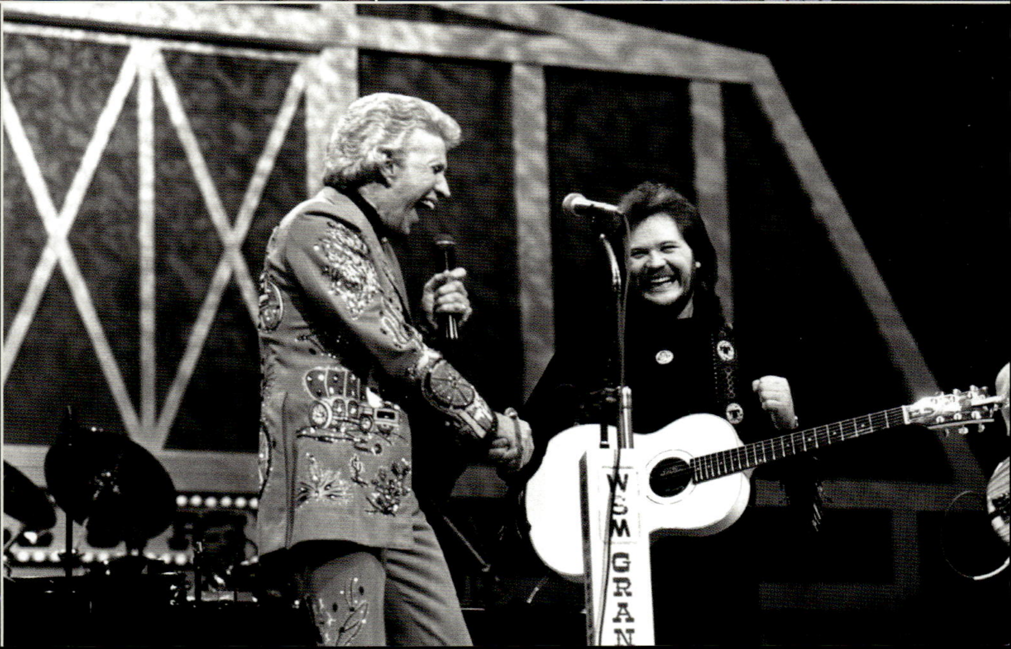
WSM

JOSH TURNER
MEMBER SINCE 2007

Combining respect for country music's traditions with a contemporary edge has made Josh Turner one of the industry's most successful young artists. He burst on the scene with "Long Black Train," also the title of his 2003 platinum-selling debut album, and has since scored such chart-topping hits as "Your Man," "Would You Go With Me" and "All Over Me."

A graduate of Nashville's Belmont University, it was Josh's songwriting that first caught the attention of Music Row and led to a publishing deal then to a record deal, as well. His debut album sold more than a million copies and his second effort, *Your Man*, debuted at No. 1 on *Billboard* magazine's Top Country Albums chart. His third album, 2007's *Everything Is Fine*, yielded the hit "Firecracker," and his fourth studio album, *Haywire*, released in 2010, spawned the chart-topping tune "Why Don't We Just Dance." His 2012 album, *Punching Bag*, produced the hit "Time Is Love."

BIRTHPLACE: Hannah, South Carolina
BIRTH DATE: November 20
OPRY INDUCTION: October 27, 2007

Q: What is your most memorable Opry Moment?
A: For me, the moment happened on December 21, 2001 when I made my debut at the Ryman Auditorium. I sang a song I wrote myself called "Long Black Train." I got a standing ovation halfway through the song and all I thought about was that I was standing in the very spot where Hank Williams had made his debut. (Hank's music was partly the inspiration for "Long Black Train.") I was completely unknown to the audience which made the moment extra special.

"I WAS FIGHTING BACK THE TEARS OUT THERE. I COULDN'T THINK STRAIGHT. I WAS TORE UP." —JOSH TURNER ON HIS OPRY DEBUT.

Inducted into the Opry in 2007, Josh says the camaraderie between artists backstage is something he treasures. "At the Opry, you just have to do a song or two and everything is already set up so it leaves time to mingle and get to know people," he says. "There's always so many artists here, it's like a reunion every weekend. You get to come here and see people you've known for a long time or you get to meet new people. It's a really cool way to network and get to know your fellow artists."

He also appreciates the way the Opry helps him connect with fans. "The Opry draws in a lot of people from all over the country," he says. "That's the coolest thing about the Opry. Many different artists — old and new — can come and showcase their talent to a new crowd every weekend. That's been a great avenue of promotion and way to stay out there in front of the people and debut new music."

CLOCKWISE FROM TOP LEFT:
1. --
2. With Ricky Skaggs
3. July 8, 2008
4. May 28, 2013
5. With the MusiCorps Wounded Warrior Band
6. With the Opry's Pete Fisher and Vince Gill, Opry induction night October 27, 2007

WSM
GRAND OLE OPRY
GRAND OLE OPRY

OLEOPRY
WSM
GRAND
GRAND

650 WSM

WSM
GRAND OLE OPRY
GRAND OLE OPRY

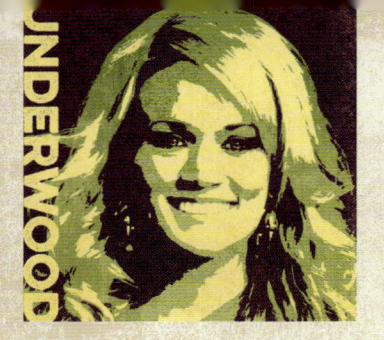

CARRIE UNDERWOOD
MEMBER SINCE 2008

Carrie Underwood was nervous the night she made her Grand Ole Opry debut. Most singers are, but the naturally shy young woman from Oklahoma had won *American Idol* just two weeks before — the first country singer to finish first on the top-rated TV show — and she wasn't sure how she'd be accepted at the venerated institution. She needn't have worried.

"It's kind of magical," she gushed on the side of the Opry stage just after finishing her two-song set. "I don't feel like I deserve this at all." But Carrie absolutely deserved the thunderous applause that night, and that sense of magic has stayed with her throughout her career — one of the most impressive in country music history.

BIRTHPLACE: Muskogee, Oklahoma
BIRTH DATE: March 10
OPRY INDUCTION: May 10, 2008

Q: What's your favorite memory from the Grand Ole Opry?
A: "It's hard to choose an absolute favorite memory. The night that I was invited to be a member and the night that I was inducted are certainly two evenings that will always shine in my mind above all others. My parents got to meet Garth Brooks which was pretty awesome!"

> "THAT WAS THE DREAM, YOU KNOW? ALL OF THE LEGENDS; THAT'S WHAT THEY DO: THEY SING AT THE OPRY, AND THEY BECOME MEMBERS AT SOME POINT."

Since that night in June 2005, Carrie has placed more than 20 singles at the top of the country charts, including "Jesus, Take the Wheel," "Before He Cheats," "Cowboy Casanova," the appropriately titled "All-American Girl," "Good Girl" and "See You Again." She has sold millions of albums worldwide. Her debut album, *Some Hearts*, is the best-selling album from any *American Idol* contestant. It spent 27 weeks at No. 1 on *Billboard* magazine's Top Country Albums chart across a three-year period, and *Billboard* ranked it as the Top Country Album of the last decade.

Carrie has become one of the most honored young singers in country music today, with a trophy tally that includes over 95 major awards including Grammys and awards from both the Academy of Country Music and the Country Music Association. She has also co-hosted the CMA Awards with fellow Opry star Brad Paisley.

Of particular significance is the award she was presented on the night of her Opry induction in 2008. "The induction award they gave me says, 'Hey, you're a part of the family,'" Carrie says. "It means a lot to me because it's the heart of country music, the church, the sacred place, the super-elite club that says you love this music."

CLOCKWISE FROM TOP LEFT:
1. Flipping the switch on "Opry Goes Pink"
2. With Brad Paisley
3. Being invited by Randy Travis to become an Opry member
4. 5th Opry Anniversary
5. Opry debut
6. June 7, 2013

WSM
GRAND OLE
WSM

WSM
GRAND OLE OPRY
GRAND OLE OPRY

5th
ANNIVERSARY

KEITH URBAN
MEMBER SINCE 2012

New Zealand-born and Australia-raised, Keith Urban moved to Nashville in 1992. His first American album came as a member of The Ranch (1997), followed by an increasingly accomplished string of Platinum and multi Platinum-selling solo albums. The 2008 compilation *Greatest Hits: 19 Kids* included such No. 1 hits as "But For The Grace Of God," "Somebody Like You," "Who Wouldn't Wanna Be Me," "You'll Think Of Me," "Days Go By," "Making Memories Of Us," "Better Life," and "You Look Good In My Shirt." He's sold more than 15 million albums, been named radio's most played country artist and won praise the world over with his electrifying sold-out concerts that have taken him from Australia to Germany, Canada, England and of course the United States.

BIRTHPLACE: Whangarei, New Zealand
BIRTH DATE: October 26
OPRY INDUCTION: April 21, 2012

Q: What's your favorite thing about being backstage at the Opry?
A: For me it's the mingling of artists, fans, friends and families. It's like everyone's hanging out together at somebody's house. I don't know of any other place where that happens.

> "I HONOR THE HISTORY OF COUNTRY MUSIC, BUT I ABSOLUTELY FULLY DEDICATE MYSELF TO THE FUTURE OF COUNTRY MUSIC, AS WELL."

Urban has been honored with multiple Grammy Awards, Country Music Association, Academy of County Music, People's Choice, and American Music awards. His remarkable musical gifts also have taken him to places where country superstars have rarely gone before, including such appearances as Live 8 with Alicia Keys, a powerful rendition of "Lean on Me" alongside Kid Rock and Sheryl Crow on the *Hope for Haiti* telethon, and *American Idol*. He was one of the first artists to appear on two episodes of *CMT Crossroads*, the first with John Fogerty and the second with John Mayer.

On April 21, 2012, Keith became an official part of the Opry after having been surprised two weeks earlier with an Opry membership invitation from Vince Gill.

Urban's philanthropic work knows no boundaries, as he's remained highly active with St. Jude Children's Hospital, appeared on numerous telethons and benefit concerts for cause-related issues, and even established the annual All For The Hall concerts, which have collectively raised millions of dollars for the Country Music Hall of Fame and Museum.

CLOCKWISE FROM TOP LEFT:
1. June 4, 2013
2. April 21, 2012
3. October 25, 2011
4. With Marty Stuart
5. Vince Gill invites Keith Urban to become an official Opry member

OPRY FAMILY MEMBERS

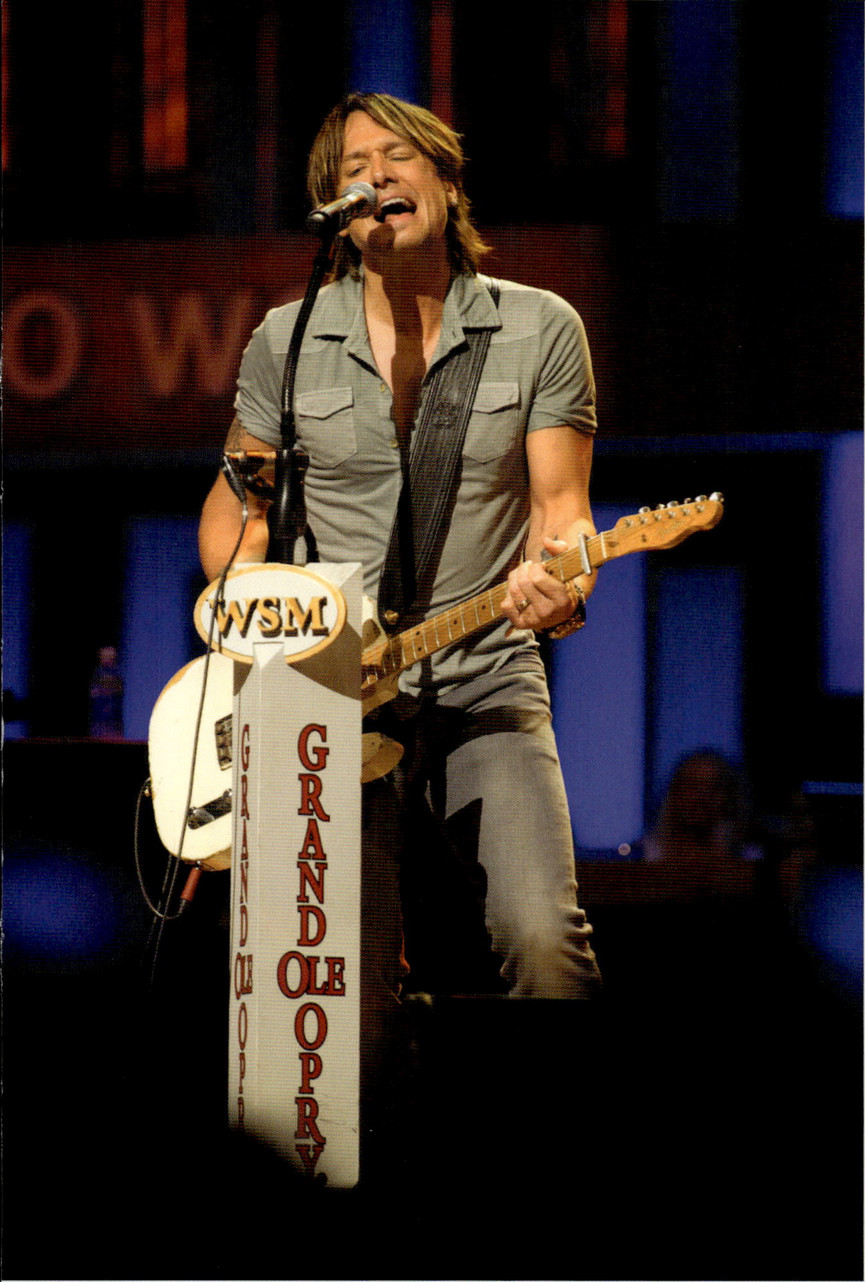
WSM
GRAND OLE OPRY

WSM

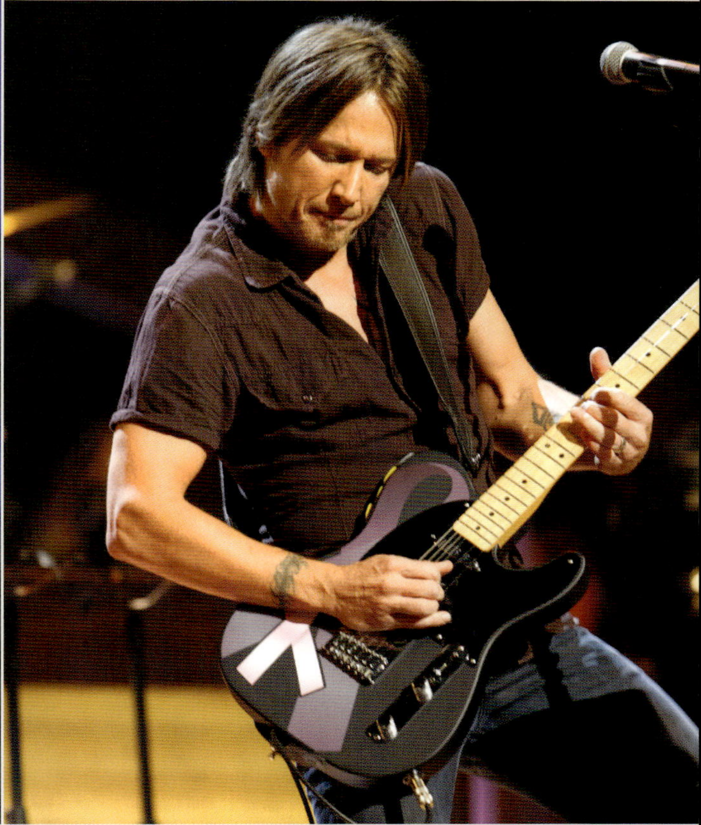

WSM
GRAND OLE OPRY

GRAND OLE OPRY
WSM
GRAND OLE OPRY

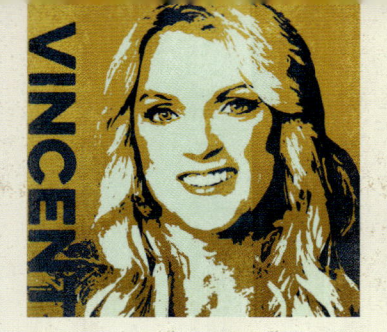

RHONDA VINCENT
MEMBER SINCE 2021

Bluegrass award-winner Rhonda Vincent started singing at age 3 with her family band The Sally Mountain Show. They made their first recording when Rhonda was 5 years old, and had a TV and radio show. She started playing mandolin at age 8, and the fiddle at age 12.

"I don't think there's any way to express to someone how the Opry has been part of my life all my life," Rhonda says.

She recalls her father tuning in to WSM Radio in Nashville early in the morning and late at night, all the way from Greentop, Missouri.

"After about 6:30 in the morning, it was all static," she says. "but it magically came back every evening."

BIRTHPLACE: Greentop, Missouri
BIRTH DATE: July 13
OPRY INDUCTION: February 6, 2021

DID YOU KNOW? In 2000, The Wall Street Journal deemed Rhonda Vincent the "New Queen of Bluegrass."

> "I LOVE EVERYTHING ABOUT THE GRAND OLE OPRY. I LOVE THE PEOPLE. I LOVE THAT IT'S A FAMILY… I CAN'T BELIEVE THAT I'M HERE … IT'S LIKE A DREAM."

In 2000, Rhonda won her first of seven consecutive Female Vocalist of the Year awards from the International Bluegrass Music Association. In 2001, she was named Entertainer of the Year and in 2002, she had the Song of the Year. In 2015, she won her eighth Female Vocalist of the Year award, and two years later, Rhonda Vincent & The Rage won a Grammy for Best Bluegrass Album.

"To me, this is a wonderful time not only for women but for bluegrass music," she said. "And for little girls and guys alike to say, 'maybe I want to play bluegrass too'."

CLOCKWISE FROM TOP LEFT:
1. Rhonda performs on stage during her induction on February 6, 2021.
2. Rhonda performs on stage on June 28, 2019.
3. Opry member Dierks Bentley joins Rhonda for a song during her induction.
4. Rhonda performs the night she was invited to join the Grand Ole Opry in 2020.
5. Rhonda introduces her grandson to the audience during a performance in 2022.
6. Rhonda faces the crowd holding her trophy during her induction.

GRAND OLE OPRY
GRAND OLE OPRY
OPRY.COM #OPRY

WSM

WSM
GRAND OLE OPRY

650 WSM
WSM
GRAND OLE OPRY

WSM
GRAND OLE OPRY

WSM
GRAND OLE

STEVE WARINER
MEMBER SINCE 1996

The combination of drive and talent that has made Steve Wariner a major country music figure showed up early. He started it all with a guitar obsession, then grew into being a singer, songwriter, painter, producer, showman, and Grand Ole Opry member.

At age nine, Steve was playing guitar, and by 10 he was playing bass in his father's country band. By the time he hit his teens, Steve had started singing publicly — just because the bands he played in needed a singer. But he didn't take it seriously until Opry star Dottie West caught his show in Indianapolis. She hired him as a bass player and introduced him to the Opry. At age 17, he was playing bass for West, by 22 for Bob Luman, and at 24 for guitar legend Chet Atkins.

Chet took on Steve as a protégé, recognizing his talents as a singer and blazing instrumentalist. He signed Steve to RCA Records in 1977, and the singer soon had a bevy of smooth country hits, including his

BIRTHPLACE: Noblesville, Indiana
BIRTH DATE: December 25
OPRY INDUCTION: May 11, 1996

DEFINITIVE STEVE WARINER:
"All Roads Lead To You"
"Life's Highway"
"The Weekend"
"Holes in the Floor of Heaven"

OPRY FACTS: Steve Wariner lent vocals to the theme song for the hit 1980s sitcom *Who's The Boss?* starring Judith Light and Tony Danza.

> "I USED TO COME HOME FOR LUNCH WHEN I WAS IN GRADE SCHOOL, AND AS SOON AS I GOT IN, I'D GO STRAIGHT TO THE BEDROOM AND START PLAYING THE GUITAR. EVERY DAY, MY MOM WOULD HAVE TO YELL AT ME, 'YOU'D BETTER EAT THIS SANDWICH AND GET BACK TO SCHOOL!'"

first No. 1, "All Roads Lead to You." Other albums and record label affiliations, including a move to a harder country direction and more self-penned hits on MCA Records, landed Steve in the country Top 10 with more than two dozen other singles and 13 more No. 1 songs.

During that period, Steve put performances on hold to concentrate on songwriting and came up with hits for fellow Opry members Clint Black, Garth Brooks, and others. Steve picked up Song of the Year honors from both the Country Music Association and the Academy of Country Music for "Holes in the Floor of Heaven," the tune that would also launch another round of professional success.

Steve continues to record, often from the studio in his Tennessee home. He also frequents the Grand Ole Opry stage, displaying the same musical prowess he first showcased on that stage at age 17.

CLOCKWISE FROM TOP LEFT:
1. With Garth Brooks
2. Kathy Mattea presents Steve Wariner with the Minnie Pearl Award in recognition of his endeavors to assist others in the country music community.
3. With Keith Urban at the Ryman Auditorium on February 3, 2012. The night marked the last night the decades-old Ryman stage on which they were performing was used before being replaced with new staging.
4. Circa 1982
5. Steve Wariner's Opry induction, May 11, 1996. With Chet Atkins

OPRY FAMILY MEMBERS   **196**

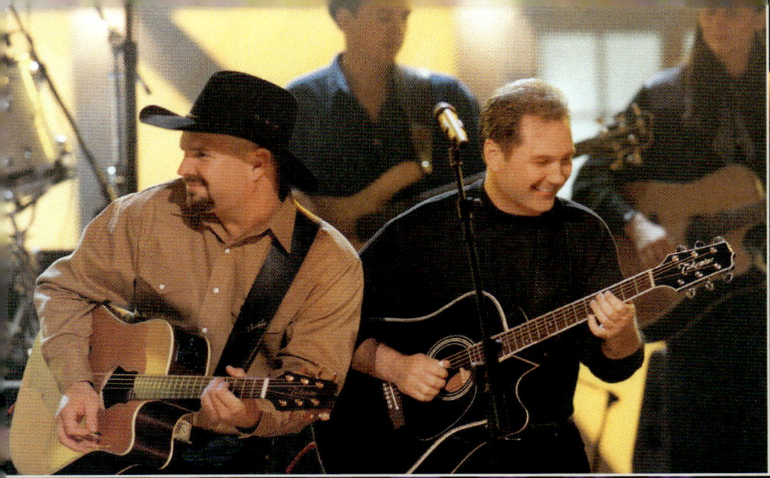

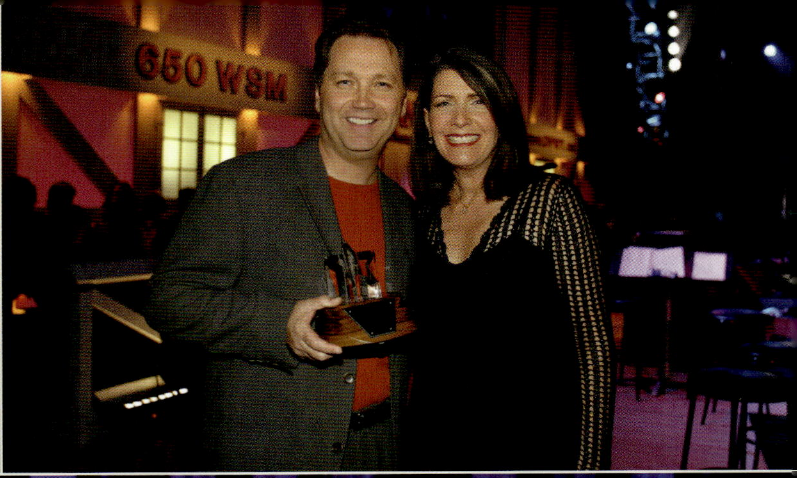
650 WSM

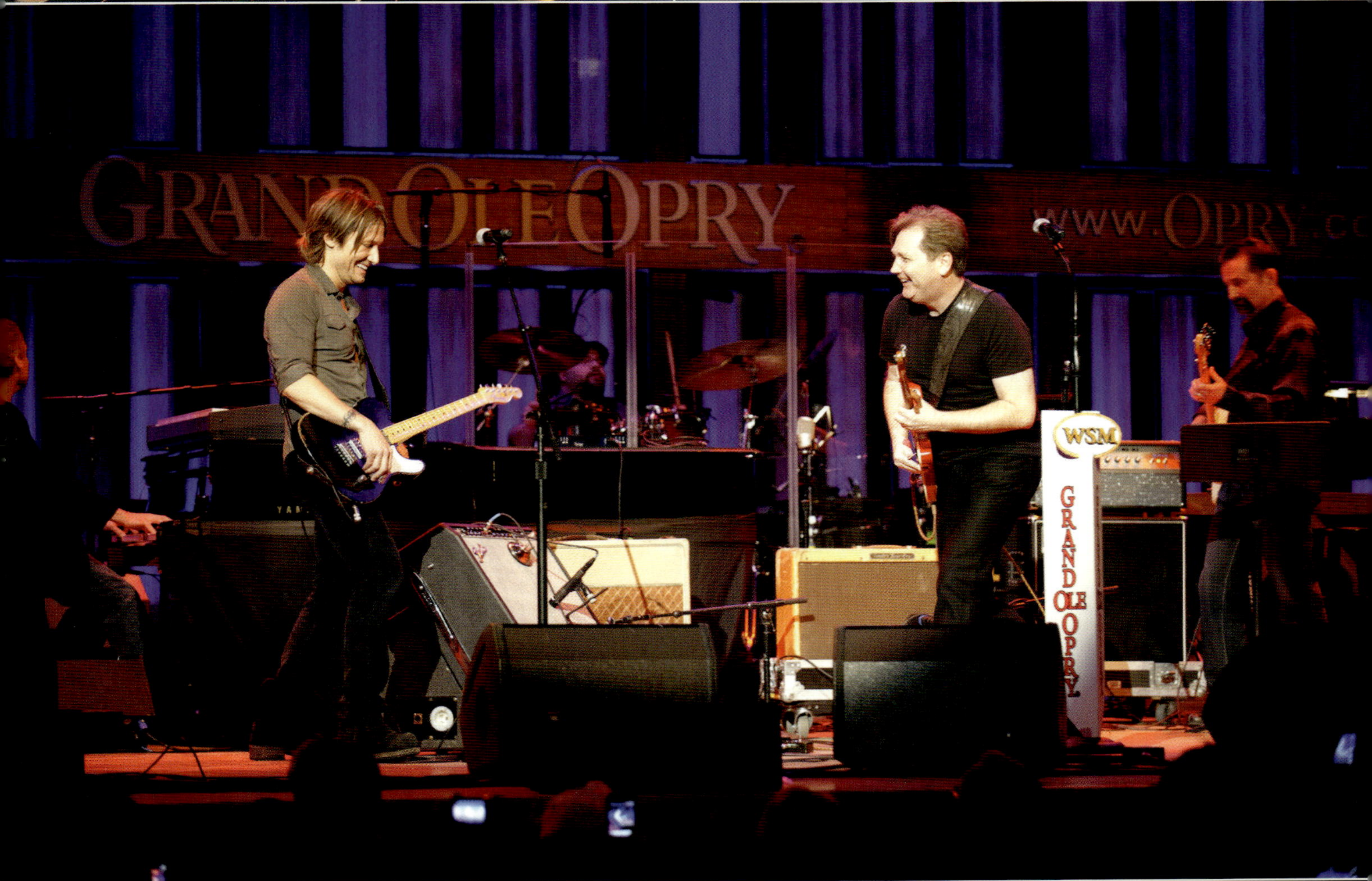
GRAND OLE OPRY
WSM
GRAND OLE OPRY

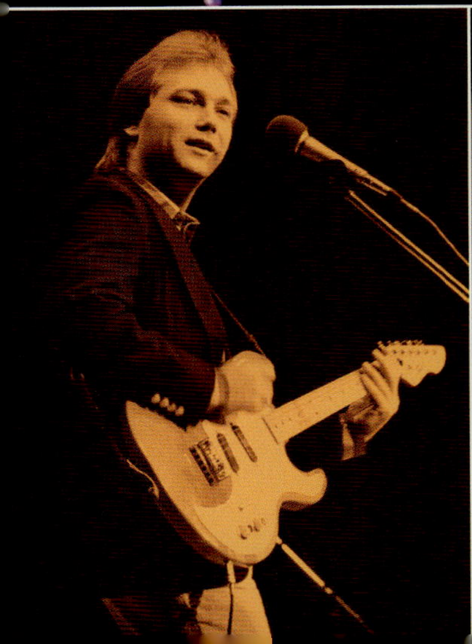

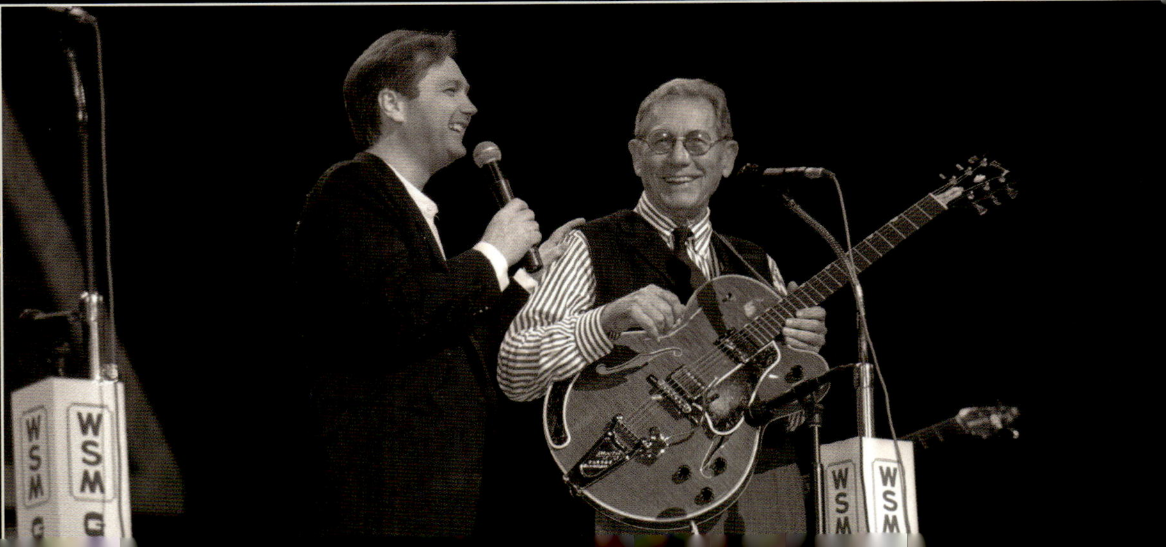
WSM
WSM

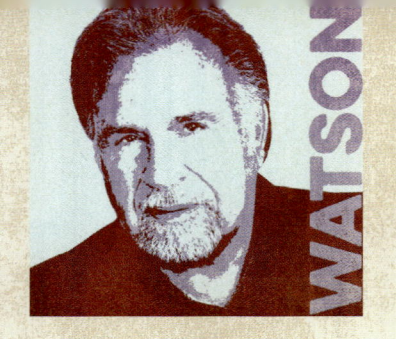

GENE WATSON
MEMBER SINCE 2020

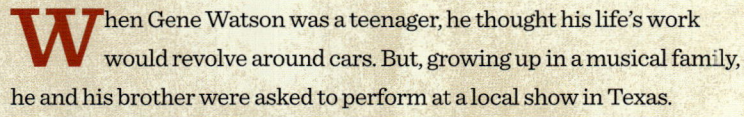

When Gene Watson was a teenager, he thought his life's work would revolve around cars. But, growing up in a musical family, he and his brother were asked to perform at a local show in Texas.

"We got paid some minimum amount but we got a standing ovation and I was hooked on the notion I could get paid for doing a little singing to help pay for a car," he said.

So he kept singing. He was working at a paint and body shop in Houston and moonlighting as a performer in 1964 when country duo, The Wilburn Brothers brought Gene to Nashville and allowed him to sing on the Grand Ole Opry stage. It wasn't until 10 years later, when Capitol Records picked up his steamy song "Love in the Hot Afternoon" for national distribution, that he hit his stride as a country music icon. It was his first of two-dozen top 10 hits.

BIRTHPLACE: Palestine, Texas
BIRTH DATE: October 11
OPRY INDUCTION: February 7, 2020

DID YOU KNOW? Before he was 10 years old, Gene and his family were itinerant workers living in a converted school bus that his father retrofitted to include a stove strapped to the exterior.

> "I LOOK AT THE GRAND OLE OPRY AS THE PINNACLE OF A COUNTRY MUSIC TRADITION. AND I JUST WANT TO DO MY PART TO UPHOLD THE TRADITION, LIKE IT DESERVES TO BE."

For almost 50 years, anytime Gene was passing through Nashville, he'd perform as a guest on the Opry. But on January 17, 2020, Opry member Vince Gill invited Gene to officially become part of the family.

"This is the best payoff that a man can have," he said. "To shake hands with somebody and say, 'I'm happy to be a member of the Grand Ole Opry,' that says it all right there. It makes everything worthwhile that you've been trying to accomplish."

CLOCKWISE FROM TOP LEFT:
1. Gene performs on his induction night on February 7, 2022.
2. Opry member Vince Gill invites Gene to join the family.
3. Opry member Steve Wariner helps induct Gene into the Grand Ole Opry.
4. Gene performs on the Grand Ole Opry.

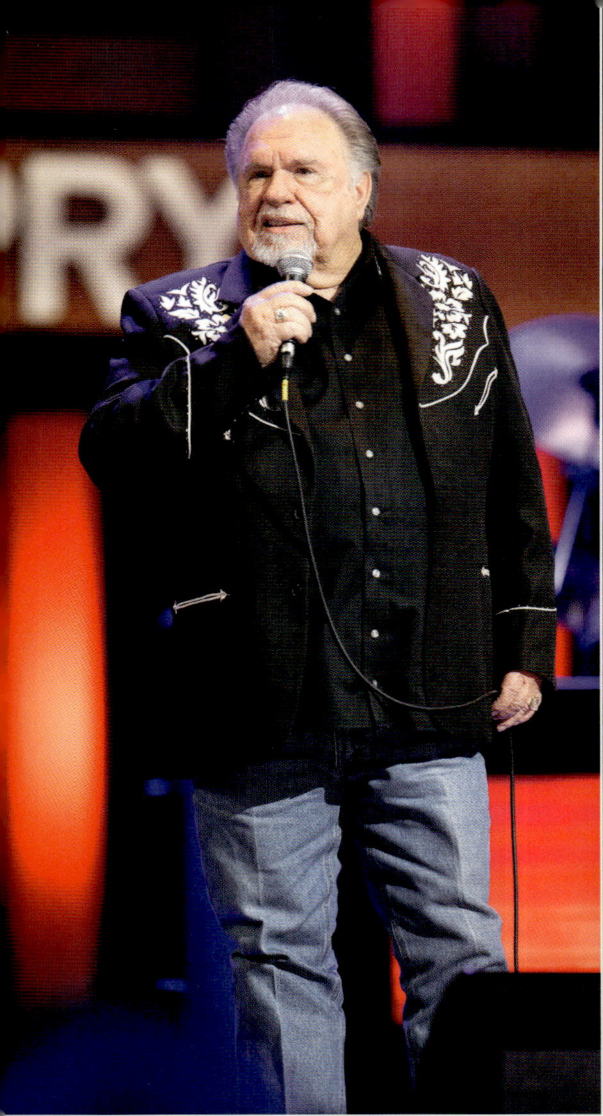
PRY

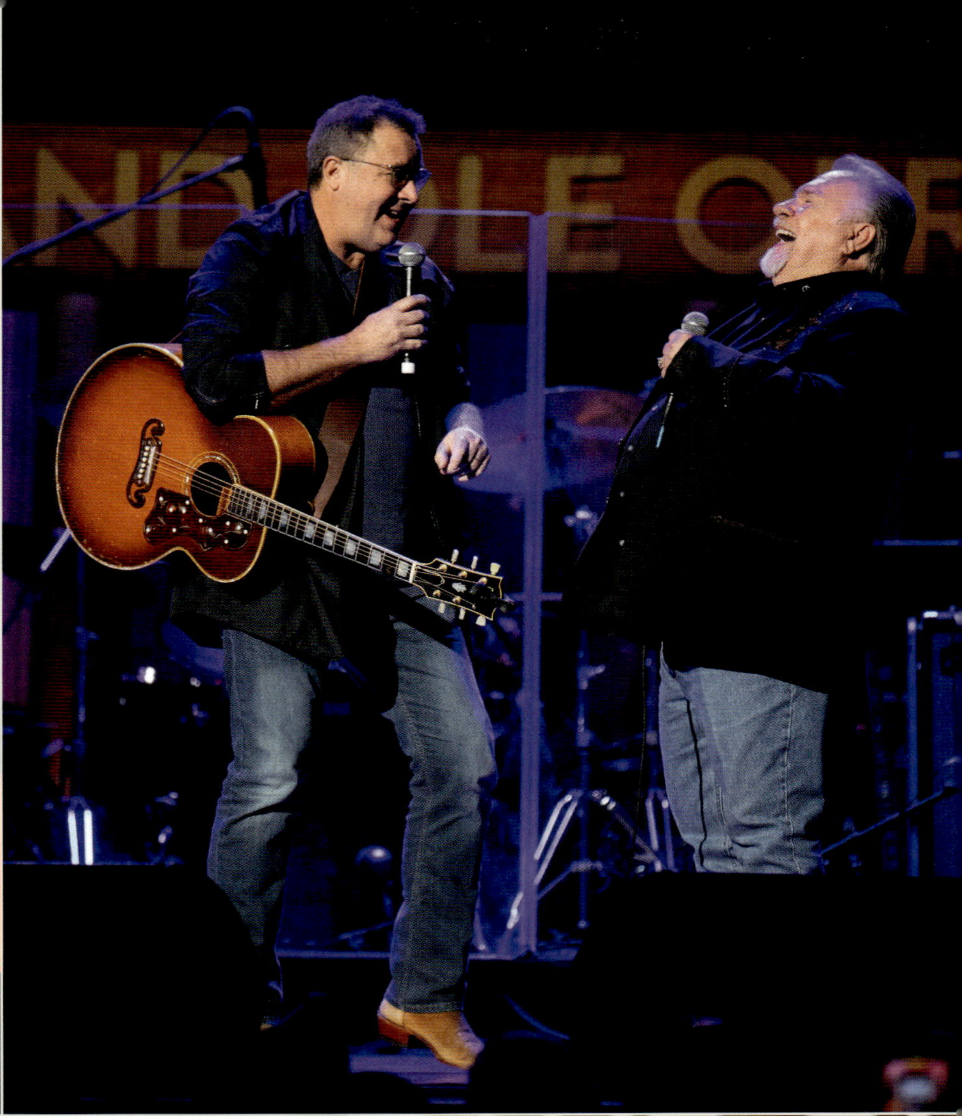
ND OLE O

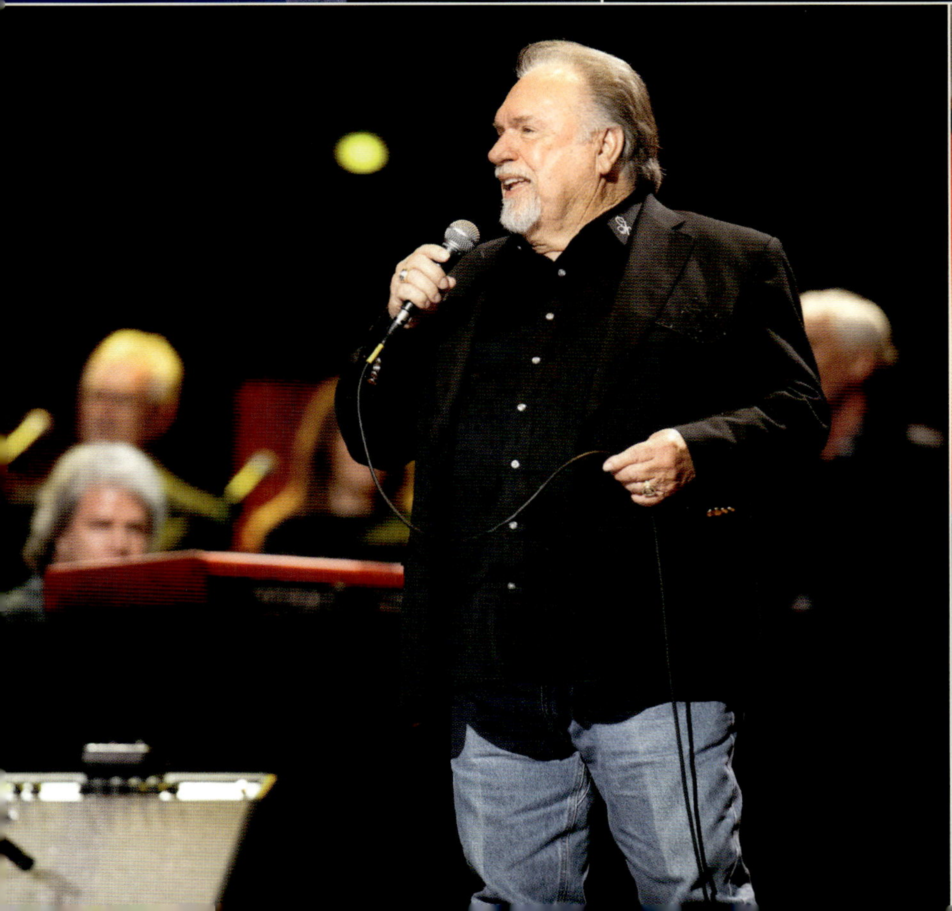

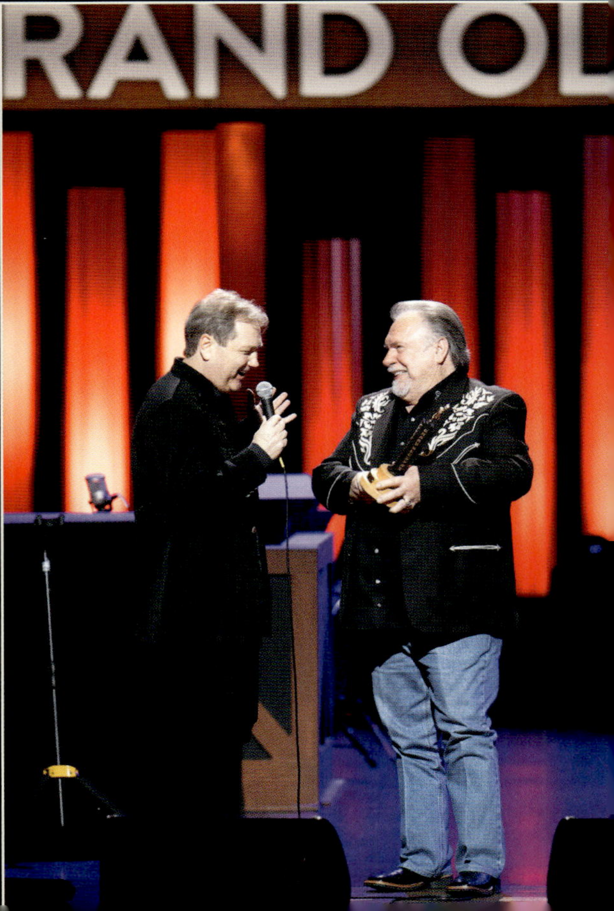
RAND OL

THE WHITES
MEMBER SINCE 1984

The Whites have been a part of the Grand Ole Opry family for more than 30 years and have been showcasing their own family harmony as a professional stage act even longer. Buck's skills on the piano landed him early gigs with the Opry's Hank Snow, Ernest Tubb and others. He married Pat Goza in 1951, and in 1962 they moved from Texas to Arkansas, where they began performing with another couple as the Down Home Folks. Their children performed as the Down Home Kids.

By the mid-'60s, the family was well known in bluegrass circles, and when the younger Whites decided they wanted to sing professionally, the family moved to Nashville in 1971. During their first years in Nashville, they performed as the Down Home Folks and recorded several bluegrass albums.

BUCK WHITE
Birthplace: Oklahoma
Birth Date: December 13

CHERYL WHITE
Birthplace: Wichita Falls, Texas
Birth Date: January 27

SHARON WHITE
Birthplace: Wichita Falls, Texas
Birth Date: December 17

OPRY INDUCTION: March 2, 1984

"I HAD DREAMS IN MY HEAD ABOUT BEING ON THE RADIO AND BEING ON THE GRAND OLE OPRY LONG BEFORE I EVER THOUGHT IT WAS POSSIBLE." —BUCK WHITE

In 1973, mother Pat retired from the group, and in 1975, The Whites played a Washington, D.C., show with Emmylou Harris. That association led to Sharon and Cheryl providing background vocals on Harris' 1978 *Blue Kentucky Girl* album. "She just opened so many doors for us and put us in front of people who had never seen us before," Sharon told interviewer Paul Edward Joyce.

In 1981, Sharon White married Ricky Skaggs, a one-time member of Emmylou's Hot Band who also co-produced The Whites' major-label debut, *Old Familiar Feeling*. The album yielded four Top 10 hits, including "You Put the Blue in Me," and "Hangin' Around." Other albums by The Whites, which blend country, folk, bluegrass, and gospel sounds include *Forever You*, *Ain't No Binds*, and *Doin' It by the Book*.

In 2000, The Whites appeared in the film, *O Brother, Where Art Thou?*, performing the Carter Family classic, "Keep on the Sunny Side," and picking up a Grammy for their efforts. The Whites were inducted into the Texas Country Music Hall of Fame in 2008, the same year their collaboration with Ricky, *Salt of the Earth*, also won a Grammy award.

CLOCKWISE FROM TOP LEFT:
1. 30th Opry Anniversary March 4, 2014
2. With Jeannie Seely
3. The Whites - Rosie, Sharon, Buck, and Cheryl
4. Roy Acuff joins The Whites outside his home in the Opry Plaza for a cameo appearance in the group's 1988 video "It's Not What You Know (It's Who You Know)."

650 WSM
WSM
GRAND OLE OPRY
WSM
GRAND OLE OPRY

WWW.OPRY.CO
WSM
GRAND OLE OPRY

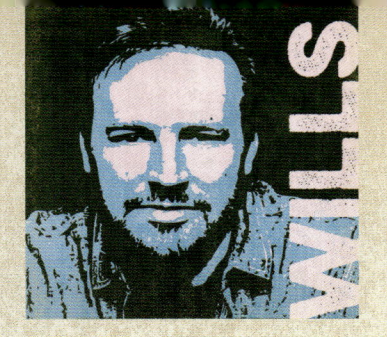

MARK WILLS
MEMBER SINCE 2019

Since making his Opry debut on August 22, 1997, Mark Wills has had an unshakeable reverence for the country music institution. Even on a night when he's not performing, you can often find him behind the curtain, watching the show with the same eager eyes as someone experiencing the Opry for the first time.

Mark understands the importance of remembering the legends who came before him. Each time he plays on the Opry stage, he makes the point to tap on the door of the dressing room dedicated to Little Jimmy Dickens out of remembrance for the icon. He also hung a picture of Jean Sheppard in his backstage locker at the Grand Ole Opry House upon learning it once belonged to her. To Mark, joining the ranks of the distinguished cast of Opry members had been a lifelong dream.

BIRTHPLACE: Cleveland, Tennessee
BIRTH DATE: August 8
OPRY INDUCTION: January 11, 2019

DID YOU KNOW? Fellow Opry member Jeannie Seely had the pleasure of introducing Mark on the night of his 1997 Opry debut and at his induction.

> "IT'S PRETTY DOGGONE COOL WHEN YOU THINK ABOUT ALL OF THE THOUSANDS WHO WANTED TO SING ON THE GRAND OLE OPRY. THERE'S REALLY NOTHING YOU CAN SAY THAT REALLY PUTS THAT INTO PERSPECTIVE ANY BETTER THAN JUST KNOWING I GET TO BE A PART OF THIS FOR THE REST OF MY LIFE."

On December 21, 2018, Christmas came early when Vince Gill asked Mark to perform a song together on stage. Little did Mark know that Vince had an even bigger question prepared: Would Mark want to become the Opry's newest member?

Speechless, Mark dropped to his knees and began to sob. "Now I like him even more. He's a crybaby like me," Vince chuckled. After a long pause, Mark composed himself and his answer was obvious: "Thank you. I would love to be the next member of the Grand Ole Opry."

Mark was inducted on January 11, 2019, performing his debut single "Jacob's Ladder" and "Phantom of the Opry," which he dedicated the show's many legends, include George Jones, whose jacket he wore that night. Everyone from his parents to his junior high chorus teacher were in attendance. After Craig Morgan presented him an Opry Member Award trophy, Mark quipped, "I slept with my ACM Award the night I won it — I'm sleeping with this tonight."

CLOCKWISE FROM TOP LEFT:
1. Mark Wills fans and newlyweds Nick and Liz saved their first dance for the Opry stage when Mark performed "I Do."
2. Mark screws in his member plaque backstage at the Opry.
3. Craig Morgan presents Mark with his Opry Member Award at his induction.
4. Joe Diffie and Mark perform together in 2017.
5. Overcome with emotion, Mark reacts to Vince Gill's invitation to become an Opry member.
6. Mark, Jeannie Seely, and Larry Gatlin embrace for a jubilant hug following Mark's induction.

OPRY FAMILY MEMBERS

0 WSM
GRAND OLE
WSM
GRAND OLE OPRY

WSM
GRAND OLE OPRY

WSM
GRAND OLE OPRY

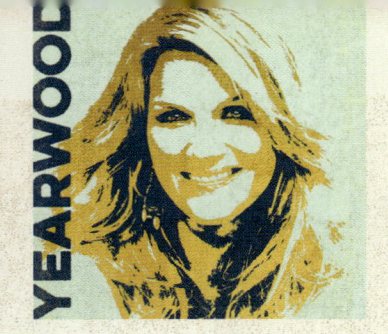

TRISHA YEARWOOD
MEMBER SINCE 1999

Whether belting out one of her signature hits on the Grand Ole Opry stage or writing a best-selling cookbook, Trisha Yearwood approaches everything she does with an abundance of passion, integrity, and talent.

The Georgia native knew she wanted to be a country singer by the time she was five years old. Winning a talent contest in Macon at 16 served to further fuel her creative desires. As a teen, she talked her parents into a family vacation in Nashville and after seeing her heroes on stage at the Grand Ole Opry, she knew there was nothing else she wanted to do.

She moved to Music City to attend Belmont University, took a job as a tour guide at the Country Music Hall of Fame, and began pursuing her dream. She worked as a receptionist at MTM Records and began

BIRTHPLACE: Monticello, Georgia
BIRTH DATE: September 19
OPRY INDUCTION: March 13, 1999

> "AT THE OPRY, YOU CAN SEE EVERY FACE, AND IT'S WONDERFUL BECAUSE YOU CAN MAKE REAL CONNECTIONS WITH PEOPLE."

singing demos. She met Garth Brooks when the two were hired to sing a duet demo for songwriter Kent Blazy. Garth introduced her to his producer, Allen Reynolds, who introduced her to Garth Fundis, who would become her friend and longtime producer. After five years in Nashville, Trisha signed with MCA Records and her first single, "She's in Love With the Boy," rocketed to the top of the country charts in 1991.

Since then, Trisha has populated country radio with such memorable hits as "Wrong Side of Memphis," "The Woman Before Me," "XXXs and OOOs (An American Girl)," "Thinkin' About You," "The Song Remembers When," "Walkaway Joe," and "How Do I Live," as well as hit singles recorded with Garth, now her husband. Trisha has won Grammy Awards and has been recognized as a top female vocalist by both the CMA and ACM.

Among all the accomplishments and accolades, being a member of the Grand Ole Opry holds special significance for Trisha. "My mother came here on her senior class trip from South Georgia," she says. "She wrote in her diary about seeing Hank Snow, Hawkshaw Hawkins and all those people. When I was inducted as a member of the Opry in 1999, she brought her diary and got Hank Snow to sign it. So it's not only about me, it's also about my whole family."

CLOCKWISE FROM TOP LEFT:
1. August 18, 2007
2. Opry Induction March 13, 1999
3. February 17, 2014
4. Opry induction with Porter Wagoner, March 13, 1999
5. Opry debut

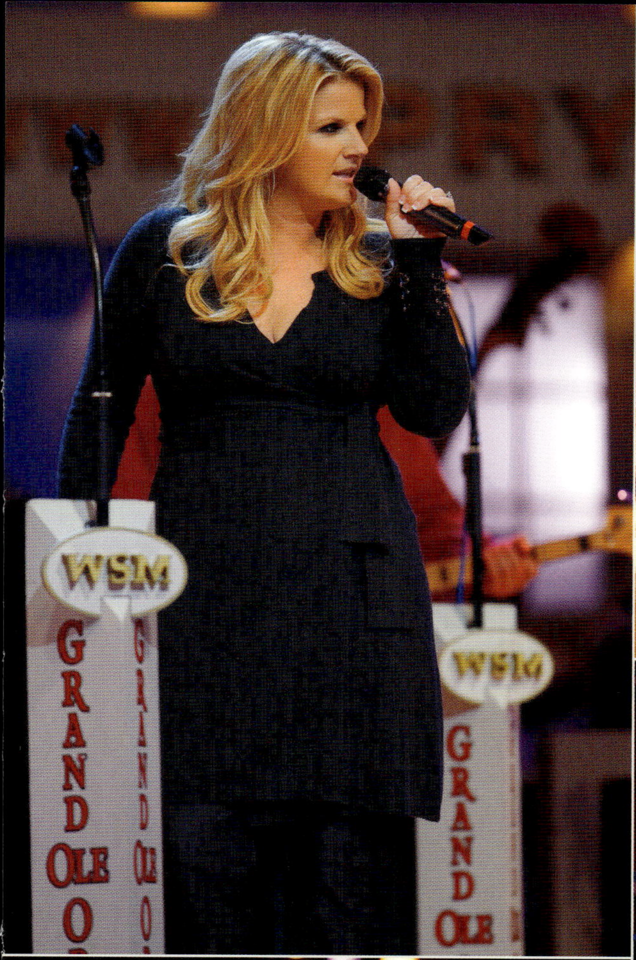
WSM
GRAND OLE
WSM
GRAND OLE

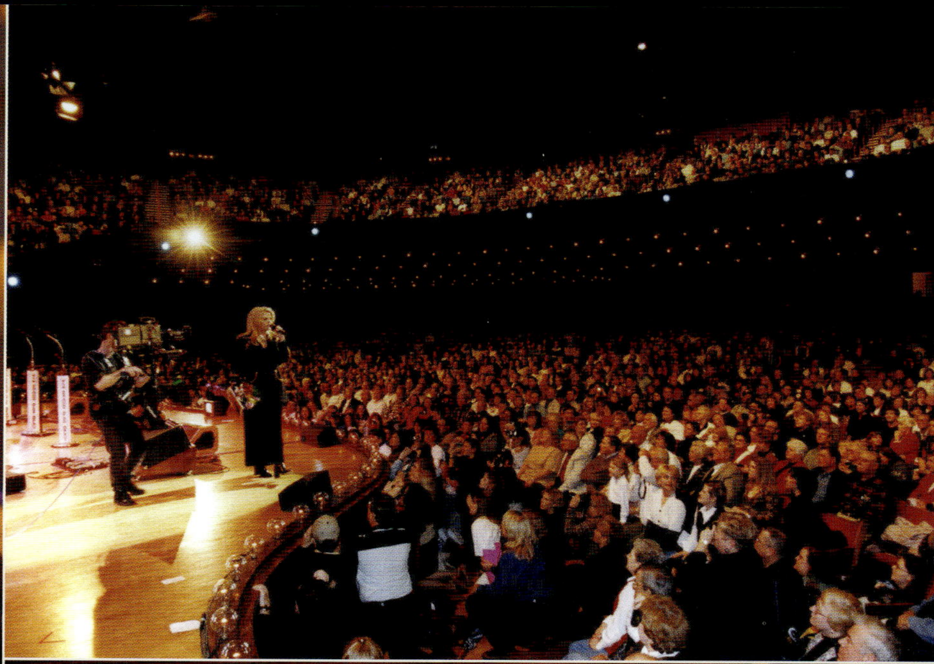

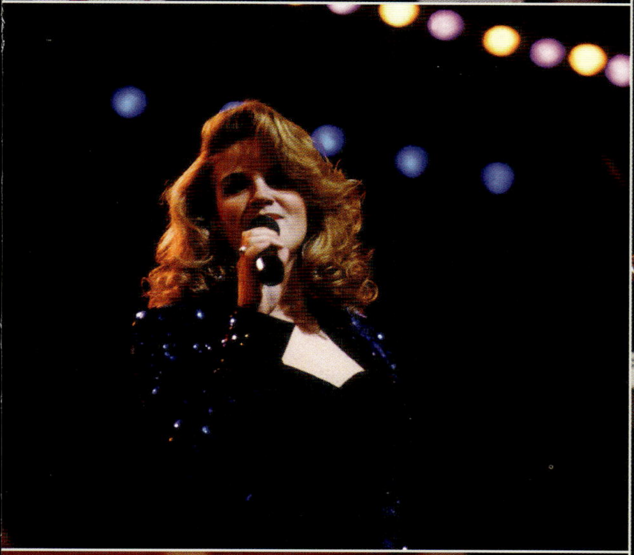

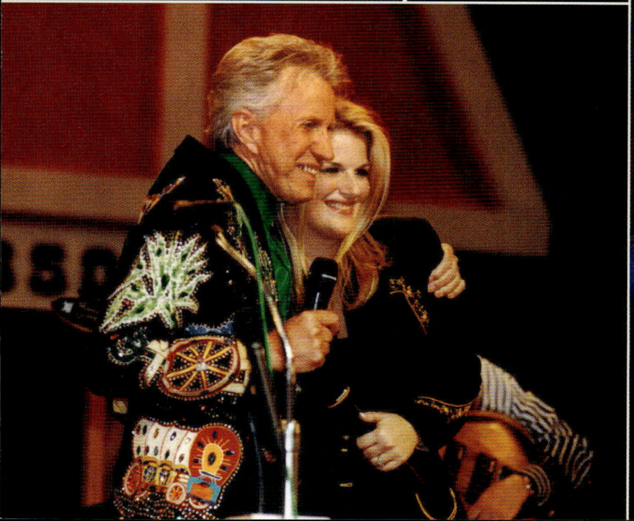

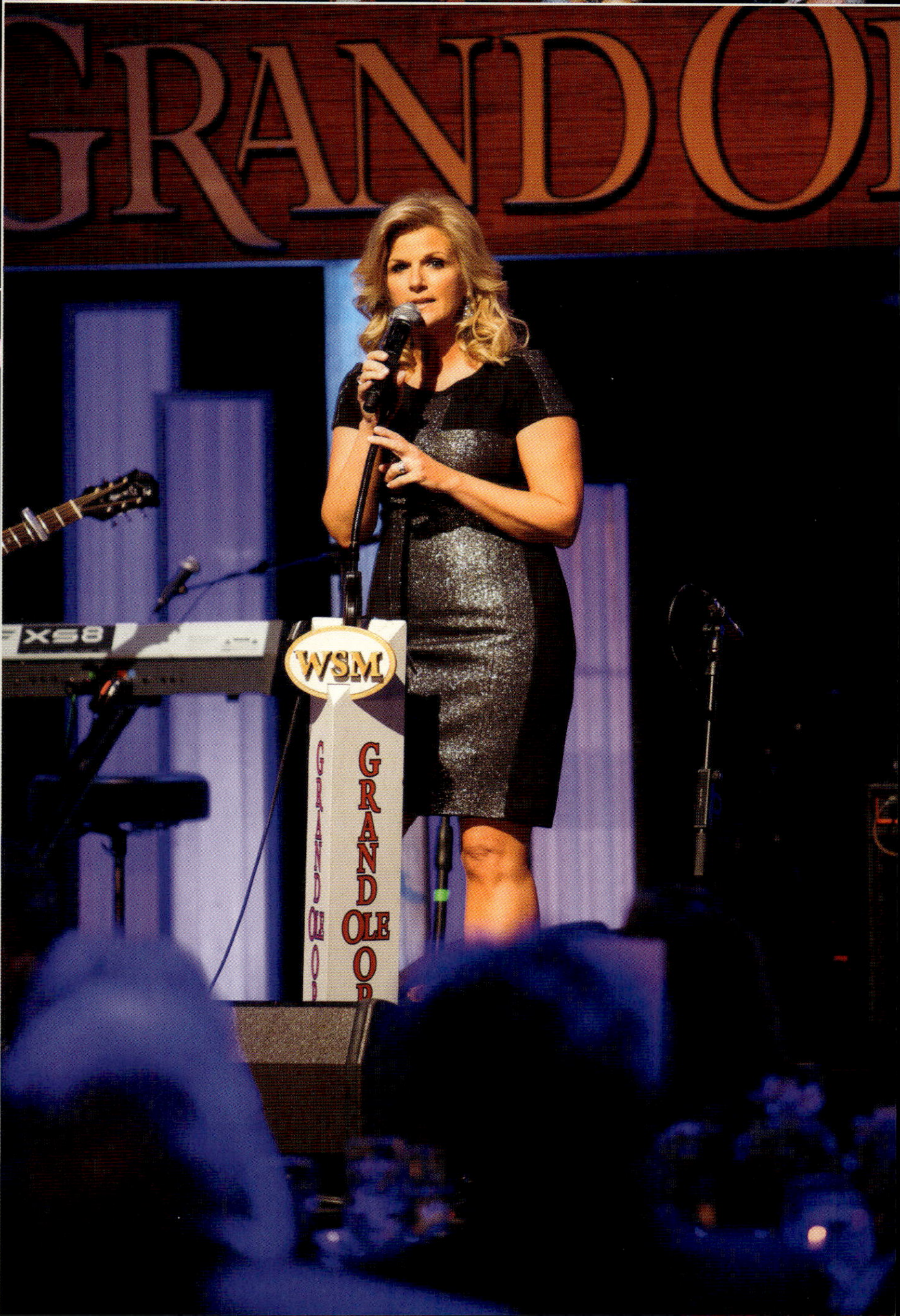
GRAND
XS8
WSM
GRAND OLE

CHRIS YOUNG
MEMBER SINCE 2017

Chris Young's rise to fame might seem meteoric, but for a hometown kid hailing from nearby Murfreesboro, Tennessee, becoming a country singer and playing on the Opry stage has been a childhood dream fulfilled.

When he was a boy, Chris sang so much around the house that his parents had to tune him out. But then puberty happened — and that tenor became a baritone.

"I was singing all of Vince Gill's stuff, and then my voice changed," Chris laughs. "For about a year there, I thought, 'Oh my God, I'm ruined. It's the end of the world!' And then I realized I could sing Randy Travis songs. It worked out well."

That's putting it lightly. After winning TV singing competition *Nashville Star* in May 2006, Chris made his Opry debut just a month later. A dynamic performer and poignant songwriter, Chris would go on to have nine No. 1 singles to his name by the time he became an

BIRTHPLACE: Murfreesboro, Tennessee
BIRTH DATE: June 12
OPRY INDUCTION: October 17, 2017

"DANG, YOU GOT ME GOOD! I LOVE YOU GUYS. I LOVE EVERYBODY HERE. I LOVE THIS PLACE." —CHRIS ON VINCE GILL SURPRISING HIM WITH AN OPRY INVITATION

Opry member, including "Tomorrow," "Aw Naw," and "I'm Comin' Over." His distinctive ballads and commanding vocals also helped him land two Grammy Award nominations, and his 2011 album *Neon* is certified platinum.

Fellow Opry member Vince Gill, whose concert fueled the musical ambitions of a 9-year-old Chris, would be the one to eventually invite him to join the Grand Ole Opry in 2017. The pair had just celebrated their chart-topping duet "Sober Saturday Night" at a backstage party earlier in the evening. When it came time to perform the song on the Opry stage, Vince deadpanned that Chris had never paid him for his work on the recording session. "I'll make you a deal," Vince said to Chris. "I'll forgive the session fees if you'll be the newest member of the Grand Ole Opry." Stunned, overjoyed, and tearful, Chris picked Vince up from the floor for an unforgettable bear hug and accepted the invitation before a standing ovation from the crowd.

CLOCKWISE FROM TOP LEFT:
1. With Little Jimmy Dickens, February 2, 2010
2. February 19, 2014
3. With the ACM Lifting Lives Campers, June 27, 2017
4. With Cassadee Pope, October 25, 2016
5. May 8, 2012
6. With Vince Gill while being invited to join the Opry, August 29, 2017
7. Chris' Opry debut, June 10, 2006

GRAND OLE
OPRY
Humana
WSM

650 WSM
GRAND OLE OPRY
OPRY.COM #OPRY

OPRY.COM
WSM

WSM
GRAND OLE OPRY

WSM

WSM
GRAND OLE OPRY

ACKNOWLEDGEMENTS

The Grand Ole Opry would like to acknowledge the fans, Opry members, guest artists, musicians, staff, and sponsors who have been a part of the Opry family over the past 97 years. You have helped create a show and tradition unlike any other. The moments recalled in this *Family Album* would not have been possible without your support.

Chris Hollo is the Grand Ole Opry's official photographer and contributed numerous photos to this *Album*. Among other contributing photographers are Erick Anderson, Kristin Barlowe, Donnie Beauchamp, Andrea Behrends, Dennis Carney, Joel Dennis, Jim Hagans, Joe Hardwick, Russ Harrington, George Holz, Robin Hood, Bill Konway, Bev LeCroy, Les Leverett, Jim McGuire, Senor McGuire, Jon Mir, Mark Mosrie, Sheryl Nields, Ivan Otis, Tom Pich, Jim Shea and Dean Tubb.

PROUD OPRY SPONSORS:

Humana

DOLLAR GENERAL
Save time. Save money. Every day!

OPPOSITE PAGE:
1. The Opry dancers with The Whites
2. The Opry band
3. Center stage at the Opry House
4. Opry announcers Eddie Stubbs, Bill Cody and Mike Terry
5. The Opry House
6. The Opry singers

M #OPRY

O WSM
GRAND OLE OPR
OPRY.CO

WSM
GRAND OLE OPRY

GRAND OLE OPRY
650

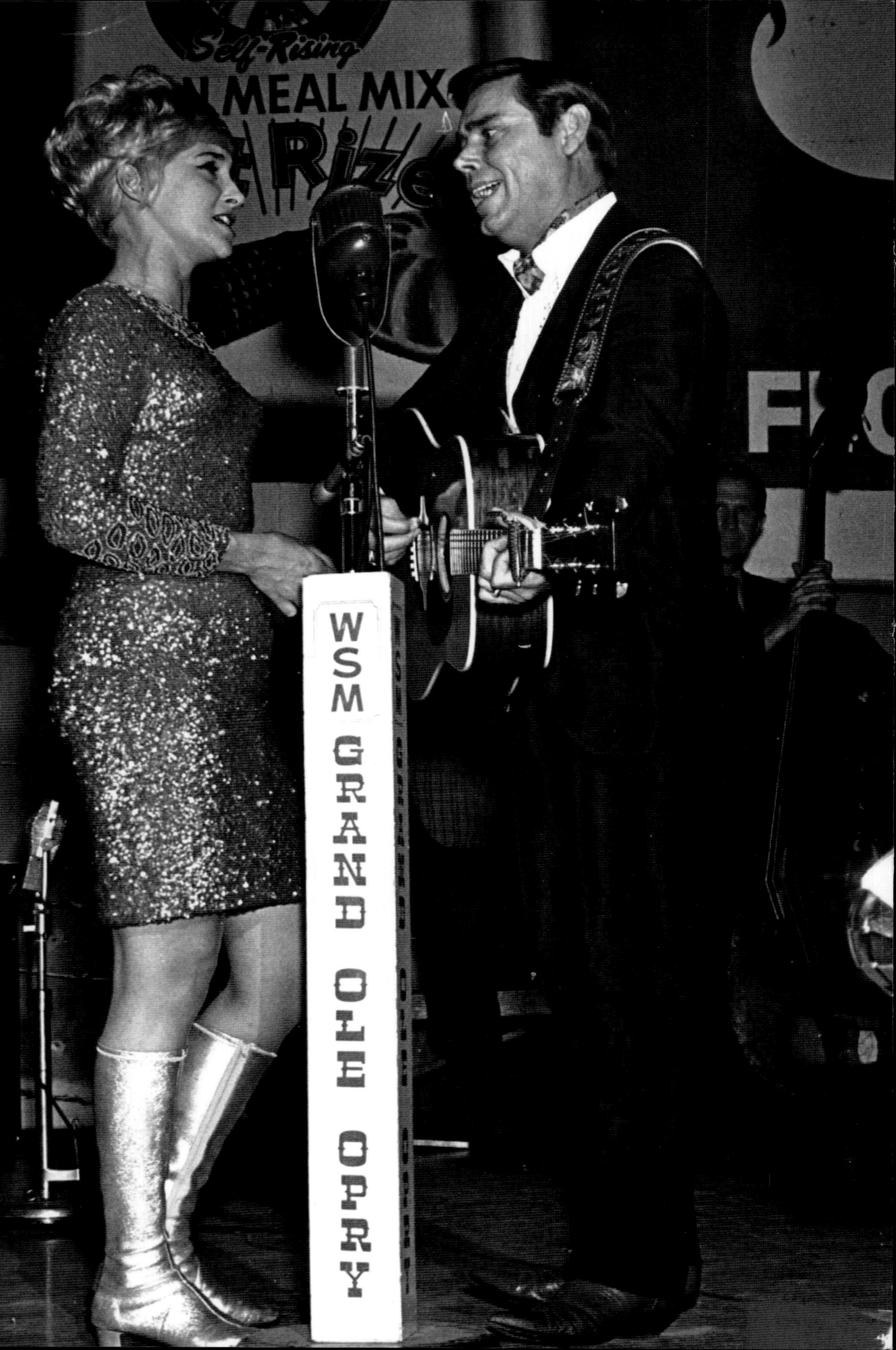
Self-Rising
MEAL MIX
WSM
GRAND OLE OPRY

THIS PAGE:
1. Curly Fox, Texas Ruby
2. Kitty Wells, Johnnie Wright
3. Porter Wagoner and Little Jimmy Dickens in wrong coats

OPPOSITE PAGE:
1. Tammy Wynette, George Jones, 1969

THIS PAGE:
1. The Fruit Jar Drinkers
2. Lester Flatt and Earl Scruggs help showcase the Opry in the 1969 Presidential inaugural parade in Washington, D.C.

OPPOSITE PAGE:
1. Hank Snow

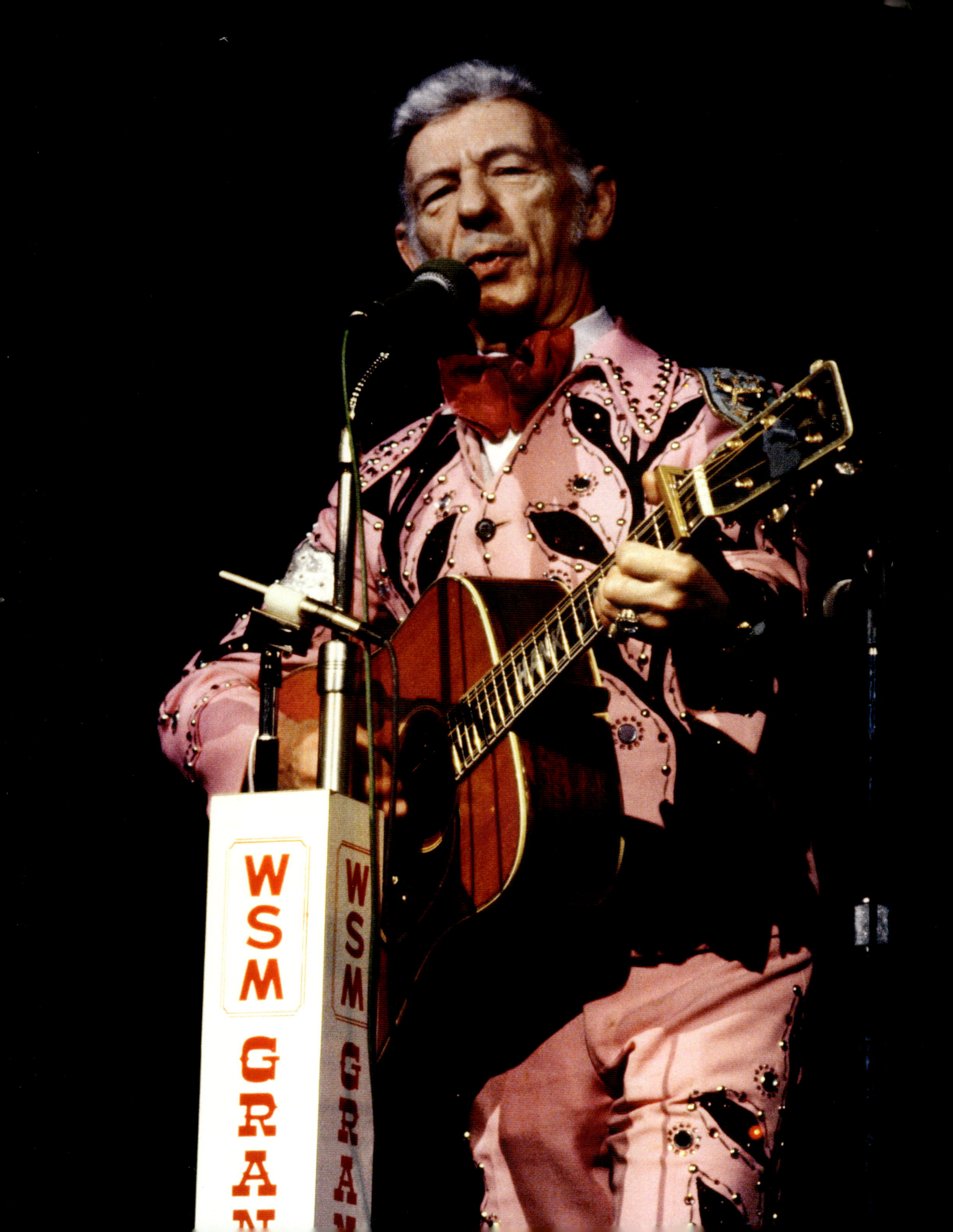

WSM
GRAN
WSM
GRAN

THIS PAGE:
1. Red Foley
2. Porter Wagoner, Willie Nelson, 2002

OPPOSITE PAGE:
1. Roy Acuff, Vince Gill on Gill's Opry induction night
2. Lorrie Morgan's first Opry appearance, December 14, 1973
3. Emmy-winning actor John Ritter, son of Opry member Tex Ritter, and Boxcar Willie, November 29, 1980

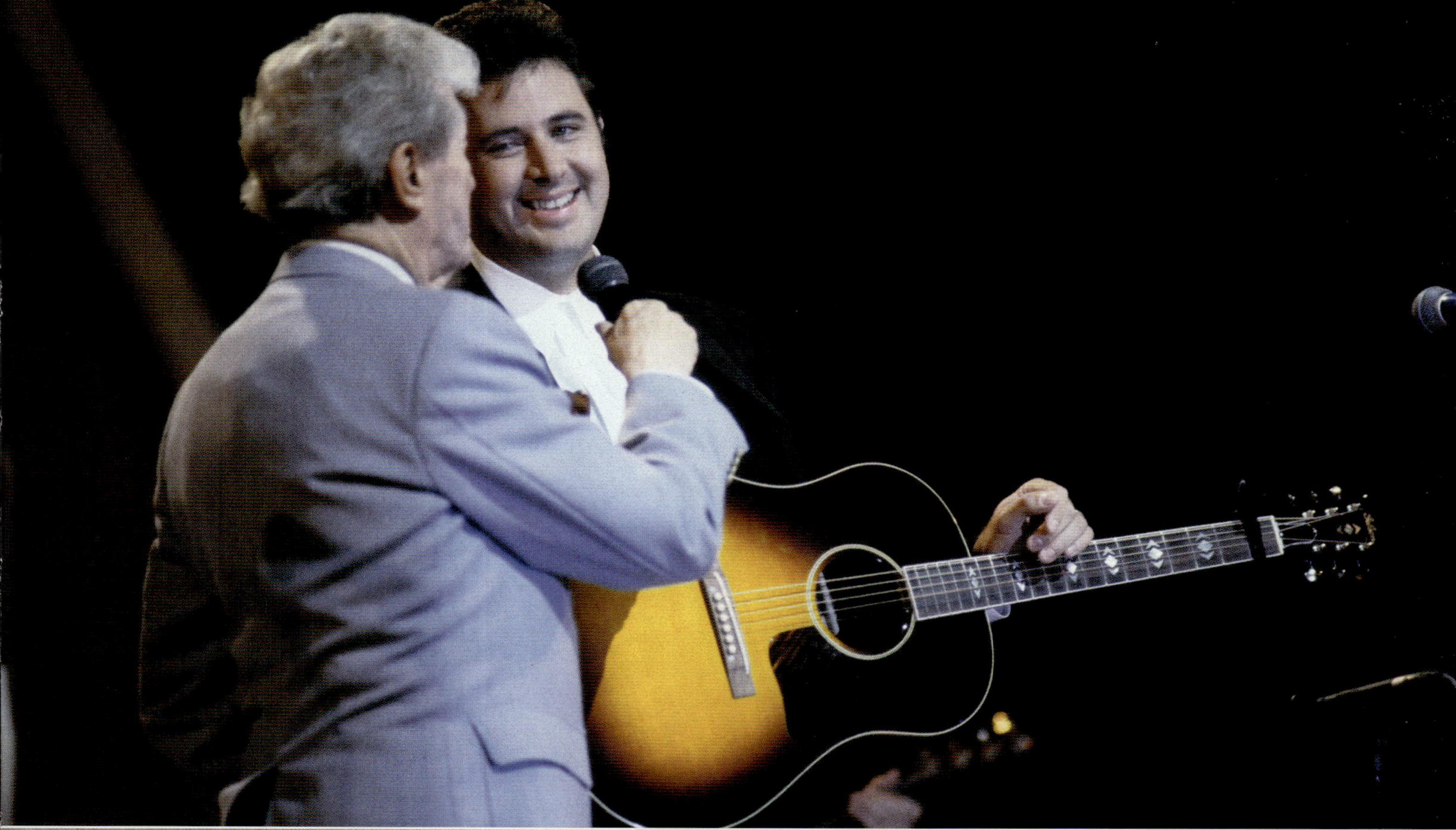

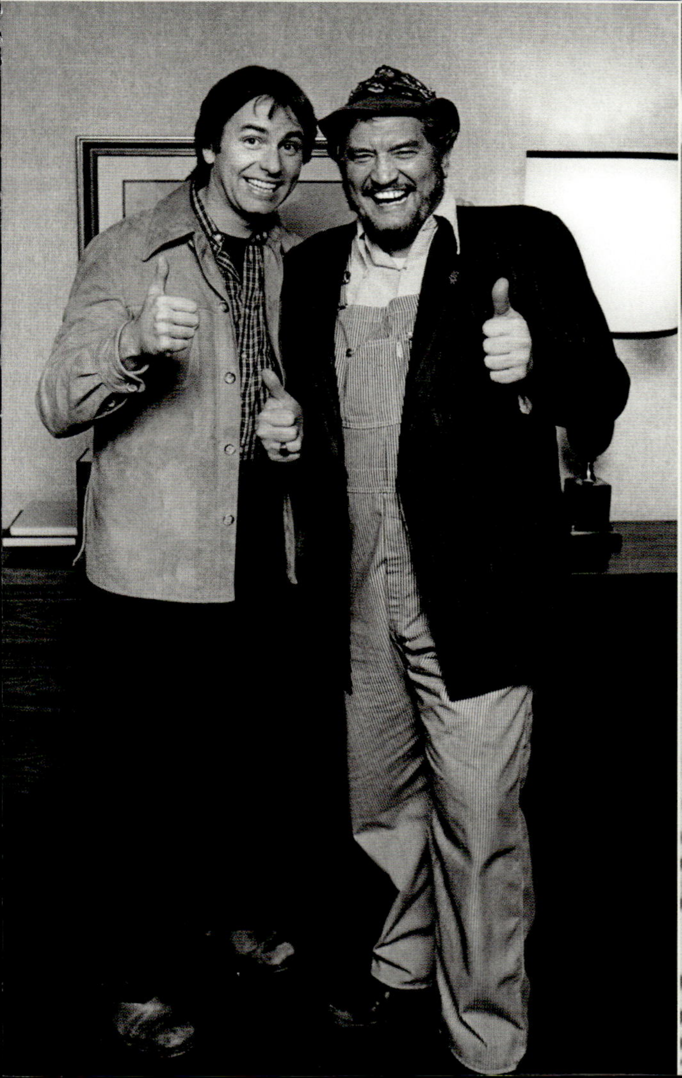

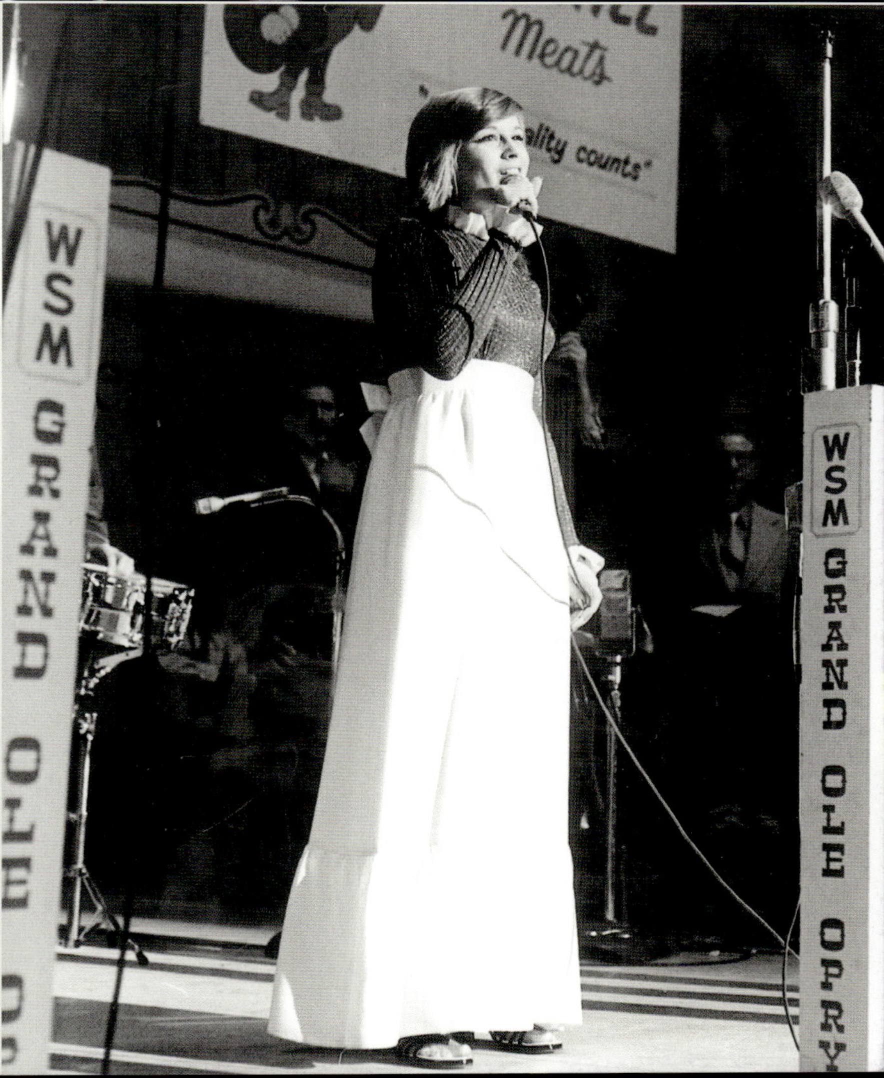
Meats
WSM GRAND OLE OPRY

THIS PAGE:
1. Lou Wilson, George D. Hay, and Sam McGee on the Opry at War Memorial Auditorium
2. Vice President George H. W. Bush visits Roy Acuff's dressing room backstage along with Jimmy Dickens and Stonewall Jackson

OPPOSITE PAGE:
1. Cover of the souvenir program from the Opry's final performance at the Ryman Auditorium
2. Tommy Colins, Minnie Pearl and Buck Owens
3. Interior of the souvenir program from the Opry's final performance at the Ryman Auditorium

SOUVENIR PROGRAM

THE GRAND OLE OPRY
THE MOTHER CHURCH OF COUNTRY MUSIC

THE RYMAN AUDITORIUM

The imposing Ryman Auditorium in downtown Nashville was the home of the Grand Ole Opry from 1943 until March 15, 1974. It was not the first home of the famous radio show that began November 28, 1925, but certainly the best known. The Opry had performed previously at WSM Studios in the National Life and Accident Insurance Company building, tents, a tabernacle, a theater and the War Memorial Auditorium in Nashville.

The Ryman Auditorium had its beginning in 1885. At that time Nashville was a community approaching 100,000 people. With a reported 900 manufacturing firms—mostly small—four cotton mills, woolen mills, extensive sawmills stretched along the Cumberland River, printing-publishing firms, railroads and steamboats. Since its founding in 1779, Nashville had been a religious city with an abundance of churches, and a leading regional educational center.

With a fruitful bed of theology already present, its not surprising Sam Jones and Tom Ryman would combine to create an auditorium for the worship of God. Jones was a Georgia preacher who regularly held tent meetings in the Nashville community. Among his converts was Tom Ryman. Immediately after his conversion, Ryman began a campaign to build an auditorium where Jones could hold his revivals. Construction on the Tabernacle was started in 1889. That same year a Charter of Incorporation was registered in the State of Tennessee under the name of the "Union Gospel Tabernacle," stating its objects and purposes as "strictly religious, non-Sectarian and non-Denominational." When Ryman died in 1904, the name was changed to the Ryman Auditorium.

The next 80 years brought many social, economic, and political changes to the community. And the famous building was influenced greatly by the turn of events. Gradually its programs were other than "strictly religious". As a consequence the building has welcomed many notables in the fields of religion, politics, and entertainment. The Ryman incurred heavy debts through the years until 1963, when it became the property of the National Life and Accident Insurance Co.

The Ryman naturally holds many memories. It has served the Grand Ole Opry well. But just as the show outgrew the other sites it occupied, the Grand Ole Opry is leaving this old structure for a new home at Opryland USA on March 16, 1974. The new Opry House, built specifically for the Grand Ole Opry and its fans, will seat 4,400 in air-conditioned comfort. It is the world's largest broadcasting studio and a truly unique theater.

Every effort has been made to make the new home spell pickin' and singing, country and western, and home folks welcome, which are Opry trademarks.

We hope you will come visit us soon. And see the Grand Ole Opry in its Grand New Home.

THE FINAL PERFORMANCE AT THE RYMAN AUDITORIUM OF THE
FRIDAY NIGHT GRAND OLE OPRY

MARCH 15, 1974

7:00-7:30 CRACKER BARRELL
ROY DRUSKY
DEL REEVES
CHARLIE WALKER
JAN HOWARD

7:30-8:00 VARALLO
BILL ANDERSON
BOB LUMAN
JIM & JESSE

8:00-8:30 ODOM SAUSAGE, U.S. BORAX
ARCHIE CAMPBELL
BOBBY BARE
DOTTIE WEST
JUSTIN TUBB

8:30-9:00 KROGER STORES
ROY ACUFF
JEAN SHEPARD
STONEWALL JACKSON
WILMA LEE & STONEY COOPER

9:00-9:30 BALTZ BROS., SCHLITZ
WILBURN BROTHERS
OSBORNE BROTHERS
JEANNE PRUETT
DEL WOOD

9:30-10:00 ACME BOOT CO., BEECHNUT CHEWING TOBACCO
JIM ED BROWN
HANK LOCKLIN
GRANDPA JONES
THE CARLISLES

10:00-10:30 CEE BEE FOOD STORES, SCHLITZ
BILLY WALKER
CHARLIE LOUVIN
STU PHILLIPS
THE WILLIS BROTHERS

10:30-11:00 SHONEYS BIG BOY
GEORGE MORGAN
THE FOUR GUYS
RAY PILLOW
LONZO & OSCAR
ERNIE ASHWORTH

GRANT TURNER & HAIRL HENSLEY—Announcers
HAL DURHAM—Opry Manager

"GOODNIGHT, MINNIE PEARL. WE LOVE YOU, TOO."
—BILL ANDERSON
EACH NIGHT AS HE LEAVES THE OPRY

A NOTE FROM THE PUBLISHER

In commemorating the great American treasure that is the Grand Ole Opry, Grandin Hood Publishers acknowledges the dedicated Book Steering Committee members who brought this story to print:

Dan Rogers, Vice President & Executive Producer, Grand Ole Opry
Emily Frans, Director of Archives
GiGi Missildine, SR Manager Buying
Katie Williams, Marketing
Paige Cushman, Creative Content

ABOUT THE DESIGNER:
Franklin, Tennessee's Jeff Carroll has been awarded numerous national and international awards for his work in book and magazine design, as well as corporate communications and brand development. www.jeffcarrolldesign.com

ABOUT THE PUBLISHER:
Grandin Hood Publishers of Nashville, founded by Pulitzer Prize-winning photographer Robin Hood, is a national award-winning publisher of commemorative books celebrating the histories and continuing stories of historic organizations, foundations, music labels, and artists. www.grandinhood.com

GRANDIN HOOD
Publishers